Literary Research: Strategi

Series Editors: Peggy Keeran & Jennifer Bowers

Every literary age presents scholars with both predictable and unique research challenges. This series fills a gap in the field of reference literature by featuring research strategies and by recommending the best tools for conducting specialized period and national literary research. Emphasizing research methodology, each series volume takes into account the unique challenges inherent in conducting research of that specific literary period and outlines the best practices for researching within it. Volumes place the research process within the period's historical context and use a narrative structure to analyze and compare print and electronic reference sources. Following an introduction to online searching, chapters will typically cover these types of resources: general literary reference materials; library catalogs; print and online bibliographies, indexes, and annual reviews; scholarly journals; contemporary reviews; period journals and newspapers; microform and digital collections; manuscripts and archives; and Web resources. Additional or alternative chapters might be included to highlight a particular research problem or to examine other pertinent period or national literary resources.

Literary Research and the Victorian and Edwardian Ages, 1830–1910

Strategies and Sources

Melissa S. Van Vuuren

Literary Research:
Strategies and Sources, No. 9

THE SCARECROW PRESS, INC.
Lanham • Toronto • Plymouth, UK
2011

Published by Scarecrow Press, Inc.
A wholly owned subsidiary of The Rowman & Littlefield Publishing Group, Inc.
4501 Forbes Boulevard, Suite 200, Lanham, Maryland 20706
http://www.scarecrowpress.com

Estover Road,
Plymouth PL6 7PY,
United Kingdom

British Library Cataloguing in Publication Information Available

Library of Congress Cataloging-in-Publication Data

Van Vuuren, Melissa S.
   Literary research and the Victorian and Edwardian ages, 1830–1910 : strategies and
sources / Melissa S. Van Vuuren.
         p. cm. — (Literary research: strategies and sources ; no. 9)
   Includes bibliographical references and indexes.
   ISBN 978-0-8108-7726-9 (pbk. : alk. paper) — ISBN 978-0-8108-7727-6 (ebook)
   1. English literature—19th century—Research—Methodology. 2. English literature—
20th century—Research—Methodology. 3. English literature—19th century—
Information resources. 4. English literature—20th century—Information resources.
5. Great Britain—History—Victoria, 1837–1901—Historiography. 6. Great Britain—
Civilization—19th century—Historiography. 7. Great Britain—History—Edward VII,
1901–1910—Historiography. I. Title.
   PR461.V35 2011
   820.7'2—dc22   2010027674

Printed in the United States of America

Contents

Acknowledgments

I would like to thank my editors—Jenny Bowers and Peggy Keeran—for their time, patience, and insightful comments. This is a better book because of them. I'd also like to acknowledge Angela Courtney for encouraging me to pursue this project and for her advice throughout the process. Writing this book was made possible by a generous summer research leave from the James Madison University Libraries; Judy Anderson for her invaluable advice about cataloging practices and use of subject headings; and my colleagues in the Public Services Department, who graciously gave me the flexibility to continue research and writing throughout the academic year. No book of this sort could be written without intensive use of library collections, and the collections at the James Madison University Libraries, the University of Virginia Library, and the Indiana University Bloomington Libraries were particularly helpful.

On a personal note, I would like to thank my family for their unending support and for always believing I was capable of what at times seemed an insurmountable task.

For the One in whom I live and move and have my being.

Introduction

The history of the Victorian age will never be written: we know too much about it.

—Lytton Strachey, *Eminent Victorians*
(New York: G. P. Putnam and Sons, 1918), v.

Although Strachey's words offer a rather cynical view of the Victorians, histories of that age have certainly been written from nearly every imaginable angle. The term *Victorian*, which is now frequently used to describe prevailing attitudes, beliefs, cultures, and norms during the reign of Queen Victoria, did not attain its connotation of prudish, strict, old-fashioned, and outdated until the early twentieth century.[1] Even if those terms are helpful for describing certain aspects of the Victorian age, no age, no matter how long or short, can be truly monolithic. Rather, varying interests, beliefs, and values coexist within any society. "In the light of all the complexities, contradictions, overlaps, and influences . . . ," Philip Davis suggests in *The Oxford English Literary History*, "the very difference and disagreements help to form between them the picture of all that is involved in this great Victorian crisis of belief."[2]

As a literary era, the Edwardian age is frequently tacked onto the end of the Victorian age or considered a mere transitional phase between Victorianism and modernism, without being a significant era in its own right. As such, scholarship on the Edwardian age is sparse at best or frequently buried within Victorian sources. Where Victorian studies abound with definitions and evaluations of what is Victorian, similar discussions are few and far between for Edwardian literature. Most frequently, the Edwardian age is characterized by opulence and moral degradation, particularly in comparison to the preceding age. However, this ready characterization no more accurately summarizes the Edwardian age than stuffiness and moral conservatism typifies the Victorian.

It is readily apparent that both the Victorian and the Edwardian ages defy easy classification. Most typically, "both/and" discussions come closer to characterizing these periods than "either/or" comparisons. The Victorian age was not sacred *or* secular, but both sacred *and* secular. Likewise, it was not agricultural or industrial, but both at once. The two extremes coexist along with various viewpoints in between. These tensions are apparent not only through historiography but also through literary history, for literature tells the story history cannot. As Davis asserts, "For the discipline of history, alone, cannot tell the inner story of the age in all its resonance of meaning, cannot give the individual experience of what is invisible, in close imaginative relation to complex and primary linguistic sources."[3] Literature illuminates what history leaves unsaid, and yet the two are inextricably connected. However, a basic knowledge of history is essential for understanding the world in which these literatures were written.

Even in the midst of her reign, pundits were already glorying in the significance and accomplishments of the age. An article in the March 1887 edition of the *New Princeton Review* proclaimed that while the "Victorian epoch in English history can hardly fail to stand out as distinct, if not as illustrious, as the Elizabethan, the Cromwellian, or any other," it will be recognized as "an era of steady, though not always rapid, advance in every department of human interests."[4] In 1830, Britain was under the rule of William IV and had already firmly established itself as a colonial power, boasting colonies in the Caribbean, Oceania, Asia, the Middle East, Africa, and the Americas. Although Victoria would not take the throne for another seven years, many movements that would define the Victorian age had already begun. The Catholic Emancipation Act had only recently passed in Parliament, and slavery in the British colonies was about to see its last days. Britain—including England, Ireland, Scotland, and Wales—would transform over the course of the century as the nation negotiated between older, traditional ways of life and new, modern ways of life. Although Britain established itself as a colonial power in the seventeenth century, not until the nineteenth century under Victoria's rule did the ideas of empire and imperialism become firmly intertwined with British identity.

Economic developments brought on by the rise of industry, science, and technology profoundly affected British society. Inventions such as the Bessemer process[5] and the compound steam engine[6] increased the speed with which goods could be produced and transported, and shifted the distribution of labor. Such inventions transformed England into the first industrial nation and earned it the title "the workshop of the world." With industrialism's rise, the British population began to migrate from the rural areas to urban centers. As population and productivity boomed and urban areas swelled, the remnants of late eighteenth- and early nineteenth-century life gave way to industrialization's spread. The tension between the agricultural past and industrial future emerges in prose works such as John Stuart Mills's essay "Civilization" (1836) and Thomas Carlyle's *Past and Present* (1843) as well as in mid-nineteenth-century industrial novels: Frances Trollope's *The Life and Adventures of Michael Armstrong, The Factory Boy* (1839), Charles Dickens's *Hard Times* (1854), and Elizabeth Gaskell's *Mary Barton* (1848) and *North and South* (1855). Despite the environmental ills and poor working conditions brought about by industrialism, industrial growth also contributed to the rise of the British middle class and the expansion of the working class. As the middle and working classes grew in economic power, they successfully agitated to gain political power. The Reform Acts of 1832, 1867, and 1884 extended voting rights to the middle class, the working class, and agricultural laborers, respectively.

In addition to debate over rights and privileges among the classes, the "Woman Question" was hotly contested throughout the Victorian age. Although women would not gain the right to vote until 1918, significant progress in women's rights was made during the nineteenth century. Suffragists such as Emmeline Pankhurst (1858–1928) and John Stuart Mill (1806–1873) contributed to increases in women's rights and the eventual granting of voting rights. Passage of the Infants and Child Custody Bill of 1839, the Matrimonial Causes Act of 1857, the Married Women's Property Acts of 1870 and 1882, the 1870 Educational Act, and the Local Government Act of 1894 paved the way for further legislation that would grant women equal rights with men. In literature, the debate over gender roles emerged in works such as Coventry Patmore's *The Angel in the House* (1854–1862) and Elizabeth Barrett Browning's *Aurora Leigh* (1856), with Patmore advocating a subservient, domestic role for women and Barrett Browning challenging traditional gender roles and highlighting social injustices.

Tension also existed between religious faith and scientific skepticism. While Christianity played a prominent role in British society, new scientific discoveries and theories posed challenges to established religious beliefs. Texts such as Charles Darwin's *The Origin of Species* (1859) and *The Descent of Man, and Selection in Relation to Sex* (1871) spurred major debates on the values and beliefs that had long underpinned British society. Skepticism and doubt pervaded the literature of poets such as Arthur Hugh Clough and Matthew Arnold while poets such as Christina Rossetti continued supporting long-held religious principles. In British fiction, Darwinian theory was woven into works such as Elizabeth Gaskell's *Wives and Daughters* (1864–1866) and Olive Schreiner's *Story of an African Farm* (1883).

In the midst of these political and social changes, British literature underwent transformations of its own. Although Keats, Shelley, and Byron died prior to 1830, Romantic poetry continued to thrive through the writings of Lord Alfred Tennyson, Robert Browning, and the Pre-Raphaelites.[7] Though the Romantic period extended to 1870, literature in the early Victorian age (1830–1851) through the mid-Victorian age (1851–1870) shifted away from Romantic ideals in response to the upheaval and societal changes brought about by Britain's Industrial Revolution. As the century progressed, Romanticism gradually gave way to the realism of the late Victorian age (1870–1901). The novel also rose in prominence throughout the nineteenth century. The novel's rise was due, in part, to the expansion of the printing press in Britain. Published first in serial form and later as triple-deckers and "yellowbacks," novels quickly gained popularity and respectability across Britain.[8] Although these formats were prevalent through most of the Victorian age, by the 1890s, single-volume novels had become the standard. Books were also increasingly more affordable for all classes of British citizenry.

Following Victoria's reign, her son Edward VII took over as Britain's ruling monarch from 1901 to 1910. Compared to earlier periods of British literature, the Edwardian age has been largely ill-defined and under-researched; however, this period was critical as a transition from late Victorian realism to early twentieth-century modernism. While somewhat difficult to characterize, this age, and its literature, "was not only progressive, it was even adventurous—but all the same it meant to keep what it had."[9] While Edwardian authors took innovative and fresh approaches, they remained mostly within the confines of traditional genres. Despite the amount of literature produced and consumed in this time period, relatively little research has been published on this literary era. Just as the public craved new literary content and literacy rates rose in the mid- to late Victorian age, reading in the Edwardian age became even more widespread and demand for reading materials increased significantly. The reading population was larger than ever, and new narrowly defined readerships emerged in the twentieth century.

In the early 1900s, the British Empire was at its peak, with nearly one-quarter of the earth's population and surface under British rule. In socioeconomic terms, the Edwardian age has often been characterized as a time of great prosperity prior to the upheaval brought about by World War I (1914–1918). The British people took great pride in the success of their empire while still valuing the traditional notion of the "country home" as representative of the English nation. In spite of the era's affluence, the Edwardian age was only prosperous for the upper and middle classes. Literary works, including H. G.

Wells's *Tono-Bungay* (1909) and E. M. Forster's *Howard's End* (1910), recognized the plight of the working class and the urban poor. They also acknowledged the spread of middle-class suburbs and the impact of city growth on British society.

During this time, Britain began to move away from the conventional values associated with the Victorian age. Building on successes from the mid- to late nineteenth century, the Women's Suffrage Movement continued to gain momentum in its goal to gain equal rights for women. Roughly 30 percent (4.7 million) of the labor force in 1901 were female, a fact reflected in the literature of the time.[10] Women became authors more frequently and were increasingly cast as the main characters in literary works. Many female writers, including Henrietta M. Batson, Julia Cartwright, Ada Leverson, Marjorie Long, Constance Smith, and Flora Annie Smith, were widely read in the early 1900s but have received little critical attention in recent decades.

Throughout the Edwardian age, theater gained in prominence as a literary form. Ironically, the major "British" playwrights of the Edwardian age were predominantly Irish. Irish playwrights such as George Bernard Shaw and John Millington Synge took center stage in the early years of the twentieth century. The founding of the Irish National Theatre Society in 1902 and Abbey Theatre in 1904 provided an outlet for Irish playwrights. Theater was not the only genre with an increase in the prominence of "non-English" authors: William Butler Yeats, another Irishman, was the major poet of the age and the driving force behind the Abbey Theatre; at the same time, Scottish playwright J. M. Barrie, Irish novelist James Joyce, Polish-born novelist Joseph Conrad, and Argentinean-born novelist W. H. Hudson enjoyed widespread popularity. English-born writers were not without representation during the Edwardian age, with science fiction writers H. G. Wells and H. Rider Haggard and novelists Rudyard Kipling, Ford Madox Ford, and E. M. Forster attracting broad readerships.

The diverse literatures of Victorian and Edwardian Britain provide a wealth of research materials for both the novice and the expert researcher. Although the body of scholarship for the Edwardian age is smaller than that of the Victorian, researchers should have no shortage of resources for learning more about the literatures of either time period. As with the other volumes of Scarecrow Press's *Literary Research: Strategies and Sources* series, this book introduces students and scholars alike to resources and research methods, both traditional and new, for exploring these British literary periods. The resources discussed in this book are organized into eleven chapters, each of which focuses on a different resource type and specific search strategies, with the exception of chapter 11, which addresses how to apply the first ten chapters to a particular research question.

Chapter 1 introduces you to the basics of online searching. The skills discussed in this chapter—using Boolean operators, reading MARC records, developing search strategies, using truncation and wildcard operators, and interpreting and evaluating search results—are necessary as you search the online catalogs and databases discussed in later chapters. Chapter 3 continues the discussion of search strategies with specific catalog searches—author, title, and subject—and provides further information on evaluating and interpreting results sets. This chapter also introduces major union and national catalogs, including *Copac*, *WorldCat*, the *National Union Catalog*, and the British Library *Integrated Catalog*.

General literary reference sources are covered in chapter 2. This chapter introduces a variety of resource types, including research guides, period-specific encyclopedias and companions, general British literature encyclopedias and companions, biographical sources, chronologies, and select reference works on individual authors or genres. These sources tend to offer background and bibliographic information to help ground your research and identify additional resources.

Chapter 4 comprises a discussion of print and electronic bibliographies, indexes, and annual reviews, all of which will direct you to relevant books, book chapters, dissertations, journal articles, and reviews. Specifically, this chapter covers major general literature bibliographies, period bibliographies for secondary resources, period bibliographies for primary resources, and era author and genre bibliographies. Chapter 5 then moves from discussing indexing sources to examining secondary-source journal literature. It highlights major scholarly journals dedicated to research on the Victorian and Edwardian ages. Journal titles are organized into five major categories: general British literature titles, the nineteenth century, the twentieth century, author-specific journals, and other nonliterary journals.

Chapter 6 addresses publishing trends in contemporary reviews and literary magazines. It also discusses resources for locating period literary magazines, locating reviews and criticism in Victorian and Edwardian periodicals, locating creative writing in Victorian and Edwardian periodicals, and author-specific sources. Complementing the previous chapter, chapter 7 addresses the history and development of Victorian and Edwardian journals and newspapers. Specific resources are for background information, locating period journals and newspapers, and locating articles. Select journal- and topic-specific sources are also included.

Just as chapters 6 and 7 focus on primary sources, chapter 8 continues that strain by introducing major microform and digital collections. Rather than simply indexing or abstracting primary source materials, these collections provide the full text, and frequently page images, of books, journals, newspapers, and other print materials. The resources discussed are either finding aids or the microform and digitized collections themselves. Chapter 9 wraps up the primary source discussion by addressing manuscripts and archives. In addition to print and online sources for locating relevant archives and manuscripts, this chapter defines archives and manuscripts, outlines "best practices" for archival research, and explains researching at the British Library.

Chapter 10 addresses an ever-moving target: Web resources. Typically, these websites' contents correspond with the traditional materials covered in the previous chapters. This chapter surveys scholarly portals, electronic text archives, author sites, contemporary newspapers and journals, current awareness resources, reference tools, and cultural and historical sources.

The final chapter outlines one way of applying the research sources and strategies discussed throughout the book. Specifically, chapter 11 looks at how to research now-obscure texts such as Flora Annie Steel's *On the Face of the Waters*, which is little known today even though it was wildly popular in its time. Addressing reference, secondary, and primary sources, this chapter explains how to use specific resources to craft a research plan.

The appendix covers major atlases, chronologies, dictionaries, encyclopedias, handbooks, guides, bibliographies, and indexes in various disciplines or areas of study, including general resources, art, historical atlases and geographical resources, history, language and linguistics, literary terms and theory, music, philosophy, religion, science and medicine, social sciences, and theater. Neither the appendix nor the chapters proper seek to be completely comprehensive, but they should provide you the necessary information to begin your journey researching the literature of the Victorian and Edwardian ages.

NOTES

1. *Oxford English Dictionary*, s.v. "Victorian," http://dictionary.oed.com (accessed April 18, 2010).

2. Philip Davis, introduction to *The Oxford English Literary History* (New York: Oxford University Press, 2002), 8:9.

3. Ibid, 8:10.

4. "The Half-Century of Victoria's Reign" in *New Princeton Review* 2 (1887), 271–77.

5. Henry Bessemer, an English engineer, invented the Bessemer process for manufacturing steel in the mid-nineteenth century. This process was "the first cheap, large-scale method of making steel from pig iron." *Hutchinson Dictionary of Scientific Biography*, s.v. "Bessemer, Henry (1813–1898)," http://www.accessscience.com (accessed April 18, 2010).

6. The compound steam engine was developed in 1845 by Scottish mechanical engineer William McNaught. Northern textile manufacturers were the primary users of these engines. *Hutchinson Dictionary of Scientific Biography*, "McNaught, William (1813–1881)," http://www.accessscience.com (accessed April 18, 2010).

7. Dante Gabriel Rossetti, William Holman Hunt, John Everett Millais, and four of their friends formed the Pre-Raphaelite Brotherhood in 1848 as a means of rebelling against the Royal Academy, the establishment of Britain's art world. Other authors associated with this movement include Christina Rossetti, William Morris, and Algernon Swinburne. David Riede, "The Pre-Raphaelite School," in *A Companion to Victorian Poetry*, eds. Richard Cronin, Alison Chapman, and Antony H. Harrison (Malden, MA: Blackwell, 2002), http://www.blackwellreference.com (accessed April 18, 2010).

8. In Victorian England, novels were published in three volumes for circulating libraries such as Mudie's Select Circulating Library. These three-volume editions were referred to as "triple-deckers." Yellowbacks were the precursors to our modern-day paperbacks. They were "frequently translations or reprints," and "when original fiction appeared in this format, it was typically by minor authors." Patrick Brantlinger and William B. Thesing, introduction to *A Companion to the Victorian Novel*, eds. Patrick Brantlinger and William B. Thesing (Malden, MA: Blackwell, 2002), www .blackwellreference.com (accessed April 18, 2010).

9. Lascelles Abercrombie, "Literature," in *Edwardian England A.D. 1901–1910: A Series of Lectures Delivered at King's College, University of London, During the Session 1932–3*, ed. F. J. C. Hearnshaw (London: Ernest Benn Limited, 1933), 187.

10. "Economically Active Population by Major Industrial Groups (in Thousands): U.K. Great Britain," in *International Historical Statistics: Europe 1750-2005*, ed. B. R. Mitchell, 6th ed. (New York: MacMillan Publishers, 2007), 168.

Chapter One

Basics of Online Searching

The world of research resources is becoming increasingly complex, and more information is readily available today than ever before. To function in this rapidly changing world, both novice and experienced literary scholars need basic search skills. While nineteenth- and early twentieth-century primary sources comprise a relatively stable body of literature, the tools through which we access them continue to evolve. Scholars need to know what sources and search strategies are available in order to improve their research efficiency and effectiveness. This chapter introduces online searching basics in order to equip scholars to use online databases and catalogs. Although resources vary from one another, these strategies should transfer to any online source. From forming questions through understanding resource types, this chapter walks you through the basic steps of scholarly inquiry. Additionally, this chapter addresses developing search strategies, reading MARC records, and interpreting and evaluating results. The later chapters in this book build on the strategies discussed here, so you may need to return to this chapter periodically to remain grounded in online searching basics.

DEVELOPING SEARCH TERMS FROM
RESEARCH QUESTIONS

Nearly all scholarship begins with a question, which then serves as the foundation for developing a search strategy. Scholars who proceed without considering how to structure their queries may not uncover the best materials and then may become frustrated at the poor results they retrieve. Taking the time to understand how questions underpin any search strategy can alleviate this problem.

Often the words that comprise a question can be turned into the building blocks for successfully finding relevant information. Online resources such as databases and library catalogs frequently refer to these terms as *keywords*. After forming your question, identify the major concepts embedded within that question. Those concepts can then be used as specific terms or elaborated on to identify synonyms and related terms. Take, for instance, the following question: "How are women's roles in marriage represented in nineteenth-century fiction?" The words *women, marriage, nineteenth-century*, and *fiction* can be pulled out of the question to serve as keywords. By identifying the question's major ideas, you have begun to create the basis for your overall strategy. In another example, the question "How is industrialism represented in mid-Victorian literature?" could be similarly broken down into the following keywords: *industrialism, mid-Victorian*, and *literature*.

Keyword Searching

Once you have identified the major terms in your question, you are ready to build on and refine your overall strategy. Begin with the basic terms you have already selected, but do not restrict yourself to these initial keywords. If you rely only on those terms, you may severely limit your results and may be less successful in your research. Beginning with the keywords from the first question (*women, marriage, nineteenth-century*, and *fiction*), brainstorm synonymous or related terms. By doing so, you will have ready alternatives in case your initial search does not produce the desired results. Synonyms and related terms for women could include *female* and *girl*, while marriage could be supplemented with the terms *matrimony* and *domesticity*. Even *nineteenth-century* is not a completely clear-cut keyword. You can also search for *1800–1899* or the narrower term *Victorian*. Fiction could also be substituted with the terms *novel* and *short story*. Table 1.1 outlines the original and alternate keywords.

Many alternate keywords are not exact synonyms for the originally identified words in your original question. Throughout your search process, look for related, broader, and narrower terms as you explore a particular topic. In the example above, *matrimony* is a synonym for *marriage* while *domesticity* is a related term. Likewise, *Victorian* is a related term to the *nineteenth-century*

Table 1.1.   Identifying keywords.

Search Term 1	Search Term 2	Search Term 3	Search Term 4
Women	Marriage	Nineteenth-century	Fiction
Female	Matrimony	Victorian	Novel
Girl	Domesticity	1800–1899	Short story

while *1800–1899* is synonymous. With the vast array of words available, the chances are rather high that an author, indexer, or cataloger chose a different word than the one you initially selected. To ensure that you get the best, most relevant results, you may often need to stray from your original terms.

Reading MARC Records

Before continuing to discuss search strategies, let's take a moment to explore the backbone underlying library catalog records—the MARC record. Although some online resources for Victorian and Edwardian literature do not base their records on this format, MARC, which stands for MAchine-Readable Cataloging, is considered a universal standard for online library catalogs. Developed in 1997 from a merger between the United States and the Canadian cataloging standards, MARC has been widely adopted for use in library catalogs around the world. Even countries that formerly maintained their own cataloging standards have begun transitioning to MARC records. For instance, until the end of 2008, the United Kingdom maintained a variant form of the MARC record (UKMARC) while transitioning to the MARC standard. With the transition complete, you should be able to search catalogs from both the United Kingdom and the United States under the assumption that the information is presented using the MARC standard.

In a nutshell, MARC records (or any catalog or database record, for that matter) are a means of representing a tangible or digital item. Rather than provide the full text of a collection's books or journals, a library catalog contains data representing both the item's contents and the physical items themselves. The MARC record format ensures that, regardless of which library catalog you use, you can expect to find information about cataloged items in a standardized format. Each part of the MARC record is assigned a specific numerical tag to facilitate locating and retrieving records. This allows you, as a scholar, not only to select your own keywords but also to specify where those terms appear. Without this coding, you could not direct the catalog's search engine to locate the words *Kim* in the title field or Rudyard Kipling in the author field.

Both books and periodicals can be represented using MARC records; however, the fields vary slightly because of the format differences. A numerical tag marks each field, forming a framework on which to hang the bibliographic data for a particular resource. Each field can be represented by an index (author, title, subject, and so forth) that allows you to focus your search in a particular way. Having a separate index for titles, for instance, enables you to look for known titles as well as keywords in titles. If you specify that your terms must appear in the title, the speed and efficiency of your search should increase, because you are querying a particular index rather than the complete catalog contents. Additionally, the results quality can be vastly improved. The following example shows a modified MARC record for a book of literary criticism, *Men in Wonderland: The Lost Girlhood of the Victorian Gentleman* by Catherine Robson (Source: James Madison University Libraries Catalog):

010 00048321
020 0691004226 (alk. paper)
050 00 PR468.G5|bR63 2001
100 1 Robson, Catherine,|d1962–
245 10 Men in wonderland :|bthe lost girlhood of the Victorian gentleman /|cCatherine Robson
246 30 The lost girlhood of the Victorian gentleman
260 Princeton, N.J. :|bPrinceton University Press,|cc2001
300 xii, 250 p. :|bill. ;|c24 cm
500 Based on the author's dissertation
504 Includes bibliographical references (p. [231]–241) and index
505 0 Of prisons and ungrown girls: Wordsworth, De Quincey, and the construction of the lost self of childhood—The ideal girl in industrial England—The stones of childhood: Ruskin's "Lost jewels"—Lewis Carroll and the little girl: the art of self-effacement—A "new 'cry of the children'": legislating innocence in the 1880s—Lewis Carroll's letter to the St. James's Gazette, July 22, 1885.
600 10 Carroll, Lewis,|d1832-1898|xCharacters|xGirls
600 10 Ruskin, John,|d1819-1900|xCharacters|xGirls
650 0 English literature|y19th century|xHistory and criticism
650 0 Girls in literature
650 0 English literature|xMale authors|xHistory and criticism
650 0 Innocence (Psychology) in literature
650 0 Gender identity in literature
650 0 Children in literature
650 0 Sex role in literature
650 0 Men in literature

The Library of Congress call number is located in the 050 field. Standard bibliographic information on author, title, and publication details is available in the 100, 245, and 260 fields, respectively. In this particular record, the title statement (245) provides the standard title for the work, while field 246 indexes a varying form of title. Records for some books may also have table of contents or summaries. This particular record contains the table of contents for the book in the 505 field, which can be queried using a basic keyword search. Subject access comes through the inclusion of the 6xx fields. Here subject headings for a personal name are listed in the 600 field, while topical subject headings are listed using the 650 field. The language used in the subject fields is referred to as a controlled vocabulary, which is a preset terminology for creating uniform catalog records in order to ensure accurate results.

The sample record for *Blackwood's Edinburgh Magazine* illustrates some of the subtle, yet significant, differences between the book and periodical MARC records, as shown in the following (Source: British Library *Integrated Catalogue*):

```
001      002831924
022 0    |a 1747-3551 |2 02
222 0    |a Blackwood's Edinburgh magazine
245 00   |a Blackwood's Edinburgh magazine.
246 14   |a Blackwood's magazine |f <July–Dec. 1895>
260      |a Edinburgh : |b William Blackwood ; |a London : |b T. Cadell and
         W. Davis, |c 1817–1905.
300      |a 178 v. : |b ill. ; |c 22–24 cm.
310      |a Monthly
362 0    |a Vol. 1, no. 1 (Apr. 1817)-v. 178, no. 1082 (Dec. 1905).
500      |a Title from caption.
500      |a This work was commenced under the title of the "Edinburgh
         Monthly Magazine" and the several numbers of vol. 1 bear a head-title
         to that effect; in consequence, however, of a dispute, the undertaking
         was relinquished by the editors at the conclusion of vol. 1, and was
         continued by the Publisher as "Blackwood's Edinburgh Magazine."
555      |a Vols. 1 (1817)-50 (1841). 1 v.
563      |a Vol. XCIII in the Collins collection is in a nineteenth century Welsh
         brown calf binding with the ticket of Catherall & Nixon of Bangor.
580      |a Issued also in an American ed., beginning in 1833.
655 4    |a Periodical publications.—Edinburgh
775 1    |t Blackwood's Edinburgh magazine (New American ed.)
780 00   |t Edinburgh monthly magazine |x 1747-356X
785 00   |t Blackwood's magazine |x 0006-436X
```

Periodical titles are in the 222 field, although you will notice that the 245 title field, which is used for books, remains in the record. As with the book record, the 260 field provides information regarding publisher and publication location and date. Although the basic dates, 1817–1905, are listed in the 260 field, the 362 field offers greater detail by including the volume and issue numbers as well as month and year. The 500 field contents, or general note field, may vary from record to record, but in this particular record, it lists title changes to *Blackwood's Edinburgh Magazine*. These title changes are more explictly identified in the 780 and 785 fields, which state the preceding and succeeding titles, respectively. According to the record, *Blackwood's Edinburgh Magazine* continues *Edinburgh Monthly Magazine* and was continued by *Blackwood's Magazine*. To enhance access to the journal's contents, the 555 field lists any available finding aids and indexing sources. As with the book records, journal records have subject headings. This particular record has a genre/form subject heading to indicate the publication type.

While this brief overview should help you to understand the bare essentials of MARC records, it has only scratched the surface of this intricate classification system. The more you use MARC records and understand their structure, the more targeted and efficient you can be in developing your search strategies. As we continue our discussion, we will build on the concepts introduced in this section on MARC records.

SEARCH STRATEGIES

Field Searching

Now that you understand the basic structure of and major fields in a MARC record, you are ready to use that knowledge to your advantage and improve your online research skills. A keyword search allows you to query several fields at once, while the standard catalog indexes—author, subject, and title—can help you look more narrowly. Note that other indexes, such as series, call number, and ISBN, may sometimes be available, but expect to find at least the three aforementioned indexes in all online catalogs. When you use an online catalog, you should have the option to specify which indexes you wish to use. For instance, if you wanted to learn more about Great Britain's relationship with India, you could look specifically for *Great Britain* and *India* in the subject fields rather than looking generally for these terms as keywords. A keyword search for these two countries will most likely produce a greater number of irrelevant results than one that uses subject headings.

Scholars may also search catalogs using classification numbers. Typically, academic and research libraries use the Library of Congress Classification (LCC) system to organize their materials into twenty-one broad classes. Language and literature are both included in the P-class, with narrower subdivisions covering specific topics: e.g., English literature books are in the PR subclass. Appearing in the 050 field of the MARC record, each call numbers is unique to a specific book in a collection. If you know a book's call number, you can search for that number to find the record for a particular work. For instance, the call number for Catherine Robson's *Men in Wonderland: The Lost Girlhood of the Victorian Gentleman* is PR468.G5 R63 2001 (see earlier in the chapter). Using this number, you could retrieve the record for Robson's book, or you could browse the catalog to find other books near this particular call number. Browsing by call number replicates examining books on the shelf and can give you a sense of what other books your library has on a given topic.

You also have the option to query multiple indexes at once. If you wanted to find a copy of W. H. Hudson's *Green Mansions*, it would be most effective to look for *Hudson, W. H.* in the author field and *Green Mansions* in the title field. While field searching can certainly be effective, there are also appropriate uses of keyword searches. You may find it helpful to use a keyword prior to field searching if you are uncertain whether a library has information on your topic or do not know the proper subject heading. This can help you to "feel out" the available resources before refining your chosen terms. Keywords may also produce a broader results set.

Boolean Operators

Both field and keyword searches can be greatly enhanced by using Boolean operators. Developed in the mid-nineteenth century by English mathematician George Boole, Boolean logic serves as the basic syntax for most online catalogs and databases. Boole devised a form of logical algebra in which the operators *and*, *or*, and *not* expressed the relationship between specific mathematical elements. While Boole probably didn't have online resources in mind when he developed his logic system, Boolean operators have been co-opted to create more complex, yet more specific queries in online catalogs and databases. Considering the sample topic outlined in Table 1.1 (representations of women's roles in marriage in nineteenth-century fiction), the keywords and their synonyms have the potential to create a messy, awkward search if improperly organized. The Boolean operators serve as tools for creating a logical search string. Without these operators, the catalog or database would not know in what order or proximity to look for the terms. The outcome could be a haphazard set of results. To demonstrate how Boolean operators bring order to an otherwise chaotic search, the following sections discuss each of the three operators in greater detail, using the terms from Table 1.1.

Boolean and Searching

The *and* operator connects specific keywords, requiring that all be present in order for a record to be included in the results set. This connector narrows the search. Beginning with your pre-identified terms, join them with the *and* operator to ensure that all terms are present in each result (i.e., *women **and** marriage* *and 1800–1899*). By searching with these terms in a database such as the *MLA International Bibliography* (*MLAIB*), a major index for literary scholarship, you can identify relevant resources for your topic (see chapter 4 for more detailed discussion of the *MLAIB*). The sample results in the following (Source: *MLAIB*, via Gale Cengage) shows the appearance of the keywords in bold. While they do not appear immediately next to one another, they are all in the same record.

Title:	'East of the Sun and West of the Moon': Victorians and Fairy Brides
Author:	Silver, Carole
Source:	Tulsa Studies in Women's Literature. 6.2 (1987 Fall), pp. 283–98.
Subject Terms:	English literature, 1800–1899, Victorian period; fiction; and poetry; treatment of **women**; **marriage**; sources in Märchen; especially fairy bride; folk literature; folk narrative; folk tale; England; **1800–1899**; treatment of fairy bride; influence on English literature.
Document Type:	Bibliographic citation; journal article

If your query fails to retrieve the desired results, then turn to the synonymous and related terms you identified previously. The shaded area in the diagram below illustrates the results set from this search (Figure 1.1).

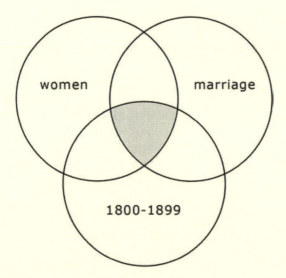

Figure 1.1.   Venn diagram of *and* Boolean searching.

Boolean or Searching

While the *and* operator narrows, the *or* operator broadens. If you were unsatisfied with the size or contents of the initial results set, you can use *or* to combine the synonymous and related terms identified in Table 1.1. The term *marriage*, for instance, could be paired with *matrimony* or *domesticity*. Combining terms such as these using *or* can improve the efficiency of your search. Rather than look for the terms separately, *or* enables you to entertain all possibilities at once. A query using *or* retrieves all results that contain at least one of the keywords present, unlike *and*, which requires all terms be present in each record retrieved.

Boolean not Searching

The *not* operator can be helpful when you need to exclude a term. In researching nineteenth-century (1800–1899) literature, you might retrieve results about literature from the Romantic period as well as the Victorian age. To limit results so that no items about the Romantic period are retrieved, you could use the *not* operator: *1800–1899* **not** *Romantic*. One potential pitfall of this particular query is that it might exclude some Romantic literature written during the Victorian age rather than simply excluding literature written in the Romantic period.

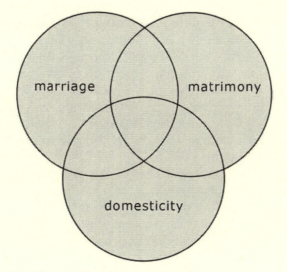

Figure 1.2. Venn diagram of *or* Boolean searching.

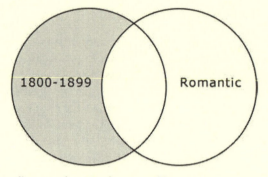

Figure 1.3. Venn diagram of *not* Boolean searching.

Truncation and Wildcard Operators

While you can use Boolean operators and nesting (a way of grouping terms, typically with parentheses) to look for word variants, most databases and catalogs recognize truncation and wildcard operators as a more efficient way of finding variants. Truncation operators enable you to look for a word's root and all of its possible endings. Wildcard operators substitute one or more letters in a given word, allowing easy identification of spelling variants. The most frequently used symbols are the asterisk (*) and the question mark (?). The exclamation point (!), pound sign (#), dollar sign ($), and plus mark (+) may also serve as truncation or wildcard operators; however, they occur less frequently than the first two. The asterisk is most often used at the end of a keyword, telling the search engine to look for a word's root followed by any number of characters. A query for *pastor** would retrieve *pastor, pastors, pastoral, pastorally,* and *pastorate* as well as any other words beginning with the root pastor. Be careful when deciding where to place the truncation mark. If you truncate too severely, you may retrieve irrelevant results. Using our previous example, if you looked for *past**, you would retrieve terms such as *pastel* and *pastry,* which are not relevant to your search. Because the truncation symbol may vary from database to database and catalog to catalog, make a habit of checking the database's or catalog's help file to determine which truncation mark is recognized.

Wildcards may be used independent of or in conjunction with truncation marks. Unlike truncation marks, which occur at word endings, wildcards are typically placed in the middle of a word. Depending on the database or catalog, the wildcard may represent no or one character. Although the symbol varies, the most typical wildcard is the question mark (?). This is particularly helpful for finding spelling variants. A search for *colo?r* will retrieve both *color* and *colour,* accounting for both American and British spellings.

STRUCTURING THE SEARCH

Building on the basics of Boolean searching, consider using various methods to further combine your terms and create more specific queries. Although *and*, *or*, and *not* are quite helpful for creating the basic structure, they sometimes do not do enough to retrieve the results you need. The following section discusses three methods for organizing and structuring your keywords: nesting, phrase searching, and proximity searching. Nesting must be used in conjunction with the Boolean operators, while phrase and proximity searching may be either independent of or in conjunction with Boolean operators.

Nesting

Nesting is a way to group a particular set of keywords in order to pair them with additional terms. Most databases and catalogs recognize parentheses, ( ), for nesting terms together. This strategy can be particularly useful for grouping synonyms and alternate spellings for terms. For instance, the terms previously identified in this chapter can be employed more effectively with both Boolean operators and nesting. By nesting the terms, you instruct the catalog or database to identify them in a particular order. Generally speaking, most databases and catalogs look for your terms in the order you enter them (i.e., left to right); however, by using the nesting technique, you can change the outcome. The two examples listed below demonstrate searches that use Boolean operators and structured without (search 1) and with (search 2) nesting.

Search 1: nineteenth century *and* marriage *or* matrimony *or* domesticity
Search 2: nineteenth century *and* (marriage *or* matrimony *or* domesticity)

If you input search 1, the catalog will look for the terms as follows:

nineteenth century *and* marriage
or
domesticity
or
matrimony

Without the parentheses, the catalog will assume you are linking marriage and nineteenth century based on word order. Because of this, your results could be about domesticity or matrimony in any time period or about marriage in the nineteenth century. Search 2, however, requires that the term

nineteenth century be present along with one of the three terms in parentheses: marriage, matrimony, or domesticity. The second query will most likely
be the better of the two in terms of quality of results. Depending on your
question, the "right" quantity may refer to fewer, targeted results rather than
more, broader results.

Phrase Searching

Another method of grouping terms is phrase searching, which uses quotation
marks (" ") to ensure that particular keywords are located in their exact order
and form. Since most catalogs look for multiple terms as individual words
rather than exact phrases, quotation marks are necessary to tell the search
engine in the catalog to find a phrase rather than discrete words. If you
searched for *Married Women's Property Act* without quotations, the catalog
would function as though you had placed *and* between each of the words,
causing all words to be found in each record but not necessarily in that order.
To retrieve these words as a phrase, search for it as the "*Married Women's
Property Act*," making sure to place the entire phrase in quotation marks.
Quotation marks may also be placed around an operator—such as *and, or,*
and *not*—in order to look for the operator as a word. By placing *not* in quotation marks, you will retrieve records containing the word *not*. Without the
quotation marks, the catalog may read the term as an operator and assume you
wish to exclude the word immediately following *not*.

Proximity Searching

At times, Boolean operators, nesting, and phrase searching do not give you
the necessary level of control. In that situation, proximity searching may
provide the direction you need. Two proximity operators are recognized by
most catalogs and databases: *near* and *with(in)*. As discussed more explicitly
below, the two operators perform similar functions but have different implications for the order in which you place your keywords. As with truncation
marks and wildcards, always check the database's or catalog's help file to
determine which proximity operators you should use.

Near Searching

The *near* operator, often signified by the letter *n*, is placed between two terms
to specify that they must occur a specific number of words from each other
in either direction. If you search for *London n2 tower*, you would retrieve
London Tower and Tower of London but not "the tower on the bank of the
River Thames in London."

With(in) Searching

The *with(in)* operator, represented by the letter *w*, is also placed between two keywords. However, the *with(in)* operator indicates that the words must be a certain distance from each other in a particular order. Searching *William w2 Thackeray* would retrieve hits for William Thackeray, William M. Thackeray, and William Makepeace Thackeray but not Thackeray, William Makepeace.

SUBJECT SEARCHING:
USING A CONTROLLED VOCABULARY

Much of our search strategies discussion has focused on keywords; however, subject headings can also be highly effective. As a scholar, you may need to employ a combination of keyword and subject headings. The trick is learning when and how to use each search type and how to use them effectively in conjunction with one another. The earlier discussion of MARC records covered the basics of subject headings, or descriptors. One of the most common sets of subject headings is the Library of Congress subject headings (LCSH). A controlled vocabulary, LCSH is used in catalog records to describe a particular work's intellectual contents. These headings are selected by subject specialists for each work and are intended to improve retrieval of relevant items by identifying a book or article's major concepts. Although originated in the United States, the British Library adopted LCSH for subject access to most catalog records created after 1971, so this structure should be useful for using British as well as American library catalogs.

While keywords may retrieve many relevant records, a keyword search is neither as concise nor as accurate as a subject search. You could use keywords to learn about property rights in Great Britain and retrieve useful results; however, if you use the proper LC subject heading, *Right of property—Great Britain*, you may retrieve additional and more highly relevant results. If you don't know the proper LC subject heading for a particular topic, a couple of strategies can help you identify the correct heading. Most catalogs and databases have a subject index, so you can browse it to find the main concept in your research. If you enter the concept in the exact form as the appropriate subject heading, then you should be able to go straight to that heading and link directly to relevant results; however, if you did not word the concept properly, often the subject index will contain a cross-listed reference to point you to the correct term. For instance, if you looked for *property rights* in the LCSH, the entry would read *see Right of property* to direct you to the appropriate heading. The second way of identifying subject headings is by using keywords to lead you to the heading. You could look for *property rights and Great Britain* as keywords.

Once your search is completed, sift through the results to find relevant ones. By examining the full records and reading through the assigned subject headings of books in your area, you should find at least one that matches your search topic. Since most online catalogs and databases contain hyperlinked subject headings, you should be able to click on the appropriate heading to bring up a list of all the books associated with that heading. This method of building on keywords to identify subject headings is known as pearling.

There are specific formats used for literature subject headings in the LCSH. Literary genres, themes, authors, and literary works may all be searched as subject headings. If you needed general information on lyric poetry, the subject heading *lyric poetry* would probably be your best starting point. Likewise, information about nineteenth-century British literature should all be classified under *English literature—19th century*. In the case of literature, however, one of the most important subject heading types is the author as subject. If you needed information about anything related to Charles Dickens (e.g., his life, correspondence, literary works, religious views, literary criticism, etc.), the best initial search would be to look for Dickens as a subject: *Dickens, Charles*. All literary authors are indexed as subjects that follow a particular form, beginning with the author's last name and followed by his or her first name, birth and death years, and any applicable subject information. Table 1.2 illustrates the form for LCSH when a person is a subject. As you can see in the example subject headings below, the heading always begins last name, first name, and birth and death years. That stem heading may or may not be followed by additional information that specifies a narrower results set. This format works for all authors regardless of period, genre, or nationality.

Table 1.2. LCSH format for a person as a subject.

Information Need	LC Subject Heading
General information on Charles Dickens	Dickens, Charles, 1812–1870.
Bibliography on Dickens	Dickens, Charles, 1812–1870—Bibliography.
Orphans in Dickens's writing	Dickens, Charles, 1812–1870—Characters—Orphans.
Dickens's correspondence	Dickens, Charles, 1812–1870. Correspondence.
Literary criticism on Dickens	Dickens, Charles, 1812–1870—Criticism and interpretation.
Encyclopedia on Dickens	Dickens, Charles, 1812–1870—Encyclopedias.
Dickens's knowledge of London	Dickens, Charles, 1812–1870—Knowledge—London (England).
Criticism on *Oliver Twist*	Dickens, Charles, 1812–1870. Oliver Twist.

Lesser-known (or less well-studied) authors will have fewer subject headings assigned to their name, but regardless of the number of headings, the form always remains the same. If you are researching an anonymous work, then there should be a LC subject heading for the title of the work, which you would search in the subject field rather than the title field.

LIMITING AND REVISING

As with good writing, good research is a recursive process. You may need to go back and revise your keywords and overall strategy as you develop deeper knowledge of your topic. This may involve setting a limiter such as language, date of publication, document type, or peer review, or it may mean identifying completely new terms. Limiting is often necessary when your initial query retrieves far too many records and you need to narrow the results to make it manageable. Remember that your first search is not always your best, so don't get stuck on certain words if they are not producing useful results.

INTERPRETING AND EVALUATING SEARCH RESULTS

Once you have a results list, your next step is to do the intellectual work of interpreting and evaluating it. The first records may not be the most relevant for your particular project, so it is important to read through all results before selecting your resources. One of the first steps is to identify what the record represents. Examine the information provided (e.g., title, table of contents, abstract or summary, subject headings, and so on) to glean pertinent information. You should be able to easily determine the work's format from the catalog record. Is it a book, an article, a sound recording, or archival material? If you need primary sources, then archival material will be better suited to your purposes than a scholarly book. Depending on your research project criteria, you may also want to consider the publication date. Resource timeliness is not always as essential in the humanities as it is in the sciences and social sciences, but regardless of your topic, examine both historic and contemporary scholarship. As for the book's actual contents, there is only so much you can tell from the catalog or database record. In a best-case scenario, you will find detailed subject headings as well as a table of contents or summary of the work. In a worst-case scenario, you may only have the bibliographic information to help you determine the work's contents. In either situation, eventually you will have to get your hands on the book or article and examine it for yourself, since online records are still inadequate for determining the item's relevance. Never underestimate the importance of serendipity in research. Even the most advanced scholars may not find all of their results through the library catalog. Many times the best results are found by browsing the books located on the shelf next to the titles you identified through the catalog.

Most catalogs and databases use relevance ranking when presenting search results. Relevance ranking, as its name suggests, is intended to move the most relevant resources to the top of the results list. Ranking varies from resource to resource, so don't assume that what is considered relevant in one catalog is equally relevant in another. The following lists some criteria used for relevance ranking in literature resources:

- Closeness of document match to search terms
- Number of search terms in the record
- Proximity of the search terms
- Uniqueness of the search terms
- Frequency of search terms
- Location of search terms in record

Some resources do not apply relevance ranking to all retrieved results, but rather limit their ranking to a specific number of initial results. Also, some do not default to or even offer relevance ranking; rather, they may sort by author, title, descending date, or ascending date. With or without relevance ranking, always evaluate your results carefully. See chapter 3 for further discussion of evaluating resources.

CATALOGS, DATABASES, INDEXES, AND SEARCH ENGINES: UNDERSTANDING THE INFORMATION RESOURCE

Equally important with understanding your results is understanding the information resource you are using. Libraries offer a variety of resource types, each intended for a unique purpose. This section surveys catalogs, databases, indexes, and search engines. Knowing the purpose of each will help you know what to expect in terms of content and functionality. Catalogs were formerly known as card catalogs, with individual records typed on index cards that were browseable by hand. Today's catalogs are searchable online and tend not to have a print counterpart. Like the card catalogs of the past, online catalogs facilitate access to and bibliographic information about a library's print and electronic holdings (see chapter 3 for more on online catalogs). In addition to the catalog, your library most likely provides access to an assortment of online databases and indexes. Databases are online repositories of intellectual content such as journal articles, primary sources, audio or video files, and datasets. Indexes generally do not include full text but contain bibliographic information that can be used to locate and eventually access various resources. The database and index contents may be created by one organization but hosted on one or more platforms. For instance, the *MLA International Bibliography*, a major literary index, is currently available on five platforms from four vendors. While the bibliography's intellectual contents are the same, the index's appearance and functionality varies from platform to platform. If you ever encounter a new database or index with an unfamiliar platform, its help menu should explain the basics of searching and using that particular resource.

Search engines are the means through which you, as a user, can access the contents of catalogs, databases, and indexes. They include the algorithms necessary to query the terms and limiters you input against the records and contents of the catalog, database, or index you are using. You are probably also familiar with the search engines publicly available on the Web. Google and Yahoo!—along with other search engines that troll the public Internet—have become household names in recent years. While they should not be your primary research tool, this type of search engine can be vastly useful in assisting the research process. Although not all information on the Web is reliable or relevant, there are many excellent resources freely available to the general public, and these engines can help connect you with those sources. As with materials found through library catalogs and databases, you must carefully evaluate any resource you find on the Web. Some of the most relevant, reliable Internet sources for the Victorian and Edwardian ages are discussed in more detail in chapter 10.

With the recent "Googlization" of information, this chapter would be lacking if it did not specifically address Google. Most people are familiar with Google and its clean interface and seemingly simple search functionality. While Google searches the Web for information in a general way, it also has specific tools for accessing scholarly information. Google Books and Google Scholar are two members of the Google family that are useful for scholars. Google Books is Google's digitization effort that makes page images and full text of books freely available to the general public. Partnering with over ten thousand publishers and authors from over one hundred countries, Google Books has full or limited access to the full text of books and some periodicals. The project also partners with major research libraries to digitize the texts from their collections that have fallen out of copyright. See chapter 10 for more on Google Books.

Another Google tool—Google Scholar—indexes scholarly literature to make citation information freely available to the public. This interdisciplinary tool grants access to citations and limited full text for peer-reviewed papers, theses, books, abstracts, and articles. Recently Google has enhanced the functionality of Scholar by working with libraries to link Google Scholar citations to the physical and digital collections as represented in library catalogs and periodical holdings. This can be a useful tool, but as is true of any resource, don't rely solely on Google Scholar, as no catalog, database, index, or search engine is completely comprehensive for any given subject area. For more on Google Scholar see chapter 4. The information found in Google Books and Google Scholar can also be found in the catalogs and databases provided by your library. Although the Google products are freely accessible and come in the familiar Google packaging, library catalogs and databases offer richer subject indexing to help you access, interpret, and evaluate the sources you find.

CONCLUSION

You should now be familiar with the basics of online searching. The strategies discussed in this chapter are built upon in later chapters that introduce specific resource types. As you go through the research process, feel free to revisit this chapter for a refresher on how to search effectively. With a rapidly changing information landscape, familiar resources continue to change, while new resources emerge on the scene. If you have a firm handle on these strategies, their strengths, and their weaknesses, you should be well prepared to adapt to those changes and incorporate new resources into your research process. The rest of this book teaches you about specific print and electronic resources and how to use them in conjunction with one another.

Chapter Two

General Literary
Reference Sources

In addition to knowing basic search strategies, familiarizing yourself with general literary reference sources will help you establish a solid foundation for researching the Victorian and Edwardian ages. This chapter specifically addresses research guides, period-specific encyclopedias and companions, general British literature encyclopedias and companions, biographical sources, chronologies, and select reference works on individual authors or genres. Resources such as these frequently provide both bibliographic information on various literary genres and periods and valuable background information about specific literary movements, authors, and texts. These general literary reference sources are an excellent starting place for any research project, whether you are a student beginning your study of Victorian and Edwardian literature or a seasoned scholar venturing into a new research area. The information they include will help you contextualize a particular author, text, movement, or literature, and they often contain valuable bibliographies that point you to seminal works on a particular topic.

RESEARCH GUIDES

Harner, James L. *Literary Research Guide: An Annotated Listing of Reference Sources in English Literary Studies.* 5th ed. New York: Modern Language Association of America, 2008. Also available online at www.mlalrg.org.

Marcuse, Michael J. *A Reference Guide for English Studies.* Berkeley: University of California Press, 1990.

A frequent companion of literature graduate students, James L. Harner's *Literary Research Guide: An Annotated Listing of Reference Sources in English Literary Studies*, now in its fifth edition, has long been the standard resource for students and scholars of literature as well as librarians. The *Literary Research Guide*, commonly referred to as Harner, is an annotated bibliography of major literary reference sources for English-language literatures. Harner emphasizes American and British literatures, as well as other literatures in English, but also includes select entries on related topics such as foreign-language literatures, comparative literature, book collecting, composition and rhetoric, linguistics, and film and literature. Each of the guide's twenty-one broad divisions—which correspond to general literary reference works, national literatures, and topics or sources related to literature—is further subdivided according to type of resource (e.g., bibliographies of bibliographies, guides to primary works, concordances, and background reading). As a whole, the *Literary Research Guide* offers a thorough overview of bibliographies, abstracts, surveys of research, indexes, databases, catalogs, general histories and surveys, annals, chronologies, dictionaries, encyclopedias, handbooks, and other print and electronic reference materials.

In total, 1,059 entries with MLA citations and objective evaluations for each resource comprise the guide. According to Harner, the resources were selected based on thoroughness, accuracy, effective organization, and adequate indexing or accessibility. Despite the vast amount of resources covered, the *Literary Research Guide* generally excludes single-author or literary work resources, which scholars can easily locate using their local library catalog. Because of the depth and breadth of resources addressed, the guide is aimed not at novice scholars but at upper-level undergraduate students through sophisticated scholars. Besides the general table of contents, each section begins with a thorough table of contents that outlines the way in which the division is organized into both subdivisions and resource types. For instance, the section on English literature is broken down according to general resources and major time periods. A Victorian scholar would thus consult the "Nineteenth-Century Literature" subdivision of the English literature section. Each narrower subdivision is then organized according to resource type and genre. Detailed indexes of persons (authors, editors, compilers, etc.), titles, and subjects enable scholars to locate a known work through the person or title indexes or works on a particular area of interest through the subject index. Recently, the *Literary Research Guide* contents became available as an online reference source, available to libraries by subscription.

A complementary resource to Harner is Michael Marcuse's *A Reference Guide for English Studies*. Marcuse is similar to Harner in scope but has not been updated since its original publication in 1990. *A Reference Guide for*

English Studies is an annotated guide to reference sources in English studies, which Marcuse defines as areas of scholarly inquiry of interest to faculty in English language and literature departments. This guide teaches students to become more "self-sufficient" in research libraries, and while helpful for beginning scholars, it is really intended for use by more experienced scholars from literary studies and allied fields. Covering English- and foreign-language materials, Marcuse aims to be highly selective in his bibliography but does include some books of "lesser quality" when a better alternative was unavailable. Only selective single-author or single-work reference materials are addressed. While the majority of entries are for book-length materials, a few are for article-length pieces. Marcuse's primary use is for locating appropriate reference materials on a particular topic; however, its secondary function—serving as a basic reference bibliography in a field or subfield of English studies and providing an overview for librarians of an English studies reference collection—is equally important. While not intended for bibliographical authority, completeness, or representative of consensus, Marcuse offers an entry point into English literary studies for those unfamiliar with the field's principal reference works.

Entries in *A Reference Guide for English Studies* generally fall into three categories: single works of scholarly reference, scholarly journals in particular fields, and frequently recommended books in a particular field. Each entry comprises a bibliographic citation, a description, and cross-referencing to supplementary and complementary works. As a whole, the entries are organized into sections addressing large topics of interest, broad classes of reference works, general categories of literary study, traditional English literary periods, and American literature. The twenty-four sections cover: general works; libraries; retrospective and current national bibliography; serial publications; miscellany; history and ancilla to historical study; biography and biographical references; archives and manuscripts; language, linguistics, and philology; literary materials and contexts; literature; English literature; medieval literature; literature of the Renaissance and earlier seventeenth century; literature of the nineteenth century; literature of the twentieth century; American literature; poetry and versification; the performing arts—theater, drama, and film; prose fiction and nonfictional prose; theory, rhetoric, and composition; bibliography; and the profession of English. Each section is further broken down according to appropriate subdivisions, and is generally arranged as follows: guides, reviews of research, closed and serial bibliographies, and reference works such as encyclopedias, companions, dictionaries, and reference histories. Sections specific to a literary period also include works on poetry, drama, prose fiction, and nonfictional prose.

The prefatory materials provide an overview of entries on journals and frequently recommended works, a list of similar guides, and a short-form listing of all main entries. This volume also contains both guides to abbreviations, acronyms, and sigla used in the entries and indexes to authors, compilers, contributors, and editors, to titles, and to subjects and authors-as-subjects. Throughout the book, extensive cross-referencing directs scholars to other pertinent resources. For Victorian and Edwardian literature, Section Q ("Literature of the Nineteenth Century") and Section R ("Literature of the Twentieth Century") are the most relevant; however, scholars should use the indexes to identify sources that are categorized in other areas such as the genre sections or general English literature section. While most of the "Literature of the Nineteenth Century" section will be relevant to the Victorian age, the "Literature of the Twentieth Century" section contains far fewer works relevant to the Edwardian age.

GENERAL BRITISH LITERARY
ENCYCLOPEDIAS AND COMPANIONS

Birch, Dinah, ed. *The Oxford Companion to English Literature*. 7th ed. New York: Oxford University Press, 2009.

Head, Dominic, ed. *The Cambridge Guide to Literature in English*. 3rd ed. New York: Cambridge University Press, 2006.

Kastan, David Scott, ed. *The Oxford Encyclopedia of British Literature*. 5 vols. New York: Oxford University Press, 2006.

Kirkpatrick, D. L., ed. *Reference Guide to English Literature*. 3 vols. 2nd ed. Chicago: St. James Press, 1991.

Serafin, Steven, and Valerie Grosvenor Myer, eds. *The Continuum Encyclopedia of British Literature*. New York: Continuum, 2003.

Now in its seventh edition, *The Oxford Companion to English Literature* is an excellent source for brief overviews of authors, literary works, critical theory, literary characters, literary terms, and literary movements. Edited by Dinah Birch for the Oxford University Press, this edition of *The Oxford Companion to English Literature* is aimed primarily at generalists and secondarily at students, scholars, and journalists. Although the main focus is English literature, as opposed to literature in English, this work covers select foreign, postcolonial, and American writers. The seventh edition has greater coverage of genres such as biography, crime fiction, fantasy, science fiction, and travel writing when compared to previous editions. This single-volume work also has four introductory essays: "Literary Culture and the Novel in the New Millennium," "Cultures of Reading," "Black British Literature," and "Children's Literature." Although this work lacks an index, the alphabetical arrangement of entries should provide sufficient access to the volume's contents. The entries are generally brief, ranging in length from a few words to a couple of pages, making this companion a good source for quick answers rather than in-depth analyses. Entries cover topics such as *Asolando*, Charles Lutwidge Dodgson, dystopia, historical fiction, the periodical *Nineteenth Century*, romance, sensation novels, and Algernon Charles Swinburne. *The Oxford Companion to English Literature*'s four appendixes comprise a chronology and lists of poets laureate, children's laureates, and literary awards. This work concludes with an "Index of New and Heavily Revised Entries by Contributor."

Edited by Dominic Head, the third edition to ***The Cambridge Guide to Literature in English*** has a broader scope than *The Oxford Companion to English Literature*. This volume is a guide to literature in English originating in English-speaking cultures from Africa, Australia, Canada, the Caribbean, India, Ireland, New Zealand, the South Pacific, the United Kingdom, and the United States. This edition emphasizes contemporary writing and incorporates 280 new entries, most of which are for living writers. Since the focus is on literatures in English, *The Cambridge Guide to Literature in English* discusses foreign-language writers only within the context of genres and movements they influenced or created, with the exception of Old English and Middle English influences. This guide's entries are arranged alphabetically and cover topics such as writers; individual plays, poems, novels, and other works; literary groups of schools; wider literary movements; critical schools or movements; literary genres; poetic forms and subgenres of drama and fiction; critical terms; rhetorical terms; theatres and theatre companies; literary magazines; and broader areas such as the Bible in English, conduct books, estates satire, libraries, pantomime, and unreliable narrator. This guide contains no index, table of contents, or appendixes.

Designed to complement *The Continuum Encyclopedia of American Literature*, ***The Continuum Encyclopedia of British Literature*** aims to be a comprehensive survey of literature that is "British in scope or origins." Edited by Steven R. Serafin and Valerie Grosvenor Myer, this encyclopedia covers literatures in English from Africa, Australia, Canada, the Caribbean, India, and New Zealand in addition to literature written in Britain and Ireland. Authors were selected based on their contribution to British literature's expansion and development. More than 1,200 entries for individual authors, literary works, and literary topics comprise the encyclopedia's contents. Author entries provide brief biographical information, a critical overview of their work, and a selective bibliography of further readings; these entries address authors such as John Buchan, Erskine Childers, G. K. Chesterton, Kenneth Grahame, Sarah Grand, and Robert Louis Stevenson. Entries for literary works are relatively few and each contains a summary alongside a discussion of its literary form and merits. The topical entries discuss varied subjects such as "Australian Literature in English," "The City and Literature," "Detective Fiction before 1945," "Gay Male Literature," "Literary Awards and Prizes," "Science Fiction," "Travel and Literature," and "Victorian Women's Poetry." Entries cross-reference to one another, and pseudonyms also cross-reference to the appropriate main entry. The articles tend to be lengthier and more in depth than those in either *The Oxford Companion to English Literature* or *The Cambridge Guide to Literature in English*. Additional features are guides to topical articles and abbreviations for periodicals in the front matter and extensive back matter, which addresses British monarchs, a historical-literary timeline, poet laureates, literary awards and prizes, a list of contributors, and an index to authors, works, and topics.

Another reliable English literature encyclopedia is ***The Oxford Encyclopedia of British Literature***. This five-volume set, edited by David Scott Kastan for Oxford University Press, has more selective coverage than the three previous reference books discussed and comprises only five hundred substantial articles about British literary history. With students as the intended audience, the articles focus on major authors and some specific genres, institutions, movements, or themes with significant impact on British literature's development. Ranging in length from four to eight pages, the articles are intended to be authoritative but not exhaustive, and include a selective bibliography of primary and secondary source materials and cross-referencing to related articles. The articles cover varied topics such as the Abbey Theatre, Matthew Arnold, Edward Bulwer Lytton, censorship, Maria Edgeworth, plagiarism, poet laureates, reading, the sensation novel, Queen Victoria, and the Victorian stage. The first volume contains a table of contents listing all articles in the five-volume set, while volume 5 has a comprehensive index to authors, works, and subjects covered in the whole set along with a contributor directory. In addition to the final index, volume 1 provides a guide to topical entries, which can be broadly categorized into the following areas: genres; schools, groups, and movements; institutions, formal and informal; and general topics. Volume 1 also offers a chronology that places the article topics in the encyclopedia in context of British and world history. Chronologies will be discussed in greater detail later in this chapter.

In its second edition, D. L. Kirkpatrick's ***Reference Guide to English Literature*** was reformatted from the first edition's eight slim volumes, which were organized first by time period and then by genre within time period, to a set of three substantial volumes organized alphabetically by author. The first two volumes serve as a guide to authors from Britain, Ireland, Australia, Canada, New Zealand, and English-speaking countries in Africa, Asia, and the Caribbean. Each author entry has a brief biographical statement that details education, military service, marriage(s), a chronological summary of the author's life, and any awards or honors the author received. This is followed by a bibliography of the author's primary source publications and selected critical studies about the author along with a critical assessment of his or her works. Both volumes 1 and 2 provide alphabetical and chronological author lists and alphabetical and chronological works lists for those covered in the set. The author-specific entries are preceded by essays that introduce and contextualize various periods in English literature, such as "The Victorian Period," "The Novel to 1900," "20th-Century Fiction," "20th-Century Poetry," "20th-Century Drama," and "Commonwealth Literature." These address the context and background of a certain genre and literary period. The third volume focuses on major literary and select historical works rather than authors. Organized alphabetically by title, the works entries list the genre, author, and publication date, and summarize the work in question. Volume 3 concludes with a title index to books included in each author entry's bibliography. Individual index entries contain information on the work's format, specifying whether it is fiction, verse, play, screenplay, radio play, or television play.

VICTORIAN AND EDWARDIAN ENCYCLOPEDIAS AND COMPANIONS

Adams, James Eli, Tom Pendergast, and Sara Pendergast, eds. *The Encyclopedia of the Victorian Era*. 4 vols. Danbury, CT: Grolier Academic Reference, 2003.

Cevasco, George A., ed. *The 1890s: An Encyclopedia of British Literature, Art, and Culture*. New York: Garland, 1993.

Marcus, Laura, and Peter Nicholls, eds. *The Cambridge History of Twentieth-Century English Literature*. Cambridge: Cambridge University Press, 2004.

Mitchell, Sally, ed. *Victorian Britain: An Encyclopedia*. New York: Garland, 1988.

Roberts, Adam C. *Victorian Culture and Society: The Essential Glossary*. London: Arnold, 2003.

Stringer, Jenny, ed. *The Oxford Companion to Twentieth-Century Literature in English*. New York: Oxford University Press, 1996.

Trodd, Anthea. *A Reader's Guide to Edwardian Literature*. New York: Harvester Wheatsheaf, 1991.

Tucker, Herbert F., ed. *A Companion to Victorian Literature and Culture*. Malden, MA: Blackwell, 1999.

Although not strictly an encyclopedia, Herbert F. Tucker's *A Companion to Victorian Literature and Culture* is a highly useful resource for both quick reference and in-depth study of the Victorian age. Part of the *Blackwell Companions to Literature and Culture* series, this volume is intended both as a reference work, by providing bibliographies for further reading and contextual and background information, and as a comprehensive guide to understanding the complexities of Victorian literature and culture. The companion covers Great Britain from 1830 to 1900 in twenty-nine topical chapters, which are organized into five broad sections: "History in Focus," "Passages of Life," "Walks of Life," "Kinds of Writing," and "Borders." Each chapter concludes with brief bibliographies of references and suggestions for further reading, both of which will prove quite helpful for scholars desiring more in-depth coverage of a particular topic. The book as a whole and the individual chapters are organized along chronological, linear lines, mimicking the steady expansion of Victorian culture and society. While this volume is quite comprehensive in its treatment of the Victorian age, several major issues such as utilitarianism, socialism, evangelicals, aesthetes, the science and religion debate, the women writers dilemma, and social classes are not treated in individual chapters but rather are recurring themes throughout the book. Scholars seeking information about a particular issue or event should use the detailed general subject index and the index of Victorian works to locate appropriate sections of the book.

Edited by James Eli Adams, Tom Pendergast, and Sara Pendergast, *The Encyclopedia of the Victorian Era* is invaluable for understanding the contexts in which Victorian literature was produced. This encyclopedia contains 627 signed essays on politics, society, and intellectual life in Britain between 1837 and 1901. While many literary sources emphasize biographies, this work not only focuses on topical essays but also includes select biographical entries for individuals who made significant contributions to the Victorian era, such as women's education pioneer Dorothea Beale, actress Ellen Terry, and novelist William Makepeace Thackeray. The entries are organized alphabetically and conclude with brief secondary-source bibliographies and occasionally list websites. To contextualize the Victorian age, this encyclopedia offers some entries on "the impact of Victorianism outside of Great Britain" to show the influence Victorian Britain had on the world and to demonstrate the global nature of the issues addressed.

The front matter of volume 1 of *The Encyclopedia of the Victorian Era* has an alphabetical list of entries, while volume 4 contains the back matter for the entire set, including three appendixes, which provide a map of the British Isles, primary documents, and selected websites. The primary documents appendix comprises selective documentation of "Domestic Life and Social Conditions,"

"Literature," "Politics and Economics," and "Religion, Philosophy, and Science." Each subsection of primary documents begins with a brief narrative situating the documents and issues within the Victorian age. Documents such as an excerpt from *Prostitution, Considered in its Moral, Social, and Sanitary Aspects*, "The White Man's Burden," an excerpt from *Imperialism: A Study*, and an excerpt from *Utilitarianism* are intended to help scholars understand the Victorian age. Another feature of this encyclopedia is a synoptic table of contents that categorizes entries into broad subjects, such as "Biographies," "Commerce and Economics," "Domestic Life and Social Conditions," "Education," "Exploration and Travel," "Medicine and Health," "Politics, Diplomacy, and War," "Print Culture," "Recreation, Leisure, and Entertainment," "Religion, Ethics, and Philosophy," "Science, Technology, and Academic Study," "Sexuality and Gender," and "Visual Arts and Architecture." A directory of contributors with their affiliations and the title of entries contributed, as well as a full index of persons, works, and subjects, concludes the volume.

Another excellent source for understanding the context and culture of the Victorian age is Sally Mitchell's **Victorian Britain: An Encyclopedia**. Published by Garland Press in 1988, this work continues to provide valuable information about the people, events, institutions, topics, groups, and artifacts of Great Britain from 1837 to 1901. *Victorian Britain* is a single-volume reference work intended to demonstrate the interdisciplinary nature of Victorian studies through the people and topics encompassed by Victoria's reign. With a broad-ranging audience—from undergraduates and general readers to graduate students and scholars—this work is useful to researchers of all levels. *Victorian Britain* offers balanced coverage of the Victorian age by shortening entries on major figures already well represented in other resources to make room for lesser-known figures. Rather than focusing exclusively on Britain, *Victorian Britain* also covers Ireland and pays specific notice to the colonies and the empire. The volume begins with a chronology of historical, cultural, and literary events in Britain between 1837 and 1901. The entries are arranged alphabetically, include bibliographies of further readings, cross-reference to related articles, and may be accompanied by illustrations. The entries cover a wide range of topics such as married women's property, decadence (1890–1900), Isabella Bird (1831–1904), birth control, the novel, the settlement movement, the social season, and William Ewart Gladstone (1809–1898). The volume wraps up with an annotated bibliography of research materials for Victorian studies that is organized according to the following broad categories: "Archives and Manuscripts," "Bibliographies," "Biography," "Dissertations," "Guides to Research," "Indexes," "Library Catalogs," "Microform Projects," "Parliamentary Debates," "Periodical Lists," and "Statistics." *Victorian Britain* concludes with a contributor list and an extensive index to topics, people, and works.

Victorian Culture and Society: The Essential Glossary is a slender volume that, in spite of its title, focuses primarily on literature but also includes
entries related to Victorian history, politics, economics, art history, and culture. Written by Adam C. Roberts, this reference book is intended for students
of all levels studying the Victorian age and for general readers. *Victorian
Culture and Society* provides factual information while giving readers a sense
of the "flavour of Victorian culture" between 1837 and 1901. The geographic
coverage is not specified; however, the entries have a decidedly British bent
to them. Arranged alphabetically, the entries address topics such as *All the
Year Round* (1859–1893), annuals, Matthew Arnold, Emily Brontë, circulating libraries, education, ghost stories, the Irish question, letters and postal
service, missionaries, opium wars, pastoral literature, religious certitude, science, and smoking. The entries cross-reference to other articles, and some
offer suggestions for further reading. Following the entries is a bibliography
of major secondary works on the Victorian age, which should prove quite
useful to beginning scholars. Also, to facilitate access to the volume's contents, an index to people, works, and topics concludes the book.

    The 1890s: An Encyclopedia of British Literature, Art, and Culture is a
more narrowly defined encyclopedia of the Victorian era. This single volume
is part of the extensive *Garland Reference Library of the Humanities* (volume
1237) and provides a focused examination of a transitional decade in British
history. The entries cover people—including actors, artists, authors, historians, journalists, music hall entertainers, philosophers, political figures, scientists, and theologians—and more than one hundred entries on major books of
the period. In addition to author and text entries, *The 1890s* contains general
topic entries covering varied subjects such as Fabianism, the Romantic nineties, the yellow nineties, absinthe, homosexuality, spiritualism, decadence,
Hellenism, and periodical literature. These signed entries vary between one-
half and two pages in length and conclude with brief bibliographies of further
readings. This encyclopedia has cross-referencing and a detailed index to
people, works, and topics.

    As we will see throughout this book, the number of resources for the Vic-
torian age and the nineteenth century far outweigh Edwardian and twentieth-
century sources. Filling an important gap in British literature reference
sources, *A Reader's Guide to Edwardian Literature* specifically addresses
the issues, texts, and contexts that characterized the Edwardian age of British
literature. Written by Anthea Trodd, this guide's seven narrative chapters
comprise "Introduction: Edwardianism," "The Imperial Identity," "The Condition of England," "The Importance of Parricide," "New Women and Mothers of Empire," "Poems, Audiences, and Anthologies," and "The New
Novel." Each chapter is then subdivided into sections that address particular

issues, themes, texts, or authors, and end with bibliographic notes. The volume also includes a summary of Edwardian writers and books such as J. M. Barrie's *Better Dead* and *Peter Pan*, Edward Carpenter's *The Art of Creation*, Marie Corelli's *Temporal Power*, and May Sinclair's *The Divine Fire*, and suggestions for further reading specific to the topics addressed in each chapter. An index to topics, texts, and authors concludes this brief yet essential guide.

A useful companion for Edwardian research is **The Oxford Companion to Twentieth-Century Literature in English**. Edited by Jenny Stringer in 1996, this companion surveys twentieth-century literature in English. Unlike many nineteenth-century resources, which are specific to England or Great Britain, this single-volume resource addresses literatures in English of the United Kingdom, Ireland, the United States, Australia, Canada, New Zealand, Asia, Africa, and the Caribbean. Most entries focus on writers, while selective entries cover philosophers, economists, and sociologists. These individuals were selected for inclusion based on literary merit, national or ethnic identity, and their representative time period. In addition to these criteria, authors must have lived beyond 1900 and published at least three significant works in the twentieth century. There are also roughly 650 topical entries on select individual works, critical concepts, periodicals, literary groups, and movements. Because of the volume's broad geographic scope and the Edwardian age's brevity, many entries will not be of specific interest to Edwardian scholars. However, authors, texts, and movements from this important period of British literature are covered by this work. *The Oxford Companion to Twentieth-Century Literature in English* is most useful for looking up known authors, texts, or movements rather than browsing to gain a sense of the age. The entries are arranged alphabetically, which is the primary mode of access as there is no index or table of contents to complement the entries proper. Some of the entries that may be of interest to Edwardian scholars include those on Joseph Conrad, Samuel Butler, *The Athenaeum*, William Somerset Maugham, D. H. Lawrence, and topographical poetry. This companion concludes with an appendix of literary prizes: the Booker McConnell Prize for Fiction, the Nobel Prize for Literature, and Pulitzer Prizes for fiction in book form, plays, and poetry.

Another general companion to twentieth-century British literature is Laura Marcus and Peter Nicholls's **The Cambridge History of Twentieth-Century English Literature**. Published in 2004, this literary history offers an overview of and commentary on the literary developments in twentieth-century England. This single-volume work comprises forty-four chapters organized into five uneven parts: "Writing Modernity," "The Emerging Avant-Garde," "Modernism and its Aftermath, 1918–1945," "Post-War Cultures, 1945–1970," and

"Towards the Millennium, 1970–2000." By far the leanest section of the book, "Writing Modernity" addresses the literary developments and culture of the early twentieth century with chapters on science and knowledge, the Victorian *fin de siècle* and decadence, empire and modern writing, and the gender of modernity. The first chapter of "The Emerging Avant-Garde" addresses the transition from Edwardians to Georgians. These carefully crafted chapters explain some of the major shifts in and characteristics of early twentieth-century British literature. The volume concludes with a select bibliography and a detailed index to the work's contents.

BIOGRAPHICAL SOURCES

Dictionary of Literary Biography. Detroit, MI: Gale Cengage, 1978. Also available online at www.gale.cengage.com.

Matthew, H. C. G., and Brian Howard Harrison, eds. *Oxford Dictionary of National Biography*. Rev. ed. 61 vols. New York: Oxford University Press, 2004. Also available online at www.oxforddnb.com.

Parini, Jay, ed. *British Writers Retrospective Supplement*. 2 vols. New York: Charles Scribner's Sons, 2001–2002.

———. *British Writers Supplement*. 13 vols. New York: Charles Scribner's Sons, 1987–2007.

Scott-Kilvert, Ian, ed. *British Writers*. 8 vols. New York: Scribner, 1979–1984.

Todd, Janet, ed. *British Women Writers: A Critical Reference Guide*. New York: Continuum, 1989.

Biographical sources are useful not only for discovering the details of an author's life but also for placing the corpus of his or her work in context of specific life events. Knowing more about a particular work's origins can be crucial to understanding the motivation behind that work. While not all texts should be read through an autobiographical lens, scholars may gain valuable insights into a text by understanding personal events from the author's life and historical events that surrounded its creation. This section discusses major biographical sources, including literary and historical biographies. Most sources covered in this section focus on authors, such as the *Dictionary of Literary Biography* and *British Writers*; however, select major biographical sources not specific to literature, such as the *Oxford Dictionary of National Biography*, are also discussed.

The Oxford University Press, in association with the British Academy, publishes the **Oxford Dictionary of National Biography** (**ODNB**), the gold standard for British biography. Most recently published in 2004, this sixty-one-volume set updates the original *Dictionary of National Biography* (*DNB*), which was published between 1885 and 1901. The original set comprises sixty-three volumes that include 27,236 articles covering the lives of 29,333 people. Following the first set's completion, three supplementary volumes were released in 1901 to update the dictionary. Supplements continued to be released from that time until 1996. In total, 36,446 articles on 38,607 people were published between the dictionary proper and its supplements. The *ODNB* builds on the work of the *DNB* to cover British biography from "the earliest times to the year 2000." Inclusion in the 2004 print set is limited to individuals who died prior to December 31, 2000. More specifically, the *ODNB* covers people who were born and lived in the British Isles, British people who gained recognition in other countries, people in former British territories while the land was under British rule, and people who immigrated to the British Isles.

The current print version comprises 50,113 entries that address the lives of 54,922 individuals. Of those entries, 38,607 were rewritten or revised from the first edition of the *DNB* and its supplements. While most of the *ODNB*'s entries address the lives of individuals, a few articles are devoted to a specific family or group. Although biographical coverage still heavily favors men, the number of women represented more than tripled from 1,758 in the original set to 5,627 in the current set. Coverage extends back to 400 BC; however, more recent centuries are more heavily represented, with 16,776 people from the nineteenth century and 15,798 people from the twentieth century included in the print version. Portraits accompany one-fifth of the articles, which generally speaking cover the activities, character, and significance of each person, and provide details as available regarding dates, key life events, parents and spouses, and places of residence. Each article concludes with a bibliography of sources, the location of any existing archives, any likenesses (images) of the person, and their wealth at death. Volume 1 contains a detailed guide to articles, which discusses entry names, order within entry names, order of articles, titles, life and activity dates, occupation or field of interest, article text, cross-references in the text, signatures, reference materials, and images. While the introduction and guide to articles are found only in the first volume, each volume has a list of abbreviations used for general terms, institutions, and bibliographic information. Although the set does not have an index to entries, volume 61 comprises an index to contributors, which lists each person who contributed to the *ODNB* along with any articles they wrote or revised.

In September 2004, an online version was released simultaneously with the print *ODNB*. The online dictionary contains the full contents of the print edition but is updated three times each year, in January, May, and October. The updates comprise new biographies from both the recent past and the "earliest times," thematic content for research and reference, updates to existing entries, enhancements to the website, and topical history and free content. New biographies are being added to the online content, as well as numerous additions and corrections to existing articles. A unique component of the online *ODNB* is the themes section, which includes reference lists such as poets laureate and masters of the king's (and queen's) music, reference groups that contain essays on well-known historical groups such as Cambridge ritualists and literary impressionists with links to their members, and feature essays that explore topics of interest such as imperial lives in the *ODNB* and political refugees in Britain, 1826–1905. These reference groups, reference lists, and features may be browsed as separate categories or through themes by field of interest such as: "Armed Forces," "Arts and Culture," "Law," "Politics: British Isles," "Politics: Overseas," "Religion," "Science and Technology," "Sport," and "Trade and Finance."

The online *ODNB* allows scholars to search content by people, full text, references, contributor, and image, and to browse biographies according to alphabetical order, birth date order, or death date order. Scholars also have the option to limit their searching and browsing by gender, illustrations, and families/groups. The search feature allows for advanced limiting by name; fields of interest; sex; life dates; place, dates, and life events; religious affiliation; image; and full text. Individual biographical records link to related biographies and to available online resources from the National Portrait Gallery, the National Register of Archives, and the Royal Historical Society bibliography. If the person's biography was also in the first edition, then the entry also links to the *DNB Archive*, which contains that biography's full text as it was published in the original *DNB*. The online version allows users to browse contributors alphabetically by last name of contributor.

No literary reference collection would be complete without the ***Dictionary of Literary Biography*** (***DLB***). Since 1978, Gale Cengage has published the *DLB* in cooperation with BCL Manly to provide high-quality biographies that address the literary achievements and development of an author's literary reputation in the context of his or her life. Although the series was originally intended to document North American literary history, it quickly expanded to include authors from Great Britain, Ireland, Germany, Canada, France, Austria, the Caribbean, Spain, Slavic nations, Japan, Greece, Italy, Denmark, South Africa, Australia, Russia, Portugal, Iceland, South Asia, Brazil, and China. Despite the broad geographic coverage, the bulk of *DLB* volumes focus on American and British authors. Select volumes are dedicated to ethnic literatures such as Native American, Latin American, African American, and Chicano; literary prizes such as the Man Booker Prize and the Nobel Prize in

Literature; specific authors such as F. Scott Fitzgerald, James Joyce, and Gustave Flaubert; and the book trade, publishing houses, and printers such as the House of Putnam, the House of Holt, and the British literary book trade.

Several new volumes are added to the *DLB* each year, with the total number of volumes exceeding 350 in early 2010. Each volume can stand alone and covers a select subset of authors; however, the series works best as a whole. Each volume's preface lists all previous *DLB* volumes by title, editor, and publication date, as well as the *Dictionary of Literary Biography Documentary Series*, which was published beginning in 1982 and merged with the *DLB* in 1999, and the *Dictionary of Literary Biography Yearbooks*, which were published between 1980 and 2002. The back of each volume also includes a cumulative index to authors covered in all previous volumes. Checking the most recent *DLB* volume's index is one of the most efficient ways to determine whether an author you are researching has been written about in the set.

The entries in the *DLB* are intended to provide objective, impersonal assessments of an author's career and reputation. Each entry begins with the author's name, birth and death dates, the name and affiliation of the contributor, and an indication whether the author has been profiled in a previous volume of the *DLB*. This information is followed by a chronological bibliography of the author's publications and translations of an author's works into English. Entries conclude with lists of letters, interviews, bibliographies, biographies, references, and papers as available. The essays, which comprise the bulk of each entry, discuss the author's life in terms of his or her career and reputation. These biographies should walk the reader through an author's life chronologically, making note of major literary works and the contemporary critical reception of those works. Many entries are accompanied by images of the person featured in the biography or facsimiles of manuscript writings. Currently, a number of *DLB* volumes cover nineteenth- and twentieth-century British literature, including volumes on *Nineteenth-Century British Dramatists*; *Late Nineteenth- and Early Twentieth-Century British Women Poets*; *Late-Victorian and Edwardian British Novelists*; *British Reform Writers, 1832–1914*; *Nineteenth-Century British Book-Collectors and Bibliographers*; and *British Travel Writers, 1876–1909*.

Depending on your local library's collection decisions, the *DLB* may be available either in print, as discussed above, or in one of two online versions. Both online versions are available from Gale Cengage: one as a part of the *Literature Resource Center* and another as a stand-alone version of the *DLB*. The version available through the *Literature Resource Center* (*LRC*) contains the majority of full text comprising the print edition. A notable exclusion from the *LRC*'s presentation of *DLB* content is the images, many of which have been excluded for copyright reasons. Even without images, the *LRC* is an excellent resource for accessing the *DLB*. Through the *LRC* search interface, scholars may search quickly and easily to determine whether a particular author is covered in the *DLB*. A benefit of searching the *DLB* through this interface is the immediate access to other *LRC* content, including literary criticism, additional biographies, topic and works overviews, reviews and notes, primary sources and literary works, and multimedia.

The other online option—*The Dictionary of Literary Biography Complete Online* (*DLB Complete Online*)—contains cover-to-cover page images of each volume of the *DLB*, the *DLB Documentary Series*, and the *DLB Yearbook*. In total, this product covers 420 volumes, 164,000 pages of content, more than 16,000 articles, and almost 80,000 images. Unlike the *LRC* version, the *DLB Complete Online* is composed of digital reproductions of each volume and allows scholars to page through the online content as if they were paging through a printed book. Every page from the front cover and front matter to the back matter and back cover is included, in addition to the biographical essays proper. Within each volume and essay, the *DLB Complete Online* offers linked contents. On the volume level, a table of contents is provided, while the essay-level contents detail the sections and illustrations that comprise the document, enabling scholars to jump quickly to the appropriate portion of the essay rather than clicking through individual pages. For instance, a scholar researching George Bernard Shaw could go straight to the overview of Shaw's life or skip to the "papers" section to learn where Shaw's correspondence and manuscripts are held.

The *DLB Complete Online* allows for searching and browsing of all *DLB* contents. The database's contents can be accessed through simple and advanced search interfaces and author and volume browse lists. The basic search screen allows searching within keyword, full text, or named author and limiting by year or series. The advanced search screen offers Boolean searching and fuzzy searching and limits for entry type and document number in addition to the basic search. The browse author and volume lists are both organized alphabetically; however, the volume browse also enables limiting by subject (e.g., British literature, World literature, etc.) or by series (e.g., *DLB*, *DLB Documentary Series*, or *DLB Yearbook*). Search results may be saved to a marked list, printed, or e-mailed.

Similar to the *DLB* in its coverage of authors and the *ODNB* in its coverage of British persons, **British Writers** is intended to introduce major authors in English literature from the fourteenth century onward. Not meant as a comprehensive resource, *British Writers* selectively includes authors based on their contribution to English literature. As such, minor authors see little representation in this series. The original series was published between 1979 and

1984 and comprised seven volumes of biographical content and an eighth volume to serve as the series' index. Since then, the set has been supplemented twice with *British Writers Supplement*, a thirteen-volume set published between 1987 and 2007, and *British Writers Retrospective Supplement*, a two-volume set published in 2001 and 2002. Ian Scott-Kilvert edited the original series while Jay Parini edited both supplements.

The entries in *British Writers* are organized chronologically by the author's birth date. Because of this arrangement, authors from the Victorian and Edwardian ages were included in volumes 4, 5, and 6 of the original series. Each volume contains a chronological table of global historical events and major literary publications that correspond to the periods in which the authors lived. The supplements initially add biographies for contemporary authors, but later supplemental volumes fill in gaps in *British Writers* throughout British literary history. The entries themselves are quite lengthy and cover the author's life, major literary output, and contemporary critical reception. Each article ends with an extensive bibliography of bibliographies, collected works, selected works, separate works, letters, biographical and critical studies, and the author's writings. Elizabeth Barrett Browning, Benjamin Disraeli, Arthur Hugh Clough, Walter Pater, Thomas Hardy, and Henry James are among the Victorian and Edwardian authors profiled in this set. The authors and literary texts from the initial *British Writers* series are indexed in the eighth volume. The supplements do not have a separate index volume, but rather each volume incorporates a cumulative index for volumes 1 through 7 of the original series, as well as all extant volumes of the supplement.

In addition to these general and literary biographical sources, there are biographical guides and dictionaries that focus on a particular subset of writers. Sources such as *British Women Writers: A Critical Reference Guide* may have biographies for minor women writers who may be otherwise overlooked in broader biographical sources. Edited by Janet Todd for Continuum Press, *British Women Writers* aims to be representative rather than comprehensive. Scholars will find these biographies markedly shorter than those found in the *ODNB*, *DLB*, or *British Writers*; however, these still provide valuable information on the authors covered in this single volume. In addition to the biographical entries, *British Women Writers* has a list of writers, a guide to abbreviations of reference works, and a thorough index to persons and subjects. The entries themselves range between a page or two in length and offer basic biographical information regarding birth and death dates and location of birth and death, as well as an overview of each woman's life and literary contributions. Any pseudonymous identities are also mentioned in these entries. Lesser-known authors such as Louisa Molesworth, Anne Manning, and Barbara Bodichon are included alongside well-known authors such as Elizabeth

Gaskell, Anne Brontë, and Olive Schreiner. In all, biographies for more than four hundred women writers from the fourteenth through the twentieth century comprise this book.

CHRONOLOGIES

Chapman, R. W., ed. *Annals of English Literature, 1475–1950: The Principal Publications of Each Year, Together with an Alphabetical Index of Authors with Their Works*. 2nd ed. Oxford: Clarendon Press, 1961.
Cox, Michael. *The Oxford Chronology of English Literature*. 2 vols. New York: Oxford University Press, 2002.

Like biographies, chronologies are important research tools for placing authors and their works in context of other literary and historical events. Understanding the culture in which a text was produced is essential for understanding the work itself, so when beginning to study a new author, work, or period within literature, you may find it helpful to consult a chronology to understand the historical background. This section only addresses two chronologies: *Annals of English Literature, 1475–1950* and its successor, *The Oxford Chronology of English Literature*. While not the only existing chronologies of British literature, these are standard sources and should thoroughly represent the historical events that coincide with literary persons, works, and movements. In addition to chronologies such as these, many of the encyclopedias, companions, and biographical sources discussed throughout this chapter contain highly useful and accurate chronologies.

The ***Annals of English Literature, 1475–1950: The Principal Publications of Each Year, Together with an Alphabetical Index of Authors with Their Works*** was initially published in 1935 with a second edition published in 1961 by Oxford University Press. The *Annals* is a compact, 380-page volume that provides a chronological outline of major British literary works between 1475 and 1950. Although the primary focus of the *Annals* is British literature, major authors from Australia, Canada, India, New Zealand, South Africa, and the United States are also included. This chronology lists major publications alphabetically by author within each year covered. The right-hand margin of each page contains notes regarding author births and deaths; newspaper, periodical, translation, editions, and compilation publication dates; and select foreign events that impacted English literary history. Each entry in the *Annals* is composed of the author's name (if known), the author's birth or death date, the title of the work, and an abbreviation to indicate whether the listed work is prose, verse, tragedy, comedy, or drama.

Entries may also make note of previous editions. In addition to the chronology, the *Annals* has a detailed authors and publications index to facilitate access to the volume.

In 2002, Oxford University Press published **The Oxford Chronology of English Literature** as the successor to the *Annals of English Literature*. In terms of both length and depth of coverage, the *Chronology* far surpasses the *Annals*. Where the *Annals* focused primarily on canonical English literature, the *Chronology* emphasizes English-language literature, both written by British authors and published in the British Isles, but selectively includes post-colonial literature in English. The new two-volume *Chronology* also expands its dates of coverage from 1474 to 2000. This resource references more authors and works, and has more contextual and bibliographical information. Despite its extensive coverage, the *Chronology* is not completely comprehensive, as it excludes certain types of works such as distributed handwritten materials. Compared with the *Annals*, more women writers are covered in the *Chronology*. Also, the *Chronology* attempts to represent all areas of British literature—low-brow, middle-brow, and high-brow. In total, the *Chronology* covers over four thousand authors and almost thirty thousand works, including fiction, poetry, drama, and non-fiction. Like the *Annals*, this chronology is organized by imprint date, beginning with 1474 and ending in 2000. Entries are organized alphabetically by author's last name within year and by title within author.

The *Chronology*'s prefatory materials include guides to using the chronology and to abbreviations. The individual entries contain the author's name, birth or death date, the standard publication title, the publisher, and an abbreviation indicating whether the work is an anthology, Bible, dictionary, drama, edition, fiction, miscellaneous, non-fiction, opera, periodical, prose retelling, prose satire, verse, verse with music, or works. Some entries also offer additional information regarding a work's publication history. Although the *Chronology* exceeds the *Annals* in coverage, the *Annals* remains a useful resource, as the two do not overlap completely. For instance, the *Annals* lists twenty-four entries for 1902 while the *Chronology* has 131. In sheer numbers, the *Chronology* surpasses the *Annals*; however, five of the *Annals*' entries are not listed among those of the *Chronology*, indicating that both volumes provide unique content.

While the discussion has focused on the heftier first volume of the set, which contains the chronology proper, the *Chronology*'s second volume is an essential part of this reference work that comprises three indexes: author, title, and translated authors. The Author Index and the Index of Translated Authors record all authors alphabetically with a chronological short-title list of works under each main name heading. Likewise, the Title Index organizes works alphabetically along with the publication date and author's name. These indexes provide invaluable help for accessing the *Chronology*'s contents. While the first volume is most useful for locating works that have known publication dates or for surveying the literary output of a particular year, the second volume will help scholars identify the corpus of an author's works or place a literary work with an unknown publication date.

INDIVIDUAL AUTHOR AND GENRE-SPECIFIC SOURCES

Alexander, Christine, and Margaret Smith, eds. *The Oxford Companion to the Brontës*. New York: Oxford University Press, 2006.

Baker, William, and Kenneth Womack, eds. *A Companion to the Victorian Novel*. Westport, CT: Greenwood Press, 2002.

Bloom, Harold, ed. *Edwardian and Georgian Fiction, 1880 to 1914*. New York: Chelsea House Publishers, 1990.

Brantlinger, Patrick, and William B. Thesing, eds. *A Companion to the Victorian Novel*. Malden, MA: Blackwell, 2002.

Bristow, Joseph, ed. *The Cambridge Companion to Victorian Poetry*. New York: Cambridge University Press, 2000.

Corcoran, Neil, ed. *The Cambridge Companion to Twentieth-Century English Poetry*. New York: Cambridge University Press, 2007.

Cronin, Richard, Alison Chapman, and Antony H. Harrison, eds. *A Companion to Victorian Poetry*. Malden, MA: Blackwell, 2002.

Hamilton, Ian, ed. *The Oxford Companion to Twentieth-Century Poetry in English*. Oxford: Oxford University Press, 1994.

Hardwick, Michael, and Mollie Hardwick, comps. *The Charles Dickens Encyclopedia*. New York: Charles Scribner's Sons, 1973.

Kemp, Sandra, Charlotte Mitchell, and David Trotter, eds. *The Oxford Companion to Edwardian Fiction*. New York: Oxford University Press, 2002.

O'Gorman, Francis, ed. *A Concise Companion to the Victorian Novel*. Malden, MA: Blackwell, 2005.

Powell, Kerry, ed. *The Cambridge Companion to Victorian and Edwardian Theatre*. New York: Cambridge University Press, 2004.

Roberts, Neil, ed. *A Companion to Twentieth-Century Poetry*. Malden, MA: Blackwell, 2003.

Schlicke, Paul, ed. *Oxford Reader's Companion to Dickens*. New York: Oxford University Press, 1999.

Taylor, Jenny Bourne, ed. *The Cambridge Companion to Wilkie Collins*. New York: Cambridge University Press, 2006.

In addition to general English literature encyclopedias, companions, biographical sources, and chronologies, author- and genre-specific reference sources are also useful research tools. Author-specific sources generally are available for major literary figures only; however, as scholarship progresses, reference sources on lesser-known authors may be published. The genre-specific sources tend to focus on one genre within a particular time period, such as the nineteenth century or the Edwardian age. The sources listed in this section do not comprise an exhaustive list of author or genre sources, but this section should give you a good sense of the available types of resources. Your local library catalog will be a useful tool for identifying which of these and other resources are available. To determine whether a reference book exists for a particular author, search for that author as a subject and look for sub-headings that include words such as encyclopedia, dictionary, chronology, biographical dictionary, or handbook. For a refresher on online searching basics, see chapter 1. For more advanced searching techniques in library catalogs, read on to chapter 3.

The Oxford Companion to the Brontës is a comprehensive introduction to the lives, writings, and culture of the Brontë sisters and their family. Edited by Christine Alexander and Margaret Smith, this companion comprises essays about the Brontës' lives, their works, the people with whom they interacted, characters and places from their writings, historical places of significance, historical events, contemporary attitudes toward social issues, and critical reception of their work. Entries for *Blackwood's Edinburgh Magazine*, early nineteenth-century divorce laws, Brontë quotations, Grace Poole, and Charlotte Brontë coexist in this single-volume reference work. The entries themselves are arranged alphabetically, with longer feature entries scattered amid more minor entries. Additionally, *The Oxford Companion to the Brontës* contains a classified list of contents that organizes entries according to the Brontës' lives, the Brontës' writings, the literary and artistic context, historical and social context, and reception and aftermath. An abbreviations list, a chronology, several maps, a guide to dialect and obsolete words, and a bibliography of the Brontës' published writings, bibliographies and reference works, biographies, background and criticism, and creative works all add value to this highly useful reference book.

One of the more than 130 volumes in the *Cambridge Companion to Literature* series, ***The Cambridge Companion to Wilkie Collins*** comprises thirteen essays on the life and works of Wilkie Collins. While a significant number of volumes in the series are relevant to the Victorian and Edwardian ages, not all of them are addressed in this chapter; rather, representative volumes, such as this one, are discussed. The individual essays are designed to stand alone, but as a whole, this companion provides a good overview both of Collins as an author and of the culture in which he wrote and lived. The chapters, which are written by scholars and graduate students in the field, cover topics such as the sensation novel, the detective novel and forensic science, the marriage plot and its alternatives, Victorian masculinity, and empire. Each chapter concludes with a bibliography of further readings, and a separate general bibliography of primary sources and reference materials, biographies, books and edited collections on Collins, essays and articles, general sources, and websites concludes the volume. This companion also contains a note on references and abbreviations, a chronology, and an index to works, people, and subjects. Additional volumes in the series address Victorian and Edwardian authors such as Dickens, Lawrence, Forster, Gaskell, Fitzgerald, Fielding, James, Joyce, Conrad, Wilde, Hardy, and the Brontës.

Throughout your research, you will find that not all sources are created equal. While similar reference books may exist on a particular author, genre, or subject, they are often designed for varied yet specific purposes. Like Shakespeare in the English Renaissance period, Charles Dickens is one of the most widely written about authors of the Victorian age. Two of the many reference sources dedicated to Dickens scholarship are *The Charles Dickens Encyclopedia* and the *Oxford Reader's Companion to Dickens*. While both works are dedicated to the study of Dickens, his life, and works, each fulfills a different scholarly purpose. ***The Charles Dickens Encyclopedia*** is the older of the two, published in 1973 by Charles Scribner's Sons, and aims to serve as a comprehensive companion to Dickens's life and writings. This single-volume work includes the publishing history, inspiration for, and synopsis of forty-one of Dickens's works; an alphabetical directory of all named characters in Dickens's works; an alphabetical directory of places in Dickens's work and life subdivided into London and the rest of the world; a time chart chronicling his life, career, and general events; a directory of his circle of friends, family, and associates; and quotations from twenty-seven of his works. The volume concludes with an index to quotations that lists memorable keywords and phrases from Dickens's quotations and names of characters. *The Charles Dickens Encyclopedia* also has a selective index to the time chart, excluding the general events, Dickens's works, and Dickens and his circle.

While *The Charles Dickens Encyclopedia* takes a microscopic view of Dickens's life and work, the ***Oxford Reader's Companion to Dickens*** offers a broader view of those same topics. Published in 1999 by Oxford University Press and edited by Paul Schlicke, the *Oxford Reader's Companion to Dickens* contains brief articles on Dickens's life, works, literary and theatrical context, reputation, and social context. A classified contents list organizes the entries under subcategories within those broader categories. Since the entries are alphabetically arranged, this organizational feature should help scholars draw connections among the various entries. Cross-referencing within entries should also facilitate research. Sprinkled throughout the entries are images of

Dickens and significant people and events from his lifetime. The volume also contains an abbreviations guide, the Dickens family tree, several maps, and a general bibliography. The bibliography comprises works by Dickens, reference books, and secondary sources and scholarly editions. Like *The Charles Dickens Encyclopedia*, this volume provides an alphabetical list of characters; however, unlike the encyclopedia, the *Oxford Reader's Companion to Dickens* does not have character descriptions. The companion's character list excludes those from Dickens's journalism, unnamed characters, those mentioned only in passing, and those that do not appear. The volume concludes with a time chart comparing Dickens's family life to historical and literary background, and a detailed index to topics covered by the companion.

The novel is arguably the Victorian age's dominant literary form. The current proliferation of companions to the Victorian novel certainly attests to that fact. Several recent works on this topic include Greenwood's *A Companion to the Victorian Novel*, Blackwell's *A Companion to the Victorian Novel*, and Blackwell's *A Concise Companion to the Victorian Novel*. Each of these companions takes a different approach to introducing, discussing, and dissecting Victorian novels, their influences, and the culture from which they emerged. Edited by William Baker and Kenneth Womack, Greenwood's *A Companion to the Victorian Novel* comprises thirty-two chapters in five broad categories: literary contexts, cultural contexts, genres, major authors, and contemporary critical approaches to the Victorian novel. Each chapter ends with a detailed bibliography of works cited and selected works for further reading. The volume concludes with a selected bibliography of further readings on the Victorian novel and an index to people, texts, and subjects discussed in the companion.

Part of the *Blackwell Companions to Literature and Culture* series, *A Companion to the Victorian Novel* has similar organization to the Greenwood companion, yet is a more substantial volume as it provides contextual and critical information about the Victorian novel. Edited by Patrick Brantlinger and William B. Theising, this companion's twenty-six chapters are organized into only three broad categories: "Historical Contexts and Cultural Issues," "Forms of the Victorian Novel," and "Victorian and Modern Theories of the Novel and the Reception of Novels and Novelists Then and Now." Unlike the Greenwood companion, which devotes a significant number of chapters to individual authors, the Blackwood companion weaves discussion of major authors throughout the chapters, making the index highly important for locating sections that address a particular author or text. Each chapter ends with two bibliographies: one for references and one of further readings.

While the first two companions address the Victorian novel with similar organizational strategies, Blackwell's *A Concise Companion to the Victorian*

Novel does not categorize its chapters but leaves the twelve chapters unlinked to one another. Covering topics such as visuality, the law, material culture, biology, and Europe as they relate to the Victorian novel, this companion takes a historical critical perspective as it attempts to situate the Victorian novel in its historical context. As in the previously discussed companions, each chapter concludes with a detailed bibliography of references and further reading. This volume includes a chronology of events from 1830 to 1901 and an index to the complete contents.

Another volume in the *Blackwell Companions to Literature and Culture* series, Richard Cronin's *A Companion to Victorian Poetry* provides a comprehensive survey of poetry from the Victorian age and the culture that produced it. Unlike many resources for Victorian literature, this work defines the Victorian age from 1830 until World War I, which makes this a useful resource for Edwardian poetry as well. The companion's chronology, however, extends only from 1827 to 1901 and charts poetry volumes, other literary and artistic events, and contexts. Rather than focusing on specific, major poets or poems, *A Companion to Victorian Poetry* contains essays that emphasize critical approaches to poetry and fall into three broad categories: "Varieties and Forms," "Production, Distribution, and Reception," and "Victorian Poetry and Victorian Culture." Prefaced by a detailed introduction on Victorian poetics, the companion's thirty essays cover topics ranging from lyric to working-class poetry, from the market to poetry and illustration, and from nationhood and empire to poetry and science. Each essay concludes with cross-references to other essays and a highly useful bibliography of references and further reading. The detailed index of people, works, and subjects will aid scholars who are looking for commentary on a particular topic.

In addition to volumes devoted to specific authors, the *Cambridge Companion to Literature* series includes volumes on literary topics. *The Cambridge Companion to Victorian Poetry* and *The Cambridge Companion to Victorian and Edwardian Theatre* are two such volumes. Edited by Joseph Bristow, *The Cambridge Companion to Victorian Poetry* gives an overview of critical developments on the poetry written during Queen Victoria's reign. For quick reference, this volume has a guide to abbreviations, a note on the texts, and two chronologies: one on poets and another on publications and events. The companion comprises thirteen chapters on topics such as poetics after 1832, Victorian meters, the Victorian poetess, poetry of Victorian masculinities, and poetry and patriotism. Each chapter has extensive bibliographic notes, and the book concludes with a glossary of poetic terms, a guide to further readings of Victorian poetry and criticism, and an index to people, works, and subjects. *The Cambridge Companion to Victorian and Edwardian Theatre* covers historic and contemporary approaches to the texts and performances of Victorian and Edwardian theater. Unlike many of the Cambridge companions, this one categorizes its fourteen chapters into the following sections: "Introduction," "Performance and Context," and "Text and Context." The individual chapters address topics such as Victorian and Edwardian stagecraft, performing identities, 1890s theater, and the fallen woman on the stage. Each chapter has extensive bibliographic notes. This companion also provides a select bibliography of secondary sources and an index.

Although few genre-specific sources on the Edwardian age have been published, Edwardian fiction has received more attention than most other genres of that period. Two such sources—*Edwardian and Georgian Fiction, 1880 to 1914* and *The Oxford Companion to Edwardian Fiction*—help to define and explain the characteristic literary works of the early nineteenth century. Edited by Harold Bloom, ***Edwardian and Georgian Fiction, 1880 to 1914*** is a collection of critical essays on British fiction from the late nineteenth and early twentieth centuries. Although it defines the Edwardian and Georgian periods as spanning 1880 to 1914, for the purposes of this book, that time period covers the late Victorian age and the Edwardian age. *Edwardian and Georgian Fiction* is part of Chelsea House Publisher's *Critical Cosmos Series*. Comprised of twenty-two critical essays arranged in chronological order by each author's birth year, this book highlights major authors, texts, and literary themes of Edwardian and Georgian fiction. This volume tends to survey major authors, such as Oscar Wilde, George Gissing, Joseph Conrad, Rudyard Kipling, and E. M. Forester, rather than little-read authors of the period. This compilation concludes with a chronology spanning the authors' lives, beginning in 1834 and ending in 1975; a guide to contributors; a bibliography of secondary sources; and an index to authors, texts, and subjects. The bibliography for general resources and works about nineteen authors should be particularly useful as a guide to further readings and sources.

Now in its second edition, ***The Oxford Companion to Edwardian Fiction*** provides critical analysis of and historical research on Edwardian authors and their works. Edited by Sandra Kemp, David Trotter, and Charlotte Mitchell, this companion comprises more than eight hundred alphabetically arranged entries on British fiction from 1900 to 1914. While most of the entries are biographical, others address specific texts and thematic topics such as Boer War fiction and invasion scare stories. Entries for major authors such as J. M. Barrie, G. K. Chesterton, and Arthur Conan Doyle are included alongside entries for lesser-known authors such as Lady Angela Forbes, Alice M. Diehl, and Basil Lubbock. This companion contains a bibliography of books frequently consulted, a short title list, an abbreviations guide, a chronology of literary and historical events, and an index to pseudonyms and changes of name.

Scholars of Edwardian and early twentieth-century poetry have several reference works available to them, including Blackwell's *A Companion to Twentieth-Century Poetry*, *The Cambridge Companion to Twentieth-Century English Poetry*, and *The Oxford Companion to Twentieth-Century Poetry in English*. The former two titles provide essays discussing and contextualizing the poets and poetry of the twentieth century, while the latter is more encyclopedic in its approach to the same topic. Like all volumes in the *Blackwell Companions to Literature and Culture* series, **A Companion to Twentieth-Century Poetry** is a substantial essay collection that offers an overview of a particular literary genre and period. This volume covers not only the poetry of England in the twentieth century but also poetry in English of the United States and postcolonial nations. The forty-eight chapters organized into five sections—"Topics and Debates," "Poetic Movements," "International and Postcolonial Poetry in English," "Readings," and "The Contemporary Scene"—address the progression of poetry and poetic movements across English-speaking nations. Each chapter concludes with a bibliography. Like Blackwell's Victorian novel companion, the volume's index is essential for locating discussions of specific poets, poems, and poetic movements. Unlike the Blackwell companion, **The Cambridge Companion to Twentieth-Century English Poetry** focuses specifically on the poetry of Britain. This book surveys English poetry in seventeen chapters in four broad sections: "Contexts," "Moderns," "Modernists," and "Later Modernities." Although the largest section of chapters emphasize the later twentieth century, the sections on "Contexts" and the "Moderns" are highly relevant to research on the Edwardian age. As with the other volumes in the *Cambridge Companion to Literature* series, each chapter ends with a bibliography of further readings. This companion also has a twentieth-century chronology and an index.

The Oxford Companion to Twentieth-Century Poetry in English is a guide to poetry in English. Edited by Ian Hamilton, this companion comprises entries for fifteen hundred poets, most of which hail from either Great Britain or the United States, with smaller numbers from other English-speaking nations. The gender and racial balances are quite uneven, with roughly two hundred women and one hundred black authors included. Any author who lived during the twentieth century, regardless of how short a time, was eligible for inclusion. The prefatory materials list poetry anthologies and offer a key to contributors. The articles are fairly brief and are arranged alphabetically, which is the only means of accessing the companion's contents as no index is provided. Most entries are for specific authors; however, a few are for specific publications or movements. Since the Edwardian age ends just ten years into the twentieth century, only a small percentage of entries are directly relevant to research of that time period. Like the *Oxford*

Companion to Twentieth-Century Literature in English, which was discussed previously, this resource is most useful for research on known authors, texts, or movements.

CONCLUSION

The resources covered in this chapter, whether encyclopedias, companions, biographies, or chronologies, should provide you with a good basis for learning the context of and history behind a particular author, text, or issue in Victorian and Edwardian literature. The resources listed here and others like them are good starting points for beginning your research, but they are generally not good ending points. The bibliographies included in these reference works and the other resources addressed throughout this book guide you through the process of conducting in-depth research of Victorian and Edwardian literatures. Throughout your research, you may need to revisit these sources as you build your knowledge of and expertise in your research area.

Chapter Three

Library Catalogs

No book on research would be complete without serious discussion of library catalogs and their functionality. Library catalogs are a crucial resource for any literary scholar, whether novice or experienced. Although indexes and databases provide the best access to journal articles, catalogs are still the best first stop for locating books on particular research topics. This chapter addresses methods of searching catalogs, including author, title, and subject searches. Chapter 1 briefly mentioned these search types as part of the MARC record structure discussion, but this chapter explains these search techniques in greater detail so that you can use each one effectively. Additionally, this chapter covers limiting and refining search results. Embedded in the discussion of author, title, and subject searches are explanations of interpreting and evaluating search results efficiently. Select union and national catalogs, including *Copac*, *WorldCat*, the *National Union Catalog*, and the British Library *Integrated Catalog*, are also addressed in this chapter.

Do not underestimate the importance of your local library catalog for discovering relevant research resources. Depending on the size and type of your library, the local holdings will vary widely in terms of the depth and selection. A library at a large research institution is bound to have more resources on hand than a library at a small undergraduate university; however, regardless of your library's size, its catalog is a good starting point for your research and may contain records for unique items. Even smaller libraries can supply access to a wealth of information resources both through materials housed in the library and by borrowing from other libraries through interlibrary loan (ILL). Take advantage of your library's interlibrary loan services, which provide access to many resources your library doesn't own, with either no or minimal cost passed on to you. Before turning to other libraries for resources, first visit your local library and search its catalog to determine what resources are already immediately available to you. Although the search functionality may vary slightly from catalog to catalog, once you have mastered the basics of searching, you can apply the skills you've acquired to any other library catalog. Remember that the help feature of an unfamiliar catalog contains valuable tips on search strategies specific to that catalog.

Although library catalogs of the past were printed card catalogs, most contemporary library catalogs are available only online. One notable exception is *The National Union Catalog: Pre-1956 Imprints*, a multi-volume reproduction of catalog cards from the Library of Congress and major research libraries in the United States. (*The National Union Catalog* is discussed in greater detail later in this chapter.) Because online public access catalogs (OPACs) are the standard for public, academic, national, and union library catalogs, this chapter focuses primarily on how they function and how to search them effectively. Building on the search basics of chapter 1, this chapter gives greater detail about the ins and outs of the catalogs and search strategies available to you. As mentioned in the first chapter, a library's holdings are represented in its catalog using MARC records. These records comprise bibliographic information (e.g., author, title, publication information, etc.) as well as descriptive information (e.g., book cover, subject headings, table of contents, summaries, etc.) about each of the items housed in the library. The search engine that provides access to the database of catalog records queries the MARC record fields to produce a list of relevant results. By understanding how to query the data in the MARC records, you will be more successful in retrieving information from the catalog.

While the MARC structure is standardized across libraries, there are still differences in how each library chooses to catalog a particular item. Typically, variances are found in the descriptive information rather than the bibliographic information. While one library may opt to include a table of contents or a summary of the work, another library may choose to exclude that information entirely. You may also notice that subject headings for an individual work may vary from catalog to catalog. While nearly all libraries use the Anglo-American Cataloging Rules (AACR2) to assign subject headings to catalog records, how those rules are implemented and interpreted is left to the discretion of individual cataloging librarians. If you compare specific item records from both your local library catalog and *WorldCat*, you will surely find differences in the amount and level of detail included in each. (*WorldCat* is discussed in greater detail later in this chapter.) With the MARC record structure underpinning the library catalog's organization, catalogs should offer the option to search by author, title, and subject. These search options can help you to search more effectively if you know how and when to use each one. Before describing specific national and union library catalogs, the chapter examines author, title, and subject searching in more depth so that you fully understand their potential in aiding your research process.

AUTHOR SEARCHES

As you research Victorian and Edwardian literatures, you may need to find works written by a particular author. In this situation, an author search is the most efficient way to retrieve all works written by a specific author included in the catalog. Unlike keyword searches, in which the order of search terms need not be exact, author search syntax is essential for retrieving the desired results set. The general structure for the author heading—beginning with the author's last name and followed by his or her first name—is the standard structure used in library catalogs. If you reverse the order of the search terms, you will retrieve either no results or a cross-reference to the proper heading. For instance, if you searched for *Annie Besant* as an author using natural order of words, then the catalog may instruct you to change your search to *Besant Annie* rather than retrieve a list of works by the author in question. Author searches tell the catalog to produce a list of any items written by the author, including novels, short stories, plays, poetry compilations, diaries, and correspondence. Depending on your local library catalog, you may find records for works that are available only in digital form, as the author search does not distinguish by format but merely seeks to match your search terms to records containing those words.

While individual catalogers have some leeway in interpreting cataloging rules, some standards exist to ensure consistency in indexing and access. One of these standards is the authority record. The Library of Congress has created authority records for names (including persons, places, meetings, and organizations), titles, and subjects, providing some level of standardization for those major index fields. Although this section focuses primarily on name authorities used for author searching, title and subject authorities are discussed in greater detail later in this chapter. Name authorities help regulate the preferred form of an author's name. Even though authorities exist for many authors, catalog records without authority records for authors, titles, and subjects remain in some catalogs because many materials were cataloged prior to the implementation of authority records.

The following examples illustrate the ways in which authority controls help assure consistency in indexing authors' names. In an ideal world, each author would have one authoritative author record assigned to him or her. However, with pseudonymous names, name variants, and name changes, cataloging authors by name is not always entirely straightforward. While some authors, such as Joseph Conrad, have one authoritative name (Conrad, Joseph, 1857–1924), others, like Elizabeth Gaskell, may be represented by multiple entries. An author search for *Gaskell, Elizabeth* in your library catalog may retrieve multiple headings, all referring to the same author, including the following options:

1. Gaskell, E. C. (Elizabeth Cleghorn), 1810–1865
2. Gaskell, Elizabeth Cleghorn Stevenson, 1810–1865
3. Gaskell, Elizabeth Cleghorn, 1810–1865
4. Gaskell, Elizabeth, 1810–1865

The first, second, and fourth entries are not authorized, which should be indicated by *see* references directing you to the third entry (Gaskell, Elizabeth Cleghorn, 1810–1865). The cross-referencing provided in library catalogs is designed to guide you to the correct form. Don't become too hung up on figuring out the authorized form of a name; rather, search using the general rule of last name preceding first name, and the catalog should do the rest of the work, directing you to the name's proper form. The following is the modified catalog record for Joseph Conrad's *Heart of Darkness* (source: James Madison University Libraries Catalog):

Author:	**Conrad, Joseph, 1857–1924.**
Title:	Heart of Darkness: complete, authoritative text with biographical and historical contexts, critical history, and essays from five contemporary critical perspectives / Joseph Conrad; edited by Ross C. Murfin.
Publisher:	Boston: Bedford Books of St. Martin's Press, c1996.
Edition:	2nd ed.
Description:	x, 315 p. ; 22 cm.
Series:	Case studies in contemporary criticism
Subjects:	Conrad, Joseph, 1857–1924. Heart of darkness.
	Psychological fiction, English—History and criticism.
	Europeans—Africa—Fiction.
	Trading posts—Fiction.
	Degeneration—Fiction.
	Imperialism—Fiction.
	Africa—Fiction.
Other Name:	Murfin, Ross C.
ISBN:	0312159013 (hardcover)
	0312114915 (pbk.)

Authors who previously wrote under pseudonyms, such as the Brontë sisters, also have multiple author entries to represent the aliases under which they have written. Although it is now commonly known that Currer, Ellis, and Acton Bell are pseudonyms for Charlotte, Emily, and Anne Brontë, respectively, entries still exist in many catalogs for the three Bells. The heading for Bell, Acton, 1820–1849 refers you to the authorized heading Brontë, Anne, 1820–1849. Likewise, the heading Bell, Currer, 1816–1855 cross-references to Brontë, Charlotte, 1816–1855, and the heading Bell, Ellis, 1818–1848 directs you to Brontë, Emily, 1818–1848. In these cases, cross-referencing helps guide you to the standard form of each author's name. With the Brontë sisters, the cross-referencing is clear and consistent. There are rare instances, however, in which authority records may exist for both the author's real name and his or her pseudonymous identity. Early nineteenth-century author Catherine Gore wrote most of her works under her given name, but also published select works under the pseudonym Albany Poyntz. Rather than providing cross-references from the Poyntz entry to the Gore entry, the records are entirely independent of each other, and both names have authority records. If you know of an alternate name for an author, consider searching both the author's given name and his or her pseudonyms or alternate names to ensure you don't miss relevant records.

If an author search does not reveal records for any works by a particular author, you may want to search for the author using a keyword search. On occasion, a work by an author may be located in your library as part of a compilation of writings, in which case the work is listed under the editor's or compiler's name rather than under each author included in the work. In this situation, a keyword search is more effective than an author search, because it searches more broadly than a record's author field. An author search for B. M. Croker will retrieve items indexed under the authorized heading for Croker: Croker, B. M. (Bithia Mary), d. 1920. However, if you search for B. M. Croker as a keyword, then you may retrieve additional relevant results. The following shows a catalog record that uses the authorized heading for Croker:

Author: **Croker, B. M. (Bithia Mary), d. 1920.**
Title: Her own people / by Mrs. B. M. Croker.
Published: London : Hurst and Blackett, 1903.
Description: 323 p. ; 20 cm.
Notes: Only edition in BM 46:136.
Notes: Publisher's ads [4] p. at end.
Notes: Bound in rose cloth, stamped in gold.

and this presents a record that contains Croker's name in the table of contents but not in the author field:

Title:	Late Victorian Gothic tales / edited with an introduction and notes by Roger Luckhurst.
Published:	Oxford; New York: Oxford University Press, 2005.
Description:	xliv, 282 p.: ill. ; 20 cm.
Other contributors:	Luckhurst, Roger.
Series:	Oxford world's classics
Notes:	Includes bibliographical references (p. [xxxiv]–xxxix).
Contents:	Lord Arthur Savile's crime / Oscar Wilde—Sir Edmund Orme / Henry James—The mark of the beast / Rudyard Kipling—**The Dak bungalow at Dakor / B. M. Croker**—Lot no. 49 / Arthur Conan Doyle—The case of Lady Sannox / Arthur Conan Doyle—Pallinghurst barrow / Grant Allen—Magic lantern / Jean Lorrain—The spectral hand / Jean Lorrain—The great god Pan / Arthur Machen—Vaila / M. P. Shiel.
Subjects:	Horror tales, English.
	English fiction—19th century.
	Gothic revival (Literature)—Great Britain.
ISBN:	0192804804 (alk. paper)

If you limited your search of Croker to the author field only, you would have missed this work of hers entirely. To avoid missing relevant texts, be tenacious in your searching, not stopping automatically after your first search but continuing to search for variants until you've exhausted your options.

TITLE SEARCHES

Title searches may also seem quite straightforward at face value, yet there are still quirks of this method that you should be aware of as you continue your research. Title searching is an ideal strategy for locating known items. If you know the title of a given work, the most efficient way to retrieve that record is to conduct a title search. For instance, to determine whether your local library owns a copy of Matthew Arnold's *Culture and Anarchy*, it is most effective to search for *Culture and Anarchy* as a title. As with name authorities for authors, title authorities dictate the preferred wording of a particular title to preserve uniformity among various records for the same work. Some publications, like Thomas Hardy's *Tess of the D'Urbervilles*, have multiple entries in a catalog's title index due to variants in the exact title wording, as shown in fig. 3.1.

Catalog Browse by Title: "tess of the d'urbervilles"

Title	Count
Tess Jaray : paintings and drawings from the eighties /	1
Tess of the D'Urbervilles /	26
Tess of the d'Urbervilles. 1994.	1
Tess of the d'Urbervilles : a facsimile of the manuscript, with related materials /	1
Tess of the D'Urbervilles : a pure woman /	16
Tess of the d'Urbervilles, a pure woman faithfully presented.	12
Tess of the d'Urbervilles : an authoritative text /	1
Tess of the d'Urbervilles : an authoritative text, backgrounds and sources, criticism /	1
Tess of the d'Urbervilles: an authoritative text; Hardy and the novel; criticism...	1
Tess of the D'Urbervilles by Thomas Hardy /	1
Tess of the d'Urbervilles : complete, authoritative text with biographical and historical contexts, critical history, and essays from fi	1
TESS OF THE DURBERVILLES NOTES INCLUDING BIOGRAPHICAL AND CRITICAL INTRODUCTION LIST OF CHARACTERS SYNOPSIS OF THE	1
Tess of the d'Urbervilles : notes, including biographical and critical introduction, list of characters, synopsis of the story, chapter	1

Figure 3.1.   *Tess of the D'Urbervilles* title variants. Source: Indiana University Libraries Catalog.

When evaluating a list of works like the one shown here, do not simply rely on the title to make your selection. While each of the variant titles for Hardy's novel refers to *Tess of the D'Urbervilles*, not all texts are equal. Obviously, you can immediately discount the work on Tess Jaray's paintings and drawings from the 1980s. The other items in the list require closer examination. To determine which text to select, click on the title's hyperlink to view the full catalog record. From there you can better evaluate the quality and relevance of each text by using the publication, contents, and subject information provided in the record. From scanning the title list, you may notice that several claim to be an "authoritative text." Any of these would be fine selections, but you should still critically evaluate any of these books and their contents rather than simply relying on the label "authoritative."

Title searches can be used not only for locating individual works but also for series. While some catalogs may index series titles under a separate index, many catalogs conflate the two types of titles and require that you use the title search to locate both. Generally, individual works that are part of a larger series have multiple title access points in the catalog: one for the individual work and one for the series. Series such as the *Dictionary of Literary Biography* (*DLB*) comprise multiple individual works that are all distinguished by unique titles, such as *British Children's Writers, 1880–1914*; *Late-Victorian and Edwardian British Novelists*; and *Victorian Poets before 1850* (see chapter 2 for further discussion of the *DLB*). By searching for the series in the title field, you will retrieve all works in that particular series. If you know the individual title, however, you will be better served by simply searching for it rather than the series. Both titles should be present in the record as is shown in the catalog record for *DLB* volume 153, *Late-Victorian and Edwardian British Novelists. First Series*, as shown here:

Title:	**Late-Victorian and Edwardian British Novelists. First series / edited by George M. Johnson.**
Publisher:	Detroit, MI: Gale Research Inc., c1995.
Description:	xxii, 420 p.: ill. ; 29 cm.
Series:	**Dictionary of literary biography; v. 153**
Note:	Includes bibliographical references and index.
Subjects:	Novelists, English—19th century—Biography—Dictionaries.
	Novelists, English—20th century—Biography—Dictionaries.
	English fiction—19th century—Bio-bibliography.
	English fiction—20th century—Bio-bibliography.
	English fiction—19th century—Dictionaries.
	English fiction—20th century—Dictionaries.
Other Name:	Johnson, George M.
ISBN:	0810357143

Combining the author and title in your search can help to weed out irrelevant catalog records. Most catalogs allow you to search like this either through the advanced search screen or through a special combined author-title search. If your catalog includes an author-title search screen, simply type the author and title information into the appropriate fields, and the catalog's search engine should pull up the desired record. The advanced search screen should work similarly; however, here you must select author and title from the appropriate drop-down boxes. This method can be particularly useful when you need to winnow out film adaptations and similarly titled books from the primary text you're seeking.

Even an author-title combined search can produce multiple records for a single title. Because a single work may be published by multiple publishers and adapted into different forms, always carefully evaluate the editions you choose. Not all editions are equal. Some may be heavily revised and edited, perhaps even significantly shortened as a children's edition, while others contain scholarly footnotes and supplementary critical materials. If you simply need the text for a course, then one of the Norton, Oxford, Penguin, or other standard critical editions should suffice. However, if you are citing the text in a manuscript that will be submitted for publication, seek out the most authoritative one available. Unfortunately there is no one source for determining authoritative editions; however, there are some methods you can employ to identify the most reliable source.

As with the *Tess of the D'Urbervilles* example above, some editions may claim in the title to be "authoritative" texts. That can be a good indicator but shouldn't be relied upon solely in making your decision. When looking at the record itself, consider the publisher and its reputation. A university press edition will generally be more scholarly than a trade publisher edition. Also, consider who the editor is and what format the work is in. By searching your local catalog or indexing sources, you get a sense of the editor's scholarly history and reliability (see chapter 4 for more detailed discussion of indexing sources). The format you choose will be largely influenced by personal preference. If you prefer reading books in print, then an electronic book or microform reproduction of the book would not be ideal selections for you. In case you can't easily distinguish among editions based on the catalog records, examine the physical book, as the introductions will often clue you in to the reliability and authority of a particular edition. You could also review some of the scholarly literature about the book and see which editions other scholars in the field consistently cite. Generally you will easily observe trends in which editions are cited in the scholarly literature and which are not. While not foolproof methods, these should help you determine which edition to select.

SUBJECT SEARCHES

The first chapter already addressed the basics of searching with Library of Congress subject headings and controlled vocabulary. Subject headings, which are terms used to describe a particular work's intellectual contents, can help you focus your search and locate highly relevant results. Topically oriented, subject headings are carefully selected and regularly updated to help define what a work is about, whether the subject is a person, geographic location, time period, mode of thought, influence, or other topic. As mentioned previously in this book, subject headings are a more specific search alternative to keywords. That said, keywords can be used to search within subject headings. Your local library catalog may allow two ways to use subject headings: through searching keywords in the subject field and through browsing the alphabetical subject-heading list. If your catalog allows for limiting your keyword search to the subject field only, then you have more flexibility in developing your search strategies. While each catalog searches for keywords in indexes such as author, subject, and title, you can specify in which of those indexes you want the keywords to occur. When keyword searching in the subject field, the syntax, or order, of your search terms does not matter as it does when you browse subject headings; rather, keyword searching only requires the presence of the search terms somewhere in the subject headings. A keyword search in the subject field for *19th century English literature* produces results containing the subject heading *English literature—19th century—history and criticism*, such as Christopher Herbert's *War of No Pity: The Indian Mutiny and Victorian Trauma*:

Author:	Herbert, Christopher, 1941–
Title:	War of no pity : the Indian Mutiny and Victorian trauma / Christopher Herbert.
Publisher:	Princeton, NJ: Princeton University Press, c2008.
Description:	334 p. : ill. ; 24 cm.
Note:	Includes bibliographical references (p. [289]–316) and index.
Subjects:	**English literature—19th century**—History and criticism.
	Politics and **literature** — Great Britain—History—**19th century**.
	Literature and history—Great Britain—History—**19th century**.
	Polemics in **literature**.
	India—History—Sepoy Rebellion, 1857–1858—**Literature** and the rebellion.
	India—History—Sepoy Rebellion, 1857–1858—Historiography.
	India—History—Sepoy Rebellion, 1857–1858—Public opinion.
	India—In **literature**.
ISBN:	9780691133324
	0691133328

Even though *War of No Pity* is specifically about the Victorian age rather than the full nineteenth century, notice that the term *Victorian* does not appear in the subject headings because the standard subject heading for British literature during that period is *English literature—19th century*. Likewise, the phrase *Edwardian literature* does not occur in subject headings, so even though the Edwardian period extended only from 1902 to 1910, the appropriate subject heading is *English literature—20th century*. Clearly, neither heading is narrow enough to research either literary period. In spite of this, they can be useful when searched in conjunction with more specific subject headings or keywords. For instance, by searching for *English literature—20th century* as a subject heading and *Edwardian* as a keyword, you can limit to works that explicitly mention that era of literature. Since *Edwardian* tends not to appear in subject headings, searching it as a keyword finds matches in the title field and any table of contents included in the record.

When searching for phrases within subject headings, use quotation marks to ensure that the words remain in the proper order. To find works on female friendship in nineteenth-century literature, you could combine the subject *English literature—19th century* with *female friendship* as a keyword phrase in the subject field. This search combines the broad heading for nineteenth-century English literature with the notion of friendship between women. Searching in this manner ensures that the terms *female* and *friendship* occur not only together in a particular order but also within subject headings.

Limiting subject search results depends a great deal on your research topic. If you are researching a particular theme within a literary period, the most useful search may combine one of the subject headings mentioned above with more specific search terms. For instance, if you needed additional information on representations of India in nineteenth-century English literature, combine the subject heading *English literature—19th century* with *India* either as a general keyword or a keyword in a subject heading. This type of searching will help you focus your results set. If you do not retrieve the desired results, consider searching with the other subject headings listed in a relevant record. Perhaps other works with the heading *India—History—Sepoy Rebellion, 1857–1858—Literature and the rebellion* are worth considering as you work through the research process. As with keyword searching, be careful not to become too set on a particular search term or phrase. Remember that searches for related, broader, and narrower concepts, and in this case subject headings, can produce some highly relevant results that would have been missed had you searched with only one subject heading.

Unlike keyword searching for subjects, which does not require words to appear in a particular order or even in the same subject heading, browsing for subject headings forces you to use the syntax and terminology set forth in the

Library of Congress Subject Headings (LCSH). For literature, there are several standard forms to which you should become accustomed. The first chapter covered how and why you should search for an author as a subject. When you place the author's last name followed by his or her first name, you can easily identify works about that author. This is the most effective subject search for locating author-specific information. There are also standard headings for researching national literatures and literary themes. Using LCSH, you would search not for British literature but for English literature, Irish literature, Scottish literature, and Welsh literature, all as distinct bodies of literature. National literature subject headings can be further broken down by time period (early modern, eighteenth-century, etc.), ethnic influences (Celtic influences, French influences, etc.), resource type (bio-bibliographies, dictionaries, etc.), and author type (black authors, women authors, etc.), among other subdivisions. These headings and their subdivisions are constructed to direct you to specific information about an otherwise large and unwieldy body of literature.

Once you know the proper subject headings for your research topic, you will find that using those headings often produces far better results than keyword searches. The cataloging librarians who create records for each work consider its main concepts and assign it particular subject headings that best represent its intellectual contents. These headings indicate that that work is substantially about a certain topic rather than simply mentioning it in passing. When you search using a heading, you can be reasonably assured that it will retrieve only works that are relevant to that topic. The precision of subject headings can be a tremendous time-saving technique, as it prevents you from sifting through irrelevant search results. On the one hand, searching for terms such as *war* and *literature* as keywords produces a large results set, most of which are completely irrelevant. Using the subject heading *war in literature*, on the other hand, brings up a significantly smaller results list; however, all of them are substantially about that topic. The discussion below highlights some other major subject heading forms that will help you search more effectively and efficiently.

To help you identify resources on literary themes, movements, and topics, there are several subject heading formats of which you should be aware. The following forms—*term in literature, term (literature)*, and *term and literature*—are all used to depict how a particular concept relates to literary studies. As mentioned previously, while LCSH are based on cataloging rules, each cataloger has some leeway in how those rules are applied, so you may find that these headings are applied unevenly at best. Even so, they are worth knowing. The *in literature* form is generally used for a concept, movement, people group, or idea as represented in literature. To find information on children within literature, search using the subject heading *Children in literature*. Likewise, works about industrialization and literature are listed under the heading *Industrialization in literature*. Another LCSH form, a term followed by *(literature)* as a qualifier, may be used to illustrate that a work is about literary aspects of a particular topic. For instance, modernism as a literary movement—as opposed to an art movement—is listed as *Modernism (literature)*. The third form, which combines a term and the phrase *and literature* is intended to express the interplay between two major concepts. A heading such as *Psychoanalysis and literature* indicates that the terms joined by *and* are roughly of equal importance. Throughout your research, bear in mind that these subject-heading forms are better understood as guidelines rather than hard-and-fast rules.

UNION CATALOGS

Center for Research Libraries. Chicago, IL: CRL. www.crl.edu (accessed 18 April 2010).
Copac: the UK and Irish Academic and National Library Catalogue. Manchester, UK: University of Manchester, at copac.ac.uk (accessed 18 April 2010).
National Union Catalog, Pre-1956 Imprints: A Cumulative Author List Representing Library of Congress Printed Cards and Titles Reported by Other American Libraries. 754 vols. London: Mansell, 1968–1981.
WorldCat. Dublin, OH: OCLC. www.oclc.org/firstsearch.
WorldCat.org. Dublin, OH: OCLC. www.worldcat.org.

The search strategies detailed earlier in this chapter and the first chapter can be used to query most online catalogs. After you have exhausted your local library's holdings, your next step is to consult any available union catalogs. A union catalog comprises the combined holdings of multiple libraries. Some union catalogs may reflect the holdings of a particular library system, representing materials held in all libraries in a university system or in a state- or region-wide library system. Other union catalogs have a national or international focus, including records from the libraries of one nation or from major libraries in nations around the globe. Regardless of the union catalog's size or scale, it should be searchable by author, title, and subject as discussed previously. Union catalogs are useful for discovering materials written on a particular topic that are not held by your local library or for identifying the location of a known work. To obtain materials found through a union catalog, consult your library's interlibrary loan department to ascertain whether a specific item can be borrowed. The following section discusses and evaluates the purpose and functionality of major union catalogs in the United States and the United Kingdom. While the Victorian and Edwardian ages encompass literatures from the United Kingdom, major American union catalogs are worth noting, as they and their holdings may be more accessible to researchers in the United States.

Available by subscription to libraries, one of the most well-known union catalogs is *WorldCat*, which was developed as a collaborative effort among libraries and librarians to enhance access to each other's holdings and increase library users' ability to locate relevant resources. *WorldCat*, a product of the Online Computer Library Center (OCLC), provides access to library holdings records from seventy-two thousand libraries worldwide and contains more than 174 million catalog records, claiming to be the world's largest union catalog. *WorldCat* is international in scope, representing 86 countries and more than 470 languages; however, the majority of the libraries represented are located in the United States. OCLC has been making concerted efforts to partner with national libraries around the world, such as the British Library, the National Library of Australia, and the National Library of New Zealand, among others. *WorldCat*'s size increased significantly in July 2006, when OCLC acquired the Research Libraries Group (RLG) Union Catalog.

While offering expanded search options, *WorldCat* can be searched using the strategies discussed previously. As with your local catalog, you still need to evaluate your results carefully and examine the records thoroughly when making your final resource selection. The default results sort is by number of libraries, meaning that books owned by the most libraries appear first, while those held by the fewest libraries fall to the bottom of the list. Just because a book is held by hundreds of libraries does not mean it has greater significance or importance than a book held by only a handful of libraries, so use a critical eye with any and all results, regardless of where they occur in the list. In addition to the default sort, you can adjust this setting to sort by date, relevance, or accession number. In *WorldCat*, relevance is determined by the number of matched search terms along with the proximity and uniqueness of those terms. These factors are used to assign each result a relevance ranking, with the highest ranked items appearing first on the list.

WorldCat has records for books, visual materials, computer files, Internet resources, serial publications, sound recordings, archival materials, articles, musical scores, and maps, so depending on your research needs, you may need to limit to a specific type of information source. As shown in the illustration below, the records themselves are similar to the records contained in your local catalog, providing bibliographic and descriptive information about a particular item (figure 3.2). The record should also indicate whether your local library owns the item and can connect directly to your library's catalog

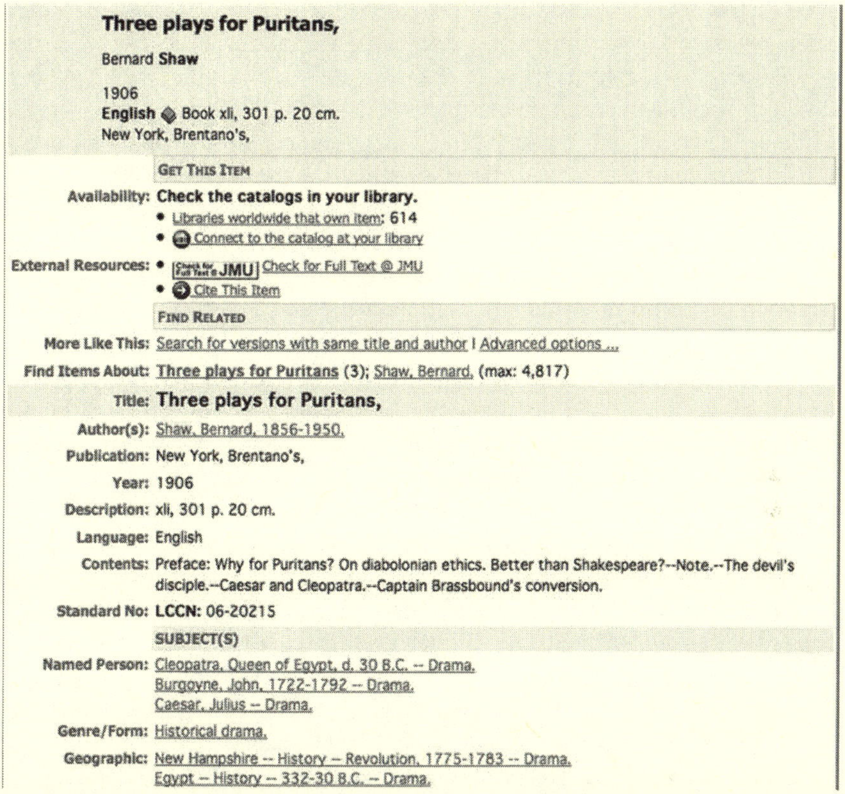

Three plays for Puritans,

Bernard **Shaw**

1906
English ◈ Book xli, 301 p. 20 cm.
New York, Brentano's,

GET THIS ITEM

Availability: **Check the catalogs in your library.**
- Libraries worldwide that own item: 614
- 🌐 Connect to the catalog at your library

External Resources: • |Find it @ JMU| Check for Full Text @ JMU
- 🔵 Cite This Item

FIND RELATED

More Like This: Search for versions with same title and author | Advanced options ...
Find Items About: Three plays for Puritans (3); Shaw, Bernard, (max: 4,817)

Title: **Three plays for Puritans,**

Author(s): Shaw, Bernard, 1856-1950.
Publication: New York, Brentano's,
Year: 1906
Description: xli, 301 p. 20 cm.
Language: English
Contents: Preface: Why for Puritans? On diabolonian ethics. Better than Shakespeare?--Note.--The devil's disciple.--Caesar and Cleopatra.--Captain Brassbound's conversion.
Standard No: LCCN: 06-20215

SUBJECT(S)

Named Person: Cleopatra, Queen of Egypt, d. 30 B.C. -- Drama.
Burgoyne, John, 1722-1792 -- Drama.
Caesar, Julius -- Drama.
Genre/Form: Historical drama.
Geographic: New Hampshire -- History -- Revolution, 1775-1783 -- Drama.
Egypt -- History -- 332-30 B.C. -- Drama.

Figure 3.2. Modified *WorldCat* record for George Bernard Shaw's *Three Plays for Puritans.* Source: *WorldCat.*

and interlibrary loan system using link-resolving technology. If your library's holdings are in *WorldCat*, then you can limit to items held by your library. This can be particularly useful if your local catalog is ever inaccessible.

Despite the vast resources cataloged in *WorldCat*, this extensive union catalog is not comprehensive, and should not be relied on as such. To be as complete as possible in your research, make a habit of searching multiple sources regardless of the size and scope of a resource. The number of catalog records can be deceptive for users who fail to realize that *WorldCat* includes multiple records for individual editions of a work. Although the catalog contains more than 174 million records, it does not have records for more than 174 million unique resources. Currently, OCLC is not always able to successfully merge records provided by various libraries, making it difficult to determine total holdings of a particular edition and track publishing histories. Because of this, you may find separate catalog entries representing the exact same edition of a book. If you need to track the publishing history and editions of a work, the *National Union Catalog, Pre-1956 Imprints* may be a better resource for accomplishing that task. In some respects, *WorldCat* can be considered as a continuation, or extension, of the *National Union Catalog*, which is discussed later in this chapter.

Recently, OCLC made the *WorldCat* records available through an open-access version of the catalog: ***WorldCat.org***—a user-centered approach to library catalogs. *WorldCat.org* allows users to search records included in the subscription version of *WorldCat* for free on the Web. *WorldCat.org* records are drawn from libraries that also subscribe to *WorldCat*. Currently, only ten thousand of the seventy-two thousand libraries have elected to participate in *WorldCat.org*. Launched in August 2006, the two catalogs offer much of the same bibliographic content but have vastly different functionality. Where *WorldCat* accepts traditional strategies such as Boolean searching, *WorldCat.org* cannot be searched using Boolean operators (*and*, *or*, *not*) or other advanced search techniques. Rather, the Web-accessible version provides a "Googlesque" search box, giving users the option to search books, DVDs, CDs, articles, and all resource tyes. The advanced search screen enables you to specify where the terms appear: as keywords or in author, title, or subject fields. From here you can also limit by format, publication date, content, audience, or language. The results display also differs from its subscription counterpart. Identical searches in the two versions of the catalog may retrieve similar results, but while *WorldCat* ranks by number of libraries, *WorldCat.org* defaults to ranking results by relevance.

The results display in *WorldCat.org* incorporates Web 2.0 technologies, allowing users to refine the results from the display screen using author, format, year, content, audience, language, and topic limiters derived from the results set. Rather than displaying all information on one screen, *WorldCat.org* presents the basic bibliographic information at the top of the screen while separating libraries, details, subjects, reviews, and tags into tabs at the bottom of the screen (see figure 3.3). By creating an individual account with *WorldCat.org*, you have the option to add tags and reviews for any item in the catalog and create private or shared lists and bibliographies based on your search results. Even if you choose not to create an account, the catalog provides links in each record to export the citation directly into either EndNote or RefWorks, and demonstrates how to cite the item in five major citation styles: APA, Chicago, Harvard, MLA, and Turabian. Enabling linking to social networking sites such as Facebook, Google Book Search, and the Web browser Firefox is another way in which OCLC has embedded Web 2.0 technologies into *WorldCat.org*.

A recent development and departure from the traditional contents held in *WorldCat*, *WorldCat.org* includes article-level citations from *JSTOR*, the National Library of Medicine's *MEDLINE*, the U.S. Department of Education's

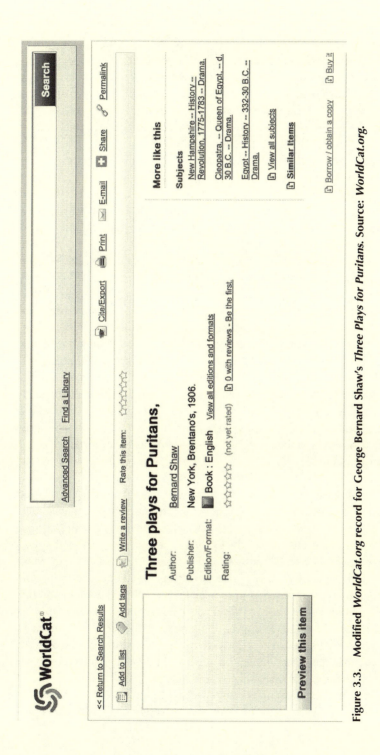

Figure 3.3. Modified *WorldCat.org* record for George Bernard Shaw's *Three Plays for Puritans. Source: WorldCat.org.*

ERIC database, the British Library *Inside* serials, the *GPO Monthly Catalog*, and the OCLC *ArticleFirst®* database. H. W. Wilson and the Modern Language Association have also agreed to include a portion of their bibliographic citations in *WorldCat.org*. The citations from the MLA will probably be the most useful for your research on Victorian and Edwardian literatures. The inclusion of article citations enhances users' access to scholarly information but does not eliminate the need to consult other sources when conducting research. Some libraries are beginning to adopt the *WorldCat.org* customization option—*WorldCat Local*—as a means of harnessing the *WorldCat.org* interface to deliver local content rather than hosting a separate, stand-alone OPAC. Early adopters of *WorldCat Local* include Cornell University Library, the State Library of Ohio, and the University of Delaware Library, but the end results of this venture remain to be seen.

A print precursor to today's online union catalogs, the ***National Union Catalog, Pre-1956 Imprints*** serves as a record of bibliographic and holdings information for materials published prior to 1956 and owned by major libraries in the United States and Canada, as well as select rare materials from other libraries. According to the 1967 *Prospectus for the National Union Catalog, Pre-1956 Imprints*, the catalog was intended to make "the important book resources of the nation accessible to the scholarly community and, so to speak, make them part of each scholar's library" and to have a "'pure' bibliographic or reference function, the identification or confirmation of the existence of a publication [. . .] the acquisition function, not in the sense of where to acquire a specific item but whether to acquire it."[1] Unlike many bibliographies of the day, the *National Union Catalog*—frequently referred to as the *NUC* or by its publisher, Mansell—is not a simple listing of citations but rather contains reproductions of physical library catalog cards, providing bibliographic and holdings information for books, pamphlets, maps, atlases, music, periodicals, and other serials. The cards are organized alphabetically by author (either personal or corporate) and by title within author. Anonymous works are listed alphabetically by title, and pseudonyms, signs, and symbols cross-reference to the author's given name. Editions of individual works are listed separately in date order, enabling researchers to track editions and publishing histories of a particular text. Each card contains bibliographic information as well as varying levels of description of the item's intellectual contents. Also, depending on the source of the card reproduced in the *NUC*, there may be a classification number in either Library of Congress or Dewey Decimal classification. Unfortunately, the *NUC* contains no subject index, so it is best used for known item searching.

This 754-volume set was published between 1968 and 1981, with the initial 685 volumes published prior to 1980 and the supplement released beginning in 1980, bringing the volume count to 754. All catalog cards included in the set contain code for the libraries that own the title in question. The key to the code is located in the front and back covers of each volume and is organized alphabetically by state. While the holdings information represented by these codes was current as of date of publication, this information should be verified using the individual library's online catalog. If that library no longer has the book in question, check *WorldCat* to see if other libraries have a copy. In this age of digital access, do not underestimate the value of the *NUC*. Although online union catalogs, such as *WorldCat*, provide records for vast amounts of resources, recent studies have shown that over 25 percent of *NUC* contents are unique.[2] As libraries are busy adding catalog records for new print and digital resources, retrospective cataloging projects sometimes go by the wayside. Because of this, the *NUC* remains a valuable resource for librarians and scholars.

Although not a union catalog, the **Center for Research Libraries (CRL)** provides scholars access to valuable research materials and, as such, is worth noting. A consortium of North American university, college, and research libraries, the *CRL* serves as a repository for preserving newspapers, journals, dissertations, archives, government publications, and other traditional and digital resources. The availability of microform sets through the *CRL* should be particularly useful for scholars, whose local libraries may not have the funds to purchase these costly sets. These materials are available through interlibrary loan and electronic delivery for scholars and researchers from member institutions. Additionally, scholars and researchers from non-member institutions may access the resource for a fee, with restrictions. The organization's catalog enables users from any institution to search for materials held by the *CRL*, and in addition to its tangible holdings, the *CRL* offers select open-access electronic collections through its website, few of which are literary in nature. If you have questions about membership in the *CRL* or desire to interlibrary-loan a resource from the center, contact your local library.

Providing free access to the catalogs of major university and national libraries in the U.K. and Ireland, **Copac: the UK and Irish Academic and National Library Catalogue** primarily contains records for the collections of Research Libraries UK (RLUK) member libraries, specialist research libraries, specialist databases, and nationally important research collections held in academic libraries. *Copac* contains approximately thirty-two million catalog records; however, like its American counterpart, *WorldCat*, it has duplicate entries for some items because multiple libraries may have contributed information for the same item and because the catalog retains records for pre-1800 unique items. Although individual entries are not linked to full text, a minority of records contains links to the open-access full text of a particular work.

Currently, even member libraries cannot borrow books, documents, or articles directly through *Copac*, but must request items through their library's interlibrary loan system, making *Copac*'s major role one of resource discovery rather than access. *Copac* may not contain 100 percent of each library's holdings, as some libraries have not loaded all of their card catalog records into their online catalogs. As a result, you may still need to consult an individual library's catalog to determine whether they own a particular item.

Similar to *WorldCat.org*, *Copac* uses Web 2.0 technologies to enhance the user's experience using the catalog. Through this search history function, you can set up an RSS feed for preferred or frequent searches, enabling ready access to citations for recent additions to the catalog that match your terms. You can download records into bibliographic management software such as Zotero, Reference Manager, and EndNote. To enable quick searching, plug-ins are available for the Internet Explorer and Firefox Web browsers that allow for access to *Copac*'s contents from a search bar embedded in the browser. *Copac* functions similarly to other union catalogs; however, lack of browseable author, subject, and title indexes makes it difficult to construct precise queries. When searching with keywords, both American and British terms and spellings should be used to retrieve the most comprehensive results set.

NATIONAL LIBRARY CATALOGS

British Library *Integrated Catalogue*. London: The British Library Board. catalogue.bl.uk.
Library of Congress Online Catalog. Washington, DC: Library of Congress. catalog.loc.gov.
National Library of Ireland *Online Catalogue*. Dublin, Ireland: National Library of Ireland. www.nli.ie/en/online-catalogue.aspx.
National Library of Scotland *Main Catalogue*. Edinburgh, Scotland: National Library of Scotland. main-cat.nls.uk.
National Library of Wales *Full Catalogue*. Aberystwyth, Wales: National Library of Wales/Llyfrgell Genedlaethol Cymru. cat.llgc.org.uk.

In addition to union library catalogs, you need to be familiar with major national library catalogs. Because research on Victorian and Edwardian literature crosses national boundaries, you may find it necessary to search multiple national library catalogs. As noted earlier, their partial contents may be included by union catalogs; however, searching a specific catalog can still be useful to learn the complete holdings of a particular library and more details about an item in the catalog. Although not technically a national library, the

Library of Congress houses a tremendous research collection and boasts the title of world's largest library. As such, no scholar should overlook the Library of Congress and its vast holdings. Researchers in the United States may already be familiar with the **Library of Congress Online Catalog**, which comprises records for approximately fourteen million books, serials, computer files, manuscripts, cartographic materials, music, sound recordings, and visual materials held by the Library of Congress. Records for materials added to the catalog between 1898 and 1980 may not be complete, and despite the general trend toward online access, the most complete information about materials added to the library prior to 1980 will be found in the print card catalog in the Library of Congress. If you are unable to travel to Washington, DC, you may try requesting items through the interlibrary loan department at your local library.

Providing basic and guided search options, the Library of Congress online catalog contains several indexes, including names, subjects, titles, notes, publications, and numbers. The detailed indexes should help you construct specific searches and retrieve highly relevant results. As with any catalog, keywords can be an effective way of beginning your search and identifying which terms and subject headings will produce the best results. If you have specific resource type needs, use the *Prints and Photographs Online Catalog* (*PPOC*) and the *Sound Online Inventory & Catalog* (*SONIC*), which are linked directly off of the catalog homepage. Since the catalog times out after five minutes of inactivity, use your time wisely.

The British Library **Integrated Catalogue** comprises records for over thirteen million items located in the British Library. Even at that, not all of the British Library's holdings are represented in the *Integrated Catalogue*. The catalog's homepage, however, provides links to collections and their respective catalogs, such as British Library *Direct*, an article database; the *Manuscripts Catalogue*; the *Sound Archive Catalogue*; *Images Online*; and other specialized finding aids. The *Integrated Catalogue* defaults to the basic search screen, which allows for simple word and phrase searching without requiring you to specify a particular field. Other options include browsing and both advanced and catalog subset searches. While the advanced search supports more sophisticated queries and lets the user specify in which fields terms appear, the catalog subset search enables the user to limit his or her search even further, focusing on subsets either individually or in combination with one another. You may also browse for a particular word or phrase in any of twelve indexes.

Depending on your research focus, you may need to search other national catalogs from the British Isles. The National Library of Ireland *Online Catalogue*, the National Library of Scotland *Main Catalogue*, and the National

Library of Wales *Full Catalogue* all contain unique resources not available in the previously discussed union and national catalogs. The National Library of Ireland **Online Catalogue** contains records for materials cataloged since 1990 as well as records for some older resources. As with the British Library, the National Library of Ireland has some additional catalogs and databases to supplement the main online catalog. The *NEWSPLAN Database*, which provides records of hard-copy and microform newspapers, the *Photographic Databases*, and the *Manuscript Collection Lists* all supplement the *Online Catalogue*. Even the *Online Catalogue* is further subdivided into *Books and Periodicals*, *Manuscripts*, *Photographs*, and *Prints and Drawings*. Within each subset of the *Online Catalogue*, alphabetical search (browse) and keyword search are the available options but the indexed fields vary from subset to subset. While the *Books and Periodicals* section has indexes for author, title, subject, series, and Irish publisher (1991–), *Prints and Drawings* has indexes for artist, title, subject, and Dewey Decimal call numbers.

The National Library of Scotland **Main Catalogue** includes more than three million records for print materials acquired by the National Library of Scotland since 1801 as well as music items, printed maps and atlases, and manuscript maps. The *Manuscript Catalogues and Guides*, the *Scots Abroad* database, the index to the *Special and Named Printed Collections* in the National Library of Scotland, and a list of *Principal Additions to the Collections* supplement the *Main Catalogue*. The *Main Catalogue* defaults to the simple search, which lets users enter words or phrases, choose a search type, and select limits for languages, resource type, and resource location. This option does not recognize Boolean operators. The advanced search allows for combining terms using Boolean operators while specifying where the word or phrase occurs in the catalog record.

Finally, the National Library of Wales **Full Catalogue** includes records for more than four million books, maps, photographs, and other materials. The *Archives* database and *National Screen and Sound Archive* main catalogue have not yet been integrated with the *Full Catalogue* and must be searched separately. Local and family history resources must also be accessed through a separate catalog. The catalog's contents and interface are available in both English and Cymraeg, or Welsh. The default language is Cymraeg but can be easily switched to English by clicking the link for "English" in the upper right-hand corner of the screen. The National Library of Wales main catalog defaults to the basic search screen but also offers keyword searching, browsing, expert searching, and external searching, which allows users to search simultaneously the catalogs of other UK and international institutions. The keyword search is similar to the advanced option in the National Library of Scotland *Main Catalogue*, which supports combining multiple terms using

Boolean operators and lets users specify in which fields their terms appear. Scholars may browse the indexes for author, title, subject, and periodical title, while the expert search should be used for command-line queries.

CONCLUSION

You should now be familiar with basic and advanced online searching techniques, as well as major union and national library catalogs. While union catalogs are an excellent source for locating hard-to-find resources, do not discount the importance of individual national catalogs and of the catalogs of research and academic libraries. Even in today's digital age, there is still no single comprehensive catalog, so never hesitate to search an individual library's online catalog, especially if that library is known to have a strong collection in one of your research areas. As illustrated in our discussion of national library catalogs, often even major libraries do not have all of their holdings represented in their main catalogs. Archival materials and manuscripts, as well as older print, microform, and government documents collections, may not be included in even the most robust online catalogs because of the time necessary to convert older printed catalog records into their digital counterparts.

NOTES

1. John W. Cronin, "History of the National Union Catalog Pre-1956 Imprints," in *Prospectus for the National Union Catalog, Pre-1956 Imprints* (London: Mansell, 1967), 11.

2. Jeffrey Beall and Karen Kafadar, "The Proportion of NUC Pre-56 Titles Represented in OCLC WorldCAT," *College & Research Libraries* 66, no. 5 (2005): 431–35; Christine DeZelar-Tiedman, "The Proportion of NUC Pre-56 Titles Represented in the RLIN and OCLC Databases Compared: A Follow-up to the Beall/Kafadar Study," *College & Research Libraries* 69, no. 5 (2008): 401–6.

Chapter Four

Print and Electronic Bibliographies, Indexes, and Annual Reviews

Regardless of your research interests in the Victorian and Edwardian ages, you should familiarize yourself with major bibliographies and indexes. Covering contemporary scholarship as well as historic literature, these resources will help you identify relevant journal articles, book articles, reviews, books, and dissertations. No matter how inclusive a particular resource seems, there is no completely comprehensive bibliography or index for either Victorian or Edwardian literature. Because the scope, time period, and specific titles vary widely from index to index and bibliography to bibliography, make a habit of searching multiple sources when conducting your research. Limiting your search to only one resource may cause you to miss highly relevant citations that would have given you a more complete understanding of your topic. While many of these resources are available as online subscription databases, your library may have access to them in print or microform rather than through their digital counterparts.

Bibliographies, generally speaking, are compilations of citations to resources about a particular topic or area of study. Varying widely in terms of length, bibliographies may comprise a page at the end of a critical article or an entire book-length work. In addition to differences in length, the amount of information provided also varies. Some bibliographies offer citation information only, while others will include annotations that explain or evaluate the intellectual contents of the cited work. Annotated bibliographies can be quite helpful in determining whether a particular book or article is relevant to your research area. Annotated or not, the best way to determine any resource's relevance is to examine the work's full text, along with any accompanying table of contents, indexes, or appendixes. Introductions that explain the bibliography's scope in terms of chronological and geographic coverage and any other limiting factors preface most bibliographies. The introduction should also indicate whether a bibliography covers primary texts, secondary texts, or both, and whether it is contemporary or historic. Indexes, like bibliographies, serve as finding aids for information about a particular topic. Generally published serially, indexes are guides to literature of a particular discipline, such as literary studies, a literary form such as biography, or an information format such as periodical literature. The apparent differences between bibliographies and indexes are rather small, but both are tremendously useful in locating additional research resources.

The best place to start is to examine the major general literature bibliographies: the *Modern Language Association International Bibliography* and the *Annual Bibliography of English Language and Literature*. Although not specific to the Victorian and Edwardian ages, these bibliographies are essential research tools for literary study. Including all time periods and genres, these bibliographies index secondary sources such as journal articles, books and book chapters, and dissertations, but neither includes citations to primary source materials. As their titles suggest, the *Modern Language Association International Bibliography* focuses on literatures from around the world, while the *Annual Bibliography of English Language and Literature* focuses on English-language literatures. In addition to these traditional bibliographies, this chapter addresses Google Scholar, *Periodicals Index Online*, and full-text resources such as *JSTOR*, *Project Muse*, and *Periodicals Archive Online*. Although not intended as bibliographies, these resources are often used as such. Because they are not traditional bibliographies or indexes, they do not contain the same depth or breadth of coverage for any particular subject. However, these resources tend to be highly accessible to students and scholars alike, providing significant amounts of full text.

After addressing the major general literature bibliographies, the chapter shifts its focus to examine major national bibliographies such as the *Index to British Literary Bibliography* and *The New Cambridge Bibliography of English Literature*, which offer bibliographic access to resources on all time periods, genres, and movements in British literature. The next section discusses period-specific bibliographies for primary and secondary resources, as well as genre- and author-specific bibliographies. On the one hand, resources such as *Victorian Database Online*, the *Annual Bibliography of Victorian Studies*, and *A Descriptive Catalogue of the Bibliographies of Twentieth Century British Poets, Novelists, and Dramatists* all offer bibliographic access to secondary sources. Resources such as the *19th Century Masterfile*, *C19: The Nineteenth Century Index*, and the *Nineteenth-Century Short Title Catalogue*, on the other hand, are excellent tools for identifying primary sources. The uneven representation of resources from the Victorian and Edwardian ages attests to the ever-increasing number of sources on the Victorian age and the still small number on the Edwardian age. The final section of this chapter discusses examples of genre-specific or author-specific bibliographies, and provides guidance for locating additional bibliographies in library catalogs.

GENERAL LITERATURE BIBLIOGRAPHIES

Annual Bibliography of English Language and Literature. Leeds: Maney Publishing for the Modern Humanities Research Association, 1921. Annual. Available online at www.chadwyck.com.

Google Scholar, Google.scholar.google.com (accessed 18 April 2010).

JSTOR: The Scholarly Journal Archive. New York: JSTOR, 1995. www.jstor.org.

Modern Language Association International Bibliography of Books and Articles of the Modern Languages and Literatures. New York: Modern Language Association of America, 1922. Annual. Available online through multiple vendors. For more information go to www.mla.org/bib_electronic.

Periodicals Archive Online. Ann Arbor, MI: ProQuest. Available online at www.proquest.com.

Periodicals Index Online. Ann Arbor, MI: ProQuest. Available online at www.proquest.com.

Project Muse. Baltimore, MD: Johns Hopkins University Press, 1993. Available online at muse.jhu.edu.

The Year's Work in English Studies. Oxford: Published for the English Association by Oxford University Press, 1919. Annual. ywes.oxfordjournals.org.

Indexing books and articles on modern languages, literatures, folklore, and linguistics, the ***Modern Language Association International Bibliography*** (***MLAIB***) is quite possibly one of the most widely used literature bibliographies available. The bibliography originated as a record of American literary scholarship and was initially published under the title *American Bibliography* as part of the journal *PMLA: Publications of the Modern Language Association of America* (see chapter 5 for more information on *PMLA*). Not until 1969 did *MLAIB* became a separate publication. The print bibliography—first published in 1922 and covering American scholarship from 1921—was available both to libraries and individuals through 2008. A print-on-demand version of the classified sections continues to be available for Modern Language Association (MLA) members. The library version was issued in two cloth-bound books: one containing five volumes with an index of editors and authors, and a second containing a list of subject terms referring to entries in the first volume. The five volumes comprising the first book included:

1. Literatures in English (American, Australian, English, English Canadian, English Caribbean, Irish, New Zealand, Scottish, and Welsh literatures),
2. Literatures in other languages (African, Asian, European, French Canadian, French Caribbean, and Latin American literatures),
3. Linguistics (history and theory of linguistics, comparative linguistics, language interaction, lexicology, phonetics, pragmatics, psycholinguistics, semantics, stylistics, syntax, translation, and teaching of language),
4. General literature and related topics (literary theory and criticism, film, radio, television, theater, manuscripts, printing, publishing, genres, literary forms, literary themes and figures, rhetoric and composition, and teaching of literature), and
5. Folklore (history and study of folklore, folk literature, folk music, folk art, folk belief systems, and folk rituals).

Since its first publication, the print *MLAIB* underwent several transitions. Until 1925, the bibliography was written in narrative form, similar to the current format of a *Year's Work in English Studies* (see discussion below). By the 1926 edition, the *MLAIB* had transitioned from a narrative assessment of scholarly contributions in literary studies to a list of bibliographic citations with select entries accompanied by brief annotations. The annotations ceased with the 1951 edition. An author index was added in 1964, greatly enhancing access to the bibliography's contents. Over the years subdivisions have multiplied, and this important resource grew in size. In 1969, the *MLAIB* divided into three volumes: General, English, American, Medieval, and Neo-Latin; European, Asian, African, and Latin American literatures; and Linguistics. By 1981, it split once more into the current five volumes.

While the print bibliography remains a useful, functional research tool, the online version offers a more efficient way to search all years going back to the 1920s simultaneously. The time saved by searching the online version as opposed to individual print volumes is invaluable to students and scholars alike. Containing more than two million citations, the online *MLAIB* is hosted on five different platforms offered by the following vendors: EBSCO, Gale Cengage (as a stand-alone or as part of the *Literature Resource Center [LRC]*), OCLC, ProQuest-CSA, and ProQuest-Chadwyck Healey (as a stand-alone and as part of *Literature Online [LION]*). In addition to availability on the aforementioned platforms, some *MLAIB* citations are searchable through *WorldCat.org*, which is discussed in greater detail in chapter 3. Regardless of platform, the database contents are provided by the MLA and should be identical. Depending on the platform, the *MLAIB* may also offer access to the *MLA Directory of Periodicals* and the *MLAIB* names and subject thesauri. The *Directory of Periodicals* comprises profiles of more than 5,500 periodicals, more than 4,400 of which are indexed in the bibliography. Like the print version, the online bibliography is a tool for locating citations to books and articles on literary topics and is not a full-text resource; however, the online version links to full text in *JSTOR*, *Project Muse*, and *ProQuest Dissertations & Theses*. Your library, however, must subscribe to both *MLAIB* and the full-text resources mentioned in order to access the full text. Citations are largely unaccompanied by abstracts; however, in April 2008, MLA began incorporating publisher-supplied abstracts for select publications. To date, the American Association of Teachers of German, Chinese Literature: Essays, Articles, Reviews (CLEAR), Intellect, *JSTOR*, the Modern Language Association of America, Monash University ePress, and *Project Muse* have granted the MLA permission to include abstracts for current and retrospective citations from their publications.

Each year, citations for more than sixty-six thousand books and articles are added to the bibliography. In addition to print journal articles and books, the *MLAIB* recently began including citations for select electronic journals, online bibliographies, electronic books, and scholarly websites. Although materials are primarily in English, the bibliography is truly international in scope, with more than sixty languages represented. Just as books are cataloged using Library of Congress subject headings (LCSH), materials in *MLAIB* are categorized according to a unique classification scheme developed by the MLA. The intellectual contents of each item added to the bibliography are indexed according to topic, place, national literature, century, author, genre, and title of the work being studied, as appropriate. MLA staff and contributors index each work according to its intellectual contents to aid in retrieval.

While the search options available in the online *MLAIB* may vary slightly from platform to platform, basic search capabilities should remain the same, and the techniques you learned in chapters 1 and 3 will be applicable regardless of platform. The search capabilities of the *MLAIB* are based on the detailed indexing done by the MLA, enabling queries by pre-determined descriptors as well as general keywords. This allows scholars to review current and past scholarship on a particular author or text easily. The descriptors, which identify major literary themes, genres, topics, geographic locations, characters, and subjects, may help guide your research path. When you identify a relevant citation in *MLAIB*, carefully examine the indexing terms (which may be referred to as subject terms or descriptors) to determine those most relevant for your research project.[1] In many *MLAIB* platforms, indexing terms are hyperlinked, which allows scholars to locate additional relevant citations easily.

The sample record shown below depicts the information types listed in an *MLAIB* entry (figure 4.1). Much of the information mirrors contents found in a library catalog, such as author, title, publication information, and subject headings. In this particular *MLAIB* version, the author and publication information,

Title: Grave Girls: Anarchic Women in Helen and Olivia Rossetti's A Girl among the Anarchists and G. K. Chesterton's The Man Who Was Thursday

Citation: "Grave Girls: Anarchic Women in Helen and Olivia Rossetti's A Girl among the Anarchists and G. K. Chesterton's The Man Who Was Thursday". Weihman, Lisa. *Journal of Pre-Raphaelite Studies*. 16. (2007 Fall), pp. 88-105.

Document Type: Bibliographic citation; journal article

Bookmark: Bookmark this Document

Library links: Check for FULL TEXT at JMU

Content Links: *The Journal of Pre-Raphaelite Studies* in Directory of Periodicals
Lisa Weihman

Subject Terms: English literature, 1900-1999; Angeli, Helen Rossetti (1879-1969); and Agresti, Olivia Frances Madox Rossetti (1875-1960); A Girl among the Anarchists (1903); novel; autobiographical novel; by women novelists; relationship to anarchism; compared to Chesterton, Gilbert Keith (1874-1936); The Man Who Was Thursday (1908).

Language: English
Publication Date: 2007
ISSN: 1060-149X

Peer-Reviewed: Yes

MLA Update: 200701
MLA Sequence: 2007-1-6178
MLA Record Number: 2007584290

Figure 4.1.   Modified *MLAIB* record for "Grave Girls: Anarchic Women in Helen and Olivia Rossetti's *A Girl among the Anarchists* and G. K. Chesterton's *The Man Who Was Thursday*." Source: *MLAIB*, via Gale Cengage.

while included, is not pulled out in a separate field; rather, it is incorporated into the citation field. Notice also that the subject terms listed here cover national literature (English literature), time period (1900–1999), authors (Helen Rossetti Angeli, Olivia Frances Madox Rossetti Agresti, and George Keith Chesterton), titles (*A Girl among the Anarchists* and *The Man Who Was Thursday*), genres (novel and autobiographical novel), and topics (by women novelists and relationship to anarchism). All of these terms are designed to help scholars locate the most relevant information as efficiently as possible. This entry also displays information about document type, language, ISSN, publication date, and peer-reviewed status. Each record may also link directly to your library's holdings so that you can easily determine whether your library owns or has access to the book or journal to which the citation refers. This form of linking has become a standard feature in most online databases to facilitate more seamless access to information resources.

The *Annual Bibliography of English Language and Literature* (*ABELL*) is another major bibliographic tool for literary research. A publication of the Modern Humanities Research Association, *ABELL* covers the English language, English literature, bibliography, and "traditional culture of the English-speaking world including custom, belief, narrative, song, dance and material culture." Unlike the *MLAIB*, which indexes scholarship on world literatures in various languages, *ABELL* provides citations for works on English language and literature exclusively, including drama, poetry, fiction, biography, literary theory, film, bibliography, traditional culture, onomastics, lexicography, and dialectology. Originating in Great Britain, *ABELL* cites more British and Continental criticism than American criticism. This bibliography is smaller than that of the MLA, boasting more than nine hundred thousand records to *MLAIB*'s more than two million records; however, *ABELL* cites unique materials and is a valuable research tool for literary studies. In addition to books and journal articles, *ABELL* indexes critical editions of literary works, book reviews, essay collections, and unpublished dissertations from 1920 to 1999. Scholars searching for book reviews will find *ABELL* a more useful tool than the *MLAIB*, as the latter does not index this type of publication.

ABELL's first edition was published in 1921, covering scholarship from 1920. The bibliography is still available in print through Maney Publishing and is compiled by a worldwide team of contributors and edited by teams in Cambridge, England, and Massachusetts. An online version containing the bibliography from 1920 to the present is also available through Chadwyck-Healey, a division of ProQuest. This version is updated prior to the release of each new annual print bibliography. The online version is available as a stand-alone database or as part of Chadwyck-Healey's *Literature Online* (*LION*), the only platform that allows subscribers to cross-search *ABELL* with the *MLAIB*.

ABELL's search interface is simpler than that of the *MLAIB*; however, it is just as powerful a research tool. With only one search interface, rather than separate basic and advanced search screens, *ABELL* offers fields for searching terms as keywords, title keywords, subjects, authors/reviewers, publication details, journals, ISBN, and ISSN. Terms for each field, with the exception of the keyword field, may be entered freely or selected from a list of possible terms. It also contains search limits for publication years, latest update, and resource type (e.g., articles, books, and reviews). This database saves your searches within a single session in its search history and allows selected records to be saved to a marked list. From the marked list, records can then be e-mailed, printed, or downloaded into a citation management program. Each record for an article or literary work provides information regarding the work's author, title, publication details, publication year, ISSN or ISBN as appropriate, subject, reference number, and additional search terms. Below is a sample *ABELL* record for Catharine R. Stimpson's article "'Do These Deaths Surpass Understanding?' The Literary Figure of the Mother Who Murders." Within the record, search terms are marked in red typeface and a red square indicator box. Review records vary slightly, containing fields for review author, review title, primary work author, primary work title, publication details, publication year, ISSN, subject categories, and reference numbers; book records contain the following fields: authors/editors, title, publication details, publication year, ISBN, subject categories for collection and all component articles, and reference number. In the results lists, reviews are indicated with the words "review of" embedded in the citation.

The **Year's Work in English Studies** (**YWES**) is an annual publication of the English Association. Since 1919, each *YWES* issue has comprised bibliographic essays that survey recent, major contributions to scholarship on the English language and on literatures written in English. While the English Association has compiled *YWES* since its first issue, this annual has changed publishers multiple times and has been published by John Murray, Blackwell Publishers, and Oxford University Press over the years. Currently *YWES* is published by Oxford and has been since 1998. Although *YWES* claims to include literatures in English, the coverage is by far heaviest on literatures of Great Britain, which takes up thirteen of the eighteen bibliographic sections. These broad sections index materials on the English language, specific periods of English literature from Old English to modern literature, American literature from colonial times to the present, new literatures in English, and bibliography and textual criticism. The sections on "The Nineteenth Century: The Victorian Period" and "Modern Literature" will be of greatest interest to Victorian and Edwardian scholars. The Victorian age section is further broken down by "Cultural Studies and Prose," "The Novel," "Poetry," "Drama," and "Periodicals and Publishing

Full Record

MARKED LIST | SEARCH HISTORY | MODIFY SEARCH | NEW SEARCH

<<Previous record | Record 2 of 3 results | Next record>>

Back to results

☑ Add to Marked List

Print View | Durable URL for this page | Download citation

ABELL

Author:	Stimpson, Catharine R.
Title:	Do these deaths surpass understanding? The literary figure of the ■ mother who murders.
Publication Details:	TriQuarterly (124) 2006, 45-62.
Publication Year:	2006
ISSN:	00413097
Subject:	English Literature: Twentieth Century: Authors: Morrison, Toni
	English Literature: Nineteenth Century: Authors: Eliot, George (Mary Ann Evans)
	English Literature: Nineteenth Century: Authors: Evans, Mary Ann (George Eliot)
	English Literature: Nineteenth Century: Authors: Wordsworth, William
	English Literature: Twentieth Century: Authors: Rich, Adrienne
Reference Number:	17643; 10054; 11718; 18239
Additional Search Terms:	Beloved
	Adam Bede
	The Thorn
	Motherhood
	Infanticide
	Criminal Law

Figure 4.2. Modified *ABELL* record for "Do These Deaths Surpass Understanding? The Literary Figure of the Mother Who Murders." Source: *ABELL*, via Chadwyck-Healey.

History." The modern literature section is divided into the following subcategories: "General," "Pre-1945 Fiction," "Post-1945 Fiction," "Pre-1950 Drama," "Post-1950 Drama," "Pre-1950 Poetry," "Post-1950 Poetry," "Irish Poetry," and "Books Reviewed." Both the Victorian and modern literature sections conclude with a composite bibliography of books reviewed.

Each *YWES* volume also has indexes to critics and to authors and subjects treated. Because of the volumes' organization, the author and subject index may be the best way to navigate *YWES* if you are researching a particular writer or topic rather than seeking to survey all current scholarship on a broad topic such as Irish poetry. *YWES* is indexed in *MLAIB* from 1955 to the present, although this indexing is only for the broad chapter level, which may not be terribly useful to scholars seeking a particular citation or researching a particular topic.

Google Scholar, while not a traditional library tool or specific to literary studies, has become a widely used resource for students and scholars alike. Created by Internet giant Google, Google Scholar is intended to search across scholarly materials from all disciplines. This tool allows scholars to look for citations to abstracts, articles, books, court opinions, dissertations, and theses. Although the exact contents of Google Scholar are not publicly listed, this resource gathers its citations by partnering with publishers, libraries, and *WorldCat.org*. Using the familiar, simple Google interface, this resource allows scholars to look within articles (with the option to include patents) or legal opinions and journals. The "Advanced Scholar Search" provides the option to search by author, publication, date, and collections; to find "all of the words," "the exact phrase," "at least one of the words," or "without the words;" and to specify where terms occur. Although you may wish to find resources from any subject area, you can use the collections limiters to look only in "Social Sciences, Arts, and Humanities" articles if you prefer. Because this uses Google's search algorithms, there is no need to use Boolean operators in Google Scholar. A search for *Collins Moonstone opiates* without limiters retrieves 108 citations, some from traditional literature journals and others from history of medicine and psychology journals. The ease of searching across disciplines is one of Google Scholar's advantages. If you conducted that same query, but limited to "Social Sciences, Arts, and Humanities" articles only, then fifty-six citations are retrieved. While Google Scholar might point you to useful citations, the full text is generally not readily available. If your library has partnered with Google Scholar, however, you should see a link to your library's digital and physical holdings. As a rule of thumb, whether using Google Scholar or any other indexing source, always consult multiple resources because none are comprehensive.

The bibliographies and indexes discussed previously in this chapter are primarily finding aids for uncovering citations to relevant resources. Generally speaking, these provide little if no full text in their print formats and very little full text in their online counterparts. Several online resources, such as *JSTOR*, *Periodicals Index Online*, *Periodicals Archive Online*, and *Project Muse*, supplement more traditional bibliographies and indexes; however, while they contain scholarly resources, they lack the indexing depth found in traditional bibliographies such as the *MLAIB* and *ABELL*. With the exception of *Periodicals Index Online*, such databases are designed to serve as full-text repositories rather than finding aids for research materials; however, many scholars use them to locate citations for relevant articles. As such, this chapter must address the contents and utility of these resources as supplementary research tools.

Perhaps the best-known journal repository, ***JSTOR: The Scholarly Journal Archive***, was developed in 1995 to archive high-quality, academic journals, while preserving scholarship, broadening access to scholarship and other materials, and reducing costs for educational institutions. Interdisciplinary in nature, the database currently archives nearly thirteen hundred titles from the humanities, sciences, and social sciences. *JSTOR* partners with university and commercial presses, scholarly and professional societies, university departments, independent journals, botanical gardens, museums, and libraries to gain the rights to distribute their content. Unlike many aggregator databases, which have journal content from a variety of sources, *JSTOR* does not offer contents from current journal issues but rather serves as a repository for journal backfiles. Each journal digitized for the collection is included from its first volume and issue up until three to five years ago, depending on the agreement *JSTOR* has established with the journal's publisher. This three-to-five year gap, known as a moving wall, ensures that libraries and scholars continue to subscribe to the current issues through the publisher. Although *JSTOR* has cover-to-cover access to the journals in its collections, the California Digital Library and the Harvard Depository serve as paper repositories to back up *JSTOR*'s digital contents.

Depending on whether your library has the complete *JSTOR* package, one or more multidisciplinary collections, or select discipline-specific collections, the journals to which you have access through *JSTOR* will vary. The multidisciplinary collections include an Ireland collection, a life sciences collection, and eight general arts and sciences collections in addition to an arts and sciences complement. In total, forty-seven disciplines are covered in *JSTOR*'s multidisciplinary collections, with more than 150 journals in "Language and Literature" specifically. Although the language and literature journals are high-quality journals, only a handful of titles are specific to nineteenth- and early twentieth-century literature, so searching only *JSTOR* would severely limit your ability to conduct a comprehensive, or even thorough, literature review. In addition to language and literature, the discipline-specific collections are for biological sciences, two business collections, ecology and botany, health and general sciences, mathematics and statistics, and music. Contact your librarian to find out which of the *JSTOR* collections you have access to through your local library.

Libraries may also subscribe to a pamphlet collection based on 19th Century British Pamphlets Project. More than twenty thousand pamphlets will comprise the collection when complete. The pamphlets are drawn from the Knowsley Pamphlet Collection at the University of Liverpool, the Cowen Tracts from Newcastle University, the Hume Tracts of University College London, the Earl Grey Pamphlets Collection from Durham University, the Foreign and Commonwealth Office Collection from the University of Manchester, selected pamphlets from the London School of Economics and Political Science, and

selected pamphlets from the University of Bristol. This addition greatly increases the number of primary sources available through *JSTOR*. These pamphlets include advertisements, annotations, cartoons, diagrams and maps, en-
gravings, letters, petitions, and portraits. Although the collection is labeled as
a nineteenth-century collection, pamphlets may date as far back as 1603.

There are two general ways to access *JSTOR*'s contents: searching and
browsing. The browse option allows scholars to locate information resources
through alphabetic listings by discipline, title, and publisher. This method will
be most useful for identifying which journals are available in your research
area. Searching *JSTOR* requires a certain amount of finesse to retrieve the
most relevant articles on your topic. Because it is first and foremost an archival repository, *JSTOR* contains no subject headings to aid in retrieving journal
articles. Rather, each journal's full text can be searched using keywords. Additionally, scholars have the option to look for their terms specifically in the
author, article title, abstract, and caption fields. Limiting by field tends to
produce more narrowly defined and highly relevant results sets; however, you
also run the risk of missing some relevant results. Scholars also have the option to limit the type of results: article, review, editorial, and pamphlets. These
limiters are invaluable for weeding out irrelevant citations. Additionally, *JS-
TOR* allows users to limit to specific disciplines. For instance, a scholar could
search only journals in "Language and Literature," or in multiple areas such
as "Language and Literature," "Religion," and "Feminist and Women's Studies" concurrently. Scholars may also revisit a previous search from their same
session and redisplay results without retyping the query. For finding known
items, *JSTOR* also includes a "Citation Locator" with fields for item title,
author, content title (i.e., journal), ISSN, volume, issue, start page, month/
season, day, and year.

If you already have a citation for an article, such as Audrey Jaffe's "Trollope in the Stock Market: Irrational Exuberance and 'The Prime Minister,'"
which was published in *Victorian Studies* in 2002, it would be easiest to use
the "Citation Locator" and search using the citation information you already
know. This is the most efficient way to find information in *JSTOR* and is most
in line with its purpose as a journal repository. When investigating a topic
without a specific citation in mind, the "Advanced Search" screen produces
more fruitful results. For instance, if you were researching inheritance in
Trollope's novels, then you would want to enter both *inheritance* and *Trollope*
in separate fields in the "Advanced Search." Because *JSTOR* articles are not
indexed, you may find that the simplest way to find variants of the word *inheritance* is by truncating the word as *inherit**, which would match with *inherit, inherits, inherited, inheritance,* and any other word beginning with the
stem *inherit*. You may need to limit to "articles only" if there are too many

editorials and book reviews in the results. If you retrieve too many citations, using the abstract, article title, and caption limiters may help narrow the pool; however, not all articles have abstracts, so you may miss relevant articles by limiting in this way. You may need to search for the same topic in multiple ways, using different limits, in order to determine whether you have located all relevant articles on your topic. Most *JSTOR* articles are in full text; however, citations for current issues of the archived journals are included without full text. As issues move behind the moving wall, *JSTOR* makes the page images available.

Like *JSTOR*, ProQuest's **Periodicals Archive Online (PAO)** is an archival product for the storage and retrieval of journal backfiles. *PAO* is the sister database of **Periodicals Index Online (PIO)**, both products of the Chadwyck-Healey division of ProQuest CSA. Formerly known as *Periodicals Contents Index (PCI)*, *PIO* indexes more than six thousand journals in more than forty languages from their first issue until 1995; run lengths vary from journal to journal, with the oldest publication dating back to 1665. Of those journals, 1,018 support literary studies and an additional 315 are general humanities publications. Even though *PIO* does not index the most recent issues, the depth and breadth of coverage makes it a valuable research tool. Scholars may search journal or article records or browse journals alphabetically, by subject, or by language. Scholars may filter their results by journal, language, date, and journal subjects. For instance, a search for *Dickens Charles* as an author retrieves 710 articles; however, if you wanted to see only results from the 1860s, the filters allow you to do this easily without starting over. Within the 214 articles from the 1860s, you could then refine down to a single year, such as 1867.

Since *PIO* relies solely on the contents of the searchable fields—keyword, article title keyword, author, journal title, language, journal subject, publication year, and ISSN—scholars should choose their terms carefully. Full-text collections, such as *JSTOR* and *PAO*, are slightly more forgiving, since terms may be searched in the document text; however, the limited data provided by the database record does not allow much room for error in selecting terms. Although *PIO* does not have full text for the journals it indexes, it links to full text in *PAO, British Periodicals, JSTOR*, and *Project Muse* for libraries that subscribe to these collections, and to library-owned content through link-resolving technologies.

While *PIO* is only an index, *PAO* provides cover-to-cover full text of select titles from *PIO*. Although *PIO* extends back to the seventeenth century, *PAO* has digital content of nineteenth- and twentieth-century periodical literature. Both generally only include periodicals until 1995. The archival product has a fraction of the journals indexed in *PIO*; however, it has digitized page images from more than five hundred journals from the arts, humanities, and social sciences. *PAO* is available as eight multidisciplinary collections and subject-specific collections on history, literature, the Spanish language, philosophy and religion/theology, literary studies, and historical studies. Between the multidisciplinary collections and the subject collections, *PAO* covers thirty-seven subject areas. Additionally, the historic *British Periodicals Collection I* and *II* are available through the *PAO/PIO* interface. See chapter 7 for more on *British Periodicals*. Check with your local library to determine to which *PAO* collections you have access.

Although *JSTOR* already offers a significant amount of digital periodical content, *PAO* contributes unique content, as the archive aims to grant access to journals not previously digitized. Coverage varies from journal to journal; each is digitized from its first volume and issue up until its terminal issue or through the issues published as late as 2000. Nothing later than 2000 is found in the archive, and the earliest journal dates to 1665. Journals must be in the arts, humanities, or social sciences. English-language titles have the heaviest representation, but select foreign language and multi-language journals are also found in *PAO*. The interface itself may be viewed in English, French, Spanish, Portuguese, German, or Italian.

Scholars may choose from "Quick," "Article," and "Find journal" searches to access the contents of the archive. "Quick" option looks for keywords in the article title and text, article title, article author, journal ISSN, or journal title, while the "Article" offers additional search and limiting options and has dedicated fields for searching in citations and article full text, citations only, or article full text only. Additionally, scholars may query fields for article title keyword(s), author(s), journal title(s), language(s), journal subject(s), years of publication, and ISSN. The "Article" option also allows scholars to limit to all content, articles, book reviews, or other, which includes unindexed front and back matter, to sort results by relevance, alphabetically by journal title, date (earliest first), and date (latest first), and set results to display twenty, fifty, or one hundred results per page. *PAO*'s "Find journals" feature allows scholars to search journal records, find journals by language or by subject, view the journal title list, and browse an alphabetical list of journal titles. This archive also offers search history and marked list features. From the marked lists, scholars can e-mail, print, and download marked citations. Scholars who opt to create a "My Archive" account may save citations for later use.

Like *JSTOR*, *PAO* articles are not individually indexed with subject headings; however, the journals themselves are assigned subject headings, which can help you identify relevant articles. Since keyword searching is the primary mode finding articles in *PAO*, the database includes additional measures for refining search results. Scholars may filter their results by journal, language, date, and journal subjects, allowing for easy exclusion of less relevant results. As with all databases, *PAO* provides detailed help files; however, the "Help" feature of *PAO* displays information specific to the screen being viewed rather than showing the full help contents. For instance, clicking the "Help" button on the article results page displays information relevant to interpreting the results screen, while the "Help" button on the find journal screen helps scholars navigate the features of that screen of the database.

Offering full text like *JSTOR* and *PAO*, Johns Hopkins University Press's **Project Muse** resulted from collaborations between libraries and publishers to provide online access to humanities and social sciences journals. Unlike the previous two archival products, *Project Muse* offers current, rather than historic, contents. *Project Muse* contains more than four hundred indexed and peer-reviewed journals from humanities and social sciences disciplines. This database supplies content to both traditional and emerging areas of study, such as literature, gay and lesbian studies, book history and print culture, history, literary magazines, philosophy, religion, and language and linguistics, among other areas. Although most journals are covered through their most recent issue, *Muse* has select titles for which publication has ceased or the publisher no longer offers new content. These are indicated by the words "archive only." Though *Muse*'s contents are mostly current, select titles link to *JSTOR* for older issues. Not all journals included in *Muse* directly pertain to nineteenth- and twentieth-century British literature; however, journals such as *ELH, English Literature in Transition 1880–1920, The Henry James Review, Journal of Modern Literature, Journal of Victorian Culture*, and *Victorian Studies* are among titles that will be of interest to Victorian and Edwardian scholars (for more on these and other pertinent journals, see chapter 5). The complete intellectual contents, excluding advertisements, are digitized in *Muse*, and each journal article and review is indexed with Library of Congress subject headings. Most journals have print counterparts; however, four are electronic only: *Advertising and Society Review, Postmodern Culture, Theory & Event*, and *Journal of Colonialism and Colonial History*.

Project Muse has several options for accessing the journals that comprise it. Scholars may either search for articles or browse for journals. The latter option not only lets scholars survey journal coverage in their research area, but it also allows them to page through a particular journal issue or volume as they would with the journal's print counterpart. The browse option allows scholars to peruse journals by title or discipline and articles by subject headings. The subject heading list for articles is comparable to subject searching for books in library catalogs. The article search option provides a different means of locating relevant journal articles. Scholars may look for terms within all fields with text, all fields except text, article text, article author, article title, subject headings, journal title, author reviewed, or title reviewed. *Muse* offers some searching flexibility by enabling scholars to add additional lines for entering terms. Scholars may also limit by content type, year, journal, discipline, and article language. Within content type, scholars may limit to "all articles and reviews," "articles only (no reviews)," "poetry," "drama," "fiction," "reviews only," "only content I have full access to," and *JSTOR* back issues. The results may be displayed as follows: relevance; date, latest first; date, earliest first; journal, a-z; and journal, z-a. Additional features include a search history and saved results option, which enable scholars to e-mail, print, or download citations. Currently, *Muse* records can be exported into EndNote or RefWorks. All in all, *Project Muse* has a fairly straightforward, user-friendly interface, but like all online resources, it has detailed help files that should be consulted for tips on more advanced searching techniques.

BRITISH BIBLIOGRAPHIES

Index to British Literary Bibliography. T. H. Howard-Hill. Oxford: Claren-
    don-Oxford University Press, 1969.
Shattock, Joanne, ed. *The Cambridge Bibliography of English Literature.* 3rd
    ed. Vol. 4. New York: Cambridge University Press, 1999.
Watson, George, and Ian Willison, eds. *The New Cambridge Bibliography of
    English Literature.* 5 vols. Cambridge: Cambridge University Press,
    1969–1977.

A multi-volume series published by Oxford University Press, the **Index to British Literary Bibliography** comprises nine volumes, each of which contains checklists and bibliographies for particular topics and periods in British literature. The initial six volumes included the *Bibliography of British Literary Bibliographies, Shakespearian Bibliography and Textual Criticism, British Bibliography to 1890, British Bibliography and Textual Criticism* (two volumes), and the *Index to British Literary Bibliographies, 1890–1969*. Since their publication, three additional volumes have been published: *British Literary Bibliography 1970–1979, British Literary Bibliography 1980–1989*, and *British Literary Bibliography 1990–1999*. As a whole, this set is an essential tool for serious literary scholars. The resource directs scholars to bibliographies published until 1999 on British literature, bibliography and textual criticism, general and period bibliography, regional bibliography, book production and distribution, forms, genres, and subjects. Each book's introduction defines the parameters of that particular volume. Each volume also contains a table of abbreviations. Scholars should consult the indexes in volume 6 and at the end of volumes 3 (to 1890), 7 (1970–1979), 8 (1980–1989), and 9 (1990–1999) to identify bibliographies on specific subjects and locate where a specific author, editor, compiler, or title is mentioned in the series. To date, a cumulative index has not been published.

Another standard literary reference source is *The New Cambridge Bibliography of English Literature* (*NCBEL*). Originally published as *The Cambridge Bibliography of English Literature* (*CBEL*) in 1940 with F. W. Bateson serving as editor, the *NCBEL* was published between 1969 and 1977 under the editing auspices of George Watson and Ian Willison. Both the *CBEL* and the *NCBEL* were published in five volumes, with four volumes of bibliographic content and a fifth volume comprising the index. Designed for use in isolation from the other volumes in the set, each bibliographic volume in *NCBEL* retains the original organization of the *CBEL* according to time period: 600 to 1660, 1660 to 1800, 1800 to 1900, and 1900 to 1950. As a whole, the set focuses on literary authors from or residing in the British Isles. It includes both primary (works by) and secondary (works about) sources, with symbols marking each type of source: §1 and §2, respectively. The bibliography is intended to be complete based on the parameters defined by the editors and, as such, excludes "unpublished dissertations and their published abstracts, ephemeral journalism, encyclopedia articles, reviews of secondary works, brief notes of less than crucial interest to scholarship, and sections in general works such as literary histories." A bibliographic citation is provided for each work.

Volume 3 (1800–1900) and volume 4 (1900–1950) should be of particular interest to individuals researching the Victorian and Edwardian ages. Volume 3 was the first volume published in the *NCBEL* and aims "to represent the whole of English studies, so far as these concern the literature of the British Isles, both in primary and in secondary materials." This volume is organized into the following sections: "Introduction," "Poetry," "The Novel," "Drama," "Prose," and "Anglo-Irish Literature." Each broad section is then subdivided into appropriate categories; for instance, "The Novel" is broken down into "General Works," "The Early Nineteenth-Century Novel," "Minor Fiction 1800–1835," "The Mid-Nineteenth-Century Novel," "Minor Fiction 1835–1870," "The Late Nineteenth-Century Novel," "Minor Fiction 1870–1900," and "Children's Books." Because it covers a shorter and more recent period of time, volume 4 has a simpler organizational structure and includes the following sections: "Introduction" (general works, book production and distribution), "Poetry" (general works, individual poets), "The Novel" (general works, individual novelists, children's books), "Drama" (general works, individual dramatists), "Prose" (critics and literary scholars, essayists, and humorists; historians, autobiographers, writers on politics, society, economics, etc.; philosophers, theologians, writers on natural science and on psychology; writers on travel, the countryside, and sport), and "Newspapers and Magazines." This volume aims to represent the state of literary studies in the first fifty years of the twentieth century as it was in 1969.

Although some of the citations are dated, the *NCBEL* remains an invaluable reference source for identifying primary sources, as well as secondary sources about authors, time periods, and genres in English literature. Each volume has an index to the primary authors with numbers referring to column number rather than page number. Individual author entries are treated with varying levels of detail, depending on each author's canonical status at the time. The final volume comprises an index to the set, listing all primary authors and anonymous works mentioned in the previous four volumes. The index's scope is broader than the indexes of the individual volumes, and lists periodicals along with their editors and proprietors, names of certain minor authors, and foreign writers in addition to authors and headings. The final volume also contains a cumulative list of contributors to volumes 1 through 4 and a guide to abbreviations used throughout the set.

While the *NCBEL* is still a highly useful source, there is no question that it needs significant updates and revisions to represent the current state of English literary scholarship. The bibliography's third edition is currently in the works with Cambridge University Press; however, to date, the only volume published is volume 4, which covers 1800 to 1900 in the new edition. Joanne Shattock is responsible for editing *The Cambridge Bibliography of English Literature* (*CBEL*), which updates the *NCBEL* and assumes the title of the original 1941 bibliography. The *CBEL* revises and augments the previous edition and introduces hundreds of authors previously omitted. The preface to the extant volume claims that the third edition will be 50 percent longer than the second edition and contains more poets, novelists, children's book authors, dramatists, and women writers. It also has a new section on political economy and an expanded philosophy section that incorporates writers on science. *CBEL* also has an abbreviation guide and a primary author index. Like the older editions, this one addresses traditional print resources, but for the first time, it also includes electronic bibliographic resources.

CBEL is an "author-based bibliography" of individuals who were natives of or resided in the British Isles and whose main corpus of work was written prior to 1900. Unlike previous editions that separated out non-English authors by nationality, this edition integrates Scottish, Irish, and Welsh authors with English authors. The bibliography is chronologically arranged, with authors assigned to sections based on their birth date. Resources within author sections are divided into primary and secondary works. Sections not devoted to specific authors, such as book production and distribution, are organized by publication date. The third edition retains some of the second edition's organizational features, but is generally expanded in its scope and coverage. Sections of the extant volume address "Book Production and Distribution," "Literary Relations with the Continent," "Poetry," "The Novel," "Drama," "Prose," "History," "Political Economy," "Philosophy and Science," "Religion," "English Studies," "Travel," "Household Books," "Sport," "Education," and "Newspapers and Magazines." These are only the top-level headings, but the bibliography has a detailed table of contents that breaks down the broader segments.

PERIOD BIBLIOGRAPHIES FOR SECONDARY RESOURCES

Chaudhuri, Brahma, ed. *Annual Bibliography of Victorian Studies*. Victoria, BC: LITIR Database, 1976.

Chaudhuri, Brahma, ed. *Victorian Database Online*. Victoria, BC: LITIR. www.victoriandatabase.com.

Chaudhuri, Brahma, ed. *Victorian Fiction: An Online Guide to Research*. Victoria, BC: LITIR. www.victorianfiction.com.

Freeman, Ronald E., ed. *Bibliographies of Studies in Victorian Literature for the Ten Years 1965–1974*. New York: AMS Press, 1981.

Lauterbach, Edward S., and W. Eugene Davis. *The Transitional Age: British Literature 1880–1920*. Troy, NY: Whitston Publishing, 1973.

Mellowin, Elgin W. *A Descriptive Catalogue of the Bibliographies of Twentieth Century British Poets, Novelists, and Dramatists*. 2nd ed. Troy, NY: Whitston Publishing, 1978.

Miller, Andrew H., and Ivan Kreilkamp, eds. *Victorian Studies Bibliography*, at www.letrs.indiana.edu/web/v/victbib (accessed on 9 April 2010).

Slack, Robert C., ed. *Bibliographies of Studies in Victorian Literature for the Ten Years 1955–1964*. Urbana: University of Illinois Press, 1967.

Templeman, William D., ed. *Bibliographies of Studies in Victorian Literature for the Thirteen Years 1932–1944*. Urbana: University of Illinois Press, 1945.

Tobias, Richard C., ed. *Bibliographies of Studies in Victorian Literature for the Ten Years 1975–1984*. New York, AMS Press, 1991.

Wright, Austin, ed. *Bibliographies of Studies in Victorian Literature for the Ten Years 1945–1954*. Urbana: University of Illinois Press, 1956.

Although general literature bibliographies are a good starting place for your secondary-source research, as your research becomes more in-depth and specialized, so will the resources you consult. This section covers period-specific bibliographies for secondary sources; the following section discusses period-specific bibliographies for primary sources. You will often find that focused bibliographies, such as those discussed in the following paragraphs, provide greater efficiency for accessing a more comprehensive resource list. Regardless of the claims of comprehensiveness made by a particular bibliography, consult multiple sources in your research. The resources discussed in this section do not comprise an exhaustive list of bibliographies on either the Victorian or Edwardian ages, but offer a sampling of resources for both periods in British literature. The *Annual Bibliography of Victorian Studies*, *Victorian Database Online*, *Victorian Fiction: An Online Research Guide*, and *Victorian Studies Bibliography* address sources for the Victorian age, while *The Transitional Age: British Literature 1880–1920* and *A Descriptive Catalogue of the Bibliographies of Twentieth Century British Poets, Novelists, and Dramatists* highlight Edwardian resources.

Published every ten years, the ***Bibliographies of Studies in Victorian Literature*** provides citations for both scholarly and popular publications on Great Britain during Victoria's reign (1837–1901). Since its origins in 1932, the bibliography has been a collaborative project between *Victorian Studies* staff and a committee of the Victorian Division of the Modern Language Association of America (see chapter 5 for more information on *Victorian Studies*). The print bibliography is organized by year, and within each year, entries are arranged according to six broad sections:

- Bibliographical materials,
- History, historiography, and historical documents,
- Economics, education, politics, religion, science, and social environment,
- Architecture, fine arts, household arts, performing arts, and city planning,
- Literary history, literary forms, and literary ideas, and
- Individual authors.

The entries include bibliographic citations and occasional notes of pertinent reviews. The bibliography concludes with an index to modern scholars, Victorian authors, figures, and non-Victorians; Victorian periodical and newspaper titles; collection names; libraries, theaters, universities, and Victorian societies and institutions; place names; and general and specific subject headings. Contents from the 1991 to 2007 *Bibliographies of Studies in Victorian Literature* are available online through the ***Victorian Studies Bibliography***. Currently, the bibliography is overseen by editors Andrew H. Miller and Ivan Kreilkamp, and serves as a guide to articles from four hundred journals, books, and reviews on the Victorian age. The online version may be browsed or searched. Scholars may browse all records or one of the six sections alphabetically by author. Unfortunately, there is no way to jump to a specific entry in the browse list or jump to a certain letter of the alphabet, both features which would greatly enhance the bibliography's usability. The simple and advanced search screens let scholars specify whether their terms appear in the entire record, the author field, or the title field. The advanced search additionally allows for date limiting. Search results are listed alphabetically by author, with each record containing citations for the work and any relevant scholarly reviews.

Available in various print accumulations, on CD-ROM, and as an online database, *Annual Bibliography of Victorian Studies* has been compiled and edited by Brahma Chaudhuri since 1976. The bibliography comprises citations to publications about the Victorian age through the beginning of World War I (1837 though 1914). Like many sources that are labeled Victorian, this one also covers the Edwardian age. The *Annual Bibliography of Victorian Studies* primarily lists publications about Great Britain but also selectively includes publications about the British colonies, as long as they relate to political or administrative affairs or discuss the cultural relationship between the colonies and Britain. The bibliography has citations for works from general and reference works, fine arts, philosophy and religion, history (both British and colonial), the social sciences, science and technology, and language and literature. The language and literature section, which is subdivided by individual authors, receives the greatest emphasis by far. Rather than cross-referencing, interdisciplinary works are listed in all applicable sections. Each entry is assigned a number and contains bibliographic information for the work. The *Annual Bibliography of Victorian Studies* also has subject, author, and title indexes. While the author and title indexes are best for known-item searching, the subject index will be helpful for locating works on a specific topic, and refers to persons as subjects, places, and topics. More recent volumes of the bibliography also include a reviewer index.

Victorian Database Online (*VDO*) is the online version of the *Annual Bibliography of Victorian Studies* and is available by personal or institutional subscription only. With over 110,000 entries for books, articles, and dissertation abstracts published between 1945 and 2009, this interdisciplinary database focuses broadly on nineteenth-century British studies, including resources from art, architecture, education, music, history, law, literature, medicine, philosophy and religion, science, sociology, technology, and women's studies. *VDO* has information on more than five hundred journals and citations for around sixty-five thousand books, periodical articles, and dissertation abstracts published from 1970 to 1997, and citations for book reviews published from 1995 to the present. Additionally, *VDO* cites recently published editions of Victorian works that contain new critical and textual notes. The database is divided into two sets—scholarship from 1945 to 1980, and from 1981 to the present—from which users must choose prior to searching the database's contents. To be listed in *VDO*, publications have to be about Victorian Britain, a term defined broadly as Great Britain between roughly 1830 and 1914.

The *VDO* "Help" file lists journal abbreviations, journals indexed, and tips for searching the database, interpreting results, and selecting and saving results. This resource's simple interface supports queries of author, title, or keyword fields. Scholars may specify publication dates and, while required to choose the desired subset to search, a scholar can also adjust the dates to include materials from the other subset. This date limit feature does not appear to be particularly accurate even when set. For example, a search for citations between 1975 and 1985 retrieves results from that time frame, but mostly retrieves entries for resources published after 1985. The results are sorted alphabetically by author's last name, and no other sort options are provided. The entries themselves are strictly citations accompanied by subject headings with no additional annotations or descriptive information. Subject headings are hyperlinked, enabling scholars to browse quickly to additional citations on a topic, and author names link all scholarship by that person. Clicking on a subject heading erases any date limiters previously set and looks within the subset initially selected (i.e., either 1945 to 1980 only, or 1981 to the present only). Although not a complete, or particularly advanced, resource, *VDO* certainly has its place in supporting Victorian scholarship. Additionally, *VDO* could be useful for tracking recent editions of a work or surveying scholarship on a particular topic in Victorian studies.

From the creators of *VDO*, **Victorian Fiction: An Online Guide to Research (VFO)** claims to index every publication on Victorian fiction from 1830 to the present. In spite of that claim, *VFO* is not comprehensive but focuses on scholarship about fifty-one specific major, minor, and under-read authors of the Victorian age. The fifty-one novelists were selected based on their inclusion in Shattock's *CBEL*, discussed previously in this chapter. The remaining 129 of 180 novelists listed in *CBEL* will eventually be added to *VFO*, making it a more robust resource for Victorian literary studies. Although *VFO* is a subscription resource, some of its information is freely available to the public through the link to "Primary Authors: Chronologies, Editions, Manuscripts, etc." (www.victorianfiction.com/primary.cfm). This section contains a chronology of the Victorian period from 1819 to 1914, a brief list of essential readings and essential websites, and a list of the fifty-one authors. For each author, a chronology of life events and publications, essential readings, and recommended editions, biographies, letters, manuscripts, and websites are given. Specific works in the author chronologies are linked to the electronic text on *Project Gutenberg* as available (*Project Gutenberg* is discussed in greater detail in chapter 10). Authors such as Mary Elizabeth Braddon, Ford Madox Ford, and George Gissing are included alongside Robert Michael Ballantyne, Mona Caird, and Amy Levy. The subscription portion of the database provides a search interface to the bibliography, which has information on manuscript holdings and citations for editions of primary works, contemporary reviews, and critical works from 1830 to the present. Currently, the database contains more than thirty-five thousand citations for books, book chapters, journal articles, and dissertation abstracts.

Victorian Fiction has the same search interface as *VDO*, and like the entries of its companion database, *VFO* entries contain citations and subject headings. Most entries do not offer full annotations but some have brief, one-sentence descriptions. The citations indicate whether an article is peer-reviewed with the designation *[refereed]* embedded in the citation text. Unfortunately there is no way to browse or search the subject headings, which minimizes their usefulness. That said, this is an excellent resource for tracking editions of specific works and surveying the scholarship on a particular author or work.

Focusing on the turn of the century in British literature, Edward S. Lauterbach and W. Eugene Davis's *The Transitional Age: British Literature 1880–1920* guides scholars through the literary developments and authors that characterized this crucial time period. This single-volume work is divided into two parts. The first part comprises four essays on important trends in the principal genres of transitional literature, including fiction (the novel, the short story, and entertainment), poetry, drama, and prose. These essays should help scholars gain a general understanding of the issues and concerns of this literary period. The second part provides selective bibliographies on 170 British authors from 1880 to 1920 and definitions of select literary terms. The author bibliographies contain a brief synopsis of the author's life and writings in relation to the period and selective bibliographies of primary and secondary sources. *The Transitional Age* covers both major and minor authors, who were all selected based on their dates of publication and the presence of transitional literature characteristics in their works. The bibliographies are arranged alphabetically by author's last name and include authors such as Algernon Blackwood, Mary Duclaux, Thomas Hardy, Hector Hugh Monro (Saki), and Mrs. Humphrey Ward. An index of names and terms enhances access to the volume's contents.

Revised from the 1972 edition, *A Descriptive Catalogue of the Bibliographies of Twentieth Century British Poets, Novelists, and Dramatists* was written as a research aid for students of twentieth-century British literature. In compiling this bibliography of bibliographies, Elgin W. Mellown selected British poets, novelists, and dramatists who were born after 1840 and published most of their work in England after 1890. Mellown uses the term *British* broadly to include English, Scottish, Welsh, Irish, and Commonwealth writers. The bibliography cites both primary and secondary sources and a range of British and American publications. Entries are arranged alphabetically by author's last name and then organized chronologically within three categories: bibliographies of primary, secondary, and general works. This resource also contains references to general twentieth-century British literature bibliographies. Because of its scope, not all authors included are relevant to the Edwardian age; however, Edwardian authors are discussed along with mid- and late twentieth-century authors. The bibliography concludes with a name index that excludes the principal entries and general bibliography authors' names.

PERIOD BIBLIOGRAPHIES FOR PRIMARY RESOURCES

19th Century Masterfile. Austin, TX: Paratext. www.paratext.com.

C19: The Nineteenth Century Index. Ann Arbor, MI: ProQuest, 2005. www.proquest.com.

Low, Sampson. *The English Catalogue of Books.* London: Sampson Low, Marston, Searle, and Rivington, 1864.

Nineteenth-Century Short Title Catalogue Extracted from the Catalogues of the Bodleian Library, the British Library, the Library of Trinity College (Dublin), the National Library of Scotland, and the University Libraries of Cambridge and Newcastle. Newcastle-upon-Tyne: Avero, 1984.

Sadlier, Michael. *XIX Century Fiction: A Bibliographical Record Based on His Own Collection.* 2 vols. New York: Cooper Square Publishers, 1969.

Wolff, Robert Lee, comp. *Nineteenth-Century Fiction: A Bibliographical Catalogue Based on the Collection Formed by Robert Lee Wolff.* 5 vols. New York: Garland Publishing, 1981.

Described as an "index of indexes," the ***19th Century Masterfile*** provides access to around sixty major and minor subject indexes prior to 1930. The indexes include a variety of resource types, including periodicals, newspapers, books, government documents, and patents. First developed in 1999, *19th Century Masterfile* began as *Poole's Plus*, an online, searchable version of *Poole's Index to Periodical Literature, 1802–1906*. Rather than simply digitize *Poole's*, Paratext enhanced the contents by adding dates, which were notably absent from the original print edition, and by normalizing the title information to make index searching more consistent and reliable. Since its origins as *Poole's Plus*, *19th Century Masterfile* has grown to incorporate additional multi-title periodical indexes as well as four other series that include book indexes, newspaper indexes, individual periodical indexes, and

U.S. and U.K. government documents. Although many of the individual title indexes are for U.S. publications, *19th Century Masterfile* indexes a significant number of British publications, particularly in the multi-title periodical indexes of Series I. Many of the indexes also include the early twentieth century and some extend coverage as far back as the eleventh century even though the database's title indicates its nineteenth-century emphasis, making this a useful resource for Victorian and Edwardian scholars alike. Because libraries can subscribe to all five series or to the first series (multi-title periodical indexes) plus any combination of the other series, you should check with your librarian to determine to which indexes you have access.

The first series, which is the collection's core, comprises ten indexes including *Poole's Index to Periodical Literature*, *Periodical Articles on Religion* (Richardson), *Index to Periodicals* (Stead), *The Psychological Index*, and *Index to Legal Periodicals* (Jones and Chipman), among other titles that together index nearly eight thousand periodicals. These resources cover the contents of multiple periodicals that span a wide variety of disciplines, making *19th Century Masterfile* essential for researching all facets of nineteenth-century life. The index's interdisciplinary design promotes serendipity in research. A scholar researching London sanitation might not purposefully search historic scientific papers and government documents, but may come across crucial primary sources by searching across indexes in *19th Century Masterfile*. Currently, the other four series supplement the periodical indexes to give fuller access to nineteenth-century printed materials. Series II—"Book Indexes"—comprises the *ALA Index to General Literature*, the *ALA Portrait Index*, *Monographs for Pre-20th Century Studies*, and *Wright American Fiction II*. Of the four newspaper indexes in Series III, only one—*Palmer's Index to "The Times" Newspaper, 1880–1890*—is for a British newspaper. Likewise, Series IV, which comprises "Individual Periodical Indexes," and Series V, which is for "U.S. and U.K. Government Documents," are largely composed of American indexes, with the exception of a few select titles. The U.S. publications indexed in *19th Century Masterfile* still have valuable information on the Victorian and Edwardian ages, particularly for understanding the reception of British works and events in the United States.

Although *19th Century Masterfile*'s purpose is to help scholars uncover citations rather than provide full text, Paratext works with link-resolving technologies to connect index entries to both library and open-access content. This index also links from citations to select open-access and subscription full-text resources, such as *JSTOR*, *Accessible Archives*, *America State Papers*, *USPTO Historical Patent File*, legal periodicals at *Hein Online*, *Congressional Record*, *American Periodical Series*, the *Making of America*, and

Wright American Fiction. Recently, Paratext added Google Books search links to the *19th Century Masterfile* search results, allowing scholars to connect easily with digitized content in Google Books. Although not all citations are currently connected with their full-text versions, Paratext intends to continue linking to full text as it becomes available. The current indexes comprising *19th Century Masterfile* have more than eleven million citations. The number of indexes and, in turn, the number of citations will grow as Paratext continues to add new resources to the existing collection. The interface allows scholars to search across the entire collection and then view any or all of the results sets, which are categorized by series and by index within series. From the results screen, scholars may sort results based on publication year, author, title, language, and classification, and may download, e-mail, or save results for further use. Scholars may also browse contents by keyword, periodical title, and author. *19th Century Masterfile* is discussed in more detail in chapter 6 for finding reviews and in chapter 7 as a tool for locating articles within period newspapers and journals.

ProQuest's ***C19: The Nineteenth Century Index*** is a recent addition to the nineteenth-century index market and claims to be the "most comprehensive and dynamic source for discovering nineteenth-century books, periodicals, official documents, newspapers and archives." Scholars will find, however, that there is little overlap between *C19* and *19th Century Masterfile*, so both should be consulted for any research on the Victorian or Edwardian ages. *C19* serves as a portal for searching across 1.5 million books and official publications, 71,000 archival collections, and 18.9 million articles from more than 2,500 journals, magazines, and newspapers. It amalgamates records from twelve bibliographic sources: *American Periodical Series*, *Archive Finder*, *British Periodicals*, *Dictionary of Nineteenth-Century Journalism*, *House of Commons Parliamentary Papers*, *The Nineteenth Century*, *Nineteenth-Century Short Title Catalogue*, *Palmer's Index to The Times*, *Periodicals Index Online/Periodicals Archive Online*, *Poole's Index to Periodical Literature*, *The Wellesley Index to Victorian Periodicals* with *The Curran Index*, and the *U.S. Congressional Serial Set*. With citations to government documents, newspapers, periodicals, and books, coverage is strong for both American and British nineteenth-century studies. Most of the sources included, with the exception of the *American Periodical Series* and the *U.S. Congressional Serial Set*, pertain to Great Britain in part if not in whole.

The interface lets scholars search across all twelve sources, in individual sources, or in specific categories of sources (archives, books, newspapers, official publications, periodicals, and reference works). Depending on which collection or collections you select, the options will vary. For instance, a search of all indexes includes fields for keyword, title keyword, author, publication date, periodical title, and periodical subject. If, however, a scholar opted to use only the *House of Commons Parliamentary Papers*, keyword, paper title, subject, chair/author, session, paper number, and year are given as fields. Additionally, the search can be limited to House of Commons papers, Command papers, bills, reports of committees, reports of commissioners, or accounts and papers. For each selected collection, scholars have the option to choose terms for certain search fields from a browseable list. More information on the *Nineteenth Century Short-Title Catalogue* is provided below, and the majority of the other collections are discussed in additional chapters of this book: *Periodicals Index Online* (see chapter 2); the *Wellesley Index* (see chapter 6); *Poole's*, *Palmer's*, the *Dictionary of Nineteenth-Century Journalism*, and *Journalism British Periodicals* (see chapter 7); *The Nineteenth Century* (see chapter 8); and *Archive Finder* (see chapter 9). *C19* is primarily an index, and excepting the *Dictionary of Nineteenth-Century Journalism*, very little full text is available here. ProQuest, however, allows linking from *C19* citations to archival products that have the document's text.

Published in three series—series 1 covering 1801 to 1815, series 2 covering 1816 to 1870, and series 3 covering 1871 to 1919—the ***Nineteenth Century Short-Title Catalogue*** (*NSTC*) was created to provide a complete catalog of British books printed between 1801 and 1918. The *NSTC* editors defined British broadly, including works published in Great Britain, the United States, and any British colonies, as well as all books printed in or translated from English. The catalog holdings of the Bodleian Library at Oxford, the Cambridge University Library, the Trinity College Library, the National Library of Scotland, the British Library, and the Newcastle University Library were combined in the creation of the *NSTC*. To enhance the catalog's usefulness, its creators chose to have a unified, single entry for each work as well as holding information for the six contributing libraries, with cross-referencing to alternate headings. Each entry contains a reference number, an author statement along with epithet and life span, a shortened form of the title, up to three Dewey Decimal classification numbers, and an edition statement regarding location of imprint, bibliographical notes, numbers of parts or volumes, information on editors and translators, and location symbols. Most *NSTC* volumes contain alphabetically arranged catalog entries. The entries are arranged by author and then by title within author. Every series has a detailed outline of the Dewey Decimal Classification Tables, which serve as the basis for the subject indexes found throughout the series. Each of the five catalog volumes of the first series has an index to its contents with a cumulative index available in volume 5. A title volume index makes up the series' sixth volume.

The second series, which is for 1816 through 1870 publications, comprises fifty-six volumes and has a more complicated organizational structure. The first forty-three volumes contain the alphabetical entry list, with indexes in every five volumes for the contents of the previous five volumes. Volumes 44 through 53 have the alphabetical title index to the second series, while volume 54 indexes volumes 36 through 38 and 40 through 43. The indexes allow scholars to see which books fall into specific Dewey Decimal Classification ranges. For instance, a scholar of nineteenth-century literary organizations could look up 806, the appropriate classification number, to identify topic-specific books. Select volumes also catalog publications issued by governmental bodies in Boston, New York, Philadelphia, Washington, DC, the United States, England, Ireland, Scotland, Wales, and London. Directories, ephemerides, hymnals, periodical publications, and liturgies are listed separately from the other publications. Series 3 of the *NSTC* was released on CD-ROM only and does not have a print counterpart. This final series, which covers 1871 to 1919, is the most useful to late Victorian and Edwardian scholars. In addition to individual entries for publications, the third series has indexes for imprints, titles, and subjects. While the CD-ROM format certainly allows for greater flexibility in searching, it still does not provide the ease of use offered by today's online resources.

The online *NSTC* is currently published by the Chadwyck-Healey division of ProQuest and is available either as a stand-alone product or as a component of *C19*. The online *NSTC* allows scholars to search across nearly thirteen million records from all three series simultaneously. In addition to the original three series, the online version incorporates a fourth series that comprises records for more than twenty-five thousand works published between 1801 and 1919 and added to the British Library's holdings after 1976. The *NSTC* editors plan to continue adding pertinent records to nineteenth-century publications from other research collections. When searched separately from *C19*, the *NSTC* may be searched by keyword, author, "living in the years," title, publication date, place of publication, publisher, NSTC subject, language, source library, NSTC number, and NSTC series. Searches for publisher and language are limited to series 3 and 4. Additionally, browseable lists are available for keywords, authors, titles, publication place, publisher, NSTC subject, language, and source library. Users may also choose how to sort results—"chronologically by earliest date," "chronologically by most recent date," "alphabetically by title," "alphabetically by author," and "relevance"—and how many results to display at once. Through either the stand-alone product or as a *C19* component, search results from the *NSTC* may be saved to a marked list, from which scholars can choose to e-mail, print, download, or save selected records. With enhanced search and browse functionalities, the online *NSTC* is much easier to use and allows for greater accuracy and efficiency in searching.

The English Catalogue of Books was printed annually, representing British publishing output from 1835 onward. In 1864, Sampson Low compiled the first cumulative volume of the *English Catalogue*, which covered 1835 through 1862. The catalog continued until 1968 with the 132nd yearly issue. In 1914, a cumulative volume for 1801–1836 materials was belatedly released. Each volume lists books printed in Great Britain during a specified year or number of years. This catalog comprises the contents of the older *London Catalogue* and *British Catalogue*, as well as major works from the United States and continental Europe. Entries are listed alphabetically by author and by title within author. In addition to basic author and title information, each catalog entry lists date, size, price, edition, and publisher. The *English Catalogue*'s earliest edition contains appendixes for works of learned societies, printing clubs, and other literary associations, for series, for periodicals, and for books in English first produced in continental Europe. Beginning with the second volume (1837–1857), an index to the catalog was issued separately from the catalog proper that listed each work by title. In the 1880s, the catalog and index were combined into one volume. The catalog also has a publisher directory that lists their contact information. The *English Catalogue* should be useful for scholars who are tracking publishing histories of particular works or for identifying contemporaneous works.

Based on the private collection of Michael Sadleir, **XIX Century Fiction: A Bibliographical Record Based on His Own Collection** is a descriptive bibliography of nearly three thousand works of nineteenth-century fiction primarily from Great Britain. Sadleir (1888–1957) was a British book collector and novelist, who began collecting first editions as an undergraduate at Oxford.[2] He eventually cataloged his collection into *XIX Century Fiction*, which categorized his books into three sections: a bibliography of authors and their first editions, the "Yellow-Back" collection, and major fiction series.[3] The first section comprises the largest portion of this two-volume set and takes up the entire first volume, leaving the remaining two sections to the second volume. Each descriptive entry, regardless of section, has information about the literary work's title and subtitle, size, author identity, publisher imprint, color of cloth used, details of cover blocking, end-paper color, publication dates, notations on blemishes of Sadleir's copies, and half-titles and pagination. While this bibliography can be used for identifying nineteenth-century fiction in general, scholars should note that the descriptions are specific to the individual volumes held in Sadleir's personal library. Presently, Sadleir's collections are dispersed among several university libraries in the United States, with his Gothic romances from 1780 to 1820 housed at the University of Virginia, his Anthony Trollope collection at Princeton University, and more than ten thousand volumes of nineteenth-century fiction at the

University of California at Los Angeles.[4] Additional features of *XIX Century Fiction* include a list of "comparative scarcities," images of select books from Sadleir's collection, a title index, and an author index.

While Sadleir's bibliography is an incomplete accounting of nineteenth-century fiction, its successor—***Nineteenth-Century Fiction: A Bibliographical Catalogue Based on the Collection Formed by Robert Lee Wolff***—offers a more complete account of nineteenth-century British fiction. Wolff, a former Harvard history professor who specialized "in Balkan affairs and East-West relations in Europe," also studied and published on Victorian literature.[5] Prior to his death in 1980, he amassed a personal library of more than eighteen thousand works of Victorian fiction.[6] Published posthumously in 1981, Wolff's five-volume bibliography follows in the tradition of and complements Sadleir's bibliography, but covers nearly eight thousand works compared to Sadleir's three thousand. The bibliography is based on Wolff's personal collection of British fiction published between 1820 and 1910. Unlike Sadleir, Wolff incorporated manuscripts into his collection whenever possible. The first four volumes comprise an alphabetical catalog of nineteenth-century authors along with their texts. In developing his collection, Wolff favored minor authors, such as Mary Cholmondeley, Matilda Barbara Betham Edwards, Percy Fitzgerald, and William Edward Norris, over canonical authors such as the Brontës, Dickens, and Trollope. The entries may provide the following information: the work's title and subtitle; publication information; the book's physical description; half-title; pagination; volumes; condition of Wolff's copy; inscriptions, dedications, and signatures; and contents. A fifth and final volume concludes the set and catalogs anonymous works, pseudonymous works, and multiple-author fiction, annuals, and periodicals. This volume concludes with an index to the entire bibliography and to illustrators. Scholars interested in researching a specific edition from Wolff's collection must visit the Harry Ransom Center at the University of Texas at Austin, where The Robert Lee Wolff Collection of 19th-Century Fiction currently resides.

ERA AUTHOR AND GENRE BIBLIOGRAPHIES

Baker, William. *George Eliot: A Bibliographical History*. New Castle, DE: Oak Knoll Press, 2002.

Beene, LynnDianne. *Guide to British Prose Fiction Explication: Nineteenth and Twentieth Century*. New York: G. K. Hall, 1997.

Mazzeno, Laurence W. *Victorian Poetry: An Annotated Bibliography*. Metuchen, NJ: Scarecrow Press, 1995.

Small, Ian. *Oscar Wilde: Recent Research: A Supplement to "Oscar Wilde Revalued."* Greensboro, NC: ELT Press, 2000.

In addition to general literature, national, and period bibliographies, author- and genre-specific bibliographies are useful tools for identifying scholarship. While the previously discussed resources should cover almost any topic pertaining to British literature, sometimes it is necessary to consult a more narrowly defined source, which may have greater depth on a particular topic. This section offers examples of author- and genre-specific bibliographies but is not intended to provide a comprehensive list. *George Eliot: A Bibliographical History* and *Oscar Wilde: Recent Research* are included as author-specific resources and *Victorian Poetry* and *Guide to British Prose Fiction Explication: Nineteenth and Twentieth Century* as genre-specific resources. To locate additional sources for a particular research topic, search your local library catalog for subject headings on a specific author, topic, or genre that contain the word *bibliography*. For instance, to locate additional bibliographies on George Eliot, use the heading *Eliot, George, 1819–1880—Bibliography*. To find bibliographies about Victorian poetry, search under *English Poetry—19th century—Bibliography*.

The two sample author bibliographies differ widely in their organization, structure, and purpose. ***George Eliot: A Bibliographical History*** by William Baker and John C. Ross is a more traditional bibliography, with annotated citations to George Eliot's literary works. As a guide to primary sources, this resource identifies and describes early British and American editions of Eliot's works, beginning with her first publication until her death on December 22, 1880. This single-volume work is organized in the following categories: major works, minor literary works, essays and reviews, miscellaneous, and collections and collected works. Each entry has a textual introduction and description, followed by a list of known editions along with bibliographic citation, collation, typography and paper, bindings, publication, printing, issue, state, designations, title page facsimile, format and sheet, signature, contents, typography, locations, notes, and reviews for each edition. Not all fields are populated for each work or edition. Additionally, *George Eliot* has appendixes on "Eliotiana," including sequels, settings for songs from *The Spanish Gypsy*, and collections of illustration, and on non-literary writings subsequently published. Two indexes conclude this work: one on works by George Eliot and a general index.

Where *George Eliot* emphasizes primary works, ***Oscar Wilde: Recent Research: A Supplement to "Oscar Wilde Revalued"*** is a narrative bibliography to recent secondary works about Wilde and his writings. Rather than listing citations, Ian Small explains and draws connections between resources in an essay format. The work is divided into eight chapters: "Wilde in the 1890s,"

"Biography," "New Paradigms in Literary and Cultural History," "Wilde the Writer," "Critical and Introductory Studies," "Editions," "Research Resources," and "Bibliography." The bibliography chapter lists citations for each work discussed in the previous chapters, allowing scholars either to browse the bibliography or to read through the narrative to understand a particular source's contents. The volume concludes with an index to critics.

The *Guide to British Prose Fiction Explication: Nineteenth and Twentieth Century* is part of G. K. Hall's series *A Reference Publication in Literature*. Edited by LynnDianne Beene, this is a bibliography of nineteenth- and twentieth-century British prose fiction explications. Although most included authors are from Great Britain, some authors, such as Katherine Mansfield, were selected based on their identification with the British Isles. Unlike many of the reference sources discussed in this section, the *Guide to British Prose Explication* does not offer contextual or biographical information but strictly limits its contents to bibliographical citations. This volume begins with the early nineteenth century and extends coverage through the late twentieth, with alphabetical arrangement by author and then by title within author. For instance, *The Fifth Queen*, *The Good Soldier*, *The Last Post*, *No More Parades*, *Parade's End*, *War and the Mind*, *When the Wicked Man*, and *Zeppelin Nights* are listed under the heading for Ford Madox Ford. Under each title, citations to criticism are provided. Rather than recording all literary criticism on specific works, Beene selected articles based on their detailed analysis of an aspect of the text in order to elucidate the text's meaning. This volume includes a detailed abbreviations guide and a bibliography of main sources consulted.

Another genre-specific bibliography—*Victorian Poetry: An Annotated Bibliography*—serves as a guide to secondary sources about Victorian poetry and poets. Written by Laurence W. Mazzeno, *Victorian Poetry* offers annotated bibliographies on general studies of Victorian poetry and the poetry of Matthew Arnold, Elizabeth Barrett Browning, Robert Browning, Arthur Hugh Clough, Gerard Manley Hopkins, George Meredith, William Morris, Coventry Patmore, Christina Rossetti, Dante Gabriel Rossetti, Algernon Charles Swinburne, Lord Alfred Tennyson, James Thomson, and Oscar Wilde. For each author, the bibliography lists general studies and studies of particular poems. The volume concludes with an author index and a subject index.

CONCLUSION

Bibliographies and indexes are essential research tools that point to other secondary sources such as scholarly books and journal articles, and primary sources such as creative works, period newspaper and journal articles, and period reviews. Regardless of your topic, you should become familiar with the resources discussed in this chapter and make regular use of them throughout your research process. The upcoming chapters will discuss in greater detail the types of resources these bibliographies point to. Remember that this chapter does not provide an exhaustive resource list, so be sure to consult your local library catalog or the union and national catalogs discussed in chapter 3 to identify additional bibliographies and indexes.

NOTES

1. Descriptor is another term for subject heading.

2. *Oxford Dictionary of National Biography*, s.v. "Sadleir, Michael Thomas Harvey (1888–1957)," http://www.oxforddnb.com/view/article/35904 (accessed April 18, 2010).

3. Yellowbacks were the precursors to our modern-day paperbacks. They were "frequently translations or reprints," and "when original fiction appeared in this format, it was typically by minor authors." Patrick Brantlinger and William B. Thesing, introduction to *A Companion to the Victorian Novel*, eds. Patrick Brantlinger and William B. Thesing (Malden, MA: Blackwell, 2002), www.blackwellreference.com (accessed April 18, 2010).

4. *Oxford Dictionary of National Biography*, s.v. "Sadleir, Michael Thomas Harvey (1888–1957)," http://www.oxforddnb.com/view/article/35904 (accessed April 18, 2010).

5. Walter. H. Waggoner, "Robert Lee Wolff, 64, a Historian," *The New York Times*, November 13, 1980.

6. "The Robert Lee Wolff Collection of 19th-Century Fiction," Harry Ransom Center at the University of Texas at Austin, www.hrc.utexas.edu/collections/books/holdings/wolff (accessed April 18, 2010).

Chapter Five

Scholarly Journals

Although books still reign in the humanities, literary scholars value journal literature as a means of keeping up with current scholarship. Because they are produced more rapidly than scholarly monographs, journals are often where new ideas about an author, literary work, genre, or literary movement are first published. It is not uncommon for a scholar to write about a topic in a journal article first and then later elaborate on that same research in a book. The bibliographies and indexes discussed in the previous chapter are the main finding aids for locating articles on a particular topic. Tools such as the *MLA International Bibliography* and the *Annual Bibliography of English Language and Literature* will help you locate articles from various journals without searching individual tables of contents for each volume and issue.

Scholarly or academic journals, which are written for scholars studying a particular field in literature, publish articles about literatures from the Victorian and Edwardian ages. In academia, journal literature that is peer-reviewed, also referred to as refereed, is viewed as having more credence than journals that are not peer-reviewed. The term peer-reviewed means that journal articles must first go through a review by a panel of experts in the field or a related field, who determine the article's quality and whether it adds to a particular scholarly discussion. Generally speaking, all peer-reviewed journals are scholarly, but not all scholarly journals are peer-reviewed. To determine whether articles from a particular journal have undergone a peer-review process, you may consult one of several available sources: the publisher's website for the journal, the *MLA Directory of Periodicals*, and *Ulrich's Periodicals Directory*. Journal literature that is not peer-reviewed may still offer valuable insights into a topic; however, these articles might not have undergone as rigorous a review process.

This chapter overviews the major journals for the Victorian and Edwardian ages. The journals are organized into five major categories: general British literature titles, the nineteenth century, the twentieth century, author-specific journals, and other nonliterary journals. Each journal entry includes information about the publisher, dates and frequency, number and length of articles and reviews, submission acceptance ranges, typical article topics, and major indexing sources. In some ways, this section could serve as a guide for determining where to submit an article for publication. The categories are intended not to provide a comprehensive list of journals but rather to discuss representative ones to give you a sense of the types currently available. Additionally, the categories are not entirely mutually exclusive, so the author used her best judgment when determining where to categorize each journal.

GENERAL BRITISH LITERATURE TITLES

ELH: English Literary History. The Johns Hopkins University Press, 1934. Quarterly. ISSN: 0013-8304. www.press.jhu.edu/journals/english_literary _history/index.html.

English Language Notes. University of Colorado at Boulder, 1963. 2/yr. ISSN: 0013-8282. www.colorado.edu/English/eln.

English: The Journal of the English Association. Oxford University Press, 1935. 3/yr. ISSN: 0013-8215. english.oxfordjournals.org.

Essays in Criticism: A Quarterly Journal of Literary Criticism. Oxford University Press, 1951. Quarterly. ISSN: 0014-0856. eic.oxfordjournals.org.

Modern Language Quarterly: A Journal of Literary History. Duke University Press, 1940. Quarterly. ISSN: 0026-7929. mlq.dukejournals.org.

The Modern Language Review. Maney Publishing, 1905. Quarterly. ISSN: 0026-7937. Former title: *Modern Language Quarterly*. maney.co.uk/index .php/journals/mlr.

New Literary History: A Journal of Theory and Interpretation. The Johns Hopkins University Press, 1969. Quarterly. ISSN: 0028-6087. www.press .jhu.edu/journals/new_literary_history/index.html.

Philological Quarterly. University of Iowa. Department of English, 1922. Quarterly. ISSN: 0031-7977. english.uiowa.edu/pq.

PMLA: Publications of the Modern Language Association. Modern Language Association of America, 1884. 6/yr. ISSN: 0030-8129. Former title: *Modern Language Association of America. Transactions and Proceedings* 1884–1888. www.mla.org/pmla.

The Review of English Studies. Oxford University Press, 1925. 5/yr. ISSN: 0034-6551. res.oxfordjournals.org.

Studies in English Literature 1500–1900. The Johns Hopkins University Press, 1961. Quarterly. ISSN: 0039-3657. www.press.jhu.edu/journals/studies_in_english_literature/index.html.

The Yearbook of English Studies. Maney Publishing, 1971. Annual. ISSN: 0306-2473. maney.co.uk/index.php/journals/yes.

This section overviews several general British literature journals. While not an exhaustive listing, it should familiarize you with some major titles currently available. Because these journals are general, many of the articles in each issue are not specific to either the Victorian age or the Edwardian age; however, each of these covers British literature from 1830 to 1910 in various capacities. Many titles discussed in this section are respected throughout literary studies.

As discussed in chapter 4, the Modern Language Association in the United States and the Modern Humanities Research Association in Great Britain produce the two major bibliographies for locating journal articles in literary studies: *MLAIB* and *ABELL*, respectively. Just as the MLA and MHRA make bibliographic finding aids, they each also publish highly respected journals that survey the state of literary studies. *The Modern Language Review* (*MLR*) has been the flagship journal of the Modern Humanities Research Association since 1905. Released quarterly by Maney Publications, *MLR* covers all modern European literatures, languages, and cultures from the medieval to the modern, including the following areas of study: general and comparative, English, American, French, Italian, Hispanic, Germanic, and Slavonic and Eastern European. Each issue's pages are divided almost evenly between peer-reviewed articles and book reviews. In a given year, *MLR* publishes between 450 and 500 book reviews. *MLR* accepts roughly two-thirds of articles submitted each year and nearly all book review submissions. One unusual feature of *MLR* is that it does not print any advertisements or any correspondence. Recent articles pertinent to Victorian and Edwardian research include those on word usage in Joseph Conrad's writings, dread in the Victorian body, healing in Rudyard Kipling's later works, and legitimacy in George Eliot's *Silas Marner.* Major indexing sources for *MLR* are *ABELL* from 1920, *MLAIB* from 1926, and *Periodicals Index Online* from 1905 to 1995.

In addition to *The Modern Language Review*, Maney Publishing produces *The Yearbook of English Studies* (*YES*) for the Modern Humanities Research Association. Printed annually, this journal comprises articles and book reviews on the English language and English-language literature. Although not peer-reviewed, *YES* is a highly regarded journal. Each issue contains between fifteen and eighteen commissioned articles and a substantial book review section that includes sixty to eighty reviews per issue. Like *MLR*, *YES* contains no advertisements or correspondence in its issues. Also similar to its counterpart, *YES* has a high acceptance rate, publishing over half of all articles submitted and all book reviews. Frequently *YES* has special topical issues such as "Time and Narrative," "Children in Literature," and "Nineteenth-Century Travel Writing." Scholars studying Victorian and *Edwardian literature may be interested in the following article topics: the significance of physical growth in late nineteenth-century medicine and fiction, women travel writers' representations of harems, and reading William Makepeace Thackeray's *Vanity Fair*. Both *MLAIB* and *ABELL* index *YES* from 1971.

PMLA: Publications of the Modern Language Association is for the Modern Language Association of America what *MLR* is for the Modern Humanities Research Association. Continuously in print since 1884, *PMLA* contains scholarly articles, professional notes, and letters in the first four issues of each year; a directory of MLA members in the fifth issue; and the MLA annual convention program in the sixth and final issue of the year. Unlike *MLR*, which publishes a significant number of reviews each year, *PMLA* does not include any book reviews. Scholarly articles pertain to the study of language and literature and are generally between 2,500 and 9,000 words long. A peer-reviewed journal, *PMLA* accepts submissions only from MLA members. Even with this submission limitation, *PMLA* receives between 200 and 320 article submissions per year; however, the journal is selective and accepts only twenty-five to thirty-five articles in a given year. The journal aims to address its members' literary interests and, as such, prints articles on all literary eras, including the Victorian and Edwardian ages. Recent article topics that may interest Victorian and Edwardian scholars are stream-of-consciousness writing in nineteenth-century novels, spectacle in Dickens's *A Christmas Carol*, women's hair in the Victorian imagination, and Lady Isabella Augusta Gregory's role in George Bernard Shaw's *The Shewing-Up of Blanco Posnet*. Not surprisingly, the primary indexing source for these and other *PMLA* articles is the *MLAIB*, which extends its indexing earlier than the 1926 beginning of the bibliography back to *PMLA*'s initial 1884 issue onward. *Periodicals Index Online* covers this journal from 1884 through 1995, and *ABELL* indexes from 1920.

Since its beginnings in 1934, **ELH: English Literary History** has emphasized English and American literature and has sought to represent the discipline's historical, critical, and theoretical concerns. Published quarterly with continuous pagination by the Johns Hopkins University Press, each *ELH* issue contains between nine and ten peer-reviewed articles. Most articles do not exceed 11,000 words in length and have brief author-provided abstracts. Each volume's final issue has a comprehensive table of contents. No correspondence or reviews are published. The journal is highly selective, with only 10 percent of each year's roughly 350 submissions accepted. *English Literary History* is fully indexed in both *ABELL* and *MLAIB* from its first volume and issue in 1934 to its most current issue. Although not exclusively about nineteenth- and early twentieth-century British literature, *ELH* has a fair number of articles for those literary periods. Recent articles of interest to Victorian and Edwardian scholars include commodity culture in Emily Brontë's *Wuthering Heights*; Robert Browning's "Caliban upon Setebos" on Darwin, natural theology, and slavery; promises in George Eliot's fiction; and anarchism and the thermodynamics of law in Joseph Conrad's *Secret Agent*.

Since 1963 by the University of Colorado at Boulder, **English Language Notes (*ELN*)** has maintained its format but recently underwent a shift in emphasis. Through the December 2006 issue, *ELN* was published quarterly and comprised brief articles on the entire canon of English and American literature; however, since the summer of 2006, the journal has focused on literary and cultural studies special topics and reduced from four to two issues per year. Despite the change in content, the journal remains committed to providing brief (three- or four-page) peer-reviewed articles. The new format also incorporates two new sections: "ELN Forums," which is designed to facilitate informal discussion on a particular topic, and "Roundtables and Reviews," which serves as a forum for book reviews and review essays. Under its new directive, *ELN* examines the relationship between literary studies and fine arts, geography, history, philosophy, science, and theology. Recent issues have covered "Photography and Literature," "Queer Space," "Literary History and the Religious Turn," and "Literature and Pseudoscience." Even with the topical focus, Victorian and Edwardian scholars should still find articles of interest in *ELN*. Gerard Manley Hopkins's poetry, serial publication of Victorian novels, and nineteenth-century spiritual sentimentalism have all been included recently. *English Language Notes* is indexed in *MLAIB* and *ABELL* in its entirety and in *Periodicals Index Online* from 1963 through 1996.

Oxford University Press publishes **English: The Journal of the English Association** on behalf of the association. Historically, each volume was composed of three issues, but as of 2009, four issues comprise each volume. *English* has peer-reviewed articles that are between 5,000 and 9,000 words in length on major English literary works and general literature topics. Additionally, *English* includes substantial book reviews and, in a highly unusual move, original poetry by contemporary poets. *English* is a selective journal, accepting only seven to nine out of the eighty to one hundred articles submitted each year. Reviews have an 80 percent acceptance rate. Unlike many humanities journals, *English* actively participates in the open-access movement, making scholarship freely available to scholars through the publisher's website, where select articles are available online prior to copyediting and typesetting.

The Oxford University Press also has freely accessible tables of contents and abstracts for every volume and issue number between 1936 and 1997, as well as for 2008. *English* is indexed in its entirety in *MLAIB*, from 1936 onward in *ABELL*, and from 1936 to 1995 in *Periodicals Index Online*.

Another Oxford University Press journal, **Essays in Criticism: A Quarterly Journal of Literary Criticism (EIC)**, covers all periods of English literature from Chaucer to the present day. *Essays in Criticism* has been published quarterly since 1951, emphasizing the importance of original interpretations of literary texts and rigorous scholarship. In addition to peer-reviewed articles, *EIC* has a lengthy book reviews and a critical opinions section. Journal articles range between 6,000 and 8,000 words in length, while book reviews tend to be between 2,000 and 3,000 words. *Essays in Criticism* is highly selective, accepting only 14 to 16 of the 80 to 120 articles submitted each year. Although *EIC*'s scope is much broader than Victorian and Edwardian literature, it offers a fair number of articles on those time periods. Recent articles relevant to Victorian and Edwardian scholars include "Auden's Goethe," "George Eliot's Grammar of Being," and "Martha Nussbaum and *The Golden Bowl*." *ABELL* and the *MLAIB* index every issue of *EIC*, while *Periodicals Index Online* indexes from 1951 to 1995.

Modern Language Quarterly: A Journal of Literary History (MLQ) comprises articles on literature and literary studies as a profession. Published quarterly by Duke University Press for the University of Washington, Seattle, *MLQ* covers all literary periods from the Middle Ages to the present and addresses all theoretical approaches to reading and interpreting literature. Periodically, this peer-reviewed journal releases special issues on varied topics such as "Influence," "Genre and History," and "Postcolonialism and the Past." Each issue, whether regular or special, includes scholarly articles of between 7,000 and 10,000 words, and book reviews of 900 to 1,500 words. Sixteen out of seventy-five to one hundred article submissions are accepted annually. "Child-Killers and the Competition between Late Victorian Theater and the Novel," "The Foreign Offices of British Fiction," and "'The Brutal Music and the Delicate Text'? The Aesthetic Relationship between Wilde's and Strauss's *Salome* Reconsidered" are among recent *MLQ* articles. The *MLAIB* and *ABELL* index *MLQ* from 1940 to the present, and *Periodicals Index Online* covers 1940 to 1995. Both the journal's and the publisher's websites (depts.washington.edu/mlq and mlq.dukejournals .org, respectively) provide select access to *MLQ*'s table of contents. The journal's website includes a list of upcoming articles and an index of every issue from 1990 to the present, with abstracts from 2000 to the present. The publisher's website allows for searching or browsing articles from March 2000 through the present.

According to the Johns Hopkins University Press, *New Literary History: A Journal of Theory and Interpretation* (*NLH*) focuses on "theory and interpretation—the reasons for literary change, the definitions of periods, and the evolution of styles, conventions, and genres." Within this broad scope, *NLH* has a heavy theoretical bent and covers literatures from around the globe and from all time periods. Since 1969, *NLH* has been issued quarterly. Each year, 40 of the 120 submitted articles are accepted. Articles are no more than 8,000 words. In addition to these peer-reviewed articles, each issue includes a list of books received. Representations of Jeremy Button in Charles Darwin's writings, bioethics in Victorian literature, and George Eliot's sequels are topics covered in recent articles. *MLAIB* indexes all issues of *NLH*, *ABELL* indexes 1970 to the present, and *Periodicals Index Online* indexes from the first issue to 1995.

Philological Quarterly (*PQ*) covers European literature and culture from the medieval times through the present day. The University of Iowa's English department has published *PQ* since 1922. Although the title indicates that *PQ* is printed quarterly, since 2006, the winter and spring issues and the summer and fall issues have been combined so that only two issues are released each year: issue 1/2 (winter/spring) and issue 3/4 (summer/fall). *PQ* is a peer-reviewed journal that incorporates scholarly articles, book reviews, and notes into its issues. Articles are a maximum of 8,000 words, while book reviews and notes are 1,500 words and 2,500 words, respectively. Less than 10 percent of the 250 articles submitted each year are accepted. Lesser-known Victorian and Edwardian authors such as Cecilia Jenkins and Elizabeth von Arnim are covered alongside heavily studied authors such as Charles Dickens, Mary Elizabeth Braddon, and Lord Alfred Tennyson. Each *PQ* issue is indexed in *MLAIB*, while *ABELL* covers 1922 through the present, and *Periodicals Index Online* covers the first issue through 1995.

Since 1925, *The Review of English Studies* (*RES*) has provided articles on all time periods of English language and literature. Rather than emphasize critical interpretation, this peer-reviewed journal gives preference to historical scholarship highlighting recently discovered sources and offering new readings of established texts. Printed five times annually, *RES* includes five to seven peer-reviewed articles and between twenty and thirty book reviews in each issue. Roughly 25 percent of articles submitted to *RES* are accepted, as are a majority of commissioned book reviews. Recent Victorian and Edwardian article topics address market forces and morality in Thomas Hardy's *The Mayor of Casterbridge*, religious symbolism and the alchemist in Christina Rossetti's "The Prince's Progress," regional dialects in William Barnes's poetry, and entropy in Joseph Conrad's *The Secret Agent*. Both *MLAIB* and *ABELL* index the complete run of *RES* from the first issue in 1925 to the present. Additionally, the publisher's website provides searchable tables of contents and abstracts for the journal's full run.

Like many general British literature journals, **Studies in English Literature 1500–1900 (SEL)** gives a broad treatment of English literature; however, in a rather unique editorial decision, *SEL* focuses each of its four issues on a different literary period: "English Renaissance," "Tudor and Stuart Drama," "Restoration and Eighteenth Century," and "Nineteenth Century." As such, the fourth issue each year should be of particular interest to Victorian literature scholars. Edwardian scholars will find *SEL* a less fruitful journal for obvious coverage reasons. Recent issues covered various topics, including Matthew Arnold's "Empedocles on Etna," Elizabeth Barrett Browning's *Aurora Leigh* as "literary self-portrait," and women's professionalization in Charlotte Mary Yonge's *The Daisy Chain*. The Johns Hopkins University Press publishes this peer-reviewed journal and accepts roughly 25 percent of submitted article manuscripts. *MLAIB* and *ABELL* provide complete indexing for *SEL*.

THE NINETEENTH CENTURY

19: Interdisciplinary Studies in the Long Nineteenth Century. University of London, 2005. 2/yr. ISSN: 1755-1560. www.19.bbk.ac.uk.

Journal of Victorian Culture. Edinburgh University Press, 1996. 2/yr. ISSN: 1355-5502. www.eupjournals.com/journal/jvc.

Literary London: Interdisciplinary Studies in the Representation of London. Literary London, 2003. 2/yr. ISSN: 1744-0807. www.literarylondon.org/london-journal/index.html.

Nineteenth-Century Contexts: An Interdisciplinary Journal. Routledge, 1987. Quarterly. ISSN: 0890-5495. Former titles: *Milton and the Romantics* 1975–1981; *Romanticism Past and Present* 1981–1987. www.tandf.co.uk/journals/titles/08905495.asp.

Nineteenth-Century Gender Studies. University of Kentucky, 2005. 3/yr. ISSN: 1556-7524. www.ncgsjournal.com.

Nineteenth-Century Literature. University of California Press, 1950. Quarterly. ISSN: 0891-9356. Former title: *The Trollopian* 1945–1949; *Nineteenth-Century Fiction* 1950–1986. www.ucpressjournals.com/journal.asp?j=ncl.

Nineteenth-Century Studies. Southeastern Louisiana University, 1987. Annual. ISSN: 0893-7931. www.english.uwosh.edu/roth/ncs.

Nineteenth Century Theatre and Film. University of Manchester Press, 1970. 2/yr. ISSN: 1748-3727. Former titles: incorporates *NCTR Newsletter*

1976–1979; *Nineteenth-Century Theatre Research* 1980–1987; *Nineteenth-Century Theatre* 1988–2000. www.manchesteruniversitypress.co.uk/journals/journal.asp?id=6.

Romanticism and Victorianism on the Net (RaVoN). St. Catherine's College, 1996. Quarterly. ISSN: 1916-1441. www.ravon.umontreal.ca.

Victorian Literature and Culture. Cambridge University Press, 1973. 2/yr. ISSN: 1060-1503. Former title: *Browning Institute Studies* 1973–1991. journals.cambridge.org/action/displayJournal?jid=VLC.

Victorian Newsletter. Western Kentucky University, 1952. 2/yr. ISSN: 0042-5192. www.wku.edu/victorian.

Victorian Periodicals Review. The Johns Hopkins University Press, 1968. Quarterly. ISSN: 0709-4698. Former title: *Victorian Periodicals Newsletter*. www.press.jhu.edu/journals/victorian_periodicals_review.

Victorian Poetry. West Virginia University Press, 1963. Quarterly. ISSN: 0042-5206. wvupressonline.com/journals/victorian_poetry.

Victorian Review: An Interdisciplinary Journal of Victorian Studies. Victorian Studies Association of Western Canada, 1972. 2/yr. ISSN: 0848-1512. Former title: *Victorian Studies Association of Western Canada. Newsletter*. web.uvic.ca/victorianreview.

Victorian Studies: An Interdisciplinary Journal of Social, Political, and Cultural Studies. Indiana University Press, 1957. Quarterly. ISSN: 0042-5222. inscribe.iupress.org/loi/vic.

Victorians Institute Journal. Virginia Commonwealth University, 1972. Annual. ISSN: 0886-3865. www.vcu.edu/vij/VIJ.html.

The following section overviews the major journals for nineteenth-century British literature. While some are specific to the Victorian age, several are for the long nineteenth century. As such, the journals may also address the early nineteenth century and British Romanticism; journals that are exclusively on the Romantic period, however, have been excluded. Likewise, some Victorian and nineteenth-century journals extend coverage into the early twentieth century and, as such, are relevant to Edwardian scholars. Grouped primarily for their emphasis on a particular time period in British literature, these journals do not exclusively publish on literary topics. While titles such as *Victorian Poetry* and *Nineteenth-Century Literature* are more overtly literary, others, including *Victorian Studies: An Interdisciplinary Journal of Social, Political, and Cultural Studies* and *Nineteenth-Century Contexts: An Interdisciplinary Journal,* are interested in examining the nineteenth century and the Victorian age from a broader, cultural perspective. Both journal subcategories should be highly useful as you conduct your research. While this list is not exhaustive, it gives a sense of the existing journal literature.

Since 1945, ***Nineteenth-Century Literature*** (***NCL***) has covered scholarship, criticism, comparative studies, and new editions in nineteenth-century English and American literature. *NCL* is a peer-reviewed, quarterly journal that has gone through a couple titular changes, beginning as the *Trollopian* in 1945 and switching to *Nineteenth-Century Fiction* in 1949 before changing to its current title in 1986. Only 5 to 6 percent of each year's 300 article submissions are accepted. In spite of its title, *NCL* does not focus exclusively on literature; rather, it contains articles on gender, history, military studies, psychology, cultural studies, and urbanism, in addition to articles on literary history and theory. Because *NCL* covers literature from 1800 to 1900, articles on the Romantic period are included alongside those on the Victorian age. Recent articles address topics such as market and manhood in Charles Reade's *Hard Cash*, rumors as fact in Anthony Trollope's *The Eustace Diamonds*, and male vanity and bourgeois desire in William Makepeace Thackeray's *Vanity Fair*. *MLAIB* and *ABELL* index from the first issue of the *Trollopian* to the most current issue of *NCL*.

Published by West Virginia University Press since 1963, ***Victorian Poetry*** (***VP***) comprises scholarly articles on British and colonial poetry written between 1830 and 1914. Because the editors define the Victorian age so broadly, this journal will also be useful for scholars of Edwardian poetry. This quarterly journal is composed of peer-reviewed articles, solicited book reviews, and a guide to the year's work. *Victorian Poetry* has a fairly generous acceptance rate of 25 percent. Recent *VP* issues have included articles on the elegies of L. E. L., Elizabeth Barrett Browning, and Felicia Dorothea Hemans; politicizing dance in late Victorian women's poetry; and the correspondence of Edward FitzGerald and Alfred Tennyson. The guide to the year's work appears in the third issue of each volume and provides bibliographies to general materials on nineteenth-century poetry, Matthew Arnold, Elizabeth Barrett Browning, Robert Browning, Thomas Hardy, Gerard Manley Hopkins, the poets of the nineties, the Pre-Raphaelites, Algernon Charles Swinburne, and Alfred Tennyson. Each volume's final issue contains an index to the volume organized by article author. *MLAIB* and *ABELL* index the contents of *VP* for the entire run, while *Periodicals Index Online* indexes from 1963 to 1995.

Titled *Browning Institute Studies* until 1991, ***Victorian Literature and Culture*** (***VLC***) prints peer-reviewed articles and review essays on all aspects of Victorian literary and cultural history. Additionally, *VLC* publishes solicited book reviews. Occasionally part or all of an issue comprises articles on a preselected editors' topic. Authors may also elect to submit chapters from books they are writing for the journal's "Works in Progress" section. The "Special Effects" section of *VLC* includes little-known and generally unavailable primary sources. This semi-annual journal seeks submissions from both new and established scholars yet is highly selective, accepting only thirty out of two hundred articles submitted each year. Recent articles cover topics such as fetishism in Mary Elizabeth Braddon's *Lady Audley's Secrets*, Oscar Wilde and the Italian Renaissance, Victorian women gardeners and the rise of gardening texts, and physiognomy in *Middlemarch*. *Victorian Literature and Culture* is indexed from its first issue in 1973 to the present in both *ABELL* and *MLAIB*. Tables of contents for volume 19 through the most recent volume are available on the journal's website (www.nyu.edu/gsas/dept/english/journal/victorian).

With its first issue published in 1996 by Edinburgh University Press, the ***Journal of Victorian Culture*** (***JVC***) is a relatively young journal. Rather than confining articles to specific disciplinary bounds, *JVC* is composed of peer-reviewed articles that critically examine interdisciplinary issues in the Victorian age. While it contains articles on literature, *JVC* seeks to also include articles on Victorian studies, including architectural history, cultural studies, economic and social history, the history of science and technology, literary studies, music, popular culture, theatre, and the visual arts. Scholarly articles, perspectives, roundtables, and book reviews comprise each issue of this semiannual journal. Recent issues have had articles on Christian manliness in Charles Kingsley's works, class and colonization in R. M. Ballantyne's stories, and clothing and commodity culture in *Household Words*. *ABELL* indexes *JVC* from 1997 through the present; however, *MLAIB* does not include *JVC*. Edinburgh University Press has also made the table of contents and full text freely available for each issue since 2000.

The official journal of the North American Victorian Studies Association (NAVSA), ***Victorian Studies: An Interdisciplinary Journal of Social, Political, and Cultural Studies*** has been published quarterly by Indiana University Press since 1957. *Victorian Studies* emphasizes interdisciplinary research with articles about comparative literature, social and political history, and the histories of economics, education, fine arts, law, philosophy, and science. In fact, articles must be interdisciplinary to be accepted. In addition to peer-reviewed journal articles, *Victorian Studies* prints review essays and book reviews. Articles range from 6,000 to 9,000 words long, while book reviews are typically 1,000 words. This journal is highly selective, accepting 14 of 125 articles submitted each year. *Victorian Studies* is an excellent source for book reviews, printing 120 each year. Recent articles have addressed topics such as authorship in late Victorian England, love and thinking in literature, emotions in animals and humans, ideals of Irish manliness, and relief work. *Victorian Studies* is indexed in *MLAIB* and *ABELL* from 1957 to the present and in *PIO* from 1957 to 2000. The *Victorian Studies Bibliography* (www.letrs.indiana.edu/web/v/victbib), which is a cumulative bibliography of publications on the Victorian age, accompanies this journal and is discussed in chapter 4.

Nineteenth-Century Contexts: An Interdisciplinary Journal (*NCC*) is a quarterly periodical from Routledge. Since 1987, *NCC* has been issued under its current name; prior to that, the journal transitioned through several identities: *Romanticism Past and Present* from 1981 until 1987, and *Milton and the Romantics* from 1975 until 1981. Currently, *NCC* offers interdisciplinary examinations of the nineteenth century, addressing diverse areas such as anthropology, art, economics, history, the history of science, literary criticism, musicology, popular culture studies, religious studies, and social history. Rather than focusing on a specific discipline, this journal aims to push on disciplinary boundaries and demonstrate the relevance of international nineteenth-century issues today. Articles are a peer-reviewed and range between 5,000 and 8,000 words in length. Special issues frequently cover specific topics such as "Reading the Past in the Nineteenth Century," "Global Formations: Past and Present," "Victorian Life Writing," and "Women's Friendships and Lesbian Sexuality." Each issue has a preliminary table of contents for the following issue and identifies whether that issue will address a special topic. Additionally, *NCC* has book reviews and notes on contributors. The journal is selective and accepts roughly 10 percent of the 150 articles submitted each year. Recent articles are on topics such as working-class autobiography, facial hair and marital values in the 1850s, and marriage in William Makepeace Thackeray's *Vanity Fair*. Tables of contents and cover images are available for the 1994 and 2006 issues on the University of Notre Dame's website (www.nd.edu/%7Encc). *MLAIB* indexes every issue, and *ABELL* indexes 1976 onward.

The interdisciplinary journal of the Nineteenth Century Studies Association, *Nineteenth-Century Studies* (*NCS*), is released annually, covering American, British, and continental subjects. Rather than focusing exclusively on literature, *NCS* contains articles on all humanistic fields, such as art history, history, the history of science, music, and the social sciences. Published by Southeastern Louisiana University's English department, this journal gives particular preference to interdisciplinary and comparative studies. In addition to submitted scholarly articles, *NCS* also prints solicited review essays that survey scholarship and events of interest to nineteenth-century scholars. Like the scholarly articles, these essays do not emphasize a single work but treat themes that run through each journal issue. Journal articles vary between 3,500 and 7,000 words in length and are peer-reviewed. According to the *MLA Directory of Periodicals*, only eight to ten of the fifty to one hundred article submissions are accepted. Recent articles of interest to Victorian scholars include "The 'Child-Woman' and the Victorian Novel," "The Politics of Pain in Charlotte Brontë's *Shirley*," "The Odd Man: Masculinity and the Modern Intellectual in George Gissing's *Born in Exile*," and "'Eyes of the Proper Almond-Shape':

Blue-and-White China in the British Imaginary, 1823–1883." The journal is indexed from 1987 onward in the *MLAIB* and from 1991 in *ABELL*, and a table of contents for each volume since the journal's inception in 1987 is available from the publisher's website.

Scholars researching theater and film efforts from the nineteenth century may find *Nineteenth Century Theatre and Film* a useful source of scholarship. This journal is printed semi-annually by Manchester University Press and has undergone several name changes in its almost thirty-year history. In 1973, it began as *Nineteenth Century Theatre Research* and incorporated *NCTR Newsletter* from 1976 through 1979; from 1980 until 1987, it was titled *Nineteenth Century Theatre*. Since 1987, the journal has been known as *Nineteenth Century Theatre and Film* and has expanded to include early film history along with theater research. Issues comprise scholarly essays, documents, bibliographies, and review essays. This peer-reviewed journal emphasizes the use of primary source materials in research and tends to focus on the performance aspects of theater. Articles are roughly 5,000 words in length with four to five articles per issue. Recent articles have covered varied topics, such as Mary Elizabeth Braddon's unpublished script fragment *The Revenge of the Dead*, the emergence of the motion picture industry in late nineteenth-century London, and York's Theatre Royal between 1803 and 1911. *Nineteenth Century Theatre and Film* is indexed from 1973 to the present in *MLAIB*, from 1975 onward in *ABELL*, and from 1973 to 1995 in *Periodicals Index Online*. The publisher's website provides select open-access content from the December 2003 issue.

While most literary journals are still available through traditional individual and institutional subscriptions, a few journals have fully embraced the open-access movement. Four such journals are *19: Interdisciplinary Studies in the Long Nineteenth Century*, *Nineteenth-Century Gender Studies*, *Romanticism and Victorianism on the Net (RaVoN)*, and *Literary London*. *19: Interdisciplinary Studies in the Long Nineteenth Century* (*19*) is a peer-reviewed, semi-annual journal of the Centre for Nineteenth-Century Studies at Birkbeck College in the University of London. *19* was first published in 2005 and, as of early 2010, has only nine issues, each of which covered a different topic: "Interdisciplinarity," "The Long Nineteenth Century," "Literature and the Press: 1800/1900," "Rethinking Victorian Sentimentality," "Verbal and Visual Interactions in Nineteenth-Century Print Culture," "Victorian Fiction and the Material Imagination," "Mind, Bodies, Machines," "Victorian Theatricalities," and "Transatlanticism: Identities and Exchanges." The journal's table of contents, full text, and images are freely available on its website. Online access is the only option, as *19* is not available in print. The journal's homepage links to additional online nineteenth-century resources in the "Debate & Research" section. As the title suggests, this journal provides interdisciplinary and international coverage of the nineteenth century. *19* accepts solicited articles only, which still undergo a peer-review process. Recent articles include "Thomas Hardy, Provincial Geology and the Material Imagination," "Moving Books/Moving Images: Optical Recreations and Children's Publishing 1800–1900," and "Feeling Dickensian Feeling." Since it is not indexed by standard sources, *19* allows scholars to sign up for e-mail notifications as new issues are released.

Nineteenth-Century Gender Studies (**NCGS**) is an equally young journal. Since 2005, the University of Kentucky has published *NCGS* as an outlet for original scholarship that addresses both gender studies and nineteenth-century literature. Initially *NCGS* was released irregularly but has since settled into a pattern of three issues, in spring, summer, and winter. In addition to peer-reviewed articles, the journal accepts book reviews. The articles range between 4,000 and 8,000 words in length, and of the fifty to sixty articles submitted each year, nine to ten are accepted. "Financial Promiscuity: Gambling on the Fallen Man in Collins's *Man and Wife*," "'And There Was No Helping It': Disability and Social Reproduction in Charlotte Yonge's *The Daisy Chain*," and "Sarah Waters's *Fingersmith*: Leaving Women's Fingerprints on Victorian Pornography" are among recent articles. In the journal's brief history, two special issues—"Papers and Keynotes from the Fifteenth Annual British Women Writers Conference" and "The New Woman and Sexuality"—have been released. Although the *MLAIB* is supposed to index *NCGS* from 2006 to the present, only one article is currently included in the bibliography. The table of contents and articles are available from the journal's website.

Slightly older than either *19* or *NCGS*, **Romanticism and Victorianism on the Net** (**RaVoN**) began as *Romanticism on the Net* in 1996. Originally focused on British Romanticism, the journal's scope expanded to include the Victorian age in August 2007 and has since been renamed to reflect its coverage. This peer-reviewed journal is released quarterly by the Université de Montréal. Essays run between 5,000 and 8,000 words in length, and roughly one-fourth of submissions are accepted. Hosted on *Érudit*, an open-access digital publishing platform created by the Université de Montréal, the Université Laval, and the Université du Québec à Montréal, *RaVoN*'s contents may be searched, browsed by issue, or accessed through the article author index on the journal's website. Since incorporating Victorian scholarship, *RaVoN* has released six special issues: "From *RoN* to *RaVoN* (*Romanticism and Victorianism on the Net*)," "Victorian Internationalisms," "Interdisciplinarity and the Body," "Modelling the Self: Subjectivity and Identity in Romantic and Post-Romantic Thought and Culture," "Science, Technology and the Senses," and "Materiality and Memory." Because of its previous focus, the early *RoN* issues are less germane than the recent *RaVoN* issues. *Romanticism and Victorianism on the Net* is indexed in both *ABELL* and *MLAIB* from 1996 to the present.

Now in its sixth volume, **Literary London: Interdisciplinary Studies in the Representation of London** is an open-access journal that began in 2003. This peer-reviewed journal is dedicated to scholarship on London and literature. While a literary journal in one sense, *Literary London* also encourages interdisciplinary approaches to understanding and studying London. Released semi-annually in March and September, each issue typically contains scholarly articles that are no longer than 5,000 words in length. Sixty percent of the twenty-five submitted articles and eight of the ten book reviews are accepted each year. In addition to scholarly essays, *Literary London* also prints poetry, review essays, book reviews, and interviews and conversations. Special issues have been produced on the following topics: "Seduced by the City: From Hogarth's London to Today," "The Thames," and "Iain Sinclair." Recent articles have covered topography, suburban ideals, vagrancy, London prophecies, and the criminal underworld. Indexing is available in the *MLAIB* from March 2003 onward, and the full table of contents and all-article text are found on the journal's website.

Victorian Newsletter (**VN**) has been published by Western Kentucky University's English department since 1952. Unlike other nineteenth-century and Victorian journals, which are highly interdisciplinary and international, this semi-annual journal accepts articles specifically on British Victorian literature. *Victorian Newsletter* provides peer-reviewed articles roughly 7,500 words in length, as well as book reviews of 2,500 words in length. Of fifty-seven articles submitted, *VN* accepts fourteen each year. Each issue also lists the upcoming issue's articles. Recent topics have included Buddhism and imperialism in Rudyard Kipling's *Kim*, stage performances of Wilkie Collins's *The Woman in White*, and art and life in Oscar Wilde's *An Ideal Husband*. *Victorian Newsletter* is indexed in *ABELL* from 1958 and in *MLAIB* from 1957. The publisher's website has tables of contents for all issues from 1952 to 2007 and annotated indexes for 1952 through 2009.

Victorian Periodicals Review (**VPR**) is the journal of the Research Society for Victorian Periodicals (RSVP) that is issued quarterly by the Johns Hopkins University Press. Previously titled *Victorian Periodicals Newsletter*, *VPR* is composed of articles, notes, book reviews, and an annual bibliography on the editorial and publishing history of Victorian periodicals since 1968. While most articles focus on British and Irish periodicals from both the Victorian and Edwardian ages, some continental and early nineteenth-century publications are also covered. *VPR*, a peer-reviewed journal, accepts most of the articles, reviews, and notes submitted each year. "Odds, Intelligence, and Prophecies: Racing News in the Penny Press, 1855–1914," "'A Charm in Those Fingers': Patterns, Taste, and the *Englishwoman's Domestic Magazine*," "Thackeray's Contributions to the Times," and "The Age of the Storytellers: British Popular Fiction Magazines, 1880–1950" are among recent *VPR* articles. This journal is indexed in *ABELL*,

MLAIB, and *Periodicals Index Online*. Tables of contents for *VPR* special issues are available on the RSVP website (www.rs4vp.org/vpr.html).

Victorian Review: An Interdisciplinary Journal of Victorian Studies (*VR*) covers interdisciplinary studies of the Victorian age, including art, culture, history, literature, and science. Published semi-annually since 1972 by the Victorian Studies Association of Western Canada, *VR* was originally titled *Victorian Studies Association of Western Canada Newsletter*. *Victorian Review* comprises book reviews, scholarly articles, and topical forums, which focus on specific subjects such as "Victorian Studies and Interdisciplinarity" and "Victorian Things: A Forum on Material Objects." Only 8 to 10 percent of articles submitted to *VR* are accepted. The articles range between 5,000 and 8,000 words in length. Recent articles include "Fading into Innocence: Death, Sexuality, and Moral Restoration in Henry Peach Robinson's *Fading Away*," "Female Gothic Motifs in Mona Caird's *The Wing of Azrael*," and "The Miser's New Notes and the Victorian Sensation Novel: Plotting the Magic of Paper Money." This journal is indexed by the *MLAIB* from 1989 to the present, by *ABELL* from 1991 to the present, and in *Periodicals Index Online*. Tables of contents from volume 25 (2000) to the most recent issue are available from the journal's website.

Published by the Department of English at Virginia Commonwealth University, **Victorians Institute Journal (*VIJ*)** began in the same year as the *Victorian Review*, 1972. *VIJ* comprises peer-reviewed articles, book reviews, and review essays on Victorian art, culture, and literature. Since 1986, *VIJ* has also had a "Texts" section, which prints unpublished Victorian works such as George Meredith's "The Friend of an Engaged Couple," Dante Gabriel Rosetti's "Roderick & Rosalba," Thomas Carlyle's "On Trades-Unions, Promoterism and Signs of the Times," and John Blackwood and Joseph Munt Landsford's "Fifteen Unpublished Letters to George Henry Lewes and George Eliot." The journal frequently has special sections over topics such as "Our Imaginary Friends," "Poetry and the Colonies," and "Ghosts of the Victorian." Each year *VIJ* accepts around ten of the forty articles submitted, as well as most book reviews. Article topics vary widely, with articles on manipulation in *Vanity Fair*, gender and art in *Jane Eyre* and "The Lady of Shalott," and the painters' role in sensation fiction. The *MLAIB* and *ABELL* index the entire run of *VIJ*; additionally, the publisher's website has tables of contents from 1972 to the present.

THE TWENTIETH CENTURY

English Literature in Transition, 1880–1920. ELT Press, 1957. Quarterly. ISSN: 0013-8339. Former title: *English Fiction in Transition, 1880–1920* 1957–1963. www.eltpress.org/thejournal.html.

Journal of Modern Literature. Indiana University Press, 1970. Quarterly. ISSN: 0022-281X. inscribe.iupress.org/loi/jml.

Modern Drama: World Drama from 1850 to the Present. University of Toronto Press, 1958. Quarterly, ISSN: 1712-5286. www.utpjournals.com/md/md.html.

Modern Fiction Studies. The Johns Hopkins University Press, 1955. Quarterly. ISSN: 1080-658X. www.press.jhu.edu/journals/modern_fiction_studies/index.html.

Twentieth Century Literature: A Scholarly and Critical Journal. Hofstra University, 1955. Quarterly. ISSN: 0041-462X. www.hofstra.edu/Academics/Colleges/HCLAS/ENGL/engl_tcl.html.

Like the previous discussion, this section emphasizes a particular time period in British literary history: the twentieth century. There are significantly fewer journals dedicated to this time period. More recent literature tends not to receive as much scholarly attention as authors and texts from earlier literary periods. It is reasonable to assume, however, that as time progresses, scholars will pay more attention to this body of literature. Even though the Edwardian age occurred in the early twentieth century, it has not been studied to the same extent as the Victorian age and the Great War, which serve as its bookends. That said, the journals discussed in this section, while not fully devoted to Edwardian literature, are useful resources for recent scholarship. Scholars of the Edwardian age should also note that many nineteenth-century and Victorian journals extend their coverage through the first ten to fifteen years of the twentieth century and, as such, are valuable sources for scholarship. Twentieth-century journals also tend to be more international in scope than their counterparts for earlier centuries. In addition to exploring interdisciplinary connections common to nineteenth-century scholarship, this selection of journals also investigates international literary relations.

As its title suggests, ***English Literature in Transition, 1880–1920 (ELT)*** comprises scholarly articles and reviews about a transitional period in English literature between the nineteenth and twentieth centuries. Originally titled *English Fiction in Transition, 1880–1920* at its inception in 1957, *ELT* assumed its current title in 1963. A peer-reviewed journal of ELT Press, *ELT* published articles and book reviews on British fiction, poetry, drama, and culture between 1880 and 1920; however, it emphasizes lesser-known authors, excludes book reviews, and does not print articles that are exclusively on Joseph Conrad, Henry James, James Joyce, D. H. Lawrence, Virginia Woolf, and W. B. Yeats. Only 10 out of 100 to 120 article submissions are accepted each year. Recent articles include "*The Hound of the Baskervilles*: Modern Belgian Masters, Paralyzing Spectacles, and the Art of Deception," "Kipling's Imperial Aestheticism: Epistemologies of Art and Empire in *Kim*," and "M. P. Shiel and

the Love of Pubescent Girls: The Other 'Love that Dare not Speak its Name.'"
This quarterly journal is indexed in *MLAIB* for its full run, in *ABELL* from
1960 onward, and *Periodicals Index Online* from 1957 until 1995.

Published quarterly by Indiana University Press, the **Journal of Modern
Literature** (**JML**) covers modern literature from all continents from 1900 to
the present. International in focus, many *JML* articles are not specific to British literature; however, it remains a useful source for Edwardian scholarship.
Each year *JML* accepts approximately thirty-five peer-reviewed articles out
of its 150 submissions. While *JML* is not strictly on Edwardian literature,
relevant recent articles include "The Spatial Imagination and Literary Form
of Conrad's Colonial Fictions," "Masculinity Amalgamated: Colonialism,
Homosexuality, and Forster's Kipling," "Pathologies of the Imperial Me-
tropolis: Impressionism as Traumatic Afterimage in Conrad and Ford," and
"Double Trouble: The Hueffer Brothers and the Artistic Temperament."
MLAIB and *ABELL* index *JML* from 1970 to the present, and Indiana University Press has tables of contents for 2001 to the present and abstracts for many
articles at the journal's website.

In the 1950s, two genre-specific journals emerged on the literary studies
scene to support scholarship on modern literature. The Johns Hopkins University Press published *Modern Fiction Studies* in 1955, followed by the
University of Toronto Press's *Modern Drama: World Drama from 1850 to the
Present*, first printed in 1958. **Modern Fiction Studies** (**MFS**) is a quarterly,
peer-reviewed journal that publishes criticism of modern and contemporary
fiction from theoretical and historical perspectives. Issues of *MFS* alternate
between general issues and special issues that focus on a specific pre-
announced topic or single author. General issues have around twenty book
reviews in addition to scholarly articles. The book reviews are organized according to the following categories: "The Americas," "British, Irish, and
Postcolonial Literatures," and "Theory and Cultural Studies." *Modern Fiction Studies* accepts twenty-five of three hundred submissions each year. The
book reviews are by commission only. Special topic issues on Ford Madox
Ford and Joseph Conrad may be of interest to Edwardian scholars. Specific
articles include "Deconstruction, Radical Secrecy, and *The Secret Agent*,"
"Oxford's Ghosts: *Jude the Obscure* and the End of the Gothic," and "The
Failures of the Romance: Boredom, Class, and Desire in George Gissing's
The Odd Women and W. Somerset Maugham's *Of Human Bondage*." Index-
ing is available through *MLAIB* and *ABELL* for the journal's full run and in
Periodicals Index Online from 1955 to 1995. Purdue University indexes all
MFS volumes (www.cla.purdue.edu/academic/engl/mfs/MFSindex.htm).

Where *MFS* focuses on narrative fictions, **Modern Drama: World Drama
from 1850 to the Present** (**MD**) emphasizes scholarship on dramatic works

from around the globe from 1850 to the present. While it covers canonical playwrights and plays, *MD* also publishes scholarship on lesser-known works. Book reviews and peer-reviewed, scholarly articles comprise each issue. Eighteen out of one hundred article submissions received each year are accepted. Articles of interest to Edwardian scholars include "Granville Barker and Galsworthy: Questions of Censorship," "Hauntings: Anxiety, Technology, and Gender in *Peter Pan*," "Mirror up to Nurture: J. M. Synge and His Critics," and "Pastoral Elements in *John Bull's Other Island*." *MD* is indexed in *MLAIB* and *ABELL* from the first issue to the present and in *Periodicals Index Online* from 1958 to 1995. The University of Toronto Press also provides tables of contents from the final issue in 2007 to the most current issue (utpjournals.metapress.com/content/120885).

Since 1955, ***Twentieth Century Literature: A Scholarly and Critical Journal*** (***TCL***) has been published quarterly by Hofstra University. Like many twentieth-century journals, *TCL* does not exclusively discuss British literature but rather has articles on modern and contemporary literatures regardless their national origin. This peer-reviewed journal comprises only scholarly articles and excludes additional content such as book reviews and correspondence. In 1984, the first index to *TCL* volumes was created, providing an alphabetic index of all *TCL* articles from 1974 and 1984. After that, indexes were released every five years, in the fourth issue in the 1989 volume and in the first issue of the 1995, 2000, and 2005 volumes. Up until 1981, *TCL* incorporated an annotated bibliography of current scholarship in modern and contemporary literature into its issues. Only 10 percent of the two hundred article submissions received each year are accepted. Recent article topics include modernism in E. M. Forster's *The Longest Journey*, the mystic self in Henry James's *The Golden Bowl*, and Joseph Conrad's *Heart of Darkness* as first published in *Blackwood's Edinburgh Magazine*. *TCL* is indexed in *ABELL* and *MLAIB* for its full run and in *Periodicals Index Online* from 1955 through 1995.

AUTHOR-SPECIFIC JOURNALS

Brontë Studies: The Journal of the Brontë Society. Maney Publishing, 1895. 3/yr. ISSN: 1474-8932. Former titles: *Brontë Society. Transactions and Other Publications* 1895–1957; *Brontë Society Transactions* 1958–2001. maney.co.uk/index.php/journals/bst.

Conradiana: A Journal of Joseph Conrad Studies. Texas Tech University Press, 1968. 3/yr. ISSN: 0010-6356. www.ttup.ttu.edu/JournalPages/Conradiana.html.

Dickens Quarterly. Dickens Society of America, 1970. Quarterly. ISSN: 0742-5473. Former title: *Dickens Studies Newsletter* 1970–1984. www.umass.edu/english/dickens.

The Gaskell Society Journal. Gaskell Society, 1987. Annual. ISSN: 0951-7200. www.lang.nagoya-u.ac.jp/~matsuoka/EG-Journal.html.

In addition to general literary and period-specific periodicals, journals may be devoted to a single author. In spite of their emphasis on an individual, they often also publish articles on other authors and texts from the same time period. The journals discussed below do not comprise an exhaustive list of author-specific journals; rather, these are simply examples of the types of journals currently available. As with the period-specific journals, the preponderance of author-specific journals discussed in this section, and in publication, relate to the Victorian age. Many author-specific journals are sponsored by societies dedicated to a particular author and serve as an outlet for the society members' scholarship. This is true for the four journals discussed below.

Brontë Studies: The Journal of the Brontë Society has been published continuously since 1895, and is the only journal devoted to the lives, writings, and cultural influence of the Brontës. *Brontë Studies* was originally titled *Brontë Society. Transactions and Other Publications* until 1958, when it changed to *Brontë Society Transactions*. The title remained the same until 2002, when it assumed its current name. This peer-reviewed journal is issued three times a year and accepts twenty-five of the forty articles submitted annually. In addition to scholarly articles, *Brontë Studies* includes book reviews and notes. Indexing is available in *MLAIB* and *ABELL* from 1958 to the present and in *Periodicals Index Online* from 1895 to 1995.

Since 1968, ***Conradiana: A Journal of Joseph Conrad Studies*** has provided Conrad scholars a source for scholarship, criticism, biographical discoveries, textual studies, and book reviews. *Conradiana*, a publication of Texas Tech University Press in cooperation with the Joseph Conrad Society of America, is peer-reviewed and printed three times per year. Only slightly more selective than *Brontë Studies*, eighteen of the fifty articles submitted each year are accepted. Indexing is available in both *MLAIB* and *ABELL* from 1968 onward and in *Periodicals Index Online* from 1968 to 1995.

Founded in 1970 as the *Dickens Studies Newsletter*, ***Dickens Quarterly*** is a peer-reviewed publication of the Dickens Society of America and has been published under that name since 1984. *Dickens Quarterly* comprises scholarly and critical essays on Charles Dickens's life, times, and works; book reviews; review essays; notes; and a quarterly bibliography of Dickens studies. The bibliography, known as the "Dickens Checklist," covers primary sources, secondary sources, recent dissertations, websites of note, and miscellaneous publications. Roughly one-fourth of the fifty articles submitted annually are accepted. *Dickens Quarterly* is indexed fully in *ABELL* and *MLAIB* and from 1970 to 1995 in *Periodicals Index Online*. Tables of contents from volume 20, issue 4 (December 2005) to the most recent issue are available on the *Dickens Quarterly* website (www.dickensquarterly.org). The website also has calls for papers and Dickens Society Symposium announcements.

Beginning publication in 1987, *The Gaskell Society Journal* is a relatively young journal. The Gaskell Society prints this peer-reviewed journal annually, and each volume includes scholarly articles, book reviews, and notes on Elizabeth Gaskell's life, works, and times. Only half of the twelve to sixteen articles submitted each year are accepted. The *MLAIB* and *ABELL* index from 1987 onward. Tables of contents for each volume from 1987 to the previous year are on the journal's website, along with indexes of authors, subjects, and book reviews.

OTHER NON-LITERARY JOURNALS

The Economic History Review: A Journal of Economic and Social History. Wiley-Blackwell Publishing, 1927. Quarterly. ISSN: 0013-0117. www .wiley.com/bw/journal.asp?ref=0013-0117.

The English Historical Review. Oxford University Press, 1886. 6/yr. ISSN: 0013-8266. ehr.oxfordjournals.org.

Historical Abstracts. ABC-Clio, 1955. 6/yr. ISSN: 1531-1120. Former titles: *Historical Abstracts* 1955–1971; *Historical Abstracts: Part A: Modern History Abstracts, 1450–1914* 1971–2003; *Historical Abstracts: Part B: Twentieth Century Abstracts, 1914 to the Present* 1971–2003. www .abc-clio.com/products/serials_ha.aspx.

The Historical Journal. Cambridge University Press, 1923. Quarterly. ISSN: 0018-246X. Former title: *Cambridge Historical Journal* 1923–1957. journals.cambridge.org/action/displayJournal?jid=HIS.

Historical Research: The Bulletin of the Institute of Historical Research. Wiley-Blackwell Publishing, 1923. Quarterly. ISSN: 0950-3471. Former title: *University of London. Institute of Historical Research. Bulletin* 1923–1986. www.wiley.com/bw/journal.asp?ref=0950-3471.

History: The Journal of the Historical Association. Wiley-Blackwell Publishing, 1912. Quarterly. ISSN: 0018-2648. www.wiley.com/bw/journal .asp?ref=0018-2648.

Journal of British Studies. University of Chicago Press, 1961. Quarterly. ISSN: 0021-9371. Former title: *Albion* 1961–2005. www.journals .uchicago.edu/toc/jbs/current.

The Journal of Imperial and Commonwealth History. Routledge, 1972. Quar-
terly. ISSN: 0308-6534. www.tandf.co.uk/journals/titles/03086534.asp.
Past and Present: A Journal of Historical Studies. Oxford University Press,
1952. Quarterly. ISSN: 0031-2746. past.oxfordjournals.org.
Social History. Routledge, 1976. Quarterly. ISSN: 0307-1022. www.tandf
.co.uk/journals/titles/03071022.asp.
Twentieth Century British History. Oxford University Press, 1990. Quarterly.
ISSN: 0955-2359. tcbh.oxfordjournals.org.

This chapter's final section addresses non-literary journals that may also be
useful for Victorian and Edwardian research. As traditional disciplines become more interdisciplinary, both in their research emphases and in their
methodologies, conducting research outside the discipline is increasingly
important. As discussed throughout this chapter, history, religion, philosophy,
women's studies, sociology, and cultural studies are a few among many areas
that have overlapping interests with literature. In addition to having their own
journals, each discipline has its own major indexing sources for locating relevant articles. Rather than address each discipline's major index, this chapter
examines *Historical Abstracts*, one of history's major indexes, as a tool for
searching the contents of many of the journals discussed. The journals included do not comprise an exhaustive list of non-literary journals that may be
germane to your research, so conducting topical searches in other disciplines'
indexes may reveal additional relevant journals. The appendix to this book
introduces important general, art, history, language and linguistics, literary
terms and theory, music, philosophy, religion, science and medicine, social
sciences, and theater resources, as well as historical atlases and geographical
resources. This is a good starting point if you need to stray outside the confines of literary studies.

   ABC-CLIO's **Historical Abstracts** and its counterpart, *America: History &
Life*, support historical research in the same way that *MLAIB* and *ABELL*
serve literary studies. While *America: History & Life* covers scholarship on
United States and Canadian history from pre-history to the present, *Historical
Abstracts* indexes scholarship on the rest of the world from 1450 to the present. *Historical Abstracts* originated as a print index in 1955 and was released
under that uniform title until 1971, when it divided into two separate indexes:
Historical Abstracts: Part A: Modern History Abstracts, 1450–1914 and *Historical Abstracts: Part B: Twentieth Century Abstracts, 1914 to the Present.*
The index continued to be issued as separate parts until the two merged into
a single index under the original title—*Historical Abstracts.* According to the
publisher, *Historical Abstracts* covers the history of education, military history, women's history, and world history, among other topics, and has some

overlap with anthropology, genealogy, multicultural studies, political science, sociology, and other disciplines. Currently, more than eighteen hundred academic journals are indexed in *Historical Abstracts*. Additionally, books and dissertations are cited in this database. With more than six hundred thousand entries already included and growing by twenty thousand new entries each year, *Historical Abstracts* is one of the most comprehensive indexes for historical research.

Although ABC-CLIO used to host the content and search interface to both *Historical Abstracts* and *America: History & Life*, in the summer of 2007 ABC-CLIO partnered with EBSCO, another major publisher. In this partnership ABC-CLIO continues to supply the indexing and abstracting that comprise the contents of both databases, while EBSCO provides the search interface and linking to their vast full-text repositories. Through the EBSCO interface, scholars continue to have access to "CLIO Notes," which comprise chronologies, bibliographies, and overviews of historical events specific to both time period and geographic location. The "CLIO Notes" for nineteenth-century Europe are on "Boundaries, Conflicts, and Nation-Building," "Expanding Overseas: Colonization and Imperialism," "The Industrial Revolution and Technology," and "Culture, Society, and Ideology." The notes for twentieth-century Western Europe begin with World War I and continue on through the century, skipping over the Edwardian age. In *Historical Abstracts*, "CLIO Notes" are available for all time periods of African, Asian, European, Latin American, and Middle Eastern history.

To facilitate historical research, *Historical Abstracts* offers the option to limit to specific historical periods by year. Additional limiters are for full text, abstract, publication, document type, references available, peer-reviewed, year, publication type, and language. This index uses subject terms extensively. These terms can be searched in the subject field or browsed through the indexes. A search for *industrialization* as a subject and either *Great Britain or England* between *1830 and 1910* produces a list of 372 citations. A survey of the results reveals scholarship on customs, wages, and workload in industrial England, Elizabeth Gaskell's industrial novels, creation of Victorian values, masculinities in industrializing societies, and industrial towns in Northern England. Figure 5.1 shows a sample record from our search on British industrialization in the Victorian and Edwardian ages. As illustrated below, each record contains basic citation information, including article title, author, journal title, year, volume and issue numbers, and inclusive page numbers. Additionally, the record locates the article in a specific historical period, offers a list of pre-assigned subject headings to describe the article's intellectual contents, and identifies the publication type, document type, and language for the source cited. The abstract gives a summary, while the notes field provides source

Title:	**MASCULINITIES IN AN INDUSTRIALIZING SOCIETY:** *BRITAIN,* **1800–1914.**
Authors:	Tosh, John.
Source:	Journal of British Studies 2005 44(2): 330-342 13p.
Historical Period:	1800-1914
Subjects:	Great Britain
	Industrialization
	Social Attitudes
	Masculinity

Abstract: Examines masculinity as a key aspect of the economic, imperialist, and gendered dimensions of *British* industrial society during the "long" 19th century. A new work ethic, an emerging domestic sphere, and rejections of physical violence among the middle and upper-middle classes were all manifestations of changing senses of masculinity that mirrored economic conditions and class consciousness. The empire gave men an opportunity to escape these emergent *British* norms of masculinity. In the colonies, men could reenact "redundant" masculine characteristics, such as violence and homosocial camaraderie, free from the obligations of domesticity and marriage. Finally, the intensified emphasis on sexual difference, often referred to by scholars as the "two-sex model," affected *British* gender ideology and sharpened criticism of effeminate and homosexual men. [V. Wish]

Notes:	Based on documents in the Killie Campbell Library (Durban, South Africa), published documents, and secondary sources; 70 notes.
Publication Type:	Academic Journal
Document Type:	Article
Language:	English
ISSN:	0021-9371

Figure 5.1. Modified *Historical Abstracts* record for "Masculinities in an Industrializing Society: Britain, 1800–1914." Source: *Historical Abstracts*, via EBSCO.

document information. If you had been researching industrial Britain in literary sources alone, you may not have found this particular article, which might contain relevant historical information to shape your thinking about this research topic. Articles such as this one and those found in the journals discussed below may prove essential parts of your literary research.

Since 1927, *The Economic History Review: A Journal of Economic and Social History* (*EHR*) has recorded changes in economic and social history along with their cultural, intellectual, and political implications. Published quarterly by Blackwell-Wiley for the Economic History Society, each issue offers scholarly articles and book reviews on British and Irish economic history as well as general economic history. Articles are peer-reviewed and do not exceed 12,000 words in length. Occasionally issues also have editorials, corrigendum, erratum, and announcements. Semi-regular features also include the "Comments and Replies" section, which offers commentary on economic history issues or a reply to a previously published article, and the "Surveys and Speculations" section, which provides an "adventurous" approach to an economic history issue. Each volume's fourth issue indexes the full volume alphabetically by author within broad categories: "Surveys and Speculations," "Articles," "Comments and Replies," "Review of Periodical Literature," "Annual List of Publications," "Book Reviews," and "General." The "Review of Periodical Literature" is printed in each volume's first issue and covers periodical literature from two years prior to the current issue. For example, the first issue of volume 62 (2009) reviewed periodical literature from 2007. These reviews are written in essay form and survey a particular period of British and Irish economic history: 400 to 1100, 1100 to 1500, 1500 to 1700, 1700 to 1850, 1850 to 1945, and since 1945. Likewise the "Annual List of Publications" is available in each volume's final issue and covers the previous year's articles. The fourth volume of 2008, for instance, listed the 2007 publications on British and Irish economic and social history. Strictly bibliographic with no annotations, this section is organized into nineteen categories, such as: "Social Structure and the Family," "Labor Conditions and Organizations," "Religion and Education," "Leisure and Popular Culture," and "Sources and Archives." Recent article topics include the cottage industry, Irish industry, British railway companies, salesmen, the grain trade, and the poor. *Historical Abstracts* indexes *EHR* from 1927 to the present, and *Periodicals Index Online* indexes from 1927 through 1995.

Published six times annually, *The English Historical Review* primarily covers British history but also addresses European and world history from the classical age to the present and the history of the Americas. Oxford University Press has printed this peer-reviewed journal since 1886, making it the oldest English-language scholarly journal in historical studies. In addition to journal articles, regular features in *The English Historical Review* include notes and documents, review articles, book reviews, and shorter notices. Each year the journal also publishes notices of periodicals and occasional publications, mainly from the previous year. This section provides brief, one- to three-sentence annotations of scholarship that was published in a select list of journals, along with a truncated citation. These listings are organized in the following broad categories: historiography, record, and archive studies; general history; Africa; Americas; Asia and Australia; East Central Europe; France; Germany, Austria, Scandinavia, and Switzerland; Great Britain and Ireland; Italy; Middle East; Netherlands and Belgium; Russia, Southeast Europe, Byzantium; and Spain and Portugal. Articles printed in *The English Historical Review* generally do not exceed 15,000 words, and notes and documents do not exceed 7,500. Recent articles have covered the laissez-faire state, anti-opium campaigns, Irish Episcopal imperialism, unions, the 1883 Corrupt Practices Act, and the British Foreign and India Offices. *Historical Abstracts* indexes this journal going back to the first issue in 1886, and *Periodicals Index Online* indexes it from 1886 to 1995. *ABELL* also selectively indexes *The English Historical Review*.

Another major source of British historical scholarship is Cambridge University Press's **The Historical Journal (HJ)**, which, since 1923, has focused on British, European, and world history from the fifteenth century to the present. Despite the inclusion of European and world history, *HJ* is primarily a journal of British history. *The Historical Journal* was originally titled the *Cambridge Historical Journal* from 1923 to 1957, when it assumed its current name. This peer-reviewed journal is published quarterly and features scholarship from both new and established scholars. Each issue's regular components include research articles, communication, historiographical reviews, review articles, and other reviews. The communication section prints scholarly responses to recent articles. Each year *HJ* accepts approximately thirty-five articles that are roughly twenty to thirty-five pages in length. Recent article topics have covered hygiene in the British mining industry, the condition of Ireland question, British surveillance in Italy, factory politics, and early twentieth-century suffragette militancy. Indexing for *HJ* is available in *Historical Abstracts* from 1923 to the present, in *Periodicals Index Online* from 1923 to 1995, and selectively in *ABELL* from 1935 onward.

Begun in the same year as *The Historical Journal*, **Historical Research: The Bulletin of the Institute of Historical Research (HR)** covers medieval and modern history from a variety of approaches, including cultural, intellectual, political, social, and urban. Wiley-Blackwell publishes this journal on behalf of the Institute of Historical Research. Like *Historical Journal*, *HR* also welcomes scholarship from authors with varied levels of academic experience, from newly minted PhDs to seasoned scholars. *HR* is a peer-reviewed journal that is released quarterly. Until 1986, *HR* was titled *University of London. Institute of Historical Research. Bulletin.* In addition to the scholarly articles printed in each issue, editorial as well as notes and documents sections are occasionally included. Each volume's final issue also contains a contents section that lists the articles, notes, or documents printed in *HR* that year. Five to nine articles ranging from ten to twenty-five pages are printed in every issue. British views on Belgium, land reform, Promenade Concerts, censuses, fire services, Gladstone's friendship with Laura Thistlethwayte, and public service rewards have all been covered in recent issues. *Historical Abstracts* indexes *HR* from 1923 to the present, while *Periodicals Index Online* covers 1923 to 1995. The journal's website also provides free access to tables of contents from 1977 to 1996, from 2003 to the present, and for forthcoming articles (www.history.ac.uk/historical).

History: The Journal of the Historical Association covers European history with a heavy emphasis on British history. *History* has been the journal of the Historical Association since 1912 and is currently published by Blackwell-Wiley. Released quarterly, articles are written from various historiographical approaches: cultural, ecclesiastical, economic, political, and social. Each issue comprises four to five peer-reviewed, critical or review articles and a substantial book review and short notices section. Editorials, notes on contributors, letters to the editor, authors' notes, and erratum are occasionally included. The volume's final issue provides an index to books reviewed or noticed in that volume. Until the July 2007 issue, the reviews and short notices were subdivided according to books regarding general, medieval, early modern, late modern, the Americas, and Africa, Asia, and Australasia, but beginning with the October 2007 issue, the reviews and short notices were printed without division by time period or geographic area. Articles vary in length between fifteen and thirty pages, while reviews and short notices tend to be one to two pages in length. The Peterloo massacre, Gladstone and Disraeli's relationship, fertility and the poor, British parliament and national identity, gambling, and the smallpox vaccine were all covered in recent issues. *Historical Abstracts* indexes *History* from the first issue onward and in *Periodicals Index Online* from 1912 to 1995.

Since 1961, the University of Chicago Press has published the **Journal of British Studies (JBS)** as the official publication for the North American Conference of British Studies (NACBS). Originally titled *Albion* from 1961 to 2005, *JBS* comprises peer-reviewed, critical articles on all time periods and aspects of British history and culture. Each quarterly issue has six to seven articles and a substantial book review section. Occasionally, issues also include a roundtable of viewpoints on a particular issue or piece of scholarship.

Articles range in length from twenty to thirty pages, and book reviews range between one and three pages. The scholarly and review articles in *JBS* cover a wide variety of disciplinary areas, including art, economics, gender studies, literature, political science, and religion. Recent issues have addressed topics such as Victorian art museums, the Contagious Diseases Acts, property ownership, globalization, Catholic identity, cosmopolitanism and nationalism, and missionaries. *JBS* is indexed in *Historical Abstracts* from 1961 onward and in *Periodicals Index Online* from 1961 to 1995. *MLAIB* and *ABELL* have spotty indexing coverage from 1961 onward.

The impact of imperialism and empire cannot be ignored in research of Victorian and Edwardian literature. For scholars particularly interested in those topics, **The Journal of Imperial and Commonwealth History (*JICH*)** is an excellent source. Currently, Routledge publishes the journal quarterly, but through 2005, it was printed three times a year. Begun in 1972, this peer-reviewed journal accepts articles on British Empire and Commonwealth history as well as the history of other European colonies. At its core, this journal comprises peer-reviewed, critical articles. Issues may contain sections on introduction, debates, review essays, book reviews, miscellany, customs, and obituary. Depending on how many additional sections are in each issue, the number of articles varies from three to twelve. Recent article topics are British color-consciousness, masculinity and missionaries, the sugar plantation economy in Mauritius, Christian-Muslim marriage, free-trade imperialism, and medical impressions of Sub-Saharan Africa. *The Journal of Imperial and Commonwealth History* is indexed in *Historical Abstracts* from 1972 until the present and in *Periodicals Index Online* from 1972 to 1995.

Since 1952, **Past and Present: A Journal of Historical Studies** is a forum for discussing cultural, historical, and social changes around the globe. Although the journal describes itself as having a global focus, in practice most articles relate to British history, culture, and society. Oxford University Press publishes the journal on behalf of The Past and Present Society, which also produces a book series for Cambridge University Press. The journal welcomes scholarship from both new and established scholars and aims to create productive scholarly debate through its articles. Each quarterly issue generally contains six or seven peer-reviewed articles and occasionally includes a debate on a particular issue, a review article, or a conference note. The articles tend to be rather lengthy, ranging from twenty-five to fifty pages. Recent articles have covered topics such as sodomy and class, the Durham diocese, Irish nationalists, regional identity, protest and politics, political posters, class in pre-war Britain, and public worship. Because of shifts in the publishing markets, *Past and Present* recently began offering an online supplement, which has essay collections that are freely available to journal subscribers.

Currently supplements have been released on "The Religion of Fools? Superstition Past and Present," "Rodney Hilton's Middle Ages: An Exploration of Historical Themes," and "The Art of Survival: Essays in Honour of Olwen Hufton." *Past and Present* is indexed in *Historical Abstracts* from 1952 to the present and in *Periodicals Index Online* from 1952 to 1995.

Another interdisciplinary journal is Routledge's **Social History (SH)**, which was first published in 1976. This peer-reviewed journal emphasizes research on the social and cultural histories of all geographic areas in all time periods, from the medieval through the twentieth century. *Social History* encourages interdisciplinary approaches and is interested in research that addresses issues of class, gender, and ethnicity. Each quarterly issue comprises abstracts, articles, reviews, short notices, and a list of books received. Occasionally, scholarly discussions, review articles, and conference reports are also included. A typical issue contains two to five articles that range in length from fifteen to thirty pages each. Recent topics are the cotton industry, images of India, the moral economy, picturesque carnivals, organized consumer movements, sanitary inspection, and master-apprentice relations. *Social History* is indexed from the first issue to the current issue in *Historical Abstracts* and from 1976 to 1995 in *Periodicals Index Online*.

First printed in 1990, **Twentieth Century British History (TCBH)** is a relatively recent addition to the corpus of history scholarship. Published quarterly by Oxford University Press, *TCBH* aims to cover all aspects of twentieth-century British history. Given the period coverage, *TCBH* is more useful for Edwardian scholars than for Victorian scholars, although even Edwardian scholars will find that many articles do not directly relate to the early twentieth century. Each issue contains four or five peer-reviewed, critical articles that range between twenty and thirty-five pages in length; additionally, the journal also has book reviews with the exact number ranging from none to thirteen reviews in a given issue. Issues occasionally include review articles, obituaries, lectures, and notes. Recent scholarly articles have covered topics such as the Treasury and the trustees of the National Gallery, juvenile courts, welfare cultures, monarchical display and the politics of empire, new Liberalism, the settlement movement, and children's education in the Jewish East End. *Historical Abstracts* indexes each issue of *TCBH*.

CONCLUSION

This chapter has given you an overview of major journals in literary studies and allied fields for studying the literature, history, and culture of the Victorian and Edwardian ages in Britain. The journals described here are representative of the journal types you should consider in your research, but are by no means intended to be either exhaustive or limiting. Other journals not mentioned here may also be valuable resources of scholarship for your particular research topic. As research becomes increasingly interdisciplinary, keeping abreast of overlaps in content and methodology between literature and other traditional academic disciplines becomes even more important. While literature and history seem to have a very natural relationship, your research may lead you into areas less closely aligned with literary studies, including the history of science and technology, religion and philosophy, economics, and psychology. The bibliographies and indexes, such as *MLAIB* and *ABELL*, previously discussed in chapter 4, will help you find specific articles and expand your knowledge base on your research topic. Likewise, indexes and bibliographies from other disciplines may help you uncover many relevant journal articles that would not typically be included in a literary resource. To learn more about major resources in other disciplines, see the Appendix at the end of this book.

This chapter and the preceding four chapters have focused heavily on the print and online resources available for finding secondary sources. Literary reference sources, library catalogs, bibliographies and indexes, and journals may help you conduct primary-source research as well, but for more in-depth, scholarly research, you must be exposed to several types of specialized resources. The following chapters will guide you through resources for finding and accessing primary sources from the Victorian and Edwardian ages. These chapters introduce you to contemporary reviews and literary magazines, period journals and newspapers, microforms and digital collections, and manuscripts and archives. Additionally, these chapters explain methods of primary-source research.

Chapter Six

Contemporary Reviews and Literary Magazines

It is by our reviews, magazines, and journals, that the vast majority of professional authors earn their bread; and the astonishing mass of talent and energy which is thus thrown into periodical literature is not only quite unexampled abroad, but is, of course, owing to the certainty of moderate yet, on the whole, sufficient remuneration.

—George Henry Lewes,
"The Condition of Authors in England, Germany, and France,"
Fraser's Magazine for Town and Country 35, no. 205 (1847): 288–89.

Although the novel has often been touted as the nineteenth century's major genre, scholars should not underestimate the importance of Victorian and Edwardian periodicals for the literary and critical reviews they printed. Most minor and major authors initially published their works in periodicals before being reprinted in triple-decker, yellowback, or single-volume form.[1] Although serialized fiction did not originate in the Victorian age, serialization became a primary mode for disseminating new, creative works as the century progressed. As Edward Bulwer-Lytton wrote in *England and the English*:

It is a great literary age—we have great literary men—but where are their works? A moment's reflection gives us a reply to the question[;] we must seek them not in detached and avowed and standard publications, but in periodical miscellanies. It is in these journals that the most eminent of our recent men of letters have chiefly obtained their renown.[2]

Some of the many authors who built readerships and developed their literary reputations through periodicals include Beerbohm, Bulwer, Carlyle, Conrad, Dickens, Eliot, Kipling, Ruskin, Swinburne, Tennyson, and Yeats. While many serialized novels were later republished in book form, others were only ever published in periodicals, making this form of publication an even more important resource for scholars. Likewise, they are also the major literary review source. These reviews are essential for helping scholars understand how contemporary critics received particular creative works. Prior to discussing specific resources, it may be helpful to review the history and development of Reviews and literary magazines as periodical types.[3]

The early Victorian age marked a crucial shift in the role of British Reviews and literary magazines. During the eighteenth and early nineteenth centuries, the Review as a distinctive periodical type was in its heyday. Major publications such as the *Edinburgh Review* and the *Quarterly Review* provided both literary criticism and political viewpoints. Reviewers wrote with seeming authority and were most often protected under the guise of anonymity, two characteristics which would fade as the nineteenth century progressed. Early nineteenth century reviews were highly esteemed; however, as Walter Graham suggests in his seminal work *English Literary Periodicals*, the "critical importance of these Reviews waned as scores of more specialized magazines and literary journals entered the field" in the mid- to late nineteenth century,[4] when Reviews declined in number and periodicals increasingly targeted niche audiences.

Whereas earlier Reviews relied on the authority of the anonymous critic, later nineteenth-century periodicals published more works by named authors. The Victorian age also saw greater integration of book reviews (as an article type) with original creative works in a single publication. At the turn of the nineteenth century, Reviews and literary magazines were quite distinguishable from one another, but by the turn of the twentieth century, "Poetry and fiction appeared in the Reviews" while "reviews became more common ingredients in magazines."[5] Genre mixing caused periodical types to be less distinctive. As the nineteenth century progressed and gave way to the twentieth century, book reviews as a discrete article format became more prevalent than the Review. Additionally, more literary magazines were published throughout the century. The increase in literary magazines was driven largely by the demands of the reading public. Both the cultural elites and the general populous craved new literary output. As novelist Wilkie Collins wrote in his essay "The Unknown Public," "the future of English fiction may rest with this Unknown Public," which will "command the service of the best writers of their time."[6] For Collins, the "Unknown Public" represented the driving force behind the literary marketplace. Reviews and literary magazines met the many demands of the reading public.

Although creative works and reviews are valuable resources for Victorian and Edwardian scholars, there are no comprehensive sources for locating them. While numerous sources index nineteenth- and early twentieth-century periodicals, they often fail to specify which periodical contributions are reviews and which are literary. This chapter surveys major resources for finding period literary magazines, literary reviews and criticism, and creative writing. A final segment discusses representative author-specific sources that index the literary criticism and contributions of particular Victorian and Edwardian authors. Although this chapter emphasizes reviews and literary magazines, the sources discussed in chapter 7 on period journals and magazines are also worth consulting. Scholars interested in period periodical publications should consult this chapter and the next in conjunction with one another. Additionally, chapters 8 through 10 guide you to full-text sources for many reviews and literary magazines found in microform and digital collections, manuscripts and archives, and Web resources.

LOCATING PERIOD LITERARY MAGAZINES

Graham, Walter. *English Literary Periodicals*. New York: Octagon, 1966.

Sader, Marion. *Comprehensive Index to English-Language Little Magazines, 1890–1970, Series One*. Millwood, NY: Kraus-Thomson Organization, 1976.

Stanton, Michael N. *English Literary Journals, 1900–1950: A Guide to Information Sources*. Detroit: Gale, 1982.

Sullivan, Alvin. *British Literary Magazines*. 4 vols. Westport, CT: Greenwood Press, 1983–1986.

Tye, J. Reginald. *Periodicals of the Nineties. A Checklist of Literary Periodicals Published in the British Isles at Longer than Fortnightly Intervals, 1890–1900*. Oxford: Oxford Bibliographical Society, 1974.

White, Robert B., Jr. *The English Literary Journal to 1900: A Guide to Information Sources*. Detroit: Gale, 1977.

Published in 1930, Walter Graham's **English Literary Periodicals** is the first survey of English literary periodicals from 1665 through the end of the nineteenth century. Rather than indexing periodical literature, *English Literary Periodicals* is a narrative guide to the history and development of literary periodicals published in England. This volume will be useful for scholars who desire to understand how a particular journal or magazine fits into English publishing history. The book begins its coverage prior to Queen Anne's reign, and throughout the volume discusses specific periodicals such as the *Tatler*, the *Gentleman's Magazine*, and the *Edinburgh Review*, and subgenres such as single-essay periodicals, critical reviews, literary magazines, and weekly journals of belles-lettres. *English Literary Periodicals* also provides an excellent bibliography of late nineteenth- and early twentieth-century scholarship on English literary periodicals, and an index to titles, authors, editors, contributors, and significant writers. Despite its early publication date, Graham's work remains the seminal book on the history and development of English literary periodicals.

British Literary Magazines surveys publications from 1698 to 1984 in four period-specific volumes: *The Augustan Age and the Age of Johnson, 1698–1788*; *The Romantic Age, 1789–1836*; *The Victorian and Edwardian Age, 1837–1913*; and *The Modern Age, 1914–1984*. The third volume is obviously the most relevant volume for Victorian and Edwardian scholars; however, *The Romantic Age* may also be of interest to scholars researching the early Victorian age. Each volume has a preface and introduction that contextualize the volume within the set's aims and describe the volume's contents. A bibliography of general works on Victorian and Edwardian newspapers, periodicals, and little magazines follows the introduction. The *Victorian and Edwardian Age* volume has eight appendixes covering titles discussed in all four volumes in the set; a chronology of social events, literary events, and British literary magazines from 1837–1913; nineteenth-century foreign reviews; Victorian comic journals; and nineteenth-century religious magazines with literary contents. The Victorian and Edwardian volume comprises profiles of ninety literary magazines and addresses 209 others in the appendixes. Due to the proliferation of nineteenth- and early twentieth-century literary magazines, only a sampling was included. Magazine entries are alphabetically arranged and discuss each magazine's history, literary contributions and significance, information sources for further research, and complete publication history. *The Bookseller*, *Cosmopolis*, *The Hobby Horse*, *The Monthly Review*, *Notes & Queries*, *The Review of Reviews*, and *Yellow Book* are among the literary magazines profiled in this resource.[7] Each volume concludes with an index of people, titles, and subjects.

For late Victorian and Edwardian publications, the ***Comprehensive Index to English-Language Little Magazines, 1890–1970*** indexes one hundred little magazines published between 1890 and 1970. Although fifty-nine are from the United States, the remaining little magazines hail from a variety of countries, including England, Ireland, Switzerland, Canada, the Netherlands, New Zealand, Australia, and Scotland. Little magazines as a genre developed from the literary magazine tradition and have frequently been the first to publish the output of the late nineteenth- through twenty-first-century literary movements. These periodicals also published many experimental and early attempts by authors who later became major literary figures. The *Comprehensive Index* is a guide to a segment of this important body of literature. This eight-volume set is organized alphabetically by subject or contributor's last name. Each entry may comprise the following information: heading, joint author, article title, translator name, article type, little magazine title, issue number, issue date, and article pagination. The article type field indicates whether each work is an article, review, poem, prose, fiction, illustration, or other form. Late Victorian and Edwardian authors such as Oscar Wilde, George Eliot, and G. K. Chesterton are all included. The first volume's preface contains a note on the resource's organization, a list of abbreviations used for the contributors' roles and type of work, and a complete list of magazines indexed. No additional finding aids are provided in this set.

Part of *American Literature, English Literature, and World Literatures in English: An Information Guide Series, The English Literary Journal to 1900: A Guide to Information Sources* and its counterpart *English Literary Journals: 1900–1950: A Guide to Information Sources* are guides to scholarship on literary periodicals' history and development. Although *The English Literary Journal to 1900: A Guide to Information Sources* emphasizes literary periodicals, Robert B. White Jr., the bibliography's author, chose to include citations for select resources on newspapers, since the early history of newspapers and periodicals overlapped significantly. The bibliography is organized into five major chapters on bibliographies and bibliographical aids, general studies, periodicals, persons, and places. The entries within each chapter provide bibliographic citations and occasional references to reviews of a particular work or a brief explanatory note. The periodicals chapter is organized alphabetically by title, with studies on a particular periodical listed under its heading. Likewise, the persons and places chapters are subdivided according to specific people or locations, respectively, with individual studies listed under each subheading. Indexes to authors, periodicals, persons, and places conclude the volume.

Following in the tradition of the previous volume, *English Literary Journals: 1900–1950: A Guide to Information Sources* annotates roughly 135 literary journals published in England between 1900 and 1950. Unlike many resources, *English Literary Journals: 1900–1950* focuses strictly on publications from England and excludes those from Scotland, Wales, and Ireland. This guide covers major publications such as the *Times Literary Supplement* and lesser-known little magazines like the *Adam International Review*. The preface overviews literary journals, their history, and development throughout the first half of the twentieth century. This slim volume is organized into two parts: journals and bibliography. The journals section has an alphabetical listing of literary periodicals, and each entry comprises the title, previous titles and accompanying dates, publication frequency, editors, and a brief description of the journal's contents and publishing history. The bibliography section lists general references; background readings; autobiography,

biography, and letters; and critical and historical commentary on individual journals. *English Literary Journals* concludes with an author and title index and a journal index.

In addition to broader guides to literary periodicals, niche resources such as J. Reginald Tye's ***Periodicals of the Nineties. A Checklist of Literary Periodicals Published in the British Isles at Longer than Fortnightly Intervals, 1890–1900*** are also useful. Published by the Oxford Bibliographical Society, this checklist began as the basis for Tye's dissertation at the University of Oxford and developed into a guide to British literary periodicals published between January 1890 and December 1899. This slender volume is organized in four parts: analysis of periodicals, publishers, printers, and editors. The largest portion is devoted to the analysis of periodicals, which lists 138 periodicals and provides information regarding title, place of publication, date, volume and number, frequency, illustration, average number of pages, price, publisher, printer, editor, and principal locations for each periodical. The remaining parts—publishers, printers, and editors—are indexes to and expansions of the information included in the first part. In spite of its brief length, *Periodicals of the Nineties* is a highly accessible overview of periodical publications from the late nineteenth century.

LOCATING REVIEWS AND CRITICISM IN VICTORIAN AND EDWARDIAN PERIODICALS

19th Century Masterfile. Austen, TX: Paratext. www.paratext.com.

Book Review Digest. New York: H. W. Wilson, 1905.

Book Review Digest Retrospective. New York: H. W. Wilson, 1905. Also available online at www.hwwilson.com.

C19: The Nineteenth Century Index. Ann Arbor, MI: ProQuest, 2005. www .proquest.com.

Cushing, Helen Grant, and Adah V. Morris, eds. *Nineteenth Century Readers' Guide to Periodical Literature, 1890–1899: With Supplementary Indexing, 1900–1922*. 2 vols. New York, H. W. Wilson, 1944.

JSTOR: The Scholarly Journal Archive. New York: JSTOR, 1995. www.jstor.org.

Periodicals Archive Online. Ann Arbor, MI: ProQuest. Available online at www.proquest.com.

Periodicals Index Online. Ann Arbor, MI: ProQuest. Available online at www.proquest.com.

Poole, William Frederick. *Poole's Index to Periodical Literature*. 6 vols. Glouchester, MA: P. Smith, 1963. Also available online through the *19th Century Masterfile* and *C19: The Nineteenth Century Index*.

Readers' Guide Retrospective: 1890–1982. New York: H. W. Wilson, 1890–1982. Available online at www.hwwilson.com.

Readers' Guide to Periodical Literature. New York: H. W. Wilson, 1900. Available online at www.hwwilson.com.

Poole's Index to Periodical Literature, which is described more fully in chapter 7, can also help you identify period book reviews and criticism. Available in a six-volume print set and electronically through *C19: The Nineteenth Century Index* and *19th Century Masterfile*, *Poole's* is not strictly a review index; however, its organization makes it an excellent tool for finding this type of article. In total, *Poole's* indexes 479 periodicals that were published between 1802 and 1906; however, roughly 35 percent are British, while the remaining 65 percent are American. All *Poole's* entries are classified under an alphabetical list of subjects. Scholars should first identify the terms that best characterize their research topic and then look under those headings to find relevant citations. A scholar researching how George Eliot's novel *Middlemarch* was received by her contemporaries could look under the heading for Eliot. Most *Poole's* volumes list her as *Eliot, George*; however, the 1882 to 1887 volume cross-lists from *Eliot, George* to the main entry: *George Eliot*. Under these headings, citations for articles about her and her works are listed. Since the novel was published serially between 1871 and 1872 and then later published in book form, you would need to look in each volume to identify all potentially relevant citations. Unfortunately, because citations are not annotated, you must make your decisions based on the publication information alone. One nice feature of *Poole's* in print is that it collocates reprinted versions of the same article. For instance, in the 1892–1896 volume, an entry for an article about George Eliot and *Middlemarch*'s main character, Dorothea Casaubon, states that the same text was printed in *Contemporary Review, Littell's Living Age*, and *Eclectic Magazine*. In addition to the print, major online indexes—*19th Century Masterfile* and *C19: The Nineteenth Century Index*—allow you to search across all *Poole's* entries and volumes. While online searching may sometimes be more efficient, it doesn't always provide the straightforward, linear organization of the print index.

When using **19th Century Masterfile** (**NCM**) to search *Poole's*, keep in mind that your terms will be matched to records in any of the sixty indexes comprising *NCM*. While many results outside of *Poole's* may also be relevant, you can choose to view only the *Poole's* citations after you have conducted the initial search. Perhaps one of the most efficient ways to use this interface to locate reviews is to search for the literary work's title and the word *review*. Based on the default settings, *19th Century Masterfile* automatically performs a Boolean *and* search and looks for both singular and plural forms of the terms. A search for *Middlemarch review* retrieves matches in *Poole's Index to Periodical Literature, Stead's Index to Periodicals, Atlantic Monthly Index,* and *North American Review.* These are all either multi-title or single-title periodical indexes. In total, fifteen reviews of *Middlemarch* are identified through this search. While most date from 1873, the same year the inexpensive "Guinea Edition" was published and the year following the four-volume edition, a couple of citations are from 1894. Another way to search for information on *Middlemarch* is to browse for keywords in all fields. Browsing for *Middlemarch* retrieves twenty-three citations dating between 1873 and 1900. While the first search required the term *review* be present in the record, this browsing technique uncovers records about *Middlemarch*, including reviews as well as early literary criticism of the novel. Because the browse keyword index only contains single word entries, it is more effective to use the term *Middlemarch* than *George, Eliot,* or a combination of the two.

C19: The Nineteenth Century Index also allows you to search *Poole's* and a different set of period indexes. Unlike *19th Century Masterfile,* which does not let you search one index at a time, *C19* enables scholars to search across all indexes or within a specific index such as *Poole's.* One efficient way to search *Poole's* through the *C19* interface is by browsing the *Poole's Index* for *Eliot George.* This reveals a number of relevant subject headings that are as general as *Eliot, George* or as specific as *Eliot, George and Dorothea Casaubon, her Theory of Realism.* Links to specific article citations are listed under each heading. There is no heading specific to *Middlemarch*; however, there are numerous headings about Eliot and Dorothea Casaubon, the novel's heroine. A search using each of the forty-two George Eliot subject headings produces a list of sixty-three articles, including criticism of *Middlemarch*, even though the novel is not explicitly mentioned in any of the headings or all of the entries. A scholar could also search *Poole's* in *C19* using *Middlemarch* as a keyword, retrieving seventeen results, most of which are book reviews. An expanded search for *Middlemarch* as a keyword in all *C19* indexes retrieves 169 citations for books, periodical articles, and reference materials. The results come from the *Nineteenth Century Short Title Catalogue, British Periodicals, Poole's, Periodicals Index Online, American Periodicals Series,* the *Wellesley Index to Victorian Periodicals,* and the *Dictionary of Nineteenth Century Journalism.* Knowing that these other indexes contain citations related to Eliot's *Middlemarch*, you might decide to search them individually to make sure that you have found all relevant, unique reviews.

Described more fully in chapter 7, the *Nineteenth Century Readers' Guide to Periodical Literature, 1890–1899* is an excellent source for locating literary reviews. While only fourteen of the fifty-one indexed periodicals are British, the *Nineteenth Century Readers' Guide* can help scholars understand how a work was received both in the United Kingdom and the United States. Although it covers only a small segment of Britain's publishing history, its clear subject organization makes it incredibly useful for scholars seeking journal articles in general and book reviews specifically. As with *Poole's*, subject entries are arranged alphabetically with citations listed underneath; however, *The Nineteenth Century Readers' Guide* takes the organization one step further. Rather than simply having a topical heading, such as *Browning, Elizabeth (Barrett) (Mrs. Robert Browning)*, this index has subdivisions as appropriate. In this case, "Influence" and "Poems about" are offered as narrower terms. Some headings have no subdivisions, while others have a greater number. For instance, scholars researching Barrett Browning's husband, *Browning, Robert, 1812–1889*, will find "About," "Bibliography," "Characters," "Criticism and interpretation," "Homes and Haunts," "Parodies," "Poems about," and "Societies" listed underneath. For each main heading and subdivision, citations are given for topic-specific articles. Amid the citations for Barrett Browning, scholars will find book reviews and early literary criticism such as T. Bradfield's "Ethical Impulse of Mrs. Browning's Poetry" (*Westminster Review* 146 [1896]: 174–84) and E. Gosse's "Origin of the Sonnets from the Portuguese" (*Critic* 25, no. 22 [1894]: 398).

The initial two-volume readers' guide was then continued by the **Readers' Guide to Periodical Literature**, which currently covers 1900 through 2008. The *Readers' Guide* is available both as an annual print index and an online database. The online version is available as *Readers' Guide Retrospective: 1890–1982* and *Readers' Guide to Periodical Literature*, which covers 1983 to the present. For Victorian and Edwardian literature, the early print volumes and retrospective online product are the relevant parts of this valuable index. **Readers' Guide Retrospective: 1890–1982** is available through H. W. Wilson and allows searching across all volumes of the *Nineteenth Century Readers' Guide* and its successor. Scholars should use the date limiters to ensure that results were published during the Victorian and Edwardian ages. One particularly nice feature of *Readers' Guide Retrospective* is the ability to specify which document type—book review, feature article, short story, or poem—will appear in the results. If you are seeking reviews or early literary criticism, then the book review and feature article document types may both be relevant. For example, if you searched for book reviews about *Sonnets of the Portuguese* published between 1890 and 1910, you would find no results. If you ran that same search but chose feature article instead of book review as document type, then the database would retrieve one result: Gosse's article mentioned above. Because you can search all words in each record, you could search for elements such as author, title, subject, and historical subject. The other highly useful component of *Readers' Guide Retrospective* is that it can connect to your library's link-resolving technology, making it easier to determine whether your library owns the document you are seeking.

Another Wilson product for locating Edwardian book reviews is *Book Review Digest*, and its online counterpart, *Book Review Digest Retrospective*. **Book Review Digest** was published in print from 1905 to 2004. While some libraries may still own the print volumes, it is currently only available online as **Book Review Digest Retrospective**, which covers 1905 to 1982, and *Book Review Digest Plus*, which includes 1983 to the present. Although its dates make it less useful for Victorian scholars, its 1905 to 1910 coverage supports Edwardian scholars. Offering searching in fields such as keyword, subject, title, personal author, review author, and LC classification, it is perhaps best for locating reviews for known texts or authors. To find reviews for a specific publication, search for that work as a title. A search for *Crystal Age* as a title and *Hudson* as a personal author retrieves records for the two editions: the original 1907 edition and a later one from 1916. Each record provides a full citation for W. H. Hudson's novel, along with citations for reviews of that edition. *Book Review Digest Retrospective* is a tremendous resource for locating book reviews, and should prove to be a timesaver for scholars.

Major interdisciplinary resources such as *JSTOR*, *Periodicals Archive Online*, and *Periodicals Index Online* can also be used to find book reviews. (These three resources are all discussed in more detail in chapter 4.) To locate book reviews in **JSTOR**, the simplest method is to run a full-text search for the author or title as phrases and limit to reviews. If necessary, you could also specify a date range. A search for *Charles Reade* and *The Cloister and the Hearth* in reviews published between 1861 and 1864 retrieves one review, from an 1864 issue of *The North American Review*. Another tactic could be to search for Reade alone, limiting to dates within his lifetime, in order to assess how his contemporaries received him and his work. A search for *Charles Reade* in articles and reviews between 1851, the year his first play was performed, and 1884, the year of his death, retrieves twenty-eight results, many of which are reviews. Because *JSTOR* can search in each article's full text, be sure to evaluate the results carefully, since not all will be relevant. Finding reviews in *JSTOR* from this time period is a hit-or-miss venture, so don't be discouraged if it does not contain a review for the text or author you are researching.

Periodicals Archive Online (**PAO**) and **Periodicals Index Online** (**PIO**) have much broader purposes than supplying book reviews and early criticism; however, like *JSTOR* they index some period journals and allow you to limit to reviews as the document type. Nineteenth-century reviews and criticism are frequently classified as articles rather than book reviews, so if you search for reviews of a particular author and title and receive no results, try including both document types. To understand responses to Matthew Arnold's *Culture and Anarchy*, you could search for *Arnold Culture Anarchy* as keywords, limiting to articles and book reviews published between 1867, the year of its publication, and 1888, the year of Arnold's death. In *PAO*, this retrieves thirty-nine articles, including reviews in the *Edinburgh Review* and the *Contemporary Review*. In *PIO*, the same search pulls up a list of eight articles, some of which are reviews and commentary on Arnold's work and some of which are Arnold's serialized writings about anarchy and culture. Because *PIO* indexes more journals than *PAO*, it may seem that it should produce more results; however, the absence of full text in *PIO* requires that search terms must match the record, where in *PAO* terms may be found in the documents themselves.

LOCATING CREATIVE WRITING IN VICTORIAN AND EDWARDIAN PERIODICALS

Boyle, Andrew. *An Index to the Annuals*. Vol. 1. Worcester: Andrew Boyle, 1967.
Curran, Eileen M. "The Curran Index: Additions to and Corrections of the Wellesley Index to Victorian Periodicals." *Victorian Research Web*. victorianresearch.org/curranindex.html. Also available online through *C19: The Nineteenth Century Index*.
Houghton, Walter E., ed. *The Wellesley Index to Victorian Periodicals, 1824–1900*. 5 vols. Toronto: University of Toronto Press, 1966–1989. Also available online through *C19: The Nineteenth Century Index*.
Vann, J. Don. *Victorian Novels in Serial*. New York: Modern Language Association of America, 1985.
Victorian Fiction Research Guide. St. Lucia, Australia: The University of Queensland, 1979–1998.

The Wellesley Index to Victorian Periodicals, 1824–1900 and *"The Curran Index: Additions to and Corrections of the Wellesley Index to Victorian Periodicals"* are valuable tools for locating creative works in nineteenth-century publications. Both are discussed in more detail in chapter 7. The print *Wellesley Index* is best for browsing the contents of a particular periodical or for consulting the contributor index (volume 5) to find what a certain author wrote. For instance, under the heading for *Gaskell, Elizabeth Cleghorn (Stevenson), 1810–1865, novelist*, fourteen brief citations are listed that cross-reference to main entries in the first four volumes. Some of these entries cover multiple periodical articles. For instance, *Wives and Daughters* was published in *The Cornhill Magazine* in eighteen installments between August 1864 and January 1866, but it is represented in one entry in the contributor index. If, then, you look in volume 1, which includes *The Cornhill Magazine*, you will find individual entries for the *Wives and Daughters* installments. While creative works are fairly easy to locate, there is no good way to identify reviews or literary criticism, as the articles are not classified by their purpose.

The *Wellesley Index* is also available online from ProQuest both as a stand-alone product and as a component of *C19: The Nineteenth Century Index*. As a separate resource, the online *Wellesley Index* allows scholars to search across all citations included in the print version, along with updates provided by the *Curran Index*. Using the same example as above, you could select *Gaskell, Elizabeth Cleghorn (Stevenson), 1810–1865, novelist* from the contributor list. Searching under her name in all dates produces thirty-seven results from periodicals such as *Fraser's Magazine for Town and Country* and *The Dublin University Magazine*. Browsing the contributor index also lets you quickly survey an individual's contributions to *Wellesley* periodicals. Alternately, you could look for a particular literary work, such as *Wives and Daughters*, in the "article title" field. This search retrieves eighteen results, each representing an installment of this serialized novel in *The Cornhill Magazine*. For both author and title searches, you can either select from a list or enter your own words into the box. On the one hand, if you browsed for *Wives and Daughters* in the article title list, then you would have the option to select any or all of that novel's installments. On the other hand, searching for the terms brings up all matches automatically. Through *C19* scholars could search in the same way, but have the option to choose whether to search *Wellesley* independently or in conjunction with other indexes.

The University of Queensland began publishing the **Victorian Fiction Research Guide** series in 1979 with *Sarah Grand: 1854–1943: A Bibliography* and concluded the series in 1998 with *Indexes to Fiction in Windsor Magazine (1850–1910)*. In total, thirty-two volumes were published in the series, covering individual authors and fiction in specific Victorian periodicals. In addition to the volumes that index a particular author's writings or a specific periodical's contents, one volume indexes the letters of G. A. Sala to Edmund Yates. Authors such as Grand, Yates, Margaret Oliphant, Mrs. Humphry Ward, and Bram Stoker[8] are indexed along with fiction in *The Quarto*, *Tinsley's Magazine*, *Pall Mall Magazine*, *Belgravia*, *The Idler*, and *The London Illustrated News*.[9] Each volume begins with a detailed introduction to the periodical's history, format, themes, readerships, and contents. The author-specific volumes list the corpus of the individual's work by genre, including both published and manuscript works, and the periodical-specific volumes index by author and by chronology. Entries contain brief, unannotated citations with author, article title, volume, and inclusive page numbers. Dates vary from periodical to periodical, with titles such as *The Idler* extending from 1892 to 1911 and *The Windsor Magazine* from 1850 to 1910. Likewise, the author coverage varies depending on the years of a specific author's literary production. These brief volumes should prove excellent resources for scholars studying a particular author or attempting to identify literary content in periodicals.

Though few guides to serialized nineteenth-century fiction exist, those that have been published are valuable sources of information on the original editions of major Victorian novels. J. Don Vann's ***Victorian Novels in Serial*** serves two primary purposes: as an introduction to serialization and as a guide to serialized Victorian novels and their installments. This slender volume begins by introducing the history of serialization, its effects on authorship, publication problems, and serial parts' endings. The bulk of *Victorian Novels in Serial* addresses the serialized fiction of Ainsworth, Collins, Dickens, Eliot, Gaskell, Hardy, Kingsley, Kipling, Bulwer-Lytton, Marryat, Meredith, Reade, Stevenson, Thackeray, Trollope, and Ward, who were selected based on their inclusion in Lionel Stevenson's *Victorian Fiction: A Guide to Research* and George Ford's *Victorian Fiction: A Second Guide to Research*.[10] In total, 192 serialized works from sixteen authors are included. The contents are organized alphabetically by author and with works by publication date under each author. For example, *Yeast*, *Hypatia*, and *Hereward the Wake* are listed as Charles Kingsley's fiction. The original publication details are recorded along with serialized parts, dates, and information on how those parts map to chapters in the volume edition of each work. Although Vann does not include publication information for editions following the original serialization, this volume is highly valuable as an amalgamation of often difficult-to-find information about serial editions. This book concludes with notes on Victorian periodicals and their publication runs, and a selected bibliography on general works and individual authors.

Published posthumously in 1967, Andrew Boyle's ***An Index to the Annuals*** covers British annuals from 1820 to 1850. The set's first volume, which indexes authors, was the only volume published. Although a second volume on artists in the annuals was intended, those plans never came to fruition, and the set remains incomplete. Despite its age and incomplete state, there are no competing indexes to early nineteenth-century British annuals. In this time period, the annuals contained predominantly literary content. Boyle's index comprises an alphabetic listing by last name of both named and identified authors to the annuals' contents. Each author's contributions are listed under his or her name, and initials and pseudonyms cross-reference to the author's full name, when known. In addition to the primary index to named and identified authors, this volume contains indexes to contributions "by the author(s) of" and anonymous contributions. *An Index to the Annuals* covers twenty-four annuals, including titles such as *Forget-me-not, Friendship's Offering, Winter's Wreath, Keepsake,* and *Christmas Box,* and published works by authors such as Benjamin Disraeli, Thomas Kibble Hervey, Leigh Hunt, Catherine Charlotte Maberly, Emma Roberts, and John Ruskin. This work concludes with three brief appendixes on the history of the following annuals: *The Bijou,* 1828–30 and *The Cameo,* 1831; *Janus* or the *Edinburgh Literary Almanac,* 1826; and *Friendship's Offering* or the *Annual Remembrancer,* 1824–44.

AUTHOR-SPECIFIC SOURCES

Churchill, R. C., ed. *A Bibliography of Dickensian Criticism 1836–1975.* New York: Garland Publishing, 1975.

Fulmer, Constance Marie. *George Eliot: A Reference Guide.* Boston: G. K. Hall, 1977.

Harden, Edgar F. *A Checklist of Contributions by William Makepeace Thackeray to Newspapers, Periodicals, Books, and Serial Part Issues, 1828–1864.* Victoria, BC: University of Victoria, 1996.

McNees, Eleanor, ed. *The Brontë Sisters: Critical Assessments.* 4 vols. East Sussex: Helm Information, 1996.

Sherry, Norman, ed. *Conrad: The Critical Heritage.* Boston: Routledge & Kegan Paul, 1973.

Among criticism bibliographies are works such as *A Bibliography of Dickensian Criticism 1836–1975* and *George Eliot: A Reference Guide,* which have citations not only for current criticism but also for contemporary criticism and reviews published during the author's lifetime. For the purposes of this chapter, these resources are important more for their historic coverage than their current coverage. ***A Bibliography of Dickensian Criticism 1836–1975*** is a thorough yet not quite comprehensive overview of Dickens criticism. The entries are organized into six broad categories: "Introduction," "General Criticism: Nineteenth Century," "General Criticism: Twentieth Century," "Criticism of Particular Works," "Aspects of Dickens," and "Critical Comparisons." Each category is further subdivided into narrower topics. For instance, the general criticism of the nineteenth and twentieth centuries are broken down by narrower time periods, and "Aspects of Dickens" is divided into subcategories such as his popularity, Dickens in Italy, his symbolism, and Dickens the journalist. The sections for nineteenth- and twentieth-century general criticism most obviously contain contemporaneous criticism, but other sections have citations to nineteenth- and early twentieth-century criticism as well, which should be easy to identify as the publications are listed according to publication date. Each entry has a bibliographic citation, and some have brief annotations. To facilitate access to the bibliography's contents, this volume offers cross-referencing and an index to chief critics and commentators.

Like the Dickens bibliography, *George Eliot: A Reference Guide* contains current and contemporary criticism of Eliot's works. *George Eliot* is an annotated bibliography to writings published between 1858 and 1971 about Eliot and her work, with entries organized chronologically. Within each year, entries are further divided according to Eliot's books and her shorter writings. Researchers should consult the section on her shorter writings even when researching one of her book-length works such as *Middlemarch*, because early criticisms often addressed the serialized publication rather than the later triple-decker and single-volume works. Because of the chronological organization, it should be easy to identify criticisms published during Eliot's lifetime. *George Eliot* concludes with an index to her works that lists reference numbers for pertinent entries, title and author indexes to writings about Eliot and her work, and a subject index to secondary texts.

Edgar F. Harden's *A Checklist of Contributions by William Makepeace Thackeray to Newspapers, Periodicals, Books, and Serial Part Issues, 1828–1864* is a guide to Thackeray's publications regardless of format or genre. This checklist records 957 certain publications and seventy-seven probable publications. Thackeray's writings are listed by year—beginning with 1828 and ending in 1864—and by specific date within year. Each citation contains full bibliographic details including page numbers. An appendix of sixty-three possible illustrations drawn by Thackeray and published in *Punch* concludes this volume.

Published by Helm Information between 1990 and 2008, the *Critical Assessments of Writers in English Series* comprises twenty-three works. Each work provides an introduction, bibliographies, chronology, and chronological overview of criticism for a particular author or group of authors. The series covers both American and British authors primarily from the late eighteenth through early twentieth centuries. *The Brontë Sisters: Critical Assessments* is one of the works specific to the Victorian age. Other volumes in the series cover authors such as Thomas Hardy, E. M. Forster, and Charles Dickens, and may also be of interest to Victorian and Edwardian scholars. Edited by Eleanor McNees, this four-volume set includes an introduction, a "Chronology of the Lives of the Brontë Sisters," bibliographies of primary and secondary sources, and a "Chronological List of Criticism Included." In addition to bibliographic resources, *The Brontë Sisters* reprints the full text of both early and recent criticism, as is standard in the series. In this volume, the earliest critical pieces include reviews of *Jane Eyre*, *Wuthering Heights*, and *Agnes Grey*, while later works represent modern literary criticism on the Brontës. This is an excellent source for locating and comparing early reviews and criticism, which can be invaluable in understanding the reception of a particular literary work.

In addition to the *Critical Assessments of Writers in English Series* discussed above, Routledge's *Critical Heritage Series* is a tremendous source for criticism of major authors from the seventeenth through the twentieth century. The series covers the authors such as Matthew Arnold, George Eliot, Ford Madox Ford, Anthony Trollope, and Oscar Wilde. **Conrad: The Critical Heritage** is one of the many books in this series. This single-volume work introduces Joseph Conrad and assesses contemporary criticism of his fiction. *Conrad* provides full-text reviews of nineteen works, such as *Almayer's Folly* (1895), *Lord Jim* (1900), *Youth: A Narrative and Two Other Stories* (1902), *Nostromo* (1904), *The Secret Agent* (1907), *Victory* (1915), and *Suspense* (1925). The number of reviews reprinted for each work varies, but as a whole, this can help scholars understand the reception of Conrad's works and save both time and effort in locating period reviews. A select bibliography and index conclude this work. To determine if your library has volumes from either series discussed here, search the catalog by series title: *Critical Assessments of Writers in English Series* or *Critical Heritage Series*.

CONCLUSION

The resources discussed in this chapter should equip you to locate and research reviews and literary magazines of the Victorian and Edwardian ages. The nineteenth- and early twentieth-century reviews are precursors to modern literary criticism that scholars so depend upon and are essential resources for gauging the critical reception of particular literary works. Serialized fiction, short stories, poetry, and other creative works published in literary magazines often constitute that work's first edition and, as such, require as much critical attention as triple-deckers, yellowbacks, and single-volume works. Scholars researching contemporary reviews and literary magazines should also consult many of the resources discussed in the following chapter on period journals and newspapers in order to be exhaustive in their research.

NOTES

1. In Victorian England, novels were published in three volumes for circulating libraries such as Mudie's Select Circulating Library. These three-volume editions were referred to as "triple-deckers." Yellowbacks were the precursors to our modern-day paperbacks. They were "frequently translations or reprints," and "when original

fiction appeared in this format, it was typically by minor authors." Only after 1894 did single-volume novels become the standard. Patrick Brantlinger and William B. Thesing, introduction to *A Companion to the Victorian Novel*, eds. Patrick Brantlinger and William B. Thesing (Malden, MA: Blackwell, 2002), www.blackwellreference .com (accessed April 18, 2010).

2. Lytton, Edward Bulwer-, *England and the English* (5th ed. Paris: Baudry's European Library, 1836), 190.

3. Throughout this chapter, Review as a periodical type is capitalized while review as an article type is in lowercase letters.

4. Walter Graham, *English Literary Periodicals* (New York: Thomas Nelson and Sons, 1930), 248.

5. Ibid., 266.

6. Wilkie Collins, "The Unknown Public," *Household Words* 18 (21 August 1858): 217–22.

7. Published between 1894 and 1897, the *Yellow Book* was a literary and art periodical edited by Henry Harland and Aubrey Beardsley. It has no connection to the yellowbacks discussed in endnote 1 above. *Dictionary of Nineteenth-Century Journalism*, s.v. "*Yellow Book* (1894-1897)," http://c19index.chadwyck.com (accessed April 18, 2010).

8. The full list of authors includes Sarah Grand, Jessie Fothergill, Edmund Yates, Mary Cholmondeley, Frances Cashel Hoey, Margaret Oliphant (volumes for fiction and non-fiction), Mrs. Humphry Ward, Rosa Praed, Rosa Nouchette Carey, Philip Meadows Taylor, Edmund Yates Papers, Elizabeth Robins, Francis Adams, Bram Stoker, Mary Fortune, Caroline Clive, Victoria Cross, and Grant Allen.

9. The full list of periodicals includes *Time, Murray's Magazine, The Quarto, The Lady's Realm, Tinsley's Magazine* (later *The Novel Review*), *Pall Mall Magazine, The Harmsworth Magazine* (later *The London Magazine*), *Cassell's Family Magazine* (later *Cassell's Magazine*), *Belgravia, Chamber's Journal, The Idler, The London Illustrated News, The Graphic*, and *The Windsor Magazine*.

10. The Brontës, Disraeli, Gissing, Butler, and Moore were also discussed in Stevenson's and Ford's guides but were excluded from *Victorian Novels in Serial* because their works were not published serially.

Chapter Seven

Period Journals and Newspapers

A man without a newspaper is half-clad, and imperfectly furnished for the battle of life. From being persecuted and then contemptuously tolerated, it has become the rival of organized governments. Will it become their superior?

—W. T. Stead, "The Future of Journalism,"
The Contemporary Review 50 (July–December 1886): 663.

Stead's words, first published in 1886 in *The Contemporary Review*—a "high-culture journal" of the late nineteenth and twentieth centuries—illustrate journalism's importance in the late Victorian age, an importance that had been building throughout the century.[1] Broader than the reviews and literary magazines discussed in the previous chapter, period journals and newspapers are excellent sources of cultural, historical, and political information on the Victorian and Edwardian ages. While not explicitly literary in nature, they too published literature, literary criticism and reviews, and information about authors' lives. Neither journals nor newspapers were nineteenth-century inventions, yet both substantially increased in readership throughout the Victorian and Edwardian ages due to the abolition of the stamp taxes in the mid-nineteenth-century, advances in printing technologies, and improved literacy rates.

Although the British press developed throughout the early nineteenth century, its expansion rate was significantly slower than other industries of the time. The greatest impediments to press growth were the so-called Taxes on Knowledge imposed by the British government.[2] Originating in the early eighteenth century, these taxes comprised a stamp tax on newspapers, an advertisement tax, and a paper tax. Burdened by these duties, newspapers, particularly, were limited in producing affordable publications and tended to cater to the wealthier British citizenry, greatly limiting circulation numbers.

One by one, the taxes were repealed with the advertisement tax abolished in 1853, the stamp tax in 1855, and the paper tax in 1861. Each repeal increased the affordability of newspapers and allowed for press growth. Because the stamp tax had specifically targeted publications containing news, periodicals were less hampered by the knowledge taxes than newspapers. As the nineteenth century progressed, technological advances in printing—transitioning from man-powered printing presses to steam printing, stereotyping, and rotary printing—and typesetting—moving from hand setting to composing machines and then the linotype machine—improved the efficiency of the presses, enabling larger press runs, which in turn increased profits. Along with printing technology advancements, papermaking processes changed in the mid-nineteenth century. Switching from rag paper to wood pulp paper decreased costs. With larger runs and reduced prices, newspapers and periodicals were available to a wider audience of readers. Working-class readers particularly benefited from the enhanced affordability of serial publications.

Another factor contributing to the growth in newspaper and periodical publications was the increasing literacy rate for the nineteenth century. The wealthier British citizenry traditionally had access to quality education and, in turn, had high literacy rates throughout the century; however, education for the working class lacked standardization and was often poor quality. Nonetheless, as the nineteenth century progressed, legislation such as the 1870 Education Act helped to improve the quality of education for working-class citizens. As education improved, literacy rates rose, and as literacy rates rose, the readerships for journals and newspapers also increased.

When using period journals and newspapers, consider consulting multiple titles in your information search. Where the large urban dailies such as *The Times* and *The Standard* provided more national and foreign news, the provincial papers such as the *Manchester Guardian* and *The Newcastle Courant* served "as critics and populisers of local government policies" and were known for "their expert handling of local economic interests."[3] Scholars should also be aware that many period newspapers and journals were highly partisan and that particular political groups or politicians financially supported many titles. A Gladstonian newspaper might present a far different story than a Whig newspaper. Understanding the political leanings of the publications you are using is crucial for conducting balanced research.

It is also important to recognize the differences between the newspapers and periodicals of the nineteenth and early twentieth centuries. Filled with topical essays, literary works, art, and policy discussions, periodicals did not fill the same news-providing role as newspapers. Much as newspapers had become engrained in British society throughout the nineteenth century, periodicals were equally important to British readers. As one anonymous author described it in 1886: "It is as hard to conceive of a time when there were no periodicals in circulation as it is to imagine the existence of a human body without any flow of blood."[4] While newspapers broadly presented the news, periodicals targeted narrower readerships and, as such, many catered to the reading interests of niche markets, including religious groups, families, women, specific occupations and commerce, professions, the arts, popular culture, workers' unions, and student groups. Scholars should also note the frequency with which these formats were published. Newspapers were often printed as dailies, weeklies, or Sunday papers, and journals frequently appeared quarterly or monthly, although many were published irregularly.

This chapter overviews the scholarly resources available for researching newspapers and journals of the nineteenth and early twentieth centuries. The resources are organized according to background information, tools for locating period newspapers and journals, tools for locating articles, journal- and topic-specific sources, and period journal and newspaper collections. The background information sources provide contextual information on the history and development of British newspapers and journals and serve as guides to more in-depth research. Sources such as *The Union List of Victorian Serials*, the *British Union-Catalogue of Periodicals*, and the *Waterloo Directories* comprise the section on locating newspapers and journals, while sources such as *Poole's Index to Periodical Literature* and the *Wellesley Index* provide article-level information. The final sections discuss representative sources that index a particular journal or a certain author's serial publications, and full-text microform and digital collections of period journals and newspapers.

BACKGROUND INFORMATION ON
PERIOD JOURNALS AND NEWSPAPERS

Brake, Laurel, and Marysa Demoor, eds. *Dictionary of Nineteenth-Century Journalism*. London: British Library, 2009. Also available online through *C19: The Nineteenth Century Index*.

Griffiths, Dennis, ed. *The Encyclopedia of the British Press, 1422–1992*. New York: St. Martin's Press, 1992.

Madden, Lionel, and Diana Dixon, comps. *The Nineteenth-Century Periodical Press in Britain: A Bibliography of Modern Studies, 1901–1971*. Toronto: Victorian Periodicals Newsletter, 1975.

RSVP Bibliography. The Research Society for Victorian Periodicals. www.rs4vp .org/bib.html.

Uffelman, Larry K., comp. *The Nineteenth-Century Periodical Press in Britain: A Bibliography of Modern Studies, 1972–1987.* Edwardsville, IL: Victorian Periodicals Review, 1992.

VanArsdel, Rosemary T. "Victorian Periodicals: Aids to Research: A Selected Bibliography." 8th ed. *Victoria Research Web.* www.victorianresearch.org/periodicals.html.

Vann, J. Don, and Rosemary T. VanArsdel, eds. *Victorian Periodicals: A Guide to Research.* 2 vols. New York: Modern Language Association of America, 1978–1989.

To understand the production history and development of British newspapers and journals, you may need to consult some research guides and background sources before beginning your research. Sources such as such as *Victorian Periodicals: A Guide to Research* offer an excellent assessment of resources and methods for researching Victorian periodicals, while the *RSVP Bibliography* introduces scholars to criticism and studies on the nineteenth- and early twentieth-century periodical press. Additionally, encyclopedias such as the *Dictionary of Nineteenth-Century Journalism* and *The Encyclopedia of the British Press, 1422–1992* provide important contextualizing information about British journalism and press history.

Although twenty years have passed since the second volume's publication, J. Don Vann and Rosemary T. VanArsdel's two-volume set—***Victorian Periodicals: A Guide to Research***—remains the standard guide to researching Victorian periodicals. The first volume, published in 1978, addresses problems and methods specific to researching Victorian periodicals published between 1824 and 1900, the same dates covered by the *Wellesley Index.* Volume 1 is organized into eight chapters, with the first chapter addressing reasons for reading Victorian periodicals and the remaining chapters addressing bibliographic control, finding lists, biographical resources, press histories, histories and studies of individual periodicals, identifying authors, and circulation and the stamp tax. Each chapter provides thorough narrative discussion of the resource type, along with bibliographic citations. An index to persons, topics, and works and two appendixes—a descriptive guide to the contents of the stamp returns, 1824–1870, and some sample circulations derived from the stamp returns, 1829–1854—conclude the first volume. The second *Victorian Periodicals* volume complements rather than updates the first. This addition has chapters on constructing the Victorian reality, periodicals of the 1890s, publisher archives, the radical and labor press, periodicals and art history, British women's serials, religious periodicals, serialized novels in magazines, magazines for children, Scottish periodicals, the Welsh periodical press, and desiderata and agenda for the twentieth century. An index and five appendixes to finding lists for Victorian periodicals, biographical resources, general histories of the press, histories and studies of individual periodicals from 1976–1986, and the *Wellesley Index* conclude the volume.

Rosemary T. VanArsdel continued her research of Victorian periodicals with *"Victorian Periodicals: Aids to Research: A Selected Bibliography."* Online and in its eighth edition, *Victorian Periodicals* resides on Patrick Leary's *Victoria Research Web*, which is discussed in greater detail in chapter 10. VanArsdel provides updated resource lists that account for recent scholarly contributions to Victorian periodical studies, and incorporates electronic resources into the bibliography. This Web guide lists citations for 192 resources categorized as general references, modern technology, biographical sources, obituaries, histories of individual periodicals, and critical commentary.

Originally published in *Victorian Periodicals Newsletter* (*VPN*) and in the *Victorian Periodicals Review* (*VPR*), the *RSVP Bibliography* is the creation of the Research Society for Victorian Periodicals (RSVP). For more on *VPN* and *VPR*, see chapter 5 on scholarly journals. The *RSVP Bibliography* is an annotated listing of articles, books, dissertations, and reviews about periodicals that were published in Great Britain between 1800 and 1914. While the bibliography is largely British in focus, select entries are included for periodicals of the United States, Ireland, and other countries. This resource surveys scholarship on Victorian periodicals in general, specific periodicals, and related topics; however, in spite of its usefulness, the *RSVP Bibliography* is not entirely exhaustive in its coverage. Each edition of the bibliography has an introduction, references, a subject index, and a title listing of journals. The references section is organized according to four areas: bibliographies, finding lists, and reports on bibliographical projects; general history of periodicals and newspapers; studies of individual periodicals and newspapers; and studies and memoirs on proprietors, editors, journalists, and contributors. Scholars may access the *RSVP Bibliography* either by consulting individual issues of *VPN* or *VPR* or by viewing select issues on the RSVP website. Although the website does not yet contain each iteration of the bibliography, it lists all *RSVP Bibliography* issues. *The Nineteenth-Century Periodical Press in Britain: A Bibliography of Modern Studies, 1901–1971* and *The Nineteenth-Century Periodical Press in Britain: A Bibliography of Modern Studies, 1972–1987* also compile and expand upon the bibliographies printed in *VPN* and *VPR*.

In addition to research guides such as *Victorian Periodicals* and the *RSVP Bibliography*, scholars may need to consult reference sources for background information. Although literary encyclopedias are discussed in greater detail in chapter 2, two encyclopedias on the British periodical press are worth mentioning here: *The Encyclopedia of the British Press, 1422–1992* and *The Dictionary of Nineteenth Century Journalism*. Both will help you better understand the history and development of British periodicals, journalism, and press. The **Dictionary of Nineteenth-Century Journalism (DNCJ)** was published in 2009 by the British Library in London, Academia Press in Ghent, Belgium, and online by ProQuest as a component of *C19: The Nineteenth Century Index* (see chapter 4 for more on *C19*). The *DNCJ* was designed to provide quick reference information about British and Irish print journalism of the nineteenth century. This resource comprises 1,620 entries about periodicals and newspapers, journalists and editors, publishers and proprietors, illustrators, printers, distributors and inventors, and topics such as answers to readers, basket boys, broadsides and chapbooks, fiction syndication, literature and journalism, and reviews. In addition to the entries, *DNCJ* has a chronology of the nineteenth-century press in Britain and Ireland from 1711 to 1896 and a bibliography of print, electronic, and archival resources on nineteenth-century journalism. This single-volume work also offers a list of acronyms, associate editors, and contributors, and an index to names, topics, and titles.

When published in 1992, Dennis Griffiths's **The Encyclopedia of the British Press, 1422–1992** became the first printed account of the history and development of British journalism and newspapers. This encyclopedia is composed of more than three thousand entries "on newspaper journalists and personalities, national and provincial newspapers, and terms, ideas, places and events connected with the British press." The entries are arranged alphabetically and tend to be rather brief, with select entries offering bibliographies. Entries cover a range of topics such as former *Sunday Times* and *Observer* editor Rachel Beer, playwright and former editor of *Punch* Sir Francis Cowley Burnand, Graham Greene, the *Sunderland Echo*, tabloid, *The Western Morning News*, and yellow journalism. *The Encyclopedia of the British Press* also has substantial essays on the history and development of British newspapers from the early newspaper press in England to the post-WWII press in Britain. Additionally, this single-volume work contains a British press chronology, national and regional circulation statistics, and guides to women and Fleet Street editors for major publications from the eighteenth century to the late twentieth century. Overviews of and contact information for major British newspaper associations and essays on editors and women in British journalism are provided in the encyclopedia's back matter. The final element is a select, thematic bibliography to resources on the British press, including general reference and history, nineteenth century, twentieth century, newspaper histories, and newspaper collecting.

LOCATING PERIOD JOURNALS AND NEWSPAPERS

Allen, P. E., comp. *Catalogue of the Newspaper Library Colindale*. 8 vols. London: British Library, 1975.

British Union-Catalogue of Periodicals Incorporating World List of Scientific Periodicals: New Periodical Titles. London: Butterworths, 1964–1981.

Doughan, David, and Denise Sanchez. *Feminist Periodicals 1855–1984: An Annotated Critical Bibliography of British, Irish, Commonwealth, and International Titles*. Brighton, Sussex, Great Britain: The Harvester Press, 1987.

Fulton, Richard D. *Union List of Victorian Serials: A Union List of Selected Nineteenth-Century British Serials Available in United States and Canadian Libraries*. New York: Garland, 1985.

Hewitt, A. R. *Union List of Commonwealth Newspapers in London, Oxford, and Cambridge*. London: Athlone Press, 1960.

Newspaper Catalogue. British Library, at www.bl.uk/reshelp/inrrooms/blnewspapers/newscat/newscat.html (accessed 20 April 2010).

North, John S. *The Waterloo Directory of English Newspapers and Periodicals, 1800–1900*. Waterloo, ON: North Waterloo Academic Press, 1994. Also available online at www.victorianperiodicals.com.

———. *The Waterloo Directory of Irish Newspapers and Periodicals, 1800–1900*. Waterloo, ON: North Waterloo Academic Press, 1986.

———. *The Waterloo Directory of Scottish Newspapers and Periodicals, 1800–1900*. 2 vols. Waterloo, ON: North Waterloo Academic Press, 1989.

Tercentenary Handlist of English & Welsh Newspapers, Magazines & Reviews. London: Dawsons of Pall Mall, 1966.

Shattock, Joanne, ed. *The Cambridge Bibliography of English Literature*. 3rd ed. Vol. 4. New York: Cambridge University Press, 1999.

Stewart, James D., et al. *British Union-Catalogue of Periodicals: A Record of the Periodicals of the World, from the Seventeenth Century to the Present Day, in British Libraries*. 5 vols. plus supplements. London: Butterworths Scientific Publications, 1955.

Stratman, Carl J. *A Bibliography of British Dramatic Periodicals, 1720–1960*. New York: The New York Public Library, 1962.

Toase, Charles A., ed. *A Bibliography of British Newspapers*. London: Library Association, Reference, Special and Information Section, 1975.

Watson, George, and Ian Willison, eds. *The New Cambridge Bibliography of English Literature*. 5 vols. Cambridge: Cambridge University Press, 1969–77.

Wiener, Joel H. *A Descriptive Finding List of Unstamped British Periodicals, 1830–1836*. London: Bibliographical Society, 1970.

Wolff, Michael. *The Waterloo Directory of Victorian Periodicals, 1824–1900*. Waterloo, ON: Wilfrid Laurier University Press, 1977.

Discussed in greater detail in chapter 2, the *New Cambridge Bibliography of English Literature (NCBEL)* and the *Cambridge Bibliography of English Literature (CBEL)* are worth mentioning here as tools for locating period-specific newspapers and periodicals and studies on them. Volume 3 in the *NCBEL*, which covers 1800 to 1900, lists resources on newspaper and magazine technical development, journalism history, the daily and weekly press, magazines and reviews, school and university journalism, and annuals and yearbooks; and for 1900 to 1950, volume 4 cites historical and general studies, journalism, accounts of individual newspaper and magazine publishing, individual newspapers and magazines, and lists, indexes, and directories. Additionally, *CBEL*'s fourth volume provides updated resource lists for nineteenth-century newspapers and magazines using the same categories as *NCBEL*'s third volume.

The *Union List of Victorian Serials: A Union List of Selected Nineteenth-Century British Serials Available in United States and Canadian Libraries* was published in 1985 as an aid for researching the Victorian age, which this volume defines as 1824 to 1900. Based on the periodicals listed in the third volume of the *NCBEL*, the *Union List of Victorian Serials* is not comprehensive but highlights the holdings of 1,779 Victorian serials in North American libraries. This single-volume work offers a guide to library codes, a user's guide, and an abbreviations guide. The union list is organized alphabetically by serial title, and each entry contains an entry number, the publication title, the *Waterloo Directory* number, the *NCBEL* number, and bibliographic description and notes related to the publishing history and title changes. This information is followed by a list of North American libraries and their exact holdings. The *Union List of Victorian Serials* is not limited to literary journals but incorporates serials from a wide variety of disciplinary areas. Literary journals such as *Bentley's Miscellany*, *The Edinburgh Review*, *Household Words*, *The Literary Gazette*, and *The Yellow Book* are included alongside non-literary journals such as *Brain: A Journal of Neurology*, *The English Chartist Circular*, *The Englishwoman's Domestic Magazine*, *The Jewish Chronicle*, and *The Musical Times and Singing Class Circular*. Since library holdings are subject to change, check the specific library's catalog to determine current holdings before travelling to research a particular serial.

Compiled by A. R. Hewitt, the *Union List of Commonwealth Newspapers in London, Oxford, and Cambridge (ULCN)* details British libraries' holdings for newspapers from former British colonies in Africa, Asia, the Caribbean, Oceania, and North America. Although this union list is somewhat dated, having not been updated since its original publication in 1960, it still is likely a useful resource for researchers interested in the British Commonwealth during the nineteenth and early twentieth centuries. The *ULCN* entries are largely comprised of newspapers held in the British Museum's Newspaper Library at Colindale, which is discussed in more detail below, with smaller collections from libraries in London, Oxford, and Cambridge represented as well. The entries are categorized by country of origin and then alphabetically within country. As with entries from the *British Union-Catalogue of Periodicals*, which is discussed below, the *ULCN* entries contain the newspaper's original title and detailed holdings information for specific libraries. The entries also mention title changes for each newspaper listed. Because of *ULCN*'s publication date, many countries have since changed names, so researchers will have to keep in mind former names for British colonies as they use this resource. A wide variety of former colonies are included, such as Australia, Bechuanaland, Ceylon, Mauritius, Rhodesia and Nyasaland, Singapore, and Turks and Caicos Islands. The volume concludes with an alphabetical title index.

The **British Union-Catalogue of Periodicals: A Record of the Periodicals of the World, from the Seventeenth Century to the Present Day, in British Libraries** (*BUCOP*) was initially published in four volumes in 1955, with a supplement added in 1962. The catalog records global periodical publication history from the seventeenth century to the mid-twentieth century, and details the location of existing periodicals in British libraries. *BUCOP* covers a variety of periodical types: magazines, journals, and reviews; acta, mitteilungen, proceedings, and transactions; research reports; yearbooks and annual publications; and miscellaneous publications such as series. Despite the broad definition this catalog uses for periodicals, several common periodical types are excluded: newspapers, variant issues of periodicals, periodicals not printed in type, administrative reports, publishers' series, and local and territorial directories, guides, handbooks, timetables, and similar publications. In total, details for 140,000 periodicals from 440 libraries are included. This set provides an arrangement and use guide, transliteration tables for Bulgarian, Russian and Ukrainian, Serbo-Croatian, and Modern Greek, and a library symbol guide. The periodical entries are arranged alphabetically by title and chronologically for periodicals having the same title. To account for name changes, each periodical is listed by its original title with mention of subsequent titles. The catalog cross-references from subsequent titles back to the main entry, which comprises the periodical's title, the dates covered, the volume and issue numbers published, and information about holdings in British libraries. The supplement updates the original set and has entries for new periodicals issued between 1955 and 1960. *BUCOP* remains a highly useful source for scholars seeking to locate historic periodicals; however, since holdings change over time, researchers should double-check the individual library's online catalog to confirm current holdings before travelling to view specific periodicals.

Following publication of *BUCOP*, the National Central Library published the **British Union-Catalogue of Periodicals Incorporating World List of Scientific Periodicals: New Periodical Titles**. As its title suggests, the new publication continues the *BUCOP* and incorporates another periodical guide: the *World List of Scientific Periodicals*. This catalog contains comparable information to *BUCOP* with information about new publications and updated holdings information. The *British Union-Catalogue of Periodicals Incorporating World List of Scientific Periodicals* was published in aggregate volumes that cover 1960 to 1968 and 1969 to 1973. Following publication of the second aggregated volume, updates were published annually from 1974 until 1980. After 1980, this work was superseded by *Serials in the British Library*, which accounts for new periodical acquisitions made by the British Library and select other major libraries since 1981.

The **Tercentenary Handlist of English & Welsh Newspapers, Magazines & Reviews** lists English and Welsh periodicals and newspapers from 1620 to 1919. Unlike *BUCOP* and *ULCN*, which contain holdings information, the *Tercentenary Handlist* simply provides a bibliographical record for newspapers, magazines, and reviews. This single-volume work is divided into two major sections: the London and suburban presses and the provincial press. Each section lists bibliographic information by year and then alphabetically within year. Both sections extend coverage until 1919; however, the first section begins in 1620, while the second begins in 1701. The two sections also have separate introductions discussing the origins and development of newspapers, magazines, and reviews in the geographic region covered. An alphabetic title index concludes each section. Each entry comprises the work's title, inclusive publication dates, known title variants, and known editors.

Serving as a basis for later Waterloo directories, **The Waterloo Directory of Victorian Periodicals, 1824–1900** was developed on behalf of the Research Society of Victorian Periodicals (RSVP) and Waterloo Computing in the Humanities to provide a single source for information on all newspapers and periodicals published in England, Ireland, Scotland, and Wales between 1824 and 1900. The introduction to *The Waterloo Directory* outlines seven major uses of this volume: to verify a publication's existence, to distinguish between similarly titled publications, to clarify each periodical's publishing history, to identify a publication's interests, to help locate particular issues of a periodical, to survey Victorian literature, and to enhance bibliographic control of Victorian periodicals. *The Waterloo Directory* draws on the *Tercentenary Handlist*, *BUCOP*, the *British Museum Catalogue of Newspapers, 1801–1900*, *Newspaper Press Directory*, and the *Union List of Serials in the USA and Canada*. Nearly twenty-nine thousand periodicals are listed. Organized alphabetically, the entries may contain information on title, subtitle, numbering, publication dates, editors and dates, publication location and dates, publisher and dates, price and dates, size, frequency, illustrations, circulation and dates, issuing body and dates, indexing, notes, mergers and dates, and subsidiary and alternate titles. Cross-references from subsequent, alternate, and subsidiary titles direct researchers back to the periodical's main entry. *The Waterloo Directory* has no holdings information, but serves as a basis for the later additions to the Waterloo directories project.

Subsequently, ***The Waterloo Directory of Irish Newspapers and Periodicals, 1800–1900***, ***The Waterloo Directory of Scottish Newspapers and Periodicals, 1800–1900***, and ***The Waterloo Directory of English Newspapers and Periodicals, 1800–1900*** have been published. Each of these directories expands on the original *Waterloo Directory*. The later directories take the contents of *The Waterloo Directory of Victorian Periodicals* and add descriptive and holdings information. Entries are assigned subject headings that correspond to the subject index found at the back of each directory. These directories contain an explanation of descriptive categories, an abbreviations guide, a subject index, a personal names index, and a place of publication index to facilitate access to the contents. The Scottish directory also includes a guide to library codes and addresses, an index to libraries, a selected bibliography, and selective illustrations. While the Irish directory was published in a single volume and the Scottish directory comprises two volumes, the English directory is available in print, on CD-ROM, or as a subscription database. Although there are currently twenty volumes of the English directory in print, the set will comprise fifty volumes once complete. To date, a Welsh directory that corresponds to *The Waterloo Directory of Victorian Periodicals* has not been published.

Located at the British Library Newspapers, Colindale, the British Library Newspaper Collections provide physical access to a substantial collection of British and Irish newspapers, overseas newspapers, popular magazines, trade papers, and comics. A more detailed overview of the collection subsets may be found online (www.bl.uk/reshelp/findhelprestype/news/blnewscoll). The newspapers are searchable through the ***Newspaper Catalogue*** of the British Library *Integrated Catalogue*. The newspaper subset comprises more than fifty-two thousand newspapers and periodicals, dating from the seventeenth century to the present. Exact dates vary title by title. The online catalog supersedes the printed ***Catalogue of the Newspaper Library Colindale***, which was published in 1975. The eight-volume printed catalog includes entries for newspapers and journals published in London, England, Wales, Scotland, Ireland, and overseas countries. It also offers an alphabetical title list of each publication in the *Catalogue of the Newspaper Library Colindale*.

Edited by Charles A. Toase, ***A Bibliography of British Newspapers*** is a series of British newspaper bibliographies compiled for the Library Association in Great Britain. Although intended to survey British newspaper production, county by county, based on counties prior to the 1974 boundary changes, the *Bibliography of British Newspapers* seems to have fallen short of its goal with only six volumes, covering eight counties, published between 1975 and 1991. The existing volumes discuss newspapers from Wiltshire, Kent, Durham and Northumberland, Nottinghamshire, Derbyshire, and Cornwall and Devon. Each volume stands independently and comprises a county section map, a guide to file locations, a newspaper bibliography, and a title index. Excepting the first volume, over Wiltshire County, each volume also has an index to places mentioned. Newspaper entries are arranged according to coverage area and chronologically within area. Each entry contains information regarding publication location, file details, library holdings, publishers' offices, collections in record offices, museums, and other British and overseas locations, and any published historical accounts. Although the series is incomplete, the existing volumes are useful research tools for scholars of those specific counties.

As you research Victorian and Edwardian periodical literature, you will find broad bibliographies that address scholarship on themes and genres within British literature, but you will also find a myriad of niche bibliographies. One of the many smaller bibliographies is *A Descriptive Finding List of Unstamped British Periodicals, 1830–1836*. Compiled by Joel H. Wiener and published by the Bibliographical Society in London, *A Descriptive Finding List* serves as a guide to periodicals published in Britain between 1830 and 1836 that were published illegally, as their publishers refused to pay the newspaper tax. This slim volume lists just over 560 unstamped periodicals. Each periodical entry may contain information about the publication location, issue dates and numbers, subsequent titles, publishers and editors, a brief description, and British, Irish, and American library holdings. The prefatory materials include a guide to institutional symbols as well as abbreviations and symbols used in the volume. *A Descriptive Finding List* concludes with a partial listing of works used in compilation and an index of publishers, printers, editors, and illustrators.

Another selective bibliography for locating periodicals is *Feminist Periodicals 1855–1984: An Annotated Critical Bibliography of British, Irish, Commonwealth, and International Titles*. Written by David Doughan and Denise Sanchez in 1987, this bibliography lists 920 periodicals by first year of publication and then alphabetically within year. Each entry contains an item number, title, title variant forms, editors, publishers, frequency, continuations and successions, location, and microform availability. Many entries also have brief, descriptive annotations about the contents of the periodical. *Feminist Periodicals* includes more than one hundred periodicals that began publication prior to 1910, such as *Victoria Magazine*, *India's Women*, *British Women's Temperance Journal*, *Women's Suffrage Journal*, and *Wom-*

en's Franchise. In addition to the entries, this bibliography incorporates a guide to references and additional reading, a name and title index, and a chronological index.

Researchers interested in theatrical performances and reception should consult Carl J. Stratman's *A Bibliography of British Dramatic Periodicals, 1720–1960*. This slender volume provides bibliographic and holdings information about 674 dramatic periodicals. Many periodicals covered by this bibliography had very short publication runs. The entries are organized chronologically and then alphabetically within year, and each contains bibliographic information, publication frequency as available, and holdings information for major U.S. and British libraries. Some of the Victorian and Edwardian titles included are *The Looking Glass; or, Daily Theatrical Mirror*, *The Manchester Dramatic and Musical Review*, *Prince of Wales Theatre*, *Rotunda Prompter*, and *Plays and Players*. This volume also has a guide to library symbols and an index.

LOCATING ARTICLES

19th Century Masterfile. Austen, TX: Paratext. www.paratext.com.

Balay, Robert. *Early Periodical Indexes: Bibliographies and Indexes of Literature Published in Periodicals before 1900*. Lanham, MD: Scarecrow Press, 2000.

C19: The Nineteenth Century Index. Ann Arbor, MI: ProQuest, 2005. www.proquest.com.

Curran, Eileen M. "The Curran Index: Additions to and Corrections of the Wellesley Index to Victorian Periodicals." *Victoria Research Web*. victorianresearch.org/curranindex.html. Also available online through *C19: The Nineteenth Century Index*.

Cushing, Helen Grant, and Adah V. Morris, eds. *Nineteenth Century Readers' Guide to Periodical Literature, 1890–1899: With Supplementary Indexing, 1900–1922*. 2 vols. New York: H. W. Wilson, 1944.

Houghton, Walter E., ed. *The Wellesley Index to Victorian Periodicals, 1824–1900*. 5 vols. Toronto: University of Toronto Press, 1966–1989. Also available online through *C19: The Nineteenth Century Index*.

Palmer, Samuel. *Palmer's Index to The Times Newspaper*. Vaduz: Kraus Reprint, 1965.

Poole, William Frederick. *Poole's Index to Periodical Literature*. 6 vols. Glouchester, MA: P. Smith, 1963. Available online through the *19th Century Masterfile* and *C19: The Nineteenth Century Index*.

Wall, C. Edward. *Cumulative Author Index for Poole's Index to Periodical Literature 1802–1906*. Ann Arbor, MI: Pierian Press, 1971.

Poole's Index to Periodical Literature was compiled by William F. Poole and published by Houghton, Mifflin, and Company in 1882. This index was subsequently revised in 1888 by Poole, correcting typographical and other errors that were printed in the original edition. Since then, *Poole's* has been reprinted multiple times: in 1938, 1958, and 1963. While a student at Yale College, Poole noted that periodical contents were not searchable through any of the library's catalogs and set out to index the contents of general periodicals. Eventually, the American Library Association partnered with Poole in this resource's creation. In total, fifty-one libraries from the United States and England collaborated in the creation of *Poole's* first volume, which indexed 232 periodicals published between 1802 and 1881, covering diverse disciplinary areas such as literature, religion, politics, and the social sciences. While *Poole's* is a useful resource for researching all aspects of nineteenth-century culture, several titles will be of particular interest to literary scholars, such as *All the Year Round, Blackwood's Magazine, Bentley's Miscellany, Bentley's Quarterly Review*, the *Edinburgh Review, Household Words*, and *Literary and Theological Review*. Other titles range from the *Englishwoman's Domestic Magazine* to the *National Review* and from the *Journal of the Statistical Society* to the *Westminster Review*. While the majority of these periodicals were published in the United States, a significant number of titles from Great Britain are also included.

Each *Poole's* volume begins with a list of cooperating libraries, a guide to abbreviations, titles, and imprints, and a chronological conspectus of serials indexed. The index is organized alphabetically by titles, subjects, and authors as subjects. Each index entry contains publication details for relevant periodical articles. Currently, six volumes of *Poole's* exist, with each representing a different time period in periodical literature. Volume 1, which was published in two parts, covers periodical literature from 1802 to 1881. Subsequent volumes address periodical literature from 1882 to 1887, 1887 to 1892, 1892 to 1896, 1897 to 1902, and 1902 to 1906. The titles indexed vary from volume to volume, so researchers should consult the prefatory material to determine which periodicals are covered in each volume. *Poole's* original volume plus the five supplements include 470 periodicals total. Although *Poole's* is an index in and of itself, use of this set may be hindered by the absence of any sort of guide or index to the set as a whole. Since each volume covers a discrete time period, a scholar could potentially need to search in multiple, if not all, volumes to determine whether he or she had located all available citations. Additionally, *Poole's* does not provide any aids to searching for articles written by a particular author. To remedy the author problem, C. Edward Wall compiled and edited a ***Cumulative Author Index for Poole's Index to Periodical Literature 1802–1906*** in 1971. Published by the Pierian

Press, the *Cumulative Author Index* alphabetically lists the authors of each article indexed in *Poole's*. Following each author's name, Wall included a code that represents the volume, page, and column where the citation is located in *Poole's*. Researchers using *Poole's* should make use of the *Cumulative Author Index* to enhance their searching. *Poole's Index to Periodical Literature* may also be searched online through the *19th Century Masterfile* and *C19: The Nineteenth Century Index*, both of which allow for greater ease and efficiency of searching. Both online resources are discussed in greater detail in chapter 4.

As suggested in **The Wellesley Index to Victorian Periodicals, 1824–1900** introduction, "the Victorian period proper has been neglected" in the scholarship of reviews, magazines, and journals.[5] Numerous sources address periodical publications for the Romantic period, yet the Victorian age, in which periodicals flourished, does not have the same depth of indexing. With five volumes published between 1966 and 1989, *The Wellesley Index* fills an important gap in the scholarship record. The first four volumes outline the contents of forty-three Victorian periodicals, comprising seventy-eight thousand articles attributed to twelve thousand authors. The one notable exclusion is that the index does not include poetry. This resource indexes titles such as *Blackwood's Edinburgh Magazine, Ainsworth's Magazine, The Rambler, The Dark Blue*, and *The London Quarterly Review*. Each periodical is introduced with a brief history of the publication, an editor list, publisher and proprietor identification, a note on attributions, and a bibliographical note. Following this introductory information, each periodical's volumes are listed chronologically, along with citations to its contents. *Wellesley Index* editors supplied author names for anonymous and pseudonymous works as far as research supports. Since roughly 90 percent of all periodical articles were published without a named author, this information is invaluable to scholars. To distinguish signed works from anonymous and pseudonymous works, the Wellesley editors inserted the term "signed" or "signature" in entries where the designation applies. The first four volumes each conclude with bibliographies of contributors, which serve as an author index to the periodicals covered in that volume; an initials and pseudonyms index; and an appendix of additions and corrections to the previous volumes. The fifth *Wellesley* volume is an epitome and index to the complete set, offering a comprehensive guide to bibliographies of contributors and to initials and pseudonyms identified in the prior volumes. This volume concludes with appendixes to alterations made in the other volumes' appendixes and to new additions and corrections.

The print *Wellesley Index* is perhaps best used either to browse periodical contents or to locate a known article citation. Each of the first four volumes comprises the chronological contents of specific Victorian periodicals.[6] One way to use *Wellesley* is browsing to gain a sense of what a particular periodical covered and why it was important. Given for each publication is a survey of its history, audience, reception, and aims; a list of editors, proprietors, and publishers; a note on attributions; and a bibliographical note. This prefatory information, along with the contents, gives a sense of a magazine's purpose. The contributor index in volume 5 is extremely useful for identifying what one particular author wrote in any or all of the titles. What *Wellesley Index* lacks most is a subject index to articles. While the existing organization and finding aids support known-item searching, they are not adequate for locating articles on a specific topic. The other feature from which this resource would benefit is the inclusion of document type indicators, so that scholars could easily ascertain whether a citation referred to a creative work, review, essay, or other mode of writing. As it is, scholars must rely on their own knowledge of nineteenth-century authors and texts to ascertain the relevance of any one citation.

Since the completion of the *Wellesley Index* in 1989, further additions and corrections have been identified, primarily through Eileen M. Curran's index. ***"The Curran Index: Additions to and Corrections of The Wellesley Index to Victorian Periodicals"*** compiles any additions and corrections published in *Victorian Periodicals Newsletter* (*VPN*) or *Victorian Periodicals Review* (*VPR*) as well as other scholarly journals (see chapter 5 for more on *VPN* and *VPR*). The *Curran Index* is available online through the *Victorian Research Web* (see chapter 10) and through the online *Wellesley Index* and *C19: The Nineteenth Century Index* (see below).

The online *Wellesley Index* comprises the original print index plus the updates made in the *Curran Index*. Contents may be searched by keyword, contributor, living in the years, pseudonym, article title, periodical title, periodical subject, publication date, and editor. You may also specify whether keywords appear in articles, contributors, pseudonyms, or periodical introductions. Where the print index only allowed browsing in a single periodical or by contributor name, this version provides greater ease and flexibility for retrieving the desired results. For instance, you could search for content edited by *John Stuart Mill* or locate articles signed with Dickens's pseudonym, *Boz*. Subscribers to *British Periodicals* and *Periodicals Archive Online* can link directly from *Wellesley* citations to the full text in those resources. In addition to searching, scholars may browse by contributors, pseudonyms, *The Curran Index to Periodical Literature*, and periodicals. For more on using the *Wellesley Index* to locate creative works, see chapter 6.

Originally published in 1925 and then reprinted in 1965 by Kraus Reprint Ltd., ***Palmer's Index to The Times Newspaper*** indexes *The Times* of London from 1790 to 1905. Successive indexing is available through *The Annual Index to The Times* from 1906 to 1913, *The Official Index to The Times* from 1914 to 1956, and *The Times Index* from 1957 to the present. Victorian and Edwardian scholars will find *Palmer's* and *The Annual Index* the most relevant for their research. From 1790 to 1840, each volume of *Palmer's* covers five-year increments, then switches to two-year increments from 1841 to 1860 and one-year increments from 1861 until 1905. Regardless of time coverage, each volume is indexed quarterly, beginning in January. Within each quarterly index, *The Times'* contents are indexed alphabetically according to subject. These subjects comprise a variety of topics such as births, criminal trials, deaths, female pickpockets, France, leading articles, mining intelligence, reviews, and theatres. Under each subject heading, subtopics and references are listed. For instance, under the heading *reviews* in the spring quarter of 1866, one of the subtopics is "Eliot, George, Felix Holt, the Radical, *26 j 6 c*." The reference indicates that the review of Eliot's *Felix Holt, the Radical* appears in the June 26 issue, page 6, column 3. The first number and letter denote the month and day, while the second number indicates the page and the second letter corresponds to the page column. This information could then be used to locate an article in a microform or digital edition of *The Times*.

While the quarterly indexing aids scholars in narrowing their search by dates of publication, researchers may find it inconvenient to search multiple indexes within a single volume. *Palmer's* retains this quarterly indexing until its final issue in 1905. In 1906, *The Times Annual Index* began offering a single index for a year, rather than subdividing the information by quarter. Neither *Palmer's* nor *The Times Annual Index* has author or title indexes. *Palmer's* is also available electronically through both *C19: The Nineteenth Century Index* and the *19th Century Masterfile* (see chapter 4), and the full text of *The Times* is available through *The Times Digital Archive* (see below). These online sources all allow for searching across multiple issues with greater efficiency than searching individual index volumes.

Overlapping with *Poole's* in terms of time coverage and title selection, the **Nineteenth Century Readers' Guide to Periodical Literature, 1890–1899** indexes fifty-one periodicals from the United States and Great Britain. Although generally the guide ceases indexing with 1899, fourteen of the titles are indexed prior to 1890 and beyond 1899. The two volumes each provide a list of periodicals indexed, an abbreviations key, and a suggestion for index use along with sample entries. Unlike *Poole's*, which has no subject headings, the *Nineteenth Century Readers' Guide* uses subject headings, cross references, and author entries to facilitate access to the guide's contents. It also indexes book reviews, short stories, novels, plays, poems, and dramatic criticism (for more on locating period book reviews and literary criticism, see chapter 6). While many of the indexed publications are American, British publications such as *Blackwood's Magazine, Contemporary Review, Cornhill*

Magazine, Edinburgh Review, English Historical Review, Fortnightly Review, Hibbert Journal, Nineteenth Century, Quarterly Review, Spectator, Westminster Review, and *Yellow Book: An Illustrated Quarterly* are also included. The subject headings allow researchers to search not only for works about a particular author but also for works on a specific topic. A researcher who needed to find contemporary commentary on the House of Lords in the late nineteenth century could look under Great Britain and then under the subdivision for House of Lords. Author entries further subdivide the citations depending on the type of work indexed. For instance, citations listed under Charlotte Brontë's entry are organized according to poems about, characters, and relics, and the entry for William Ewart Gladstone has a list of works he wrote as well as works about him.

Robert Balay, who also oversaw the creation of the Balay's *Guide to Reference Books* (see appendix), compiled **Early Periodical Indexes: Bibliographies and Indexes of Literature Published in Periodicals before 1900** to assist researchers in locating contemporary commentary in periodical literature published prior to 1900. In this volume, Balay provides an annotated listing of bibliographies and indexes that focus on pre-1900 periodical literature. The bibliographies and indexes themselves are broadly categorized according to general resources, humanities, history and area studies, social and behavioral sciences, science and technology, and library and information science. Each broad category is further subdivided into more specific disciplinary areas. Entries are arranged alphabetically within each subdivision and contain full bibliographic information along with a descriptive annotation of the bibliography's or index's contents and functionality. To facilitate access, *Early Periodical Indexes* has indexes for authors, titles, subjects, and dates of coverage.

Scholars should also consult two major indexes—**19th Century Masterfile** and **C19: The Nineteenth Century Index**—when researching nineteenth-century newspapers and periodicals. These indexes allow for simultaneous searching across archives, books, newspapers, official publications, periodicals, and reference works, or more specialized searching within a specific resource. Particularly, *British Periodicals, Periodicals Index Online, Poole's Index to Periodical Literature, Wellesley Index to Victorian Periodicals,* and *Palmer's Index to the Times* in *C19* and the indexes such as *Poole's, Stead's Index to Periodicals,* and individual newspaper and magazine indexes in *19th Century Masterfile* are useful for journal and newspaper research. Because of their broad indexing coverage, you may need to consult the *19th Century Masterfile* and *C19* frequently for almost any Victorian or Edwardian research project. Both are discussed in greater detail in chapter 4 and in chapter 6 as tools for locating reviews and literary criticism.

JOURNAL- AND TOPIC-SPECIFIC SOURCES

Lanser, Mark Samuels. *The Yellow Book: A Checklist and Index*. London: The Eighteen Nineties Society, 1998.

Lohrli, Anne. *Household Words: A Weekly Journal 1850–1859*. Toronto: University of Toronto Press, 1973.

Palmegiano, E. M. *The British Empire in the Victorian Press, 1832–1867: A Bibliography*. New York: Garland Publishing, 1987.

———. *Crime in Victorian Britain: An Annotated Bibliography from Nineteenth-Century British Magazines*. Westport, CT: Greenwood Press, 1993.

Occasionally, you may come across an index to a particular periodical either in its entirety or for a select number of years. While this chapter cannot discuss all such works, it addresses two examples: *The Yellow Book: A Checklist and Index* and *Household Words: A Weekly Journal 1850–1859*. Published in 1998, Mark Samuels Lasner's ***The Yellow Book: A Checklist and Index*** details the contents of all thirteen volumes published between April 1894 and April 1897. The checklist was created to fill a gap in the indexing of this important *fin de siècle* periodical, which published works such as Max Beerbohm's "A Defence of Cosmetics," Kenneth Grahame's "The Roman Road," William Butler Yeats's "The Blessed," and Henry James's "She and He: Recent Documents." In total, 576 works of art and literature are indexed in *The Yellow Book: A Checklist and Index*. Each volume has separate lists for both literature and art, organized in page order. Lasner filled in pseudonymous identities and initials to increase the usefulness of the checklist to scholars. This work concludes with an index to authors and titles.

Anne Lohrli's ***Household Words: A Weekly Journal 1850–1859*** indexes the contents of Charles Dickens's periodical *Household Words* and serves as a guide to its contributors. This single-volume work begins with a detailed and lengthy introduction about *Household Words* as a periodical, its contents, its contributors, the *Household Words* office book, and a bibliographical note on the periodical's publication history. The index portion of this work is organized chronologically, beginning with volume 1, which was printed between March 30, 1850, and September 21, 1850, and ending with volume 19, which was published between December 4, 1858, and May 28, 1859. Within each volume, every issue, including extra Christmas issues, is listed chronologically, along with its contents in page order. The bibliographic citations contain the printed title of the article, a category or summary notation, inclusive page numbers, length in columns, payment, Office Book authorship ascription, and the author's full name. The second part of the volume—"*Household Words* Contributors"—comprises a complete listing of writers and their contributions.

This section is organized alphabetically by author's last name. Entries list the contributor's name as recorded in the Office Book, his or her address of residence or address to which payment was sent, an identification note with references to sources when available, and a list of each item contributed to *Household Words*. This resource ends with a title index, a table of volumes, numbers, and dates, a list of abbreviations used, and a bibliography.

In addition to sources that index a particular publication, there are also topical guides to the contents of periodicals, including *The British Empire in the Victorian Press, 1832–1867* and *Crime in Victorian Britain*. Part of Garland Publishing's *Themes in European Expansion* series and the larger *Garland Reference Library of Social Science*, Eugenia M. Palmegiano's **The British Empire in the Victorian Press, 1832–1867: A Bibliography** highlights the ways in which the press made the Empire visible to the citizens of Great Britain in the mid-nineteenth century. This bibliography is organized into three major sections: an introduction and two checklists. The introduction provides a detailed overview of imperial themes in the Victorian press, sea routes to the East, and specific geographic regions of the British Empire: India, the Indian Ocean, the Far East, the Pacific Ocean, British North America, the Caribbean and South America, and Africa. The first checklist covers thirty-six London magazines dealing with the British Empire from 1832 to 1867, ranging from *The Anti-Slavery Reporter* to the *Australasian Gold Fields* and from *Captain Pidding's Chinese Olio and Tea Talk* to *The Friend of Africa*. Each journal entry may comprise run dates, publisher, subtitle, supersession, editor, sponsor, publication frequency, price, and location inspected. The second checklist is composed of articles on empire in British periodicals from 1832 to 1867. This list contains historically significant journals such as all those listed in the *Wellesley Index to Victorian Periodicals*, sixteen journals from *Poole's Index*, and *The Monthly Repository*. In total, sixty-two periodicals are indexed in the second checklist, which lists 2,859 articles about the British Empire. The entries are organized by source periodical and chronologically within periodical. An index of article authors and an index to territories and article topics conclude this bibliography.

A second bibliography by Palmegiano—***Crime in Victorian Britain: An Annotated Bibliography from Nineteenth-Century British Magazines***—is part of Greenwood Press's *Bibliographies and Indexes in World History* series. This resource guides scholars to articles published on crime in forty-five Victorian periodicals between 1824 and 1900, such as *All the Year Round, The Cornhill Magazine, Murray's Magazine*, and *Tait's Edinburgh Magazine*. The entries are organized alphabetically by title and chronologically within title. Each entry comprises a bibliographic citation and a brief annotation. The volume begins with an informative introduction on rates, types, and causes of crime, law and enforcement, prosecution of criminals, sentences for crimes, classes of crime, and crime in the United Kingdom. Coverage is not limited to England but includes Ireland, Scotland, and Wales. *Crime in Victorian Britain* concludes with an author index, a select personnel index, and a subject index.

PERIOD JOURNAL AND NEWSPAPER COLLECTIONS

19th Century British Library Newspapers. Farmington Hills, MI: Gale Cengage. www.gale.cengage.com.

19th Century U.K. Periodicals. Farmington Hills, MI: Gale Cengage. www .gale.cengage.com.

British Periodicals. Ann Arbor, MI: ProQuest. www.proquest.com.

Early British Periodicals, 1681–1921. 902 microfilm reels. Ann Arbor, MI: University Microfilms International, 1970–1979.

English Literary Periodicals, 1681–1914. 969 microfilm reels. Ann Arbor, MI: University Microfilms International, 1951–1977.

Hoornstra, Jean, and Grace Puravs, eds. *A Guide to the Early British Periodicals Collection on Microfilm with Title, Subject, Editor, and Reel Number Indexes.* Ann Arbor, MI: University Microfilms International, 1980.

Puravs, Grace, Kathy L. Kavanagh, and Vicki Smith, eds. *Accessing English Literary Periodicals: A Guide to the Microfilm Collection with Title, Subject, Editor, and Reel Number Indexes.* Ann Arbor, MI: University Microfilms International, 1981.

Rare Radical and Labour Periodicals of Great Britain. 72 microfilm reels. Brighton, Sussex: Harvester Microform, 1978–1983.

Times Digital Archives, 1785–1985. Farmington Hills, MI: Gale Cengage. www.gale.cengage.com.

Times Literary Supplement Historical Archive, 1902–2005. Farmington Hills, MI: Gale Cengage. www.gale.cengage.com.

Today's scholars are fortunate to have a variety of microform and digital collections of period journals and newspapers. These collections range from multi-title compilations such as *British Periodicals* and *19th Century British Library Newspapers* to single-title and niche collections such as the *Times Digital Archive* and *Rare Radical and Labour Periodicals of Great Britain.* This is not an exhaustive assessment of available collections, but the resources discussed here should help you gain a sense of what is available. Microform and digital collections are discussed in greater detail in chapter 8.

Comprising 969 microfilm reels, **English Literary Periodicals, 1681–1914** provides access to 341 literary periodicals published in Great Britain from the seventeenth through the nineteenth centuries. The collection contains literary reviews and miscellanies as well as theatrical journals, satire and humor periodicals, political magazines, religious magazines, and women's magazines. While most of the periodicals were published in England, several titles, such as the *Belfast Monthly Magazine* and *Edinburgh Magazine*, were published in either Ireland or Scotland. *English Literary Periodicals* has titles such as *Ainsworth's Magazine, Figaro in London, Merry England*, the *New Monthly Magazine*, the *Westminster Review*, and *Yellow Book*. A guide entitled ***Accessing English Literary Periodicals: A Guide to the Microfilm Collection with Title, Subject, Editor, and Reel Number Indexes*** accompanies the collection and is the best means of identifying the collection's contents. While the title and editor indexes are most effective for locating known items, the subject index should help researchers find information on a particular topic within the collection. For instance, the subject heading *19th Century—Book Reviews* will aid a researcher in quickly locating which periodicals published reviews. Unfortunately, subject indexing is only at the periodical-title level and does not delve deeper into each issue. The reel number index gives a comprehensive overview of all 969 reels' contents.

The ***Early British Periodicals, 1681–1921*** collection complements *English Literary Periodicals*. Where *English Literary Periodicals* emphasized literature, *Early British Periodicals* has broader subject coverage. With 902 microfilm reels and more than three million pages, this resource comprises 160 English periodicals covering the fine arts, history, literature, philosophy, science, and the social sciences in the eighteenth and nineteenth centuries. Literary journals such as *The Bee, Belgravia, Bentley's Miscellany, The Kaleidoscope*, and *The Literary Magazine* are included alongside journals from other disciplinary areas such as *The Badminton Magazine of Sports and Pastimes, The Economic Review, The Home Friend, The Journal of Sacred Literature*, and *Judy, or the London Serio-Comic Journal*. ***A Guide to the Early British Periodicals Collection on Microfilm with Title, Subject, Editor, and Reel Number Indexes*** provides additional information about the collection's contents. As with the guide to *English Literary Periodicals*, the indexes to *Early British Periodicals* only go to the periodical title level.

ProQuest's ***British Periodicals*** offers online, full-text access to the complete contents of the UMI microfilm collections *Early British Periodicals, English Literary Periodicals*, and *British Periodicals in the Creative Arts*. *British Periodicals* is divided into two collections, which may be purchased together or separately. *British Periodicals Collection I* comprises the *Early British Periodicals* microfilm collection, and *British Periodicals Collection II* is composed of *English Literary Periodicals, British Periodicals in the Creative Arts*, and select other titles. In total, the database consists of more than 460 journals and more than five million pages of digitized material from 1681 through 1920. While the content replicates the microform collections, *British Periodicals* allows for unprecedented searching across major and minor periodical titles from a wide variety of disciplines, enhancing the efficiency with which scholars search. This online collection is searchable by keyword, article title keyword, author, journal title, journal editor, journal subject, and place of publication. Scholars may also limit by publication date, publication frequency, content type (e.g., advertisements, articles, front matter, poems, recipes, etc.), and articles containing cartoons, comic strips, illustrations, maps, music, and photographs. From the article search results screen, scholars can additionally filter their results by journal, journal subject, date, publication frequency, journal editor, and article type. When viewing individual results, scholars may choose to view the document as a grayscale JPEG image or to download the document either as a grayscale JPEG or as a grayscale/black-and-white PDF file. Results may also be saved to a list, from where you can e-mail, print, download, or save to "My Archive." The "My Archive" feature, which requires the creation of an individual username and password, allows scholars to save both their searches and their selected records for future use. *British Periodicals'* contents can also be accessed through the "Find Journals" feature, which lets scholars browse journals by title, subject, and publication frequency. It allows for searching journal records and browsing a full title list.

Scholars who need to access periodical literature should consult Gale Cengage's *19th Century U.K. Periodicals* (*NCUKP*). When complete, this collection will comprise around six hundred periodicals that cover twenty-three subject areas. The titles were selected based on their inclusion in major finding aids such as *The Wellesley Index*, *The Waterloo Directory of English Newspapers and Periodicals*, and the *Cambridge Bibliography of English Literature*, and were sourced from the British Library, the National Library of Scotland, and other major research collections. *NCUKP* covers the full run for each title whenever possible and incorporates title changes. Periodical records are linked to *Waterloo Directory* head notes, which provide descriptive information regarding editors, proprietors and publishers, frequency, title changes, print runs, and circulation. Unlike most other digital and microform collections, which are typically in black-and-white or grayscale, many of *NCUKP*'s contents are in full color, since they were scanned from original print sources. Currently, only two of the five planned series have been released: "New Readerships: Women and Children, Sports and Leisure, Humour and Satire" and "Empire: Travel and Anthropology, Economics, Missionary and Colonial." The final three series will cover "Culture: Literature, Visual and Performing Arts," "Working Life: Agriculture, The Professions,

Trade and Industry, and Medicine," and "Knowledge: Academic, Field Sciences, Philanthropic, Political, Religious and Scientific Journals."

When using *NCUKP*, scholars may search in the complete contents or limit to specific series, subject categories, publication sections, publication frequency, or articles with illustrations. Scholars can select from the basic, advanced, or Command Control Language (CCL) advanced search interfaces. While the basic option allows for simple queries in keywords or the full text, the advanced and CCL advanced options allow for more complex and specific searches. In addition, *NCUKP* offers a publication search to help scholars identify specific titles. The periodicals contained in this database are an excellent resource for information on the political, cultural, and literary state of the United Kingdom in the nineteenth century. Scholars will find literary output from authors such as Charles Dickens, Olive Schreiner, and Mary Elizabeth Braddon. As there is no indexing at the article level, full-text searching is the primary means of accessing the periodicals' contents. Because of this, scholars should remember to use nineteenth-century British terminology and pseudonyms and variants of author names to retrieve the most comprehensive results. Taking advantage of the "fuzzy search" feature can also enhance results, particularly to account for spelling variants.

In addition to broad periodical collections, there are also smaller collections that focus on specific readerships, ideologies, or subgenres. One representative collection is ***Rare Radical and Labour Periodicals of Great Britain*** from Primary Source Microfilm. This resource was published in two series, with series 1 covering the nineteenth century and series 2 covering the late nineteenth and early twentieth centuries, 1875–1933. In total, seventy-two microfilm reels comprise the set and represent various political and social viewpoints, such as social democrat, anarchist, pacifist, trade unionist, syndicalist, and communist. Periodicals such as the *Labour Union Journal* and *Journal of the Working Classes* and views of authors such as George Bernard Shaw and Annie Besant are included.

Scholars needing British newspapers of the nineteenth century should consult Gale Cengage's ***19th Century British Library Newspapers***. Newspaper digitization has been particularly useful to scholars, as it has made resources otherwise only accessible on microform available through a searchable online interface. In total, forty-nine titles from England, Ireland, Scotland, and Wales comprise this archive. *19th Century British Library Newspapers* contains national, regional, and penny newspapers, and highlights newspapers that were influential in social and political movements. Each paper's full run has been digitized, including titles such as the *Derby Mercury*, the *Hull Packet*, *Lloyd's Illustrated Newspaper*, the *Pall Mall Gazette*, and the *Poor Man's Guardian*. The newspapers' contents may be searched through either basic or advanced search screens. Scholars can choose to search for their terms in keywords, the entire document, document title, document number, publication title, publication date, and day of week. Additional limits are for date, title, place, section, and frequency of the publication; language; and documents with images. Scholars may also browse by publication title and place, which organizes the newspapers by country of origin and then region within country. The record for each newspaper contains a head note regarding the history and political or social leanings of the publication. Individual article search results may be saved to a marked list and downloaded as HTML. From the results screen, scholars also have the option to view the article, the page, and information about the publication, and to browse the issue. Results may be further narrowed by publication section if desired.

Because of funding from the Joint Information Systems Committee (JISC), the *19th Century British Library Newspapers'* complete contents are available for free to Further and Higher Education Institutions in the United Kingdom. For all other institutions, page images are only accessible through subscription from Gale Cengage. The archive's indexing and search interface, however, is available to the general public (newspapers.bl.uk/blcs). Scholars may still search the full text to all forty-nine newspapers included, but can only see an extract containing their search terms rather than the entire article. The full text is available for select pages in the open-access version, and scholars have the option to purchase individual articles. Additionally, scholars can access the chronology and other research tools, use the basic and advanced searches, browse publications by location, use the search history feature, and save records to the marked list for printing, e-mailing, and downloading.

In addition to archival products that search across multiple titles, some collections focus on a single title. One such single-title product is Gale Cengage's *Times Digital Archives, 1785–1985* (*TDA*), which provides facsimiles of each page of *The Times* of London from 1785 to 1985. One of Gale's earlier digital archives, *TDA* offers full-text searching of each article, advertisement, and caption from *The Times*. The contents may be searched by keyword, title, date, text, author, category, subcategory, illustration, page, day of week, issue, and record number. Additionally, searches may be limited by date or by section (e.g., "Advertising," "Business," "Editorial and Commentary," "Features," "News," "People," and "Picture Gallery"). Each section is further divided into subcategories. For instance, "People" is subcategorized by births, business appointments, deaths, marriages, obituaries, and official appointments and notices, while "Features" is divided according to arts and entertainment, reviews, sport, and weather. Search options include advanced, relevance, and keyword. Additionally, *The Times* may be browsed by date. Browsing allows scholars to peruse an issue of *The Times* much as one would page through a printed newspaper. The results display allows scholars to view the article in isolation or in context of the entire page. Results may also be downloaded as PDF files. Scholars can add relevant items to a marked list for printing or e-mailing.

Another publication-specific, full-text resource is the ***Times Literary Supplement Historical Archive, 1902–2005***, which was digitized by Gale Cengage. This resource offers access to all *TLS* issues from 1902 to 2005 and is an excellent tool for locating articles, creative works, letters, obituaries, reviews, speeches and lectures, and unpublished works in older issues of the *TLS*. The *TLS Historical Archive* will be particularly useful for Edwardian scholars. The *TLS Historical Archive* is a valuable resource not simply for its full-text search capabilities but because it reveals the identities of otherwise anonymous contributors. Both the basic and advanced search options allow scholars access to *TLS* contents. The basic search simply supports finding keywords in the full text. From the advanced screen, terms may be combined using Boolean operators, limited by date and article type and searched in specific fields: full text, keyword, author, contributor, book title, editor, article title, translator, illustrator, publisher, place of publication, and document type. In addition to searching, scholars may browse the *TLS Historical Archive* by issue, book title, author, contributor, illustrator, editor, or translator. Results display with a page thumbnail, publication details, and links to the issue, specific page, and article PDF. Additionally, this resource saves a scholar's search history for the session and allows records to be saved to "My Marked List" or "My Archive."

CONCLUSION

Although more resources are available than ever before for researching period newspapers and journals, significant gaps remain in the research record. As such, there is no one comprehensive source for locating and identifying the contents of Victorian and Edwardian serial publications. Not only will scholars need to consult many of the sources identified in this chapter, but they also will need to examine the resources discussed in chapter 6, the microform and digital collections of chapter 8, and many of the standard bibliographies, indexes, encyclopedias, and other sources discussed throughout this book. Just as period journals and newspapers were not written in a vacuum, neither should scholars confine their research to the sources discussed in this chapter. Thorough research requires you to work with multiple resource types in a recursive, repetitive process. While period newspapers and journals may be an important piece in your research process, they should not be the only sources you consult.

NOTES

1. *Dictionary of Nineteenth-Century Journalism*, s.v. "Contemporary Review (1866–1988)" (by Anthony Cummins), c19index.chadwyck.com (accessed April 18, 2010).

2. The phrase "Taxes on Knowledge" was initially used in the 1830s to describe the Stamp Acts, which were first introduced in 1712.

3. Lucy Brown, "The British Press, 1800–1860," in *The Encyclopedia of the British Press 1422–1992*, edited by Dennis Griffiths, 24–32 (New York: St. Martin's Press, 1992).

4. "Periodicals," *Bow Bells* 45, no. 1153 (September 1, 1886): 251.

5. Walter E. Houghton, "Introduction," in *The Wellesley Index to Victorian Periodicals, 1824–1900* (Toronto: University of Toronto Press, 1966), 1:xxii.

6. Volume 1 comprises *Blackwood's Edinburgh Magazine, The Contemporary Review, The Cornhill Magazine, The Edinburgh Review, The Home and Foreign Review, Macmillan's Magazine, The North British Review*, and *The Quarterly Review*. Volume 2 contains *Bentley's Quarterly Review, The Dublin Review, The Foreign Quarterly Review, Fraser's Magazine, The London Review, The National Review, The New Quarterly Magazine, The Nineteenth Century, The Oxford and Cambridge Magazine, The Rambler*, and *The Scottish Review*. Volume 3 includes *Ainsworth's Magazine, The Atlantis, The British and Foreign Review, The London Review, The London and Westminster Review, The Modern Review, The Monthly Chronicle, The National Review, The New Monthly Magazine, The New Review, The Prospective Review, Saint Pauls, Temple Bar, The Theological Review*, and *The Westminster Review*. Volume 4 provides *Bentley's Miscellany, The British Quarterly Review, The Dark Blue, The Dublin University Magazine, The London Quarterly Review, Longman's Magazine, Tait's Edinburgh Magazine*, and *The University Magazine*.

Chapter Eight

Microform and
Digital Collections

While all libraries have limits regarding the types and quantity of information they house, microform and digital collections enable libraries to offer extensive and often rare collections that would otherwise be relatively inaccessible and require significant amounts of space. The humanities have benefited greatly over the past decades as publishers first began releasing major microfilm collections and, in more recent years, creating vast digital archives of primary sources. This chapter introduces you to major microform and digital collections that support research in the Victorian and Edwardian ages. Many collections discussed here may be used in conjunction with the research tools developed for studying period reviews, literary magazines, journals, and newspapers, which were discussed in the previous two chapters. While the tools of chapters 6 and 7 often serve as finding aids to primary sources, this chapter describes the primary sources themselves, or at least representations thereof. No reproduction can truly replace the original physical artifacts; however, many scholars will find microform and digital surrogates more readily accessible and affordable. Younger scholars particularly may not have the funding to visit major archives and libraries in either the United Kingdom or the United States. As substitutes, these collections provide unprecedented access to previously isolated research materials and may facilitate research that would not happen otherwise. Likewise, certain primary sources have been "rediscovered" through their microform or digital reproduction.

Of the two formats, microforms certainly have a longer history as information storage mechanisms than their digital counterparts, and while they are the less user-friendly of the two, microforms continue to have a pertinent place among research resources. The earliest microforms were developed in Manchester, England, in 1839 as daguerreotype plates.[1] Throughout the nineteenth century, microforms were used primarily for photography with limited discussion of their use for printed materials. Around World War II, microform gained popularity as storage for archival materials. So promising did microform's future appear that in 1937, H. G. Wells proposed the creation of a "Permanent World Encyclopaedia" that would be "a world synthesis of bibliography and documentation with the indexed archives of the world."[2] The preferred format for this encyclopedia, of course, would be microfilm. Although Wells's vision never came to fruition, microforms greatly increased in use and availability from the 1930s through the 1970s as the format proliferated into microfilm, microfiche, microcards, and ultra-fiche. As technology advances changed the library resource landscape, however, microforms began to intermingle with their digital counterparts. Even today, scholars must navigate both microform and digital resources, since many materials have yet to be digitized. Both collection formats provide surrogate access to books, images, manuscripts, newspapers, periodicals, pamphlets, and other archival materials. Perhaps one day digital resources may completely replace microforms, but until then scholars must be proficient in using both.

Even though fewer microform collections are being created, older microform sets are finding new life through digitization. Many recently created digital collections have been sourced from standard microform sets. For example, Pro-Quest's *British Periodicals* was sourced from the UMI microfilm collections *Early British Periodicals*, *English Literary Periodicals*, and *British Periodicals in the Creative Arts*. Digitizing existing microforms is a faster, more cost-effective way of creating a digital collection than making new digital scans from the original materials. Even so, some publishers are beginning to create digital collections from newly scanned documents, allowing for higher resolution and greater clarity of images and creating full-color scans as opposed to the black-and-white or gray-scale microform images. Digital collections may present their contents in a variety of file formats, including PDF, TIFF, JPEG, and GIF formats, each of which allows for different uses and display options. In addition to providing page images, collections frequently have transcripts of source documents, which enhance the text's readability. Transcripts are created either by rekeying texts by hand or through optical character recognition (OCR) software. Optical character recognition is used to obtain a character-by-character version of a text from computer-scanned page images. While OCR creates transcripts far faster than manual rekeying, older fonts can be particularly difficult for the technologies to parse accurately. Because of this, scholars should always double-check the transcript against the digital image or even the original document if possible. Depending on the publisher, digital collections may be searchable by keyword or in specific fields, such as author, title, publisher, and subject. As a whole, digital collections tend to be easier to search than microform collections, which are often better for locating known items.

Both microforms and digital collections pose particular access problems. Often the collection as a whole may garner a single catalog entry, but the individual contents may or may not have individual records. This can hinder scholars who may be searching for a particular item but do not realize it is available in a larger collection. Some libraries, however, may purchase or create MARC records at the title level to facilitate access to and promote use of these materials. In this situation a scholar might find a record for a particular book or newspaper on microform that indicates the collection to which it belongs and a microform number that will help in locating the physical item. When only the collection-level record exists, scholars must consult any printed, microform, or digital guide that accompanies the set. Lacking even a guide, scholars should consult the indexing resources discussed in chapters 6 and 7 for period reviews, literary magazines, journals, and newspapers. This chapter identifies several tools for finding microform and digital collections and highlights some of the major collections for the Victorian and Edwardian ages. If you come across a microform collection that your library does not own, you could either request that your library purchase it or contact your library's interlibrary loan department to borrow it from another library. To access digital collections not provided by your local library, you may need to visit a nearby library that already has access, or lobby your librarian to add the resource to your library's digital holdings.

FINDING MICROFORM AND DIGITIZED COLLECTIONS

"Bibliographies and Guides." *Library of Congress Microform Reading Room*, 3 March 2009, online at www.loc.gov/rr/microform/bibguide.html (accessed on 19 April 2010).

Dodson, Suzanne Cates, ed. *Microform Research Collections: A Guide*. 2nd ed. Westport, CT: Meckler Publishing, 1984.

Frazier, Patrick, ed. *A Guide to the Microform Collections in the Humanities and Social Sciences Division of the Library of Congress*. Washington, DC: Library of Congress Humanities and Social Sciences Division, 1996. Online at www.loc.gov/rr/microform/guide (accessed on 19 April 2010).

Guide to Microforms in Print. 2 vols. München, Germany: K. G. Saur Verlag, 1978.

WorldCat. Dublin, OH: OCLC. www.oclc.org/firstsearch.

While most literary scholars prefer to use original primary-source materials, sometimes geographic and financial realities prohibit you from traveling to the library or archive that houses the resource in question. Fortunately, microform and digital collections are more readily available than ever before, and the number of reproduced materials increases with each passing year. Although microform sets continue to be created, the publishing trends are moving away from microform and toward digitization. Digital collections provide more ubiquitous access in a user-friendlier environment, and are often the more attractive of the two formats. That said, microforms are not completely obsolete. Even with the shift toward digital resources, microforms maintain an important position in the research process. This section discusses some of the major guides to locating these collections. Since digital collections are relative newcomers to the field, these finding aids deal exclusively with microform collections. To identify existing digital resources, however, scholars may find it most helpful to browse the websites of major humanities publishers, including Adam Matthew Digital, Gale Cengage, and ProQuest.

In 1996 the Humanities and Social Sciences Division of the Library of Congress published *A Guide to the Microform Collections in the Humanities and Social Sciences Division of the Library of Congress*, which combined two previous editions and added two hundred new collections held by the Library of Congress. This single-volume work comprises an alphabetical title listing of microform collections. Each entry may contain a bibliographic citation, a microform number, a brief contents listing, a collection description, and appropriate Library of Congress subject headings (LCSH). The collections outlined in *A Guide to the Microform Collections* cover all cultures and time periods within the humanities and social sciences. The guide includes an "Index by Format and Subject," which is arranged alphabetically with relevant titles listed under the appropriate format or subject entry. For instance, *Playbills from the Harvard Theatre Collection* is listed beneath the heading for *Playbills—England—19th c.* Likewise, *Archives of the Fabian Society* and *Bernard Shaw Diaries, 1885–1897* falls under the heading *Shaw, George Bernard*. This guide has since been updated in an online form (www.loc.gov/ rr/microform/guide). The online edition of *A Guide to the Microform Collections* contains the 1996 edition's contents and updates holdings with microform collections added since 1996. The online version also has an alphabetical title listing as well as an "Index A-J" and an "Index K-Z" for both subject and format.

In addition to the online *A Guide to the Microform Collections in the Humanities and Social Sciences Division of the Library of Congress*, the Library of Congress Microform Reading Room has a useful *"Bibliographies and Guides"* section. This webpage links to several guides on "Using Research Materials in Microform" and "Using Books in Microform" as well as select subject-specific guides such as "British Government Documents in the Micro-

form Reading Room of the Library of Congress." While many of the microform collections held by the Library of Congress focus on the United States
and North American interests, scholars of the Victorian and Edwardian ages
will find many pertinent collections, since not all manuscripts of British origin
have remained in Great Britain.

Published annually since 1978, the *Guide to Microforms in Print* provides
subject access to microforms from around the globe. It is organized according
to the Dewey Decimal Classification System and is designed to help researchers and librarians identify resources available in microform. Within each
Dewey class, entries are arranged alphabetically by title. Entries may comprise the following information: title; subtitle; author(s); editor(s); place,
publisher, and date of both the original and the microform; series; collation
information; type of microform; price; ISBN or ISSN; distributor or co-
publisher information; additional title information; order number; publisher
code; and subject classes. The set contains country-of-publication codes, currency symbols, key to abbreviated series, general abbreviations, a survey of
Dewey classes, publishers and distributors; and an index to publishers and
distributors. Although other subject areas may be pertinent as well, Dewey
class 420—English language and literature—will be of particular interest to
scholars of Victorian and Edwardian literature. The second volume includes
an index of persons as subjects, which should also be useful for scholars seeking microform resources on a particular author or individual from nineteenth-
and early twentieth-century Britain.

Now in its second edition, *Microform Research Collections: A Guide* offers
an overview and reviews of microform collections available to librarians and
scholars. This guide does not comprehensively treat microforms but highlights
representative collections in the arts, humanities, sciences, and social sciences.
Unlike the *Guide to Microforms in Print*, which simply lists microforms and
their publication data, *Microform Research Collections* provides detailed information regarding the title, publisher, format, price, reviews, arrangement and
bibliographical control, bibliographies and indexes, and scope and content. The
added information in *Microform Research Collections* should help researchers
determine whether they need to seek out a particular microform collection. In
addition to the entries proper, this volume contains a detailed table of contents,
a publisher list, and an index to authors, compilers, editors, and titles of microform collections and their guides. Although not all collections in this guide
pertain to literary studies in general or Victorian and Edwardian literature in
particular, many of the collections are highly relevant, including: *British Culture: Series One, 18th and 19th Century*; *English and American Plays of the 19th
Century: English Plays 1801–1900, American Plays 1831–1900*; *The English
Gift Books and Literary Annuals, 1823–1857*; *English Literary Periodicals*;

Religion, Radicalism, and Freethought in Victorian and Edwardian Britain; and *Victorian and Albert Museum, Early Rare Photographic Collection.*

A final source for locating microform and digital collections is ***WorldCat.*** Discussed in more detail in chapter 3 on library catalogs, *WorldCat* allows scholars to easily search the holdings of multiple libraries and to limit their searching to microforms. To find microforms using *WorldCat*, use the same search techniques discussed in chapter 3, but set the subtype limit from "Any Format" to "Microform." For example, a quick keyword search for *George Bernard Shaw* with the subtype limited to "Microform" returns 230 microform results related to Shaw. Scholars in search of a known item could also use this catalog to verify the microform's existence and location, since *WorldCat* provides location details for known copies of items. If your library does not own a particular collection, you should either request the item through interlibrary loan or consider taking a trip to use the collection at another library. Because *WorldCat* does not always represent 100 percent of any library's holdings, double-check in the library's online catalog prior to travelling to use its resources.

MICROFORM AND DIGITIZED COLLECTIONS

British Literary Manuscripts Online, c. 1660–1900. Farmington Hills, MI: Gale Cengage. www.gale.cengage.com.

The Correspondence and Literary Manuscripts of Margaret Oliphant (1828– 1897) from the National Library of Scotland. 20 microfilm reels. Wiltshire, England: Adam Matthew Publications, 1999.

English Gift Books and Literary Annuals, 1823–1857. 697 microfiche. Teaneck, NJ: Somerset House, 1976–1977.

Gaskell and the Brontës. 7 microfilm reels. Wiltshire, England: Adam Matthew Publications, 2003.

India, Raj, and Empire. Wiltshire, England: Adam Matthew Digital. www .amdigital.co.uk.

The John Johnson Collection: An Archive of Printed Ephemera. Cambridge, U.K.: Chadwyck-Healey. johnjohnson.chadwyck.co.uk.

Literary Manuscripts (Berg). Wiltshire, England: Adam Matthew Digital. www.amdigital.co.uk.

The Microbook Library of English Literature. 7,000 ultra-microfiche. Chicago: Library Resources Inc., 1970.

The Microbook Library of English Literature, Basic Collection: Author Catalog and Title Catalog. Chicago: Library Resources, Inc., 1972.

The Microbook Library of English Literature. Basic Collection, Shelf List. Chicago: Library Resources, Inc., 1972.

The Nineteenth Century. 49,480 microfiche. Alexandria, VA: Chadwyck-Healey, 1986–1994. Index online at c19.chadwyck.co.uk and on CD-ROM.

Nineteenth-Century Fiction. Ann Arbor, MI: ProQuest. www.proquest.com and on CD-ROM.

Nineteenth-Century Literature and Culture. Charlottesville, VA: University of Virginia Press. rotunda.upress.virginia.edu (accessed 19 April 2010).

Nineteenth Century Literary Manuscripts. 122 microfilm reels. Wiltshire, England: Adam Matthew Publications, 1996–2005.

Nineteenth Century Women Writers. 25 microfilm reels. Wiltshire, England: Adam Matthew Publications, 2006.

Oliphant: The Collected Writings of Margaret Oliphant (1828–1897). 106 microfilm reels. Wiltshire, England: Adam Matthew Publications, 1995.

Popular Stage: Drama in Nineteenth Century England. 208 microfilm reels. Brighton: Harvester Microform; Reading: Research Publications, 1985–1989.

Ruskin and Victorian Intellectual Life: Manuscripts of John Ruskin (1819–1900) from the Ruskin Library, University of Lancaster. 18 microfilm reels. Wiltshire, England: Adam Matthew Publications, 2004.

Sensation Fiction. 10 microfilm reels. Wiltshire, England: Adam Matthew Publications, 2003.

Victorian Popular Culture. Wiltshire, England: Adam Matthews Digital. www.amdigital.co.uk.

Women and Victorian Values, 1837–1910: Advice Books, Manuals, and Journals for Women. 144 microfilm reels. Wiltshire, England: Adam Matthew Publications, 1996.

Yang, Cecil Y., ed. *The Letters of Matthew Arnold: A Digital Edition*, at rotunda.upress.virginia.edu/arnold (accessed 19 April 2010).

The collections below include a selection of major, unique, and representative microform and digital collections available for Victorian and Edwardian scholars. While some collections such as *Victorian Popular Culture* strictly cover the time period in question, others such as *The Microbook Library of English Literature* are broader collections that survey additional British literary periods. This is not a comprehensive overview of available collections, but these collections, along with the guides discussed previously, should help you locate relevant resources in your field of study. The collections and any associated finding aids are listed in the bibliography above and discussed in the text below. Collections of period journals and newspapers are not discussed below but in the previous chapter.

The Microbook Library of English Literature (**LEL**) is a selective ultra-microfiche collection of 1,400 years of English literary history from the earliest times to 1900. Although the collection was intended for undergraduate and high school students, *LEL* should prove useful to both graduate students and researchers because of the wide variety of literary texts it contains. While many major literary texts may be widely accessible in printed form, works less readily available in print make this collection valuable to scholars. In addition to primary-source texts such as *The Works of John Ruskin* and H. Rider Haggard's *She*, *LEL* includes periodicals such as *The Spectator*, standard reference sources such as the *Oxford English Dictionary*, correspondence, literary biographies, and early literary criticism. This microfiche set contains scanned page images from all of the books in the collection, as well as the complete author and title catalogs. Two guides—***The Microbook Library of English Literature, Basic Collection: Author Catalog and Title Catalog*** and ***The Microbook Library of English Literature. Basic Collection, Shelf List***—were published in 1972 as finding aids for *LEL*. The author and title guide comprises two alphabetically arranged catalogs of works included in *LEL*. Each author catalog entry may list the *LEL* ultrafiche number, a complete bibliographic citation, descriptive information, table of contents, and Library of Congress subject headings. Title catalog entries contain the *LEL* ultrafiche number, a complete bibliographic citation, and a cross-reference to the proper entry in the author catalog. These two resources are also available at the beginning of the ultrafiche collection. The shelf list offers more basic information than the author and title catalogs, comprising a short title list of works organized by *LEL* number.

The Nineteenth Century is a microfiche collection of books and pamphlets published in the English language between 1801 and 1900 from around the globe, with the exclusion of North America. Comprising six collections—general; linguistics; publishing, the book trade, and the diffusion of knowledge; visual arts and architecture; women writers; and children's literature—*The Nineteenth Century* is intended to provide access to publications that have permanent research value. Each record in the general collection is organized according to broad subject classifications, including agriculture, economics, education, family life and household management, geography and topography, history and archaeology, jurisprudence, medicine, philosophy, politics, psychology, recreation, religion, science, and technology and useful arts.

Supplementing *The Nineteenth Century* microfiche are *The Nineteenth Century on CD-ROM* and *The Nineteenth Century* online catalog. Both resources are guides to the general and specialist collections included in the microfiche set. The CD-ROM allows for searching within keyword, title, title keyword, author, author keyword, broad subject, names and LC subject, publication place, publisher, publisher keyword, publication year, printer, printer keyword, and microfiche number. Every record both comprises details regarding the title, imprint, collation, notes, microform editions, topical subjects, NC series, name added entry, and location, and corresponds to a work in *The Nineteenth Century* microfiche. In addition to searching, the CD-ROM allows for index browsing. The disc is accompanied by a print manual that explains how to use the program and contains appendixes to subject classifications, stop words, and command keys. The online catalog allows scholars to search across all collections or within a particular subset, such as "The General Collection," "Women Writers," "Children's Literature," "Books on British Colonization," and "Books on Linguistics." Like the CD-ROM records, the online catalog records correspond to the original microfiche. Scholars will find the online version much easier to access and search than the CD-ROM.

One full-text digital collection is ***Nineteenth-Century Fiction***. A ProQuest product, this database contains 250 literary works originally published between 1782 and 1903 in Great Britain and Ireland. The collection represents works by major authors of the period, gothic novels, the "Silver Fork" school,[3] the "New Woman" novels,[4] popular fiction, and *fin de siècle* fiction. Given the collection's composition, non-canonical authors such as Sabine Baring-Gould and Meadows Taylor are represented along with canonical ones such as George Eliot and Sir Walter Scott. Most works are either rare or out of print. Each work is included in its full text; however, the text is displayed as HTML with page divisions marked, rather than as downloadable PDF files. In addition to reading nineteenth-century novels, scholars can use *Nineteenth-Century Fiction* to search for occurrences of specific words or phrases in the full text. Scholars may access the contents either by browsing an alphabetical list of authors and their works or by searching for keywords in the work, title, or author fields. Additionally, results may be limited according to publication date, years living, gender, nationality, ethnicity, and work section. A CD-ROM version is also available from ProQuest.

Adam Matthew Publications' ***Nineteenth Century Women Writers*** is a microfilm collection of popular writings by nineteenth-century British women. While many of these authors were widely read in their time, most are little known by today's readers, and libraries hold few copies of their published works. Although the set is not exhaustive, *Nineteenth Century Women Writers* offers a good overview of popular nineteenth-century women writers. Series I, which contains twenty-five microfilm rolls, covers the writings of Matilda Betham-Edwards, Annie Edwards, Florence Marryat, Helen Mathers, Charlotte Riddell, Dora Russell, Adeline Sergeant, Annie Hall Thomas (Mrs. Pender Cudlip), Lucy (Bethia) Walford, John Strange Winter (Mrs. Arthur Stannard), Emma Jane Worboise, Eglanton Thorne (Elizabeth Emily Charlton), and Ann Manning. This collection merely highlights the work of these women. For instance, the prolific Emma Jane Worboise wrote more than fifty works in her day, but only five were filmed for this set: *Thornycroft Hall,*

Robert Wreford's Daughter, *Sissie*, *Helen Bury or the Errors of my Early Life*, and *Heart's Ease in the Family*. Series II has not yet been completed but is intended to emphasize correspondence, autograph manuscripts, and literary manuscripts. A digital guide—composed of an editorial introduction, a publisher's note, biographical notes on the authors, and reel contents—is available online (www.adam-matthew-publications.co.uk/digital_guides/nineteenth _century_women_writers_part_1/Contents.aspx).

Other microform collections, such as **Sensation Fiction**, cover a particular genre of literature. Ten microfilm reels comprise the first part of *Sensation Fiction*, which is the only portion currently published. These reels focus exclusively on Mary Elizabeth Braddon's diaries, notebooks, and literary manuscripts that are housed at the Harry Ransom Humanities Research Center at the University of Texas at Austin. Braddon's manuscripts are part of the Robert Lee Wolff Collection. Some specific works include the manuscript novel *Before the Knowledge of Evil*, the story *Tom Pearsons Last Party*, and miscellaneous notes on African explorers. Additional information about Wolff's collection as detailed in *Nineteenth-Century Fiction: A Bibliographical Catalogue Based on the Collection Formed by Robert Lee Wolff* can be found in chapter 4. Once complete, *Sensation Fiction* should provide a wealth of information for scholars of this genre.

Nineteenth-century British drama scholars should consult **Popular Stage: Drama in Nineteenth Century England**. With 208 microfilm reels organized in three series, this collection was published originally by Harvester Microform and Research Publications, which are now Gale Cengage's Primary Source Media. This collection was filmed from *The Frank Pettingell Collection of Plays* in the University of Kent at Canterbury's Templeman Library (library.kent.ac.uk/library/special/html/specoll/petting.htm), which acquired them from the widow of English actor Frank Pettigell. Arthur Williams, a late Victorian and Edwardian popular comedian, originally developed the collection. The first series (113 reels) is subdivided into five parts and covers manuscript and typescript plays, the second series (20 reels) incorporates pantomimes, and the third series (75 reels), which is organized in three parts, contains rare printed plays. In all, more than one thousand manuscript and typescript plays, more than three hundred pantomime librettis, and more than five thousand rare printed plays comprise *Popular Stage*. The guides and detailed descriptions for this collection are available in print and are located online (microformguides.gale.com/GuideLst.html).

Manuscripts are some of the most valuable resources for literary scholars and are often the most difficult to access. Previous generations of scholars could only use them through travelling to specific archives and special collections; however, today's scholars have greater access through collections such as the ones discussed below. One recent digital collection is Adam Matthew Digital's *Literary Manuscripts (Berg)*. This resource comprises the Victorian manuscripts housed in the Henry W. and Albert A. Berg Collection at the New York Public Library (NYPL). The physical Berg Collection at NYPL is much broader than Victorian literature, covering printed materials and manuscripts from English and American literature, 1480 through the twentieth century. As such, *Literary Manuscripts (Berg)* represents only a fraction of the complete Berg Collection. Manuscripts are included for fifteen Victorian authors: Matthew Arnold, Emily Brontë, Elizabeth Barrett Browning, Robert Browning, Wilkie Collins, Joseph Conrad, Charles Dickens, George Eliot, George Gissing, Thomas Hardy, Henry James, Dante Gabriel Rossetti, John Ruskin, Alfred Tennyson, and William Makepeace Thackeray. This collection contains unique items such as holograph poems by Emily Brontë from the 1840s, a manuscript draft of Joseph Conrad's will, and several of John Ruskin's letters to Elizabeth Barrett Browning. These digitized manuscripts are an invaluable resource for students and scholars of Victorian literature. Adam Matthew Digital does not provide transcripts for the manuscripts, so scholars must grapple with handwritten texts just as they would when using the physical collection. In addition to the manuscripts proper, *Literary Manuscripts (Berg)* contains biographies with lists of notable works and links to related content in the *Oxford Dictionary of National Biography* and *VictorianWeb*, and chronologies of historical events, cultural events, literature, and each author's life. Chronologies may be viewed separately or simultaneously. Scholars interested in the larger Berg Collection at NYPL should consult the collection's website (www.nypl.org/locations/schwarzman/berg-collection-english-and-american-literature) for finding aids and information on accessing the collection.

Another manuscripts source is Gale Cengage's *British Literary Manuscripts Online, c. 1660–1900 (BLMO)*. This archive was created from digitized microform sets, including the following nineteenth-century collections: the *Brontë Manuscripts*; the *Charles Dickens Manuscripts*; the *Forster & Dyce Collections, c. 1800–1900*; *Literary Manuscripts of William Morris from the British Library, London*; *Literary Manuscripts of William Morris from the Huntington Library, San Marino, California*; the *National Library of Scotland, c. 1800–1882*; and *The Oscar Wilde Collection*.[5] The collection comprises roughly four hundred thousand manuscript pages from sources such as letters, diaries, and drafts of novels, plays, poems, and other literary works. As in Adam Matthew's *Literary Manuscripts (Berg)*, the *BLMO* manuscripts are unaccompanied by transcriptions and, as such, the full text cannot be searched. Rather, searching relies on indexing of fields such as author, work title, document type, manuscript number, person-about, year, source library, collection in library, and source microfilm collections. Search results may be marked for printing, downloading, or e-mailing. A citation generator that allows scholars to format a citation in MLA, APA, or plain text with bibliographic tags, or to export the citations into EndNote, ProCite, Reference Manager, and RefWorks is also linked from the marked documents page. In addition to searching, the contents may be browsed alphabetically by author. The browse author list contains cross-references from variant forms and pseudonymous names to the authorized name entry. To help scholars use the manuscripts, *BLMO* includes a dictionary search of the *Merriam-Webster's Encyclopedia of Literature* and the *Merriam-Webster's Collegiate Dictionary.* Additionally, links are provided for related resources on paleography courses, portraits and images, digital scholarship, catalogues and bibliographies, maps and place-names, and select subscription-only sites.

One major microform manuscript collection is *Nineteenth Century Literary Manuscripts* from Adam Matthew Publications. Seven parts in 114 microfilm reels currently comprise this resource. Each part focuses on a different set of documents from an author, editor, or publisher: manuscripts from Browning, Eliot, Thackeray, and Trollope; the correspondence and records of Smith, Elder, and Co.; Arthur Hugh Clough's correspondence and literary manuscripts; John Gibson Lockhart's correspondence and papers; Caroline Bowles and Robert Southey's papers; Archibald Constable's correspondence and papers; and Robert Cadell's correspondence and papers. While the papers of Lockhart, Bowles, and Southey relate more directly to the Romantic period, the other subsets pertain to the Victorian age. The manuscripts were originally sourced from libraries such as the British Library, the National Library of Scotland, and the Bodleian Library, depending on the collection. *Nineteenth Century Literary Manuscripts* should be of particular interest to scholars of textual, publishing, and literary history as the contents illuminate the relationship between major literary authors and publishers of the day. Digital guides are available for all seven parts (www.adam-matthew-publications.co.uk/digital_guides/n.aspx).

The University of Virginia has created *Nineteenth-Century Literature and Culture* as part of Rotunda, which is the electronic imprint for the University of Virginia Press. This resource provides primary and secondary source materials from nineteenth-century American and British literature. Publications include "born digital" resources, which have no print counterpart, and digital versions of print resources. Scholars may either search or browse the collection, depending on their research needs. *The Letters of Matthew Arnold, The Letters of Christina Rossetti*, and *Journal of Emily Shore: Revised and Expanded* should be of particular interest to Victorian scholars. Each collection contains an introduction, the documents' full text, manuscript transcripts, and extensive footnotes. Although the collection is small, it should prove to be a valuable resource.

Because literature and literary research do not exist in a vacuum, scholars may need to access non-literary and ephemeral texts in support of their research. Recently, more collections of this nature have been digitized. One such resource is ProQuest's *The John Johnson Collection: An Archive of Printed Ephemera*, which was created in cooperation with the University of Oxford's Bodleian Library. The Bodleian houses the physical ephemera digitized for this database (www.bodley.ox.ac.uk/johnson/johnson.htm). The collection was originally compiled by John de Monins Johnson, a British classical scholar, ephemerist, and printer, who finished printing the *Oxford English Dictionary* in 1928 in addition to being an avid collector of printed ephemera.[6] When complete, this resource will comprise more than sixty-five thousand ephemeral publications relating to nineteenth-century entertainment, the book trade, popular prints, advertising, and crime, murders, and executions. The items were digitized in full color and at high resolutions, which allows scholars to examine the page images in great detail. Although some items date to earlier centuries, the bulk of the ephemeral items were published in the eighteenth, nineteenth, and twentieth centuries.

The included ephemera may be either searched or browsed. Scholars may browse by the five categories—advertising, book trade, crime, entertainment, and prints—and have the option to drill down into the categories, which mimic the organization of the Bodleian collection. For instance, "Broadsides: Murder and Execution folder," "Crime," and "Harding B" are listed as subcategories under "Crime." The interface allows you to search within one or all categories using keywords, names, title/first line, subject, illustration subject, place, document type, printing process, printer/publisher, engraver/lithographer, date, shelfmark, physical form, or special features. Scholars may save images to the "Lightbox" but must create a profile to do so. The profile allows you to save images for future use. The "Lightbox" displays thumbnail images of ephemeral publications that can be printed, e-mailed, downloaded, moved to another lightbox, or removed from the lightbox. Scholars may set up multiple lightboxes to organize their search results for specific research projects. Those who do not wish to set up an account may use the "My Archive" feature to accomplish the same tasks as the "Lightbox." The main difference between the two features is that "My Archive" only saves marked items for the duration of your session, while the "Lightbox" saves them indefinitely.

Scholars with broader research interests will find *Victorian Popular Culture* an excellent resource for cultural materials. Created by Adam Matthew Digital, *Victorian Popular Culture* will eventually comprise resources on

"Spiritualism, Sensation, and Magic," "Circuses, Sideshows, and Freaks," and "Music Hall, Theatre, and Popular Entertainment." Currently only the first two sections are available. The third section is scheduled for release in late 2010. "Spiritualism, Sensation, and Magic" provides primary-source material and essays on mesmerism, psychical science, secular, and magic spiritualism from America, Britain, and Europe between 1779 and 1930. Divided into three subsections—"Popular Enchantments: Magicians, Conjurors, and Illusionists," "Spiritualism: Mediums, Psychics, and Spirits," and "From Mesmer's 'New Science' to Animal Magnetism, Hypnotism, and Psychical Research"—this material was based on "Entertaining the Supernatural: Rare Printed Sources from the Harry Price Library of Magical Literature at Senate House, University of London" and "The History of Magic Scrapbooks from the Houdini Collection with related material from the Harry Ransom Humanities Research Center." "Circuses, Sideshows, and Freaks" is based on collections at the University of Sheffield's National Fairground Archive. It covers topics such as World's Fairs, freaks and oddities, and fairground rides. The database's contents may be browsed by title, author, or publication date, or searched with keywords or terms in title, date, publisher, publication place, author, source library, document type, and document subtype fields. Scholars may search using word stemming or proximity. *Victorian Popular Culture* also contains canned popular searches for topics, such as escape artist and prestidigitation, and names, such as Cardini or Cosmo the Mystic. Supplementary material offered by this database includes a slideshow gallery, chronology, biographies, bibliography, glossary, external links, and editor's choice, which highlights select materials in the collection. Documents may be read in the database's interface or downloaded as PDF files.

Adam Matthew Digital recently collaborated with the National Library of Scotland to produce *India, Raj, and Empire*, a digital collection of manuscripts on Great Britain's relationship to India from 1600 to 1947. In spite of the coverage dates, this collection is strongest for the eighteenth and nineteenth centuries. The documents cover "The East India Company: Government and Administration c. 1750–1857," "Agriculture and Trade c. 1750–1857," "Society, Travel, and Leisure c. 1750–1857," "The Mysore and Maratha Wars, the Indian Uprising 1857–58," "The Raj: British Government and Administration of India after 1858," "Agriculture and Trade after 1858," "Society, Travel, and Leisure after 1858," and "India: Literature, History, and Culture." While the collection is largely historical, literary scholars interested in British imperialism and colonialism should find it a useful, informative resource. In addition to searching, scholars can browse topics and key people. Images, maps, a chronology, a glossary, and external links to additional resources are included along with facsimiles of diaries and journals, official and private papers, letters, sketches, paintings, and original Indian documents. Because the emphasis is on the primary-source materials, transcripts are generally not provided.

In addition to broad microform collections, niche collections are also available to help meet specific research needs. One such collection is Adam Matthew's ***Women and Victorian Values, 1837–1910: Advice Books, Manuals, and Journals for Women***. Arranged in four parts on 144 microfilm reels, this collection contains primary sources that address changes in and the development of gender in the nineteenth and early-twentieth centuries. Although the title specifies the Victorian age, this collection is just as relevant for research on the Edwardian age and serves as a continuation of *Women Advising Women*, a microfilm collection of advice literature and journals for women from 1577 to 1837. Researchers who are interested in the early Victorian age should consult both collections. While this particular resource is not specific to literature, it provides invaluable information about the cultural expectations and norms for women in Victorian and Edwardian Britain. It has cover-to-cover page images of advice books, manuals, and journals for women and addresses the following broad areas: cookery and domestic life; etiquette; education; entertainment; fashion, society, and beauty; language and literature and letter writing; marriage and divorce; miscellanea; mothers and daughters; religion and morality; travel; women and work; women's health; and women's rights and status. A variety of titles are included, such as *Every Girl's Guide to Sport, Occupation, and Pastime* (1897), *Domestic Economy, and Cookery, for Rich and Poor* (1827), *Matrimony Made Easy* (1913), and *Marriage with a Deceased Wife's Sister* (1849). A print guide to the use and contents of the microform reels accompanies the collection. This guide is reproduced at the beginning of the first reel.

Another niche collection is ***English Gift Books and Literary Annuals, 1823–1857***. On 697 microfiche, this resource will be of particular interest to early Victorian literary scholars as it pulls together twenty-three gift book and literary annual titles that were originally published between 1823 and 1857. This set contains titles such as *Friendship's Offering, Janus; or, the Edinburgh Literary Almanac, Winter's Wreath, Aurora Borealis, Bijou,* and *Forget Me Not*. These gift books and literary annuals provide scholars with a wealth of primary-source material in early Victorian literature.

The papers of many Victorian and Edwardian authors are also available as archival collections. At this point, scholars will find more microform collections than digital collections dedicated to a single author or select group of authors. Several examples include *Gaskell and the Brontës, The Correspondence and Literary Manucripts of Margaret Oliphant (1828–1897) from the National Society of Scotland,* and *Ruskin and Victorian Intellectual Life,* all published by Adam Matthew Publications, and the University of Virginia Press's *The Letters of Matthew Arnold*. Collections such as these are excellent for in-depth research on a specific author's life and writings.

Cecil Y. Lang's ***The Letters of Matthew Arnold: A Digital Edition*** is composed of only correspondence. Comprising nearly four thousand letters, this archive is an invaluable resource for scholars of Arnold and Victorian poetry and criticism. The University of Virginia Press published both the print and online editions of *The Letters of Matthew Arnold*.[7] The two are largely the same; however, the online version consolidates the front matter, regularizes opening and closing elements of the correspondence, presents letters consistently across volumes, places all letters in chronological order, includes Greek characters with diacriticals, and corrects errors in the printed edition. The front matter from the printed edition contains acknowledgements, an introduction, editorial principles, short titles and abbreviations, and chronology. The letters may be browsed chronologically, beginning in 1829 and ending in 1888. They may also be searched by keyword or phrase, with limiting options for both author and recipient. A cumulative alphabetical index is provided. Although not apparent from the online edition's homepage, this is a subscription resource. If your institution does not subscribe, individual scholars may set up a free 48-hour trial.

Gaskell and the Brontës combines contents of two archival collections held by the Brotherton Library at the University of Leeds. Among other documents, the collections comprise Gaskell's letters, Gaskell's journal from 1835 to 1838, an autograph manuscript of *Sylvia's Lovers*, Branwell Brontë's manuscript works, Charlotte Brontë's poetry manuscripts and exercise books, and correspondence about, from, and to the Brontës. Seven microfilm reels contain the collection, with three reels dedicated to Gaskell and four to the Brontës. A fifty-six-page guide is available in print and online (www.adam-matthew-publications .co.uk/digital_guides/gaskell_and_the_brontes/Contents.aspx). The guide includes a publisher's note, an editorial introduction, the reel contents, and a detailed listing. While the Gaskell and Brontë parts of the collection do not have natural connections, both sets of material provide a wealth of information about the works and lives of literary women in Victorian Britain.

Unlike *Gaskell and the Brontës*, ***Oliphant: The Collected Writings of Margaret Oliphant (1828–1897)*** focuses on a single author's literary production. Lesser known today than either the Brontës or Gaskell, Margaret Oliphant was certainly a more prolific writer, penning ninety-eight fictional works, twenty-six non-fiction, more than fifty short stories, and more than three hundred articles and reviews. This microfilm collection provides scholars with the entire corpus of her literary output, both fiction and non-fiction. *Oliphant* is available in four parts, with twenty microfilm reels in each part. A guide to the collection is online (www.adam-matthew-publications.co.uk/digital_guides/oliphant

_collected_writings_parts_1_to_4/Contents.aspx). Scholars of Oliphant may also want to consult *The Correspondence and Literary Manuscripts of Margaret Oliphant (1828–1897) from the National Library of Scotland*. Another Adam Matthew Publications collection, this set supplements *Oliphant* and comprises twenty microfilm reels of primary-source materials about her life and literary output. The collection's digital guide is available online (www .adam-matthew-publications.co.uk/digital_guides/oliphant_the_correspondence _and_literary_manuscripts/Contents.aspx).

Ruskin and Victorian Intellectual Life: Manuscripts of John Ruskin (1819–1900) from the Ruskin Library, University of Lancaster is divided into two parts with part 1 covering "Diaries, 1835–1888" and part 2 covering "Correspondence with Joan Severn, 1864–1899." Unlike the previous authors discussed in this section, John Ruskin was a major Victorian critic rather than a literary author; however, his influence on Victorian culture and society is undeniable. This collection contains twenty-nine diaries written between 1835 and 1888, and more than three thousand letters written from Ruskin to his cousin Joan Severn between 1864 and 1899. The collection's two parts complement each other well as they provide insights into the mind and life of Ruskin. A digital guide comprising a publisher's note, technical note, reel contents, detailed listing, and chronology is available online (www .adam-matthew-publications.co.uk/digital_guides/ruskin/Contents.aspx).

CONCLUSION

Microform and digital collections are essential resources for scholars of Victorian and Edwardian literature. Although using the original primary-source material is always the preferable option, financial, geographic, and time constraints often necessitate that scholars consult facsimiles. The collections described in this chapter may help address research needs that otherwise would go unmet. If you are researching a topic that does not seem to be covered in the specific resources discussed above, consult finding aids such as *Guide to Microforms in Print* or *Microform Research Collections: A Guide*, or ask your librarian. These and other sources should point you to available, pertinent collections. While many major and minor collections have been filmed or digitized, the materials you need may only be available in their original form. Even if your research resources are available on microfilm or digitally, you may still have to consult the physical objects. If you require archival materials to complete your research, consult the following chapter, which discusses best practices for use of and tools for locating archives and manuscript collections.

NOTES

1. S. J. Teague, *Microform Librarianship* (Boston: Butterworths, 1977), 2.

2. H. G. Wells, "The Idea of a Permanent World Encyclopedia," in *World Brain* (Garden City, NY: Doubleday, Doran, and Co., Inc., 1938), 85.

3. The "silver-fork school" was a derisive term used to describe nineteenth-century British novelists "who emphasized gentility and etiquette." William Harmon. "Silver-Fork School," in *A Handbook to Literature*, 11th ed. (Upper Saddle River, NJ: Prentice Hall, 2009), 514.

4. The term "new woman novel" referred to works written by women novelists that "challenged the conventional representations of women's lives that limited a woman's space to the domestic sphere and idealized self-sacrifice as a noble female trait." Michael R. Molino. "New Woman Novel," in *The Oxford Encyclopedia of British Literature*, Vol. 4 (New York: Oxford University Press, 2006), 98.

5. Additional microform collections incorporated into *British Literary Manuscripts Online, c. 1660–1900* include *British Library Series I: c. 1500–1700*; *British Library Series II: c. 1700–1800*; *Edward Gibbon Manuscripts*; *Folger Shakespeare Library, c. 1500–1700*; *Forster & Dyce Collections, c. 1500–1800*; *National Library of Scotland, c. 1300–1700*; *National Library of Scotland, c. 1700–1800*; *The Sir Walter Scott Manuscripts*; and *William Cowper and Other Eighteenth Century Literary Manuscripts*.

6. *Oxford Dictionary of National Biography*, s.v. "Johnson, John de Monins," http://www.oxforddnb.com/view/article/34203 (accessed 19 April 2010).

7. *The Letters of Matthew Arnold*, ed. Cecil Y. Lang, 6 vols. (Charlottesville: University Press of Virginia, 1996–2001).

Chapter Nine

Manuscripts and Archives

Although you may begin in the library, your research will frequently lead you into the archives as you delve deeper into your topic. While archival research may be time-consuming and costly, it is one of the most exciting steps in the research process, as it grants you access to original primary-source materials. In spite of increases in accessibility and availability of microform and digital collections, as discussed in chapter 8, many materials remain only in their original form, requiring you to visit a particular repository. Even when materials have been reproduced, sometimes you will find that there is no good substitute for examining the original, physical artifact. Certain features of a document, such as watermarks, may not be evident in a reproduction, or the reproduction itself may not clearly depict the text on the page. Difficult-to-read typefaces and handwriting may be decipherable in the original but incomprehensible in the microform or digitized edition. Additionally, the unquantifiable experience of handling original manuscripts and rare texts cannot be replicated in any other format.

Often housed within libraries, particularly on university campuses, archives are also found in businesses, governments, historical societies, museums, newspapers, and other repositories, so you may need to visit a variety of establishments to access the resources you need. While a particular repository may hold a significant number of items written by or related to a particular author, it is improbable that one archive will contain 100 percent of the materials you require. More frequently, collections and sometimes even individual manuscripts will be divided among multiple locations. You will find that archival research takes patience, persistence, and time as you track down the manuscripts and archives necessary to complete your research. Just as locating manuscripts may be more challenging than locating typical library holdings through online catalogs, using manuscripts requires a different set of skills. You may need to decipher difficult-to-read handwriting, complete with bleed-through, fading, and blotting, or the text you are reading may require special care and handling to prevent brittle pages from crumbling. These conditions may significantly slow down the rate at which you can read a particular passage.

This chapter overviews what archives are, how they differ from libraries, and what strategies are most effective for researching archival materials. Although each archive differs from the next, there are general principles and policies that should apply to most collections. By familiarizing yourself with best practices for archival research and knowing what general expectations exist for using rare and sensitive materials, you will be better equipped to use both archives and manuscripts in your research. Additionally, this chapter covers major resources for locating relevant archives and manuscripts, including sources such as Beal's *Index of English Literary Manuscripts*, the *National Union Catalog of Manuscript Collections*, and the *Location Register of Twentieth-Century English Literary Manuscripts and Letters*. The final section addresses online resources for locating archival and manuscript collections. This part focuses on subscription resources such as *Archive Finder* and *ArchiveGrid* as well as open-access resources like *Repositories of Primary Sources* and the many online finding aids for identifying resources in the collections of the British Library and the British National Archives.

DEFINING ARCHIVES AND MANUSCRIPTS

Although both libraries and archives amass, store, and preserve materials for future use, they are not identical in either their purposes or their collections, nor are the research methods employed the same. While libraries purchase published resources item by item, archives tend to acquire materials as complete collections rather than individual titles. You will often need to sift through a large collection to find pertinent documents, but this may also help you discover related resources that would otherwise remain unknown to you. Archives have unpublished resources such as organizational records, personal papers, and oral histories, whereas libraries focus on published works, such as books, films, journals, and microforms. Similar content may be found in both published and unpublished materials, but the format likely differs. For instance, a library might own a published edition of Wilkie Collins's collected letters, but the actual manuscript letters are housed in an archive. Likewise, many published copies of George Eliot's *Middlemarch* can be found in libraries around the world; however, an archive holds the original handwritten manuscripts for the novel. When a library does not have the materials needed, you can access them as simply as submitting an interlibrary loan request. If an archive does not contain all the papers or manuscripts of a particular author, then you must then visit whichever other archive does have the materials in question, as archives tend not to loan out their resources. Unlike libraries, which generally have open, circulating collections, archives have closed, non-circulating collections, meaning that materials may not be removed from the premises and must be retrieved by the archival staff on duty.

On the one hand, libraries tend to acquire resources to provide the greatest access to those materials. Archives, on the other hand, collect not only to grant access but also to preserve rare and valuable materials for posterity. Because preservation is such a major part of the archival mission, archives may place more restrictions on use of their materials than libraries do. One major restriction, alluded to previously, is that scholars cannot freely browse the collection for research materials; rather, they must use finding aids to identify pertinent materials and then request access from the archivist. Along this vein, generally you may only access one item at a time, which will be served to you by the archivist or archive's staff. Typically, scholars must supply proof of identification prior to using materials; however, some collections even require letters of introduction from known scholars who can vouch for your research purpose or institutional affiliation prior to granting you access to any resources. These policies vary from archive to archive, so always investigate access requirements prior to visiting any repository. Archives often keep more limited hours than libraries, so plan your time wisely and schedule your visit ahead of time if at all possible. Advanced research and preparation into matters such as usage policies, hours, and restrictions can enhance the efficiency with which you use a particular collection.

Online library catalogs are the primary means of accessing libraries' physical holdings. Not so with archival materials. Some archives may represent their materials in a library catalog; however, these records are often inadequate for describing either archives or manuscripts. Where library materials are cataloged using MARC records (see chapters 1 and 3), archives and manuscripts are described in finding aids using Encoded Archival Description (EAD). While MARC records work best for creating catalog records, archivists and manuscript curators prefer EAD for inventorying full-text materials in online finding aids because it provides a structure for descriptive information while giving archivists and manuscript curators the flexibility needed to represent unique archival and manuscript collections. Finding aids are often not included in online catalogs but may be available from the archive's website or in print at the archive. Occasionally you may come across materials without finding aids. In this situation, your best source of information is the archivist for the collection. You may also consult various guides to locating archives and manuscripts, such as those discussed below; however, for the most accurate information about any archive's holdings, always contact the archive for the collection. Since most repositories have websites, your first step should be to check the website for online finding aids as well as contact information and hours. In the event that a repository has no Web presence, then an old-fashioned phone call will do the trick. In speaking directly with the archivist, you may learn about uncataloged collections that are pertinent to your research.

In addition to archives and libraries, another critical distinction is between archives and manuscripts. Both terms can be used to describe collections; however, they are not completely synonymous. Archives originate from an organization or institution, while manuscripts are acquired from or donated by an individual or family. The individual pieces of an archival collection are referred to as records, and the specific holdings of a manuscript collection are called papers. Additionally, the term *archives* tends to refer to a collection of materials, while *manuscripts* alludes to handwritten or draft documents. To confuse matters, archives may house manuscripts, and both are organized as collections. Rare printed and manuscript materials may also be housed in special collections within a larger research library. Understanding the distinction between these terms should help you navigate the world of archives and manuscripts.

"BEST PRACTICES" FOR ARCHIVAL RESEARCH

Prior to using any archival or manuscript materials, prepare in advance by doing any necessary secondary research to build a body of knowledge to contextualize your project. Like all things, manuscripts and archival collections were not originally created in a vacuum, so learning about the context in which individual documents were written could give you a better understanding of their significant aspects. Additionally, knowing background information prior to using archival materials enables you to use your time with them more effectively. Being better informed about your topic will help you know where you should focus your attention in a text. Your research will not only help you understand a particular manuscript's significance, but it may also reveal other archives and manuscripts you should consult. Along these lines, be sure to note the introductions and acknowledgements of both biographies and standard editions, as these often refer to archival materials and manuscripts. Both introductions and acknowledgements frequently mention the collections that were most helpful to their research. Often those same collections will be relevant for your research as well. Doing this could save you time and may help you identify existing archives and manuscripts when you don't have access to some of the subscription resources discussed below.

Typically, archives are open during set hours only, and although some archives accommodate walk-in visitors, it is best to make an appointment prior to your visit to ensure that the materials are available. (Archives often store materials in a different physical location, requiring the materials to be brought to the reading room from an off-site facility.) Additionally, if you schedule your visit in advance, the archivist should have the materials ready when you arrive, saving valuable research time that otherwise would have been wasted waiting for the items' retrieval. Even if you request all the materials you need in advance, you will most likely have access to only one manuscript at a time. As you finish using one manuscript, you must return it to the archivist before being allowed to view subsequent documents. Because these materials are often fragile, you may be required to use a cradle to hold them. In archives, cradles made of foam are designed to support a book's spine while allowing you to browse carefully through its pages. When working with archival materials and manuscripts, you are not allowed to write with pens or other writing instruments that leave permanent marks; rather, you must use pencil only when using these sensitive materials. While earlier generations were limited to pencil and paper for taking notes about their research materials, today's scholars are frequently allowed to bring a laptop into the reading room. Another change in archival practice relates to whether rare materials should best be handled with white gloves or clean bare hands. Previously, the standard practice was to wear white cotton gloves to prevent oils and dirt from transferring to the page; however, gloves greatly reduce a scholar's dexterity and can often do more harm than good as scholars inadvertently damage pages in their struggle to turn them. Today most archives recommend using materials with clean, bare hands. That said, you should always check an individual archive's policies to see what is preferred.

Just as handling materials is subject to guidelines, what you bring with you into an archive is frequently restricted by archival policies. Many repositories do not allow backpacks, large bags, or even jackets in their reading room, but often provide storage lockers for you to stash your belongings while using their facilities. Although laptops are allowed, cameras are not as widely accepted. Some archives may permit non-flash photography, while others restrict use of cameras altogether. Since this varies from archive to archive, be sure to check with the archivist prior to taking photos of any materials. You can request to have materials scanned or photocopied; however, the archive's staff typically does this, and generally there is a per-page cost. One final restriction to note: since spilled drinks or crumbs from food could do irreparable damage to irreplaceable materials, food and liquids are not normally allowed in any archive's reading room.

While these guidelines may seem restrictive to some, their intent is not to make research overly cumbersome or difficult. Rather, they are in place to protect and preserve archival materials. By controlling how archives and manuscripts are used, archivists ensure that the resources will be available well into the future, preserving the cultural heritage those documents represent. As stated previously, the guidelines vary from archive to archive, so always double-check on a particular repository's policies rather than assuming they adhere to the established standards. As a way of applying this information, the following section walks you through using the British Library's collections.

THE BRITISH LIBRARY

Any scholar researching Victorian and Edwardian literature may at some point need to consult the research materials housed in the British Library. While the British Library collections are extensive, it will likely not be the first stop on your research path; rather, you should have explored all other avenues and completed a significant amount of your research prior to visiting the British Library. To gain admittance to reading rooms at two British Library locations—St. Pancras and British Library Newspapers at Colindale—you must first register for a Reading Pass, which is granted based on need of specific resources in the library's collections.[1] Scholars may register onsite and receive their pass immediately. Those seeking to use the collections must provide two original identification documents: one as proof of home address and the other as proof of signature. Having proper identification is essential so that you make the best use of your time. If you only bring your passport as identification, for example, you will only be eligible for a day pass and will be required to reregister each day of your visit, wasting valuable time that could have been spent using research materials. Scholars who have limited time for visiting the British Library and need to access materials stored off-site may also request items in advance and prior to registering for the Reading Pass. More details on acquiring a pass are available on the British Library's website.

Because the collections are so broad in focus, the British Library's St. Pancras location—which houses the main collections excluding newspapers, which are at Colindale—is organized into eleven subject-specific reading rooms, including the African and Asian Studies Reading Room, the Business and Intellectual Property Centre, the Humanities Reading Rooms, the Manuscripts Reading Room, the Maps Reading Room, the Rare Books and Music Reading Room, the Science Reading Rooms, and the Social Science Reading Room. While the individual research project will dictate which room is most appropriate, scholars of Victorian and Edwardian literature will probably find the Humanities Reading Rooms (post-1850 printed books and journals), the Manuscripts Reading Room (Western-language handwritten manuscript collections), and the Rare Books and Music Reading Room (pre-1851 printed books) the most helpful. Subject-specific reference teams staff each reading room to provide expert research assistance to scholars. The team members are available to help you access and make the best use of the library's resources.

Once you have gained admittance to the reading rooms, be aware of restrictions on using the space and collections. Any materials that may damage the collections—including pens, food, drinks, candy, chewing gum, glue, ink bottles, correction fluid, cleaning liquids, scissors, knives, highlighter pens, scanner pens, adhesive tape, and umbrellas—are prohibited. Like most archives, the British Library allows only pencils for writing; however, scholars should be sure not to mark or write in any of the materials even in pencil. Likewise, tracings and rubbings of materials are prohibited without special, explicit permission from the British Library staff. While copies can be made of most materials using the library's copying equipment, visitors to the library may not bring their own scanners, copiers, or cameras to duplicate any materials. Scholars must request access to British Library materials, which are then delivered by library staff. The issued materials may only be used in the reading room where they are first delivered and may not be removed to any other room. When finished using materials, you must return them to the desk where they were first issued to you. Additional information about using the British Library reading rooms and collections is on the library's website.

WEBSITES FOR LOCATING ARCHIVES AND MANUSCRIPT COLLECTIONS

Abraham, Terry. *Repositories of Primary Sources*. University of Idaho. www .uiweb.uidaho.edu/special-collections/Other.Repositories.html (accessed 19 April 2010).

Access to Archives. The National Archives. www.nationalarchives.gov.uk/a2a (accessed 19 April 2010).

Archive Finder. Ann Arbor, MI: Chadwyck-Healey. archives.chadwyck.com (accessed 19 April 2010).

ArchiveGrid. Dublin, OH: OCLC. www.archivegrid.org (accessed 19 April 2010).

ARCHON Directory. The National Archives. www.nationalarchives.gov.uk/ archon (accessed 19 April 2010).

The Catalogue. The National Archives. www.nationalarchives.gov.uk/ catalogue (accessed 19 April 2010).

DocumentsOnline. The National Archives. www.nationalarchives.gov.uk/
documentsonline (accessed 19 April 2010).
Manuscripts Catalogue. The British Library. molcat.bl.uk (accessed 19 April
2010).
The National Archives. www.nationalarchives.gov.uk (accessed 19 April 2010).
National Register of Archives. The National Archives. www.nationalarchives
.gov.uk/nra (accessed 19 April 2010).

Currently, many major archives make their catalogs and finding aids available
online, which greatly eases the process of searching for archival materials.
While the print resources discussed later in this chapter remain useful, online
resources can be updated more easily and frequently, and thus are often more
current. Some print resources, such as the *Location Register of Twentieth-
Century English Literary Manuscripts and Letters* and the *NUCMC*, are already updated through online counterparts. This section covers gateway
websites such as the University of Idaho's *Repositories of Primary Sources*,
Chadwyck-Healey's *Archive Finder*, and OCLC's *ArchiveGrid*. The catalogs
and finding aids from the British Library and the British National Archives
are also discussed in detail below.

Compiled by the University of Idaho's Terry Abraham, **Repositories of
Primary Sources** is a guide to more than five thousand websites for archives,
manuscripts, historic photographs, rare books, oral histories, and other primary-source materials. The online resources indexed by *Repositories of Primary Sources* come from around the globe and are categorized geographically
by Western United States and Canada; Eastern United States and Canada;
Latin America and the Caribbean; Europe; Asia and the Pacific; and Africa
and the Near East. Within each category, repositories are listed by geographic
location (state, province, or country) and alphabetically by repository name
within location. The repository lists do not include descriptions of the major
archival holdings, but simply link to the website of the archive, library, museum, or other location. This site offers additional lists of general and coun-
try-specific repositories, and has indexes to states, provinces, and countries
and an integrated index of all geographic categories that displays in a sidebar
while the repository list displays in the center of the screen. Currently, browsing is the only means of accessing the repositories linked from this resource.

While *Repositories of Primary Sources* can be accessed by all scholars
through the Internet, other resources, such as *Archive Finder* and *ArchiveGrid*,
are available only to subscribers. Published by the Chadwyck-Healey division
of ProQuest, **Archive Finder** is a descriptive directory of archives in the United
States, including 206,000 collections in 5,750 repositories. *Archive Finder*
draws its information from the *NUCMC* from 1959 to 2006, the *National Inven-*

tory of Documentary Sources in the United States (*NIDS*), the *National Inventory of Documentary Sources in the United Kingdom and Ireland* (*NIDS UK/ Ireland*), descriptions submitted by repositories, and online finding aids. *Archive Finder* is the only online archival finding aid that contains the complete contents of the *NUCMC*. This resource is available as a stand-alone product or as a component of *C19: The Nineteenth Century Index*, which is discussed in more detail in chapter 4. *C19* indexes a subset of *Archive Finder*'s contents, specifically, 71,000 records for nineteenth-century materials. Collections of papers that begin in the nineteenth century and extend into the twentieth century are included in the *C19* subset of *Archive Finder* records.

The stand-alone *Archive Finder* has options to search collections, repositories, or both simultaneously. Collections may be searched by keyword, collection name, repository name, repository city/town, repository state (U.S.), repository county (U.K.), repository country, *NIDS* fiche number, *NUCMC* number, index terms, and collection dates, while repositories may be searched by repository name, city/town (U.S.), county (U.K.), country, and holdings keyword. The collections and repositories indexed come from England, the Republic of Ireland, Scotland, the United States, and Wales. In spite of the inclusion of *Archive Finder* records in *C19*, the two do not produce identical results for nineteenth-century topics. A simple keyword search for "Mary Elizabeth Braddon" in both resources produces one result in *C19* and five in *Archive Finder*. The major difference in the results is that *C19* results exclude the *NIDS* results incorporated into *Archive Finder*.

Like *Archive Finder*, OCLC's **ArchiveGrid** is a database of collection descriptions that enables scholars to search across the holdings of multiple archives simultaneously. Indexing the contents of more than 3,800 archives, *ArchiveGrid* provides access to almost one million archive records. The collections indexed in here are not strictly literary in nature but cover correspondence, family histories, historical documents, manuscripts, and personal papers. The interface appears quite simple, with only one input box for terms; however, the search engine behind the interface recognizes phrase searching, Boolean operators, wildcards, and nesting. Additionally, scholars can indicate the importance of a particular search term by marking it with a caret (^) and a number greater than one. Search results are relevance-ranked based on frequency, field length, number of search terms, and indicated emphases. The records' contents are drawn from OCLC's *WorldCat* catalog records (see chapter 3 for more information on *WorldCat*). Each record may contain details about the collection's size, arrangement, and finding aids; the repository's contact information; collection notes and summaries; and a list of relevant subject headings. From the results screen, scholars can choose to sort the results by relevance, date, title, archive, or location, and refine results by archives or locations.

In addition to resources that search across multiple locations, the finding aids for manuscripts and archives in the British Library and the British National Archives are worth addressing in this section. While print resources such as M. A. E. Nickson's *The British Library: Guide to the Catalogues and Indexes of the Department of Manuscripts* and the *Index of Manuscripts in the British Library* can help scholars locate manuscripts held by the British Library, some may find it more convenient to search these holdings online through the British Library *Manuscripts Catalogue*. Contents of the *Manuscripts Catalogue* may be searched in two main ways: the index search and the descriptions search. The former allows scholars to look for particular terms in the following fields: name, additional name, descriptive adjunct, index entry, language, state, start year, end year, and name, adjunct, and index entry. The descriptions search enables keyword searching of manuscript collection descriptions. While most of the British Library's manuscripts are included in the online *Manuscripts Catalogue*, several collections are not yet represented here and must be searched through the print catalogs.

In addition to the British Library, scholars of any British literary era should be familiar with *The National Archives* and its online catalogs and directories. *The National Archives* serves as the official archive of the United Kingdom government, covers nearly one thousand years of history, and comprises materials from the Public Record Office, the Historical Manuscripts Commission, the Office of Public Sector Information, and Her Majesty's Stationery Office. The collection contains more than ten million records to archival materials such as manuscripts, photographs, and maps. The *National Archives* website links scholars to several major finding aids for British archival materials: *The Catalogue, Documents Online, ARCHON Directory, National Register of Archives*, and *Access to Archives*. These tools are indispensible for locating research materials in the National Archives and other British archives.

The Catalogue of the National Archives is the primary search mechanism for eleven million descriptions of British government and legal records. The catalog entries are arranged according to department of each document's origin. Each item fits into a specific hierarchy developed for the catalog, which, from top level to bottom level, is organized as follows: department, division, series, subseries, sub-subseries, piece, and item. Additionally, items are assigned department codes to indicate the department of origin. For example, publications by the Foreign Office are labeled "FO," while Railway and Canal Companies publications are labeled "RAIL." To aid scholars in researching in *The National Archives*, the catalog also contains nearly three hundred detailed research guides on varied topics such as "Australia, 1787–1868, Transportation to," "Divorce Records After 1858," "Lunatic Asylums, 18th–20th Centuries," "Maps in the National Archives," and "Poor Law Records, 1834–1871." Scholars may search the catalog by word or phrase, year range, and department or series code. Places, prominent people, and subjects are pulled out in an alphabetical list that may be either searched or browsed. Each item in the list is linked to general information about the place, person, or subject, and has a unique "Search" button assigned to it that automatically queries the archive holdings for that topic. The catalog's full contents may be browsed according to reference or title.

While the National Archives' *Catalogue* is simply a catalog without any full-text materials, ***DocumentsOnline*** provides a searchable collection of scanned public documents that may be downloaded. The *DocumentsOnline* contents may be searched either by quick search, which allows for keyword searching in specific date ranges, or by advanced search, which enables searching by keyword in first name, last name, place, or other keyword. Advanced searches can be limited by date range, categories, and media types. Contents are browseable by collection. Relevant items may be added to the "Shopping Basket" for purchase at a minimal cost. Because only a selection of documents is included in *DocumentsOnline*, scholars should consult *The Catalogue* to conduct a more comprehensive search.

Since the National Archives do not contain all British archival materials, scholars should also consult the ***ARCHON Directory***, which the National Archives: Historical Manuscript Commission maintains. Preceded in print by *Record Repositories in Great Britain* from 1964 to 1999, the *ARCHON Directory* supersedes all print volumes and comprises contact information for archives, libraries, the records office, and other institutions holding significant manuscript collections throughout the United Kingdom and overseas. The repositories may be either browsed alphabetically within geographic area or searched by repository name or *ARCHON* code. Each repository entry may include a numerical code, contact information, access information, information specific to the repository recorded in the National Register of Archives, and accessions for the previous five years.

While the *ARCHON Directory* is useful for identifying repositories, the ***National Register of Archives*** (***NRA***) indexes more than 44,000 catalogs and records lists for locating archival materials. Also maintained by the National Archives: Historical Manuscript Commission, the *NRA* has been available online since 1995. Indexes are the primary means of accessing the *NRA*'s contents. Five online indexes—business, organisations, personal, families and estates, and diaries and papers—organize the records according to provenance rather than subject. Each of these is searchable by corporate name (combines business and organisations), personal name (combines personal and diaries and papers), family name, and place name. The personal name search, particularly, is best for researching a specific author. A search for *Mary Elizabeth Braddon* as a personal name retrieves archival information that directs scholars to related collections and historical information about Braddon. When available, the historical information section links to a pertinent *Oxford Dictionary of National Biography* (*ODNB*) entry (for more on the *ODNB*, see chapter 2). Likewise, the corporate name search can be useful for locating publishers' archives. Scholars should employ the *NRA* as a finding aid to point them to specific archives and collection-level descriptions. For more detailed information, scholars should consult the finding aids created by the archive holding a particular collection.

One final source for searching archival collections is ***Access to Archives*** (***A2A***). Much like the *NRA*, *A2A* is a database of catalogs for other archival collections. Currently, approximately four hundred repositories' records are included in *A2A*, roughly 30 percent of all archival collections in England and Wales. The site's contents may be searched by a keyword or by an advanced search from where scholars can limit by date, place, repository, and region, and specify whether "all these words," "one or more of these words," or "this exact wording or phrase" must appear in the search results. Unlike *NRA* results, which have collection descriptions but not finding aids, *A2A* results list specific documents contained within a particular collection. The item-level descriptions will be particularly useful for determining whether a collection is relevant to a specific research project.

PRINT SOURCES FOR LOCATING
RELEVANT ARCHIVES AND MANUSCRIPTS

Ash, Lee, and William G. Miller. *Subject Collections: A Guide to Special Book Collections and Subject Emphases as Reported by University, College, Public, and Special Libraries and Museums in the United States and Canada.* 7th ed. 2 vols. New Providence, NJ: R. R. Bowker Co., 1993.

Beal, Peter, ed. *Index of English Literary Manuscripts.* Vol. 4. New York: R. R. Bowker, 1982–1999.

British Library. Department of Manuscripts. *Index of Manuscripts in the British Library.* 10 vols. Teaneck, NJ: Chadwyck-Healey, 1984–1986.

Dictionary of Literary Biography. Detroit, MI: Gale Cengage, 1978. Also available online at www.gale.cengage.com.

Foster, Janet, and Julia Sheppard, eds. *British Archives: A Guide to Archive Resources in the United Kingdom.* 4th ed. New York: Palgrave, 2002.

Great Britain. Public Record Office. *Guide to the Contents of the Public Record Office.* 3 vols. London: H. M. Stationery Office, 1963–1968.

Index to Personal Names in the National Union Catalog of Manuscript Collections, 1959–1984. Alexandria, VA: Chadwyck-Healey, 1987–1988.

Index to Subjects and Corporate Names in the National Union Catalog of Manuscript Collections, 1959–1984. Alexandria, VA: Chadwyck-Healey, 1994.

Matthew, H. C. G., and Brian Howard Harrison, eds. *Oxford Dictionary of National Biography.* Rev. ed. 61 vols. New York: Oxford University Press, 2004. Also available online at www.oxforddnb.com.

National Union Catalog of Manuscript Collections. 29 vols. Washington, DC: Library of Congress, 1959–1993. Also available online at www.loc .gov/coll/nucmc.

Nickson, M. A. E., and Julian Conway. *The British Library: Guide to the Catalogues and Indexes of the Department of Manuscripts.* 3rd ed. London: The British Library, 1998.

Storey, Richard, and Lionel Madden. *Primary Sources for Victorian Studies: A Guide to the Location and Use of Unpublished Materials.* London: Phillimore, 1977.

Storey, Richard. *Primary Sources for Victorian Studies: An Updating.* Leicester: Victorian Studies Centre, 1987.

Sutton, David C., ed. *Location Register of English Literary Manuscripts and Letters: Eighteenth- and Nineteenth-Centuries.* 2 vols. London: British Library, 1995.

———. *Location Register of Twentieth-Century English Literary Manuscripts and Letters: A Union List of Papers of Modern English, Irish, Scottish, and Welsh Authors in the British Isles.* 2 vols. London: British Library, 1988. Online supplement available at www.reading.ac.uk/library/about-us/ projects/lib-location-register.asp.

WorldCat. Dublin, OH: OCLC. www.oclc.org/firstsearch.

Originally written by Richard Storey and Lionel Madden, ***Primary Sources for Victorian Studies: A Guide to the Location and Use of Unpublished Materials*** is an excellent guide to literary and non-literary research sources and methods in Victorian Studies. Designed with students in mind, this guide will also be useful to scholars who are researching the Victorian age for the first time or who are just now exploring a new aspect of the period. *Primary Sources for Victorian Studies* is organized into nine chapters that discuss research materials, methods, collections, and reference resources. This volume introduces and overviews the Historical Manuscripts Commission and the National Register of Archives, local and national British repositories, and select overseas (non-British) repositories. Particularly valuable are the research guides to nineteenth-century architecture and the visual arts, business history, education, imperialism, literature, military and naval history, politics, postal history, publishing, religious history, science and technology, transport, and visual sources. An index to topics concludes this brief yet helpful guide.

Ten years after its initial publication, Storey updated the guide with *Primary Sources for Victorian Studies: An Updating*. Although both guides are somewhat dated, they both retain value for their concise, coherent presentation of historic resources and research methods for Victorian studies.

Edited by Peter Beal, the fourth volume of the *Index of English Literary Manuscripts* set covers literary manuscripts of thirty-four British and Irish authors of the nineteenth century. These authors were selected based on their inclusion in the *Concise Cambridge Bibliography of English Literature* (*CCBEL*), although several authors listed in the *CCBEL* had to be excluded for space and time reasons. While this volume of the *Index to English Literary Manuscripts* by no means presents a comprehensive listing of nineteenth-century English literary manuscripts, it provides as complete as possible a record for each author. Divided into three parts, volume 4 covers Arnold, Austen, the Brontës, the Brownings, Butler, Byron, Carlyle, Carroll, Clare, Clough, Coleridge, Collins, DeQuincy, Dickens, Disraeli, Edgeworth, Eliot, FitzGerald, Gaskell, Gissing, Hardy, Hazlitt, Hopkins, Keats, Kipling, Lamb, Landor, Meredith, Morris, Pater, and Patmore. Each part includes a list of repositories, a list of auction houses and booksellers, facsimiles, a glossary and guide to symbols, and a guide to abbreviations. This work is arranged alphabetically by author. For each author the manuscripts are divided according to verse, prose, dramatic works, works edited by, diaries and notebooks, and marginalia in printed books and manuscripts. An introduction to the manuscripts, an abbreviations guide, and a guide to the arrangement of manuscript entries preface each author's section. When known, provenance and manuscript numbers are listed for the entries. Since the publication of the *Index of English Literary Manuscripts*, ownership of various manuscripts may have changed, so researchers should always verify the provenance before seeking to examine a particular manuscript.

Edited by David C. Sutton for the British Library, the *Location Register of English Literary Manuscripts and Letters: Eighteenth and Nineteenth Centuries* catalogs eighteenth- and nineteenth-century literary manuscripts and letters located in British libraries and archives. The *Location Register* defines English rather broadly as authors of British or Irish birth, those who spent significant time in Britain or Ireland, and those who renounced their British citizenship. Major authors such as Arthur Hugh Clough, Benjamin Disraeli, and Elizabeth Gaskell are addressed alongside lesser-known authors such as Mary Cowden Clarke, John Forster, and Francis Turner Palgrave. Authors are organized alphabetically by last name with their literary manuscripts and letters listed alphabetically under the main author heading. Each entry may comprise the work's title and subtitle, a brief description, provenance, and manuscript number. The second volume concludes with an appendix of institutional addresses.

The *Location Register of Twentieth-Century English Literary Manuscripts and Letters: A Union List of Papers of Modern English, Irish, Scottish, and Welsh Authors in the British Isles* is a union list of papers from modern English, Irish, Scottish, and Welsh authors in the British Isles from the past century. Also edited by David C. Sutton, this two-volume set lists manuscripts and letters for any twentieth-century British literary author, deceased or living, that are in any publicly available collection in the British Isles. Because any author who lived during the twentieth century was included, there is some overlap between this set and the *Location Register of English Literary Manuscripts and Letters: Eighteenth and Nineteenth Centuries*. Some authors whose work spans the *fin de siècle*, such as Mary Elizabeth Braddon and Thomas Hardy, appear in the location register for the twentieth century rather than the eighteenth- and nineteenth-century set, so researchers may need to consult both location registers to find the holdings of a particular author. The entries in the twentieth-century location register are arranged alphabetically by author and then by title within author. Entries contain brief summary descriptions of the item and a provenance statement with a manuscript number. The second volume concludes with an appendix to the full addresses of institutions referenced in the set. In 2003, an online supplement to the *Location Register of Twentieth-Century English Literary Manuscripts and Letters* was published as an open-access resource. The online supplement, hosted by the University of Reading, updates records published in 1988 and adds records for holdings acquired by British and Irish libraries between 1988 and 2003.

Scholars looking for archival and special collections materials in the United States and Canada should consult *Subject Collections: A Guide to Special Book Collections and Subject Emphases as Reported by University, College, Public, and Special Libraries and Museums in the United States and Canada*. Compiled by Lee Ash and William G. Miller, *Subject Collections* is currently available in its seventh edition, which was released in 1993. Although this two-volume set is slightly dated, it remains a valuable resource for literary scholars. This reference work comprises 65,818 entries for collections held by 5,882 libraries and museums. Entries are arranged by Library of Congress subject headings and alphabetically under each heading. The organization should help scholars easily locate relevant archives and special collections, whether they pertain to authors, newspaper or periodical publications, geographic locations, historical events, literary movements or periods, or other topics. Each entry lists the repository name, address and contact information, holdings, and notes. Because the repositories provided content for many of the entries, the detail level varies widely from entry to entry. *Subject Collections* has a guide to abbreviations but does not have any additional indexing or other means of accessing its contents other than the LCSH arrangement.

Now in its fourth edition, **British Archives: A Guide to Archive Resources in the United Kingdom** is edited by Janet Foster and Julia Sheppard and remains the primary print reference source for locating archival materials in Great Britain. Scholars planning a trip to the British Isles may want to consult this work to determine where relevant archives are housed. However, since this work has not been updated since 2002, scholars should also confirm with the individual archive to ensure that the materials in question are still housed in that location. *British Archives* comprises 1,231 entries and covers archival collections from 478 institutions. Each entry lists the repository's name, parent organization, address and contact information, website, enquiries, hours of operation, access, historical background, acquisitions policy, major collections, non-manuscript material, finding aids, facilities, conservation, and publications. The entries are organized by postal districts for London locations and alphabetically by town for the rest of Great Britain. *British Archives* contains an index to repositories, parent organizations, major predecessor organizations, and collections. Additionally, the editors included a subject guide and appendixes to institutions that have transferred their archives, institutions reported having no archives, and institutions that did not respond, requested not to be included, or supplied insufficient information. This guide also directs scholars to useful organizations, websites, and publications for the following areas: general resources; archival practice and conservation; arts, architecture, and design; business records; directories; education; family history; labour history; literature; local history; military/naval history; other media; overseas; politics; religion; science and medicine; social history and social science; surveys; and transport. Literary scholars may find the main index the best way to identify archival holdings on a particular author.

Scholars planning to visit the British Library to use its manuscript collections may want to consult M. A. E. Nickson's *The British Library: Guide to the Catalogues and Indexes of the Department of Manuscripts* prior to going. Now in its third edition, *The British Library* guides scholars through the many individual collections and resources available through the Department of Manuscripts, much of which is not accounted for in the British Library *Integrated Catalogue* (see chapter 3 for more on this catalog). This slender guide outlines the foundation collections (Cotton, Harley, and Sloane), other closed collections (Royal, Lansdowne, Hargrave, Burney, King's, Arundel, Stowe, Ashley, Yates Thompson, and Zweig), and collections currently being added to (Additional, Egerton, and manuscripts on loan). Each collection is listed along with a statement about its origins and history, a brief description of its contents, and a reference for any existing catalogs or indexes to the collection. *The British Library* includes a table depicting the contents of the printed *Catalogues of Additions to the Manuscripts* and related catalogs, and guides to play collections, charters and rolls, seals, papyri and ostraca, and reproductions of manuscripts. Descriptions of the *Index of Manuscripts in the British Library*, *The Class Catalogue*, *The Singer Index*, and special interest catalogs are provided. An overview of reference books in the Manuscripts Reading Room and an index conclude this volume.

Published between 1984 and 1986, the ten-volume **Index of Manuscripts in the British Library** draws on older catalogs and indexes of the British Library and the British Museum to detail the manuscript holdings of the British Library up until 1950. The *Index of Manuscripts* not only serves as a compilation of holdings identified in other sources but also normalizes spelling variants of names. Whenever possible, the index collocates entries relating to a specific person or place. The entries are arranged alphabetically by person or place with place-names preceding personal names. Each entry contains the manuscript's title or description, dates (when known), and a manuscript and folio number. The *Index of Manuscripts* is not limited to the nineteenth and early twentieth centuries, so researchers will find entries for Medieval and Renaissance manuscripts mixed in with entries for Victorian and Edwardian documents. Likewise, literary works are listed along with correspondence, journals, deeds, wills, and other legal documents. No additional indexes are included to enhance access to the *Index of Manuscripts*.

The **Guide to the Contents of the Public Record Office** provides bibliographic and descriptive information about the legal records, state papers, and departmental records of the British government. This three-volume set describes historic documents in the first two volumes and documents transferred between 1960 and 1966 in the third volume. Legal records comprise those of the Exchequer, the Court of Common Pleas, the Court of Wards and Liveries, and the Office of Queen Anne's Bounty, among others. State papers and departmental records consist of, but are not limited to, those of the Admiralty, the Colonial Office, the Ministry of Education, the Registry of Friendly Societies, the Lands Tribunal, the Lord Chamberlain's Department, and the National Coal Board. Each category is prefaced by an introduction to the office or department and a discussion of its role in British government and society. An annotated bibliography of records follows each of these introductions. For instance, under Court of Common Pleas, there are entries for items such as *Certificates of Acknowledgements of Deeds by Married Women* from 1834 to 1875 and *Plea Rolls, Placita de Banco, or De Banco Rolls* from the reigns of Edward I to Victoria. Volumes 1 and 2 each contain a key to regnal years with chronological index to statutes cited in the text, an abbreviations list, a persons and places index, and a subject index. Volume 1 also includes a guide to special collections of documents. The third volume has corrections and additions to the first two volumes.

Between 1959 and 1993, the Library of Congress printed the ***National Union Catalog of Manuscript Collections*** (***NUCMC***) in a twenty-nine-volume set. The printed *NUCMC* comprises roughly 72,300 manuscript collections held in 1,406 repositories in the United States. Around 1,085,000 entries for subjects and personal, family, corporate, and geographic names, in addition to name, subject, and repository indexes, are contained in the print version. As with the *National Union Catalog* (see chapter 3) the *NUCMC* entries resemble printed Library of Congress catalog cards. Entries are organized by manuscript number, and each has a main heading, a title, a physical description, location, scope and content, and other information as available regarding collection descriptions, restrictions to access, literary rights, and provenance. Although the *NUCMC* is no longer available in print, it is continually updated in its online version.

The online *NUCMC* provides access to content from 1986 to the present. While there is some overlap between the online and print *NUCMC*, the print retains its value, as content prior to 1986 is only available through the print volumes. Currently, there are no plans to add the pre-1986 volumes to the online catalog. The online records may be searched either through the *NUCMC* gateway to archival records in OCLC's ***WorldCat*** (www.loc.gov/coll/nucmc), or by searching *WorldCat* directly by using the "Archival Materials" limit. (See chapter 3 for additional discussion of *WorldCat*.) The gateway available through the *NUCMC* website may be searched by title, notes, subjects, and all names. The records themselves are similar to those in the print volumes. Despite the ease of online searching, finding the location of specific archival holdings requires the scholar to consult either the "OCLC Participating Institutions List" or the "MARC Code List for Organizations," which are both linked from the *NUCMC* search interface.

The two-volume ***Index to Personal Names in the National Union Catalog of Manuscript Collections 1959–1984*** complements and enhances the *NUCMC*'s usefulness. Containing roughly two hundred thousand names, the *Index to Personal Names* lists all personal and family names referenced in the *NUCMC* in alphabetical order. Each entry may list the name, an epithet, birth date, death date, flourish dates, and a two-part citation number referring to the relevant manuscript number and the sequential number of that manuscript. Maiden names and variant names are cross-referenced to the individual's main entry. Like the *Index to Personal Names*, the ***Index to Subjects and Corporate Names in the National Union Catalog of Manuscript Collections 1959–1984*** facilitates access to the *NUCMC*. This three-volume index provides an alphabetic listing of topics, places, and corporate names in the *NUCMC*. Each entry includes appropriate subdivisions as necessary and a two-part citation number that refers to the volume in which the collection is located and the sequential number for that collection. Combined, these two indexes enhance researchers' access to *NUCMC* contents and aid in locating relevant manuscript collections.

When specialized guides to archives and special collections are unavailable, general resources such as the ***Dictionary of Literary Biography*** (***DLB***) and the ***Oxford Dictionary of National Biography*** (***ODNB***) are also helpful for locating archival and special collections. *DLB* entries typically mention major holdings of correspondence and manuscripts in the "Papers" section, while *ODNB* entries include a detailed listing of archives for a particular person. For more on these resources, see chapter 2 for further information on both the *DLB* and the *ODNB*.

CONCLUSION

Although archives and manuscripts may present some of the greatest research challenges, they can also provide some of the greatest rewards. The sources you uncover in archival collections may give your research the edge it needs to make unique and groundbreaking contributions to scholarship in your field. The print and online resources addressed in this chapter should help you identify appropriate manuscript and archival collections, but they are merely a starting point. The real work and intellectual engagement happens when you begin using original primary-source materials in your research. While essential to the research process, the sources in this chapter simply show you the path to the specialized materials needed to complete your research.

NOTE

1. The third British Library location is the Boston Spa Reading Room and does not require a Reading Pass.

Chapter Ten

Web Resources

While previous chapters have emphasized more traditional resources, this one emphasizes new developments in open-access, online sources. The databases discussed in other chapters also have Web interfaces, but they are generally available from publishers and require libraries to subscribe to or purchase the content to gain access. More so than the other resource-specific chapters, this chapter just scratches the surface of Victorian and Edwardian Web resources. Websites are an ever-moving target as new ones emerge, existing ones shift focus, and established ones disappear without notice. Even so, reliable, scholarly Web resources are more common than they were even five years ago and are rapidly gaining acceptance among literary scholars. Although the humanities in general have been slower than other disciplinary areas to embrace the digital revolution, many websites are now being recognized for their contributions to literary scholarship. Earlier chapters have nodded to select online resources, and indeed, most traditional resource types now have online counterparts. Secondary sources such as peer-reviewed, scholarly journals and online dictionaries are gaining acceptance. Additionally, primary sources, including scholarly editions of literary works and digital editions of period newspapers and journals, are more readily available than ever before.

Since online resources do not always undergo the same rigorous editorial and peer-review processes as other resources, make a habit of evaluating your sources carefully before incorporating them into your scholarship. Materials you locate through library catalogs and databases like the *MLA International Bibliography* also require evaluation; however, you may more readily trust resources published through traditional means. Regardless of format, you should consider the following factors when choosing a new resource to incorporate into your research, particularly when you identify it through an Internet search engine:

Accuracy. Can the information presented be verified by other sources? Are there any inconsistencies?

Authority. What are the author's credentials? Is there evidence that the author has expertise in the topic?

Currency. When was the resource published? Has it been updated to account for new developments and information since it was first released? Has the site's author or editor maintained links?

Objectivity. Is there an inherent bias in the resource? Are multiple perspectives presented?

Scope. What does the resource contain? What dates, authors, or geographic locations are covered? Do the contents match with your research objectives?

The remainder of this chapter introduces you to major, reliable scholarly portals, electronic text archives, author websites, contemporary newspapers and journals, current awareness tools, reference tools, and cultural and historical resources available on the Web. Like print resources, these websites serve a variety of functions including directing scholars to relevant citations, providing background information, and situating a body of literature in its historical context. Often these resources point you toward additional scholarly websites that could not be represented in this book.

SCHOLARLY PORTALS

Landow, George P. *The Victorian Web*, at www.victorianweb.org (accessed 16 April 2010).

Leary, Patrick. *Victoria Research Web: Scholarly Resources for Victorian Research*, at www.victorianresearch.org (accessed 16 April 2010).

Liu, Alan. *Voice of the Shuttle*, at vos.ucsb.edu (accessed 16 April 2010).

Lynch, Jack. *Literary Resources on the Net*, at andromeda.rutgers.edu/~jlynch/Lit (accessed 16 April 2010).

If you are just beginning research on Victorian and Edwardian literatures or a new topic within those literary periods, you may want to start in online scholarly portals. These portals may be general and cover any literary topic—*Voice of the Shuttle* and *Literary Resources on the Net*—or they may focus on a particular area in literary studies: *The Victorian Web* and *Victoria Research Web*. Although there is no portal site for Edwardian literature, both the general and Victorian portals should touch on Edwardian topics, texts, and authors to some extent. In some ways, these websites are similar to print reference sources in that they provide background information and point you to other relevant sites.

Maintained by the University of California, Santa Barbara's, Alan Liu, *Voice of the Shuttle* (*VoS*) is perhaps the oldest portal, going back to 1994. Although previous *VoS* versions were static webpages, the current version is a dynamic, database-driven site that allows for greater ease and efficiency of updating and improved searching for users. Intended for use by humanities scholars, *VoS* contents are organized according to disciplinary areas such as "General Humanities Resources," "Anthropology," "Cultural Studies," "Gender and Sexuality Studies," "History," "Literature (in English)," "Literary Theory," and "Philosophy." The "Literature (in English)" section links to websites pertaining to topics such as "General English Literature Resources," "Victorian," "Modern (British and American)," "English Literature by Genre," "History of the Book," and "Courses in English and American Literature." In addition to general and electronic resources, the Victorian and modern sections contain links to author-, work-, or project-specific Web resources, which may include primary- or secondary-source materials. Other subsections in these areas list information on selected writers on social issues, course syllabi, criticism, journals, listservs and newsgroups, and conferences. While *VoS* does a significant service to the profession by organizing these Web resources, you may frequently find dead links for sources which have changed addresses or been removed from the Internet altogether. When you find dead links, use an Internet search engine to determine whether a resource still exists.

Focusing more specifically on literature than *VoS*, **Literary Resources on the Net** aggregates information about literary studies sources. Maintained by Jack Lynch of Rutgers University's Newark campus, *Literary Resources on the Net* is organized into categories such as: "Victorian British," "Twentieth-Century British & Irish," "Theatre and Drama," "Theory," "Women's Literature & Feminism," "Ethnicities & Nationalities," and "Bibliography & History of the Book." One notable exception within these categories is that "Eighteenth-Century" comprises a separate archive rather than a subset of *Literary Resources on the Net*. Not surprisingly, while other sections may be relevant, the Victorian and twentieth-century subsections will be the most useful to Victorian and Edwardian scholars. The Victorian literature sources are categorized according to general, women authors, theatre, pre-Raphaelitism, societies and institutes, journals, and authors. Likewise, twentieth-century British literature sources are organized in the following groups: general, the Great War, and authors. As when using *VoS*, you will find more than a few bad links on *Literary Resources on the Net*, so you may need to determine whether a resource remains active. Scholars may search the site's contents for single words. Although multiple-word searches are possible, single-word searches have far better results. For instance, searching for *Dickens* retrieves links for five websites, while a search for *Charles Dickens* retrieves only one site. Although the search feature is useful, it is limited by the fact that only Lynch's annotations are searched. Many relevant websites, particularly general ones, will not be retrieved even though their contents pertain to the research topic.

Nineteenth-century scholars benefit from having two well-respected sites devoted to scholarship in their area: *The Victorian Web* and the *Victoria Research Web*. Founded and edited by Brown University's George Landow, **The Victorian Web** provides background and scholarly information on the culture, history, and literature of Victorian Britain. The website's contents are organized according to the following categories: "The Victorians," "Political History," "Social History," "Gender Matters," "Philosophy," "Religion," "Science," "Technology," "Genre and Technique," "Authors," "The Visual Arts," "Theater and Popular Entertainment," "*Victorian Web* Books," "Victorian Texts," "Bibliography," "Economic Contexts," "Periodicals," "Places," "Related WWW Resources," "Book Reviews," "What's New," and "Neo-Victorianism." While *Victorian Web* certainly contains links to outside websites, most of its contents are full-text essays written specifically for the site by scholars and occasionally undergraduates. Additionally, select Victorian images and texts, full-text scholarly books, and book reviews are included.

Scholars will find *Victorian Web* useful whether they need ready background information or brief bibliographies of relevant works. A section like "Authors," for instance, comprises a list of Victorian authors with varying amounts of information about each one. A biography, works bibliography, literary relations essay, and cultural contexts are given for an author such as Catherine Gore; entries for major authors like Gerard Manley Hopkins comprise biography, works, political history, social history, science, genre and mode, literary relations, visual arts, religion, themes, imagery, poetic structure, bibliography, related Web resources, and leading questions, which highlight major issues in Hopkins's work. Although there is great disparity in coverage of minor and major authors, this highlights gaps in the scholarship record, which could help scholars identify new research areas. Other sections, such as "Social History," have topical essays. This section organizes the essays according to "Public Health," "Conditions of Life and Labor," "Race, Class, and Gender Issues," "Education and the Lives of Children," "Leisure and Amusements," "Victorian Cities, Towns, and Countryside," "Miscellaneous," and "Economic History." Individual essays are signed and link to relevant *Victorian Web* content to contextualize an issue. In addition to browsing through contents, scholars may search for an individual word or phrase in order to locate relevant information quickly. A search for *sensation fiction* retrieves 111 hits, each marked with one to four stars indicating the strength of the match, with the best matches appearing first.

Patrick Leary's ***Victoria Research Web: Scholarly Resources for Victorian Research*** (*VRW*) is a guide to "Research Resources," "Books," "Discussion Groups," "Teaching," and "Other Victorian Resources." Leary, who also founded and manages *VICTORIA List*, created *VRW* in 1996 as a research tool for all aspects of the Victorian age (for more on *VICTORIA List* see below). The site is valuable for any serious scholar and has substantial sections on archives, printed sources about libraries, serials, pictures, and books, and tips for planning a research trip to Great Britain. Leary's website is particularly helpful because he not only links to highly relevant sources but also explains how and why they are useful and draws connections between them. Among the many helpful components of *VRW* are the VanArsdel bibliography on Victorian periodicals (see chapter 7), the *Curran Index* (see chapters 6 and 7), and *At the Circulating Library*, which is discussed in greater detail below. Scholars who need information on archives and researching Victorian periodicals will find this site particularly relevant since Leary provides detailed discussion on each topic's nuances. Additionally, the journal guide contains information on major scholarly journals and book series focused on the nineteenth century. The discussion group section directs scholars to major listservs and blogs in this area, which should help scholars keep abreast of trends and concerns in Victorian literature. Teaching faculty will benefit from the *VRW* syllabi and teaching resources. The syllabi are organized according to history, literature surveys, the novel, poetry, and special topics. The final *VRW* section comprises links to general guides, Victorian studies organizations, major websites, and other resources of interest.

ELECTRONIC TEXT ARCHIVES

Digital Book Index: A Union Catalog of Electronic Books, Texts, and Documents, at www.digitalbookindex.org (accessed 16 April 2010).

Drake, Alfred J. *The Victorian Prose Archive*, at www.victorianprose.org (accessed 16 April 2010).

Goodridge, John, ed. *Labouring-Class Writers Project*, 17 April 2008, at human.ntu.ac.uk/research/labouringclasswriters/Index.htm (accessed 16 April 2010).

Google Books, at books.google.com (accessed 16 April 2010).

Lancashire, Ian. *Representative Poetry Online*, at rpo.library.utoronto.ca/display/index.cfm (accessed 16 April 2010).

The Modern English Collection, 2 January 2008, at etext.lib.virginia.edu/modeng/modeng0.browse.html (accessed 16 April 2010).

NINES: Nineteenth-Century Scholarship Online, at www.nines.org (accessed 16 April 2010).

Project Gutenberg, 31 August 2009, at www.gutenberg.org (accessed 16 April 2010).

Thorne-Murphy, Leslee. *The Victorian Short Fiction Project*, 14 March 2009, at vsfp.ctlbyu.org (accessed 16 April 2010).

Timney, Meagan. *Factory Girls and Serving Maids: Victorian Working-Class Women Poets Archive*, 9 January 2009, at wcwp.english.dal.ca (accessed 16 April 2010).

Victorian Plays Project, at www.worc.ac.uk/victorian/victorianplays (accessed 16 April 2010).

Victorian Women Writers Project, 24 April 2003, at www.indiana.edu/~letrs/vwwp (accessed 16 April 2010).

Chapter 8 covered microform and digital collections that are available as subscriptions or for purchase. This section supplements that discussion of proprietary collections with an introduction to some of the many open-access, full-text resources currently available on the Internet. These electronic-text archives include general archives such as *Project Gutenberg* and Google Books alongside niche archives such as *The Victorian Women Writers Project*. Such archives provide a vast amount of primary-source material that would be difficult to access otherwise.

The first free online book archive, **Project Gutenberg**, has been around since 1971, when founder Michael Hart first invented the e-book. Currently, *Project Gutenberg* hosts nearly thirty thousand e-books that can be read online or downloaded to a PDA or e-book reader. Approximately four hundred new titles are added each month. Although this archive primarily contains e-books, some digitized music, videos, and audio books are also included. Because works must be in the public domain, typically *Project Gutenberg* texts are pre-1923 imprints, making it an excellent resource for Victorian and Edwardian primary-source materials. The majority of works—twenty-five thousand books—are in English. Works by Sir Arthur Conan Doyle, Henry Rider Haggard, and R. M. Ballantyne are available alongside works by J. M. Barrie, Louis Becke, and Olive Schreiner. Scholars can access the contents with the basic author and title word searches, by using the advanced search, or by browsing the catalog. From the advanced option, you can search by author, title, subject, language, category, Library of Congress Classification (LoCC), file type, etext-number, or full text. According to the LC Classification breakdown, more than thirty-seven hundred works are in English literature. Unfortunately, there is no way to search specifically for texts written between 1830 and 1910 since there is no date limit or means to use narrower LC ranges than PR (English literature). If you know the appropriate Library of Congress subject heading (LCSH), the subject field will help narrow your results; however, the archive does not have a browseable or searchable LCSH list. The browse feature allows users to peruse *Project Gutenberg*'s contents by author, title, language, category, or recently posted. Individual records contain information on the author, illustrator, title, language, LC Classification, subject, etext-number, release date, copyright status, base directory, and full text of the work. One drawback of *Project Gutenberg* works is that they do not provide publication details such as publisher, date, or edition. For Victorian and Edwardian scholars, this resource may be best for known-item searching rather than browsing for works. Additionally, *Project Gutenberg* does not have the authoritative editions, so they should not be cited in scholarly works.

A relative newcomer compared to *Project Gutenberg*, **Google Books** has surpassed its predecessor in both size and reputation. Containing millions of books, Google Books takes a different approach at online books, providing page views rather than rekeyed HTML or text files. For this project, Google partnered with authors, libraries, and publishers to offer ubiquitous access to printed texts from around the globe. Google's founders—Sergey Brin and Larry Page—first conceived this project at Google's inception in 1996; however, the digitization initiative that became Google Books did not begin until 2002. Currently twenty libraries, including those of Harvard University, Oxford University, the University of California, the University of Michigan, and the University of Virginia, have joined with Google to digitize public-domain books from their collections. Additionally, publishers such as Cambridge University Press, Oxford University Press, and Penguin have agreements with Google to promote their works through Google Books' snippet view, which allows scholars to view a portion of the book rather than the entire contents.

You may browse Google Books by various fiction, non-fiction, and random subjects. You may also find information using the basic or advanced book search screens. The basic option appears on the homepage and allows for keyword searching in all records and content. The advanced book search enables you to specify where terms appear and limit by various parameters. Looking for terms "with all of the words," "with the exact phrase," "with at least one of the words," or "without the words" can help you retrieve more relevant results. Likewise, you can search all books, limited preview and full view, full view only, or public domain only, or limit to all content, books, or magazines. Other fields include language, title, author, publisher, subject, publication date, ISBN, and ISSN. Because Google has broad digitization goals, scholars will find copies of literary works like Elizabeth Gaskell's *Cranford* alongside non-fiction such as Matthew Arnold's *Culture and Anarchy* and periodicals such as *Household Words*. While Google Books contains a wealth of information, scholars must often employ creative search techniques to find the resources they need. For instance, modern periodicals such as *Life* are browseable by issue, whereas historic periodicals like *Household Words* are erroneously classified as books, making it difficult to locate subsequent issues. If you search for *Household Words* as a periodical, it appears as though this title has not been digitized for Google Books, even though many issues are available. Indexing mistakes like this one are not uncommon, so scholars should search in multiple ways before assuming Google Books does not have what they are seeking. Scholars looking for digital books should also consult the *Hathi Trust Digital Library*, which is discussed below in the section on contemporary newspapers and journals.

Despite its clunky interface, the **Digital Book Index: A Union Catalog of Electronic Books, Texts, and Documents** is a highly useful website for finding full-text e-books. As its title and subtitle suggest, the *Digital Book Index* does not contain full text but indexes other major online repositories. Sources such as *Project Gutenberg*, the Library of Congress, and the British Library are all indexed here. In sum, the site links to over 145,000 e-books from the following areas: the arts, children's books, history, law, literature and languages, math and sciences, medicine and health, philosophy and religion, reference books, social sciences, and other topics. Roughly twelve thousand texts fall into the literature and languages category. Visitors to the site must select from one of two mirror servers and log in prior to using the website. Although the site is free, it requires a login as a means of tracking usage and gathering information on visitors. Scholars can search the *Digital Book Index* by author, title keywords, or author and title. When searching by author, you will retrieve the best results if you begin with the last name. The title keyword options include "all words" or "any words," each of which produces different results. "All words" narrows the results, while "any words" expands the results. You may also browse by subjects, authors, American studies, publishers, and *NetLibrary* by subject. The benefit of the *Digital Book Index* over Google Books and even *Project Gutenberg* is the detailed subject indexing and the ability to locate relevant books across multiple e-book providers. While it indexes fewer titles than Google Books holds, the *Digital Book Index* allows for more targeted searching, which enhances the speed with which a scholar can identify relevant sources.

Covering the long nineteenth century (1770–1920), **NINES: Nineteenth-Century Scholarship Online** bridges nineteenth-century primary resources to twenty-first-century digital scholarship. *NINES* has three overarching goals: to peer-review digital work, to support priorities and best practices for digital research material creation, and "to develop software tools for new and traditional forms of research and critical analysis." Rather than create new resources, *NINES* collocates existing digital scholarship on the nineteenth century and provides a search interface and the technology needed for individual scholars to create exhibits. Currently, more than four hundred thousand peer-reviewed digital objects from seventy-eight federated sites comprise *NINES*. Scholars may search by title, author, editor, publisher, year, and key-word to identify relevant resources and may use the limits at any time to browse or narrow down the results. The limits are for resource type, genre, and access. Once scholars have created a free account, they may save selected resources by clicking the "collect" button. The collected items may be saved for later use along with searches, tags, discussions, and exhibits. The exhibits feature allows you to create an online exhibit of collected items to share with other scholars. Scholars can then insert their own text and draw connections between print and digital works. *NINES* enables scholars to search across websites including the *Letters of Christina Rossetti*, *The Rossetti Archive*, *The Poetess Archive*, *Letters of Matthew Arnold*, *Morris Online Edition*, and *Collective Biographies of Women*. While much of the content is open access, some is proprietary, such as *JSTOR* journal articles and ProQuest's *Nineteenth-Century Fiction*. For these resources, indexing is available but not the full text. *NINES* also has a forum section where members can pose questions and engage each other in scholarly debate.

A narrower collection than those previously discussed, **The Modern English Collection** provides selected digital reproductions of drama, fiction, illustrations, letters, manuscripts, newspapers, non-fiction, and poetry published from 1500 to the present. This archive was created by the University of Virginia Library's Electronic Text Center and can be searched or browsed by author's last name or by area of interest. Although not all texts are relevant to Victorian and Edwardian scholarship, works by Charlotte and Emily Brontë, Wilkie Collins, Charles Dickens, Elizabeth Gaskell, John Stuart Mill, John Ruskin, and other authors of those periods will be. Additionally, *The Modern English Collection* includes a selection of bestsellers from 1900 to 1930, many of which will be useful for Edwardian scholars.

Additional poetry is available through the University of Toronto Libraries' **Representative Poetry Online (RPO)**, which was founded and continues to be edited by English Professor Ian Lancashire. *RPO* contains the 3,162 English poetic works by five hundred poets from the Old English period to the present day. The initial basis for *RPO* came from the book *Representative Poetry* (Toronto: University of Toronto Press, 1912). The website contains the original book's contents as well as supplementary information added since 1994. Most but not all of the poems were written by British authors. Scholars can browse poets either by last name or chronologically, and poems by title, first line, or last line. *RPO* also offers a timeline of poets, poems, and events, and a calendar of the year's days, both of which link to appropriate authors and their texts. The timeline has subsets for the Victorians (1833–1903) and the Georgians (1903–1920) among other literary periods. Edwardian scholars will need to consult both of these sections to identify relevant poets and poems. Contents can also be searched by keywords. Scholars should find the biographical information about poets and original printed editions of poems particularly useful. Additional *RPO* features include a glossary of poetic terms and forms, writings on poetry, and a bibliography and links to other poetry websites.

The *Victorian Plays Project* is a digital play archive based on T. H. Lacy's *Acting Edition of Victorian Plays* (1848–1873), which is a series of plays published in the mid-nineteenth century by Samuel French. Comprising a complete catalog of Lacy's plays, an alphabetical index of digitized titles, and a search interface to enhance access to the site's contents, the *Victorian Plays Project* is a valuable resource for Victorian theater scholars. Currently the project contains 350 plays out of the almost fifteen hundred published in the original series, including titles such as Dion Boucicault's *The Queen of Spades* (1851), Frederick Hay's *Caught by the Cuff* (1865), George Roberts's *Idalia; or, The Adventuress* (1867), and William Leman Rede's *The Rake's Progress* (1833). The catalog is organized chronologically by volume and lists each play along with first performance date, playwright, title, subtitle, and first performance place. Titles link to full text as available. Basic, advanced, and type-specific searches are provided. The basic option searches title, author, and year, and the advanced searches titles, names, places, quotes, stage, song lines, cast, and keywords, while type-specific produces a list of pre-defined keywords related to places, names, quotes, stage directions, and titles. The *Victorian Plays Project* also offers links to general and playwright-specific websites on nineteenth-century theater.

Scholars should find *The Victorian Prose Archive* a limited yet useful resource. Maintained by Alfred J. Drake, an English literature professor at the University of California, Irvine, *The Victorian Prose Archive* comprises select prose works by Matthew Arnold, Thomas Carlyle, James Anthony Froude, Francis W. Newman, Cardinal John Henry Newman, Walter Horatio Pater, J. J. Thomas, and Oscar Wilde. Although the website indicates plans to add works by additional authors including Walter Pater, Thomas Carlyle, and Algernon Swinburne, so far no content seems to have been added to the site since 2003.

The *Victorian Short Fiction Project* (*VSFP*) comprises annotated editions of British short fiction written between 1837 and 1901. Students at Brigham Young University created *VSFP* contents under English Professor Leslee Thorne-Murphy's direction. Sixty short-fiction works by forty-three authors, such as Margaret Gatty's "Unopened Parcels," Mrs. James Whittle's "Helen Fairfax," Artemus Ward's "On Kremashun. A Posthumous Paper," and Lady Augusta Gregory's "The Legend of Diarmuid and Grania," are included. Each work contains the story's full text, a PDF of the original when available, a brief introduction contextualizing the journal and short story, and annotations. Additionally, *VSFP* offers a select list of seventy-eight journals that printed short fiction, all of which are drawn from the BYU Harold B. Lee Library holdings, such as *All the Year Round, Blackwood's Edinburgh Magazine, The Englishwoman's Domestic Magazine*, and *Man in the Moon*. The title, editor, publisher, background, and table of contents for volumes consulted are provided for each journal. Although a relatively small collection, *VSFP* is an excellent resource for introducing scholars to Victorian short fiction, which has received significantly less critical attention than the Victorian novel.

Developed by Dalhousie University's Meagan Timney, **Factory Girls and Serving Maids: Victorian Working-Class Women Poets Archive** was created to increase the availability of poetry by lower-class women in Victorian Britain. Because of this, works by poets such as Elizabeth Barrett Browning and Christina Rossetti are not included. Not yet comprehensive in its survey of lower-class women poets, *Factory Girls and Serving Maids* currently covers eighteen poets and the full text of almost fifty poems. Because of its small size, the website's contents can be easily browsed, so the lack of a search interface should not impede scholars from identifying relevant texts. Original publication information accompanies each poem. Additionally, this site contains a bibliography of online resources and print sources such as anthologies and journal articles. Scholars interested in working-class literature should also consult the **Labouring-Class Writers Project**, which comprises a database of fourteen hundred male and female authors who wrote in Great Britain and Ireland between 1700 and 1900. The database is currently under construction, so even though the bibliography of authors is available, the search interface is not yet working.

The Library Electronic Text Research Service (LETRS) at Indiana University Bloomington created the **Victorian Women Writers Project** (**VWWP**) in 1995. Originally edited by Perry Willett, *VWWP* is a full-text archive of anthologies, children's books, novels, poetry, political pamphlets, religious tracts, verse drama, and other works written by women writers of the Victorian age. Nearly two hundred works by more than forty authors appear in this collection. While some works are from the early Victorian and Edwardian ages, most were mid- to late-Victorian publications. Texts by well-known authors such as Mary Elizabeth Braddon, Sarah Stickney Ellis, and Olive Schreiner appear alongside those by forgotten authors like Josephine Butler, Ada Cambridge, and Caroline Norton. The *VWWP* contains titles such as the following: *A Lady's Life in the Rocky Mountains*; *Tarantella*; *Lady Audley's Secret*; *Criminals, Idiots, Women, and Minors*; *The Soul of Lilith*; *Ballads and Lyrics of Socialism*; *Xantippe and Other Verse*; and *Papers on Aggressive*

Christianity. Scholars access *VWWP* contents by either browsing a list of works available or by searching the full text. Texts may be viewed in either HTML or TEI. This website also contains a valuable list of online resources, which are categorized as journals, essential starting points, electronic-text projects, nineteenth-century American literature, women's studies, societies, syllabi, and other. Although it had been some years since this resource has been updated, the Digital Library Program, libraries, and English department at Indiana University are currently collaborating to improve both the functionality and the interface of the *VWWP*.

AUTHOR SITES

The Brownings: A Research Guide, at www.browningguide.org (accessed 16 April 2010).

GladCAT, at www.st-deiniols.com/the-library/gladcat.htm (accessed 16 April 2010).

McGann, Jerome J. *The Complete Writings and Pictures of Dante Gabriel Rossetti: A Hypermedia Archive*, June 2008, at www.rossettiarchive.org (accessed 16 April 2010).

Walsh, John A., ed. *The Swinburne Project: A Digital Archive of the Life and Works of Algernon Charles Swinburne*. April 16, 2010, at swinburne archive.indiana.edu (accessed 16 April 2010).

Author-specific websites are abundantly available yet vary widely in terms of contents and quality. These resources tend to range from popular sites to carefully crafted digital scholarship created by libraries and scholars. This section highlights several reliable websites but does not seek to present a comprehensive overview of author sites. To find additional websites, consult the scholarly portals discussed earlier in this chapter. While it is possible that no reliable website exists for an author you are researching, most major and many minor authors have sites devoted to them and their works.

Edited by Jerome G. McGann—an English professor at the University of Virginia and the founder of *NINES* (see above)—***The Complete Writings and Pictures of Dante Gabriel Rossetti: A Hypermedia Archive*** comprises digital reproductions of existing Rossetti manuscripts, proofs, original editions, drawings, paintings, and designs. This resource is more frequently referred to as the *Rossetti Archive*. Editorial commentary, notes, and glosses supplement these primary-source materials, making the *Rossetti Archive* an indispensible resource for Rossetti scholars. The archive's contents are indexed both alphabetically and chronologically according to the following categories: double works, pictures, poems, prose, translations, books, manuscripts, correspondence, and material design. Each category contains text that introduces and contextualizes the resources within it. For each Rossetti writing or image, the archive may provide scholarly commentary, page images, transcripts, general description (date, genre, rhyme, meter), a production description (document title, author, composition date, manuscript type, collation, scribe, and corrector), provenance, and physical description. In addition to browsing works, scholars may access the archive's contents either through "free form" or "structured" searching. "Free form" searches any word or phrase in the collection introductions, text introductions, image records, or text transcriptions, as specified. Scholars may opt to make terms case sensitive. The structured search allows scholars to choose from the following options: title, Boolean, phrase, genre, name, or date. Each option offers a "help" link that leads the user to topic-specific information. While browsing can help you understand what materials are available or locate a known item, through searching you may make connections among multiple Rossetti texts and images. The *Rossetti Archive* also contains a bibliography of works used and cited in the archive, and a brief discussion of standard bibliographies and guides.

Published by Indiana University's Library Electronic Text Resource Service (LETRS) and Digital Library Program, ***The Swinburne Project: A Digital Archive of the Life and Works of Algernon Charles Swinburne*** gives access to Swinburne's works and contextual materials such as contemporary criticism, biographies, and Swinburne's art criticism. John A. Walsh, a library and information science professor at Indiana University, edits the collection, which comprises the following ten volumes of Swinburne's poetry and letters: *Atalanta in Calydon*; *Erechtheus*; *Poems and Ballads, First Series*; *Poems and Ballads, Second Series*; *Songs before Sunrise*; *Songs of the Springtides*; *Studies in Song*; *A Tale of Balen*; *Tristram of Lyonesse*; and *Uncollected Letters of Algernon Charles Swinburne*. Scholars may browse by volume or by title. Eventually, the collection will contain Swinburne's prose works, which are currently available at another site (www.letrs.indiana.edu/swinburne/contents.html). In addition to browsing, scholars may search by keyword or by bibliographic information. Transcripts, rather than page images, are provided for each text along with document information. The *Swinburne Project* also has a brief reference section with a chronology and supplementary materials to Terry Meyers's *Uncollected Letters of Algernon Charles Swinburne* (3 vols. London: Pickering and Chatto, 2005).

The Brownings: A Research Guide was created by the Armstrong Browning Library at Brown University to support research on both Robert Browning and Elizabeth Barrett Browning and their circle. *The Brownings* comprises the Browning collections, correspondence, contemporary reviews, printed works, supporting documents, Lady Layard's journal, and the Joseph Milsand archive. Based on the 1913 Sotheby's auction catalog of estate holdings, the Browning collections section includes records for the Brownings' library, first works, presentation volumes, manuscripts, likenesses, works, other association manuscripts and documents, other association volumes, and works of art, household, and personal effects. Each section in *The Brownings* can be searched individually. While the site serves primarily as an index and bibliography, full text is provided for select correspondence and Lady Layard's journal. Scholars of either Elizabeth Barrett Browning or Robert Browning and their contemporaries will find this a tremendously useful resource.

Unlike most author-specific websites, **GladCAT** is not a full-text archive but a catalog of works originally owned by William Ewart Gladstone. Created by the St Deiniol's Library in Wales and the University of Liverpool, *GladCAT* should benefit scholars of Gladstone, nineteenth-century literature and culture, and the history of the book and reading. This resource is hosted on the St Deiniol's Library website but remains separate from the main catalog. While the catalog is open access, scholars must request a username and PIN from the library. *GladCAT*'s holdings are restricted not simply to titles Gladstone owned but to the exact copies from his personal library. The catalog records reflect specific features of these copies, such as notes on Gladstone's handwritten annotations and indexes. The catalog offers both basic and advanced search options. The basic is a simple keyword search, while the advanced supports Boolean searching for terms in specific fields or media. You may also opt for either a summary or detailed view of the results. *GladCAT* records may contain the following information for each work: standard number, title, authors, imprint, keywords, subjects, medium, class, edition, language, notes, series, price, collation, accession, loan type, location, status, and shelf mark. The notes field tends to include information identifying the work as Gladstone's, dedications, textual annotations, Gladstone's handwritten index, and diary entry references.

CONTEMPORARY NEWSPAPERS AND JOURNALS

Athenaeum Index of Reviews and Reviewers: 1830–1870, October 2001, at athenaeum.soi.city.ac.uk/reviews/home.html (accessed 16 April 2010).

The Athenaeum Scientific Material: 1828–1830, October 2001, at athenaeum .soi.city.ac.uk/scientific/athsci.html (accessed 16 April 2010).

de Montluzin, Emily Lorraine. *Attributions of Authorship in the Gentleman's Magazine, 1731–1868*, April 21, 2008, at etext.virginia.edu/bsuva/gm (accessed 16 April 2010).

Hathi Trust Digital Library, at catalog.hathitrust.org (accessed 16 April 2010).
Internet Library of Early Journals, at www.bodley.ox.ac.uk/ilej (accessed 16 April 2010).
The Modernist Journals Project, at dl.lib.brown.edu/mjp (accessed 16 April 2010).
Modernist Magazines Project, at www.cts.dmu.ac.uk/exist/mod_mag/index.htm (accessed 16 April 2010).
Nineteenth-Century Serials Edition, at www.ncse.kcl.ac.uk (accessed 16 April 2010).
Science in the Nineteenth-Century Periodical, 18 December 2007, at www.sciper.org (accessed 16 April 2010).
Seton, David. *Missionary Periodicals Database*, research.yale.edu:8084/missionperiodicals/index.jsp (accessed 16 April 2010).

The following resources offer either full text or indexing for nineteenth- and early-twentieth-century journals and newspapers. While chapter 7 addressed print and online sources for locating and searching period journals and newspapers, this section supplements that information with open-access resources. Indexing sites—the *Athenaeum Index of Reviews and Reviewers: 1830–1870*; *The Athenaeum Scientific Material: 1828–1830*; *Attributions of Authorship in the Gentleman's Magazine, 1731–1868*; *Science in the Nineteenth-Century Periodical*; and *Modernist Magazines Project*—are discussed alongside the following full-text resources: *Internet Library of Early Journals*; the *Nineteenth-Century Serials Edition*; and *The Modernist Journals Project*. The *Missionary Periodicals Database*, which has descriptive information about periodicals, is also included. Although not discussed in this section, Google Books (see above) contains some period journals, so scholars may want to consult that resource as they search for the full text of particular titles.

The Yale University Divinity School Library hosts the **Missionary Periodicals Database**, which records British periodicals on foreign missions from the eighteenth century through the 1960s. Listing nearly six hundred periodicals, the *Missionary Periodicals Database* began as part of two University of Cambridge projects: "North Atlantic Missiology Project" and "Currents in World Christianity." The database contents may be browsed by region or periodical title, or searched for specific terms. To browse by region, scholars may click on world and regional maps to identify periodicals about missionary efforts in a particular geographic area. Periodicals such as the *General Baptist Missionary Society Annual Report*, *Medical Missionary*, and *South American Missionary Magazine* are listed in the database. Browsing by periodical title allows scholars to scan an alphabetical list. Scholars may also search by title, issuing body, denomination, place, publisher, region, or keyword. The search interface links to a list of terms used within the database to refer to "denomination," "region of work," "field of activity," "target readership," "illustrations," "principal locations," and "features." In individual records, these terms are hyperlinked to help scholars easily find related publications. A repository list is also provided. Each periodical record contains the following fields: title, issuing body, other entries, denomination, place, publisher, volume numbers, date, frequency, price, region of work, illustrations, principal locations, features, and comments. Each record identifies which repositories hold a particular title and the comprehensiveness of their holdings. Although the *Missionary Periodical Database* is not strictly literary, the journals listed may contain contents of interest to Victorian and Edwardian scholars. Scholars seeking information on the history of Christianity and empire in Britain will find this a tremendously useful resource.

Following the eighteenth- and nineteenth-century practice, the *Gentleman's Magazine*, like many contemporary publications, printed unsigned articles. Today's scholars may find that convention hampers their research. Emily Lorraine de Montluzin's ***Attributions of Authorship in the Gentleman's Magazine*** compiles three sources that identify authors: *Gentleman's Magazine: An Electronic Version of James M. Kuist's The Nichols File of the Gentleman's Magazine*; *Attributions of Authorship in the Gentleman's Magazine, 1731–1868: A Supplement to Kuist*; and *A Synthesis of Finds Appearing neither in Kuist's Nichols File nor in de Montluzin's A Supplement to Kuist*. This resource is provided by the University of Virginia's Electronic Text Center. *An Electronic Version of James M. Kuist's The Nichols File of the Gentleman's Magazine* is a database of almost fourteen thousand authorship attributions that Kuist and his researchers transcribed from marginal notes in the Folger Shakespeare Library's copy of the *Gentleman's Magazine*. Of these entries, more than 5,300 are from the early Victorian age. This electronic version can be searched by word or phrase, title, and year. A "compound search" option is also offered, which enables proximity searching and limiting to specific entry types. The contents can be browsed by volume year or synopsis by author; however, this feature seems to be inconsistently available. De Montluzin's *A Supplement to Kuist* adds four thousand new or corrected author attributions to Kuist's work. These contents may also be searched or browsed by date or synopsis by contributor. The supplement compiles six articles on the *Gentleman's Magazine* published in *Studies in Bibliographies* in the 1990s.[1] The final component—*A Synthesis of Finds Appearing neither in Kuist's Nichols File nor in de Montluzin's A Supplement to Kuist*—adds 1,850 unique authorship attributions. In total, the three databases index just fewer than nineteen thousand attributions. Detailed introductions are included for each section of this website.

Published weekly from 1828 to 1923, the *Athenaeum* covered literary, political, and scientific topics, and, as was typical in that time period, published unsigned book reviews. The ***Athenaeum Index of Reviews and Reviewers: 1830–1870*** supplements the periodical by providing details on book reviews and reviewer biographies during the early and mid-Victorian age. The *Athenaeum Index* can be browsed by author, title, or contributor, or searched by title or name. The name search supports Boolean operators and truncation (indicated by a period [.]) and should be used to find both authors and reviewers. Author entries list works written by the individual and published in the *Athenaeum*, while contributor entries contain biographical details of the reviewer—dates, sources of characteristics, characteristics, and mark—and a list of reviews attributed to them. The title search retrieves results based on words, phrases, or complete titles, and supports Boolean operators. The records are quite brief, with fields for title, author, contributor, mark, and reference information. The mark field corresponds to the "marked" copy of the *Athenaeum* held by City University Library, London, which is the only extant run that includes handwritten surnames. This copy allows researchers to identify authors of both reviews and articles written for this periodical. A second *Athenaeum* index—***The Athenaeum Scientific Material: 1828–1830***—comprises 345 book reviews and 1,370 articles. Although coverage is prior to 1830, it remains pertinent to research on the early Victorian age.

Another index of nineteenth-century scientific literature is ***Science in the Nineteenth-Century Periodical*** (***SciPer Index***). Rather than focus on one publication, *SciPer Index* covers scientific content in select years of sixteen periodicals: *The Academy*; *La Belle Assembleé*; *The Black Dwarf*; *Blackwood's Edinburgh Magazine*; *The Boy's Own Paper*; *The Christian Observer*; *The Comic Annual*; *The Cornhill Magazine*; *The Englishwoman's Domestic Magazine*; *The Edinburgh Review*; *Harper's New Monthly Magazine* (European edition); *The Mirror of Literature, Amusement, and Instruction*; *Punch*; *The Review of Reviews*; *The Wesleyan-Methodist Magazine*; and *The Youth's Magazine*. A descriptive introduction that identifies title, sequence, editor, publisher, printer, price, format, pages, frequency, circulation, indexes, and copies is provided for each journal, as are notes on indexing and a brief bibliography. Scholars may browse the *SciPer Index*, people, authors, illustrators, books, periodicals, institutions and societies, and unidentified pseudonyms. *SciPer Index* not only indexes scientific articles but also fiction, poetry, and news articles containing scientific references. For that reason it is unique among nineteenth-century periodical indexes. Individual index entries may include information regarding title, serial parts, author, genre, publications reviewed or extracted, relevant illustrations, illustrators, subject, descriptions, reprints, cross-references, subarticles, and people, publications, and institutions mentioned. *SciPer Index* also offers four search options—simple, standard, advanced, and register—so that scholars can search with varying levels of specificity.

In addition to indexing sites like the ones previously discussed, newspaper and periodical archives are freely available on the Internet, but they tend to be significantly smaller than subscription or purchase archives such as *British Periodicals* and *19th Century British Library Newspapers*. One open-access archive is the **Nineteenth-Century Serials Edition** (**NCSE**), which contains six nineteenth-century newspapers and periodicals. Created by the University of London, King's College London, the British Library, and Olive Software, *NCSE* does not simply offer the full text but is a collection of scholarly editions. *NCSE* comprises the *Monthly Repository* (1806–1837) and *Unitarian Chronicle* (1832–1833), *Northern Star* (1838–1852), *Leader* (1850–1860), *English Woman's Journal* (1858–1864), *Tomahawk* (1867–1870), and *Publishers' Circular* (1880–1890).[2] With the exception of *Publishers' Circular*, the complete run of each title is provided. Digital facsimiles, transcripts, and keywords related to persons, places, and institutions help scholars access the content. Scholars may browse issues and articles from specific serials, or they may search across multiple publications simultaneously. *NCSE* allows keyword searching in articles, pictures, and advertisements with the option to limit to specific publications, date ranges, and metadata: issue title, volume/series, issue number, edition, page, price, geographic location, and size. Results may be viewed as snippets, articles, and pages in either digital facsimile or OCR text.[3] Although containing only a select group of titles, *NCSE* is an excellent resource for cultural, historical, and literary research of the nineteenth century. In addition to the newspaper and periodical contents, *NCSE* provides each serial publication's history, editorial commentary, a project history, and a references section.

A collaborative venture by the Universities of Birmingham, Leeds, Manchester, and Oxford, the **Internet Library of Early Journals** (**ILEJ**) comprises digitized editions of three eighteenth-century and three nineteenth-century journals. The journals included are *Annual Register*, *Gentleman's Magazine*, *Philosophical Transactions of the Royal Society*, *Blackwood's Edinburgh Magazine*, *The Builder*, and *Notes and Queries*. The latter three are from the nineteenth century, specifically covering 1843 to 1869. At least twenty consecutive years of issues were digitized for each title, giving scholars a substantial body of periodical literature to research. Scholars may browse periodicals by volume and issue/date within volume. Individual issues may also be paged through, enabling scholars to see the original composition and organization. Excepting *The Builder*, each journal may be searched by full text, subject index, title index, or author index. Not all search methods are available for each journal, so scholars should check the *ILEJ* "Help" file for title-specific details. The results list publication information for the relevant issues along with a snippet of text containing the search terms. Unfortunately, in the search results, multiple hits in a single article are not listed together, and author and title information is not given. Another drawback to *ILEJ* is the inability to search across journals. Additionally, while the main search page indicates that fuzzy searching, which would account for spelling variants and misspellings, is available, the "Help" section of the website indicates that this form of searching is currently not possible for any of the six journals. Page images rather than rekeyed text are provided for each issue.

Even though several of the previously discussed contemporary newspaper and journal sites extend coverage into the early twentieth century, Edwardian scholars will find *The Modernist Journals Project* and the *Modernist Magazine Project* more germane to their research. **The Modernist Journals Project (*MJP*)** was developed collaboratively by Brown University and the University of Tulsa to capture modernism in English-language periodical literature. With journals dating from 1890 to 1922, *MJP* will be useful for Edwardian scholars as well as those of the late Victorian age. Currently fourteen journals are digitized. While many are from the later modernist period, several— *Dana*, *The English Review*, *The New Age*, and *Le Petit Journal des Réfusées*—are from the Edwardian and Victorian ages. In addition to modernist journals, this website includes essays from and about the modernist period and scholarly books on related topics. To facilitate access to these resources, *MJP*'s search interface enables scholars to look for keywords as words or phrases. Scholars can specify whether terms appear in the full text, author/ editor/artist, title, or all metadata fields, and whether to limit to periodicals, biographies, essays, images, or all. Complementing these full-text resources is a periodical database that lists nearly six hundred English-language literary and artistic journals from 1890 to 1922. Name, country, type, periodicity, date started, date ended, and notes are given for each journal. This is a tremendous resource not only for full text but also for identifying modernist journals.

The **Modernist Magazines Project** complements *The Modernist Journals Project*, but indexes rather than provides full text. Under the direction of Peter Brooker (University of Sussex) and Andrew Thacker (De Montfort University), the *Modernist Magazine Project* indexes "modernist magazines, bibliographical and biographical data, selected contents and web links." Covering 1880 to 1945, many of the indexed periodicals are pertinent for Victorian and Edwardian scholars, including *Beltaine*, *The Chameleon*, *Dana*, *The Dial*, *The Evergreen*, *The Germ*, *The GreenSheaf*, *The Oxford and Cambridge Magazine*, *The Pageant*, *Samhain*, *The Savoy*, *The Studio*, and *The Yellow Book*. This website has a magazine index and an author index. The former index lists forty modernist publications. Each entry links to a list of issues, which leads to a table of contents. The author index comprises an alphabetical list of individuals who were published in these resources. Each name connects to a chronological bibliography of specific works. The *Modernist Magazine Project* also has a search interface, where scholars may look for keywords in either the author or title fields. The project will also result in a book—*Critical and Cultural History of Modernist Magazines* (3 vols. New York: Oxford University Press, 2009–2010)—and an anthology.

Although not specifically focused on either the Victorian or the Edwardian age, the **Hathi Trust Digital Library** also contains digitized nineteenth- and early twentieth-century journals. The *Hathi Trust* began as a collaboration among thirteen universities and the University of California system with the intent to archive and share digital collections. Currently, twenty-six institutions have joined in this venture. More than 845,000 of the 5.5 million volumes are in the public domain and can be viewed by the general public. The remaining volumes are still under copyright and will be made available as laws permit. Generally speaking, this site comprises books and journals, most of which are in English. Scholars may browse or search the collections. The Advanced Search screen allows for the most flexibility in finding relevant publications. Here, you can limit by language and original format, and can search for terms in the following fields: title, author, subject, publisher, series title, year, ISBN/ISSN, or all. For instance, searching for *literary*periodical** and limiting to English language and newspapers or journals retrieves 273 results, ninety-eight of which are from the United Kingdom, England, Scotland, or Wales, and sixty-four dating between 1830 and 1910. Title such as *Ainsworth's Magazine, The Jewish Literary Annual*, and *The Bookwork: A Literary and Bibliographical Review* are included. Scholars can refine results by viewability, subject, author, language, place of publication, date, original format, and original location. The *Hathi Trust* also offers a full-text search, but this option does not allow for sorting or limiting options.

CURRENT AWARENESS RESOURCES

Calls for Papers, at call-for-papers.sas.upenn.edu (accessed 16 April 2010).
A Discussion of English Literature, Culture, and Society 1880–1920, at listserv.temple.edu/archives/elcs-l.html (accessed 16 April 2010).
Literature Conferences Worldwide, at www.conferencealerts.com/literature .htm (accessed 16 April 2010).
Miller, Andrew H., and Ivan Kreilkamp, eds. *Victorian Studies Bibliography*, at www.letrs.indiana.edu/web/v/victbib (accessed on 16 April 2010).

New Books in Nineteenth-Century British Studies, at newbooksonline.org (accessed 16 April 2010).
VICTORIA List, at listserv.indiana.edu/archives/victoria.html (accessed 16 April 2010).

To stay abreast of scholarly trends, you should familiarize yourself with several current awareness resources. RSS feeds, listservs, calls for papers, conferences, and bibliographies all serve to inform scholars of new articles and developments which help them keep up with research trends. Staying current can be time consuming, so these tools are essential for increasing efficiency of information gathering. This section is not comprehensive but covers some of the major current awareness resources such as the University of Pennsylvania's *Calls for Papers* and listservs like *VICTORIA List* and *A Discussion of English Literature, Culture, and Society, 1880–1920*. Additionally, technological tools like RSS feed are addressed here.

Maintained by the University of Southern California's English Department, **New Books in Nineteenth-Century British Studies** is "an interdisciplinary guide to scholarship on nineteenth-century Britain." This resource pertains to both the Romantic era and the Victorian age and lists publication information, tables of contents, cover art, prices, ISBN, and links to online bookstores for each work. Approximately forty reviews and two hundred scholarly books dating between 1996 and 2008 are indexed in *New Books in Nineteenth-Century British Studies*. This resource is not comprehensive, even for the years covered, but is still a useful resource for scholars. In addition to browsing books and reviews, scholars may search by title, author first name, author last name, keywords, ISBN, publisher, and publication year. Book entries include abstracts and tables of contents along with publication details. Review entries contain the same information in addition to the review's full text. Another useful source for current Victorian scholarship is the **Victorian Studies Bibliography**, which is discussed in more detail in chapter 4. Connected to the Indiana University Press, the North American Victorian Studies Association (NAVSA), and the journal *Victorian Studies* (see chapter 5), this bibliography is an essential tool for Victorian scholars. This resource cites works published between 1991 and 2008.

Not exclusive to any particular resource, RSS (or really simple syndication) is an excellent tool for scholars to customize the information they receive and monitor it at their leisure. RSS feeds are frequently found on news sites, blogs, journals, podcasts, and even UPenn's *Calls for Papers* (see below). To use these feeds, you first need to choose an RSS reader such as *Bloglines*, My Yahoo!, or Google Reader. You may also receive RSS feeds through a desktop e-mail client such as Mozilla Thunderbird or Microsoft Outlook. After choosing where you wish to receive notification, you simply subscribe by clicking on the orange RSS button that appears in your browser when you are at a site that contains a feed. Subscribing to RSS feeds has several advantages. Gathering information through RSS allows you to consult one source for updates from numerous sites. If you want to stay abreast of recent articles in journals such as *Victorian Studies* or *ELH: English Literary History*, RSS feeds notify you of new issues and their contents without you having to check the journal websites repeatedly. Also, RSS allows you both to control when you read particular notifications and to easily share items of interest with colleagues. Although this tool may not fit with everyone's workflow, those who choose to use it will find it to be a tremendous time saver and an easy way to keep up with new developments in their research areas.

Provided by the University of Pennsylvania's English department, ***Calls for Papers*** (***CFP***) is an incredible tool for scholars of any literary topic. Currently, scholars have the option to browse or subscribe to all *CFP* posts or specific categories. The categories include topics such as "bibliography and history of the book," "cultural studies and historical approaches," "film and television," "gender studies and sexuality," "poetry," "postcolonial," "romantic," "theory," and "travel writing." Browsing allows you to sort through all existing calls for papers online, while subscribing to RSS feeds for all or select categories allows you to receive automatic notification of new calls. As the topics mentioned previously illustrate, *CFP* defines literary studies quite broadly, encompassing cultural and area studies along with traditional literary topics. Victorian and Edwardian scholars will find the categories for "Victorian" and "twentieth century and beyond" the most pertinent, although other sections may be relevant, depending on specific interests. You may submit a new call for papers on the *CFP* website. Each call contains a title, a full name or organization name, a contact e-mail, *CFP* categories, and a description. If browsing and RSS feeds do not help you find relevant calls for papers, you can also search the website by keyword. All scholars, even those still in graduate school, should familiarize themselves with *CFP*.

In addition to *CFP*, scholars should identify relevant listservs, which are e-mail distribution lists that allow subscribers to communicate with other people interested in similar topics. These can be particularly useful for sharing ideas and gathering peer feedback, noting recent publication, perusing conference listings, and networking with other scholars. While many listservs for Victorian and Edwardian literature exist, this section addresses two representative lists: *VICTORIA List* and *A Discussion of English Literature, Culture, and Society, 1880–1920*. ***VICTORIA List*** is hosted at Indiana University and is for all aspects of Victorian studies, not just the period's literature. You may choose to receive list updates in real time or have them sent in digest form so that you receive less frequent messages. Past discussions are archived on the *VICTORIA List* website by week and may be browsed by list members and non-members alike. Recent topics have included Gothic sites of violence, Japan in the British mind, *Lady Audley's Secret*, Victorian conduct manuals, and Victorian sources for *Peter Pan*. Typically, original messages and their responses are listed together in the archives. Scholars of late Victorian and Edwardian literature should find the information shared on *A **Discussion of English Literature, Culture, and Society, 1880–1920** (**ELCS-L**)* relevant to their research. Like *VICTORIA List*, scholars may subscribe to the list's contents in both regular and digest form. Also, *ELCS-L* provides the archives on its website, so that scholars may browse topics without subscribing. The archives are presented in reverse chronological order by month. *ELCS-L* is not as active as *VICTORIA List*, and many recent posts have been announcements about new online and print publications.

Literary scholars should also be aware of major and minor conferences in their research areas. Although they are frequently announced on listservs, you can also consult **Literature Conferences Worldwide**, a website that aggregates conference announcements. You may either browse by date or subscribe to receive automatic e-mail alerts about upcoming events. The site's contents are organized beginning with the current month, followed by subsequent months. Because this resource is for literary studies and related fields, not all of its contents will be relevant for your research interests. Victorian and Edwardian literature conferences are listed alongside ones for areas such as Spanish literature, early modern English literature, and popular culture. Each entry includes the dates, location, website, contact name, description, organizing body, and deadline for abstracts/proposals. Scholars may also search the site by keyword. This is not a comprehensive listing, so you should also consult the listservs and *Calls for Papers* discussed above.

Keep in mind that small academic societies and organizations may have their own listservs and host their own conferences. Organizations such as the *Gaskell Society*, *The Shaw Society*, and the *Pre-Raphaelite Society* focus on one author or a particular group of authors. These can also be important current awareness resources, particularly if your research interests are highly specialized. In addition to having their own listservs and conferences, many of these societies also publish their own journals, which can provide excellent publishing opportunities for scholars whose research interests match with the society's purpose.

REFERENCE TOOLS

Bassett, Troy J. *At the Circulating Library: A Database of Victorian Fiction, 1837–1901*, March 17 2010, at victorianresearch.org/atcl/index.php (accessed 16 April 2010).

Bibliography of Scottish Literature, at www.arts.gla.ac.uk/STELLA/biblio graphy (accessed 16 April 2010).

Centre for Research into the English Literature and Language of Wales. *Bibliography of Welsh Literature in English Translation*, at www.bwlet.net (accessed 16 April 2010).

Garside, Peter, Anthony Mandal, Verena Ebbes, Angela Koch, and Rainer Schöwerling. *The English Novel, 1830–1836: A Bibliographical Survey of Fiction Published in the British Isles*, 26 January 2006, at cardiff.ac.uk/encap/journals/corvey/1830s/index.html (accessed 16 April 2010).

Matsuoka, Mitsu. *Hyper-Concordance*, at victorian.lang.nagoya-u.ac.jp/concordance (accessed 16 April 2010).

Reading Experience Database, 1450–1945, 15 June 2009, at www.open.ac.uk/Arts/reading (accessed 16 April 2010).

Wright, Julia M. *Bibliography of Nineteenth-Century Irish Literature*, 19 May 2008, at irish-literature.english.dal.ca (accessed 16 April 2010).

Internet reference sources, like their print and database counterparts, provide essential background and contextual information. Equivalent published print and electronic resources are discussed in more detail in chapter 2, which covers general literary reference sources, and chapter 4, which discusses bibliographies, indexes, and annual reviews. This section includes a selection of secondary- and primary-source bibliographies, databases that contextualize literary circulation and reading, and an online concordance.

The English Novel, 1830–1836: A Bibliographical Survey of Fiction Published in the British Isles, as its title suggests, is a bibliography of early Victorian British fiction. This project was created by Cardiff University's Centre for Editorial and Intertextual Research (CEIR) in collaboration with the Paderborn University's Projekt Corvey team. This resource extends Peter Garside, James Raven, and Rainer Schöwerling's *The English Novel, 1770–1829: A Bibliographical Survey of Fiction Published in the British Isles* (New York: Oxford University Press, 2000). Although the site's introduction states its purpose is to complete the bibliography of Romantic-era publications, it is also useful for researching the early years of the Victorian age. Works by Scott and De Quincey are indexed alongside those by Dickens and Disraeli. Because it is based on a published bibliography, this site has a clearly defined structure, a thorough introduction complete with an abbreviations guide, and a standardized entry format. The bibliography was compiled from examining original first editions when available, secondary sources such as Sadleir's and Wolff's bibliographies (see chapter 4), advertisements and notices in period newspapers and periodicals, the *Nineteenth-Century Short-Title Catalogue* (see chapter 4), and *WorldCat* (see chapter 3). Entries are arranged chronologically by imprint year and alphabetically by author and title within year. Generally speaking, the entries comprise the following fields: entry number; author name(s); full title; publication place and imprint details; pagination, format, and place; contemporary listings; location and shelf-mark of copy examined and references to other catalogues and copies; and notes. *The English Novel, 1830–1836* can be browsed by year or viewed in its entirety in HTML, rich text, or PDF format. Two appendixes of additional works and indexes to author, title, and publisher supplement the main entries. Much like a print resource, this website has no search mechanism, so scholars must rely on traditional organizational structures and indexes to find pertinent information.

Victorian scholars will find *At the Circulating Library: A Database of Victorian Fiction, 1837–1901* (*ATCL*) a useful resource for bibliographic information on Victorian authors, novels, and publishers. Comprised of 5,282 titles by 1,781 authors, this database combines information on three-volume novels from sources such as *The English Catalogue of Books* and the British Library *Integrated Catalogue*, and serialization information from more than sixty Victorian periodicals. *ATCL* is part of the *Victoria Research Web* and was created by Troy J. Bassett, who intended this resource to pick up where *British Fiction, 1800–1829: A Database of Production, Circulation, and Reception* (www.british-fiction.cf.ac.uk) and *The English Novel, 1830–1836: A Bibliographical Survey of Fiction Published in the British Isles* end. Lesser-known authors such as Marion Agnes Bengough, Annie Keary, and Henry Sedley are included alongside well-known authors like Wilkie Collins, George Meredith, and Mary Elizabeth Braddon. Scholars may browse by author, title, publisher, year, serial, and genre, and may search by keyword for author and title. Entries for authors comprise the name, alternate names, biography, references, and titles of works. Title entries have fields for author and title, serialization, first edition, edition size and price, summary, and references. Additionally, *ATCL* provides a list of sources and abbreviations.

Scholars interested in Irish, Scottish, and Welsh literatures in addition to English literature should consult the *Bibliography of Nineteenth-Century Irish Literature*, the *Bibliography of Scottish Literature*, and the *Bibliography of Welsh Literature in English Translation*, respectively. Dalhousie University's Julia M. Wright created the *Bibliography of Nineteenth-Century Irish Literature*, which lists both English-language and Irish-language authors and their texts. This site is primarily a bibliography, with select titles linking to the full text. In addition to the main author lists, this site includes contextual resources such as a bibliography of scholarship on nineteenth-century Ireland, the Act of Union between Ireland and Great Britain (1800), and nonfiction prose on colonialism and related issues outside of Ireland. Indexes to authors and texts are also provided.

Unlike the Irish bibliography, the Scottish and Welsh ones are not specific to the nineteenth century. The Department of Scottish Literature at the University of Glasgow created the ***Bibliography of Scottish Literature***, which addresses Scottish literature from the medieval age to the present. The site's contents are broken down by time period, with post-1945 literature further subdivided according to genre. The section "Victorian and Edwardian Scottish Literature" includes discussion of general histories and historical and cultural background sources, and bibliographies of general works and texts specific to the following topics: George MacDonald; James Young Geddes, John Davidson, and Scottish poetry; James Thomson; Robert Louis Stevenson; Margaret Oliphant; George Douglas Brown; and J. M. Barrie and the Scottish theater. Each section lists original and recent editions as well as criticism and biography. The ***Bibliography of Welsh Literature in English Translation*** covers literary works from the eighteenth century through the present. With interfaces in both English and Cymraeg, this resource enables scholars to search across keywords, author, title, publisher, dates, published in, and notes fields with Boolean operators. The records contain information regarding title, secondary title, author, page numbers, dates, published in, book type, reference type name, keywords, publisher, abstract, and URLs. Unfortunately there is no way to browse the site's contents. The *Bibliography of Welsh Literature in English Translation* also provides links to websites on translation studies, institutions, and publishers and booksellers.

Created at Open University in 1996, the ***Reading Experience Database, 1450–1945 (RED)*** compiles data about "reading experiences of readers of all nationalities in Britain and those of British subjects abroad from 1450 to 1945." To date, *RED* has nearly twenty-nine thousand entries. *RED*'s contents are taken from published and unpublished sources. Individuals can add entries on what, where, and when British people read and what they thought of their readings by going to the "Contribute" section of the website. Scholars may browse by either author of text or reader's name, and may search the database's contents. The basic search looks for keywords in all fields including evidence. The advanced option searches for keywords in evidence with the option to limit to century of experience, reader/listener/reading group, text being read, and reading experience. *RED*'s contents should help scholars understand the culture of reading in Britain and how texts were received.

Created by Mitsu Matsuoka of Nagoya University in Japan, the ***Hyper-Concordance*** is a searchable, full-text collection of American, British, and Irish literary works. While this site has works by authors from all eras, its strengths lie in Victorian literature. Some of the authors included are W. H. Ainsworth, R. D. Blackmore, Marie Corelli, Margaret Oliphant, Walter Pater, and C. M. Yonge. Scholars can access the *Hyper-Concordance* contents by selecting an author from the list and then choosing a text. For instance, if you chose Margaret Oliphant, you could then search the contents of *A Belea-guered City*, *The Open Door*, *A Little Pilgrim*, *Old Lady Mary*, *Jeanne d'Arc*, or *The Library Window*. After selecting a book, you must search for a term in the full text with options to limit to case sensitive, non-alphabet character sensitive, head length, and tail length. The results provide information on total text lines, word count, and query result. Each instance of a word or phrase is shown in context with the number of characters specified in the head and tail lengths appearing before and after it, respectively. Links from the text line number and matching word or phrase connect to the literary work's full text. Because of the full-text searching capabilities, this resource is excellent for locating specific passages or word occurrences. Unfortunately, there is no way to get to the text without searching for a particular phrase. As with *Project Gutenberg* above, the *Hyper-Concordance* does not offer publication or edition details for the source texts, which is a significant drawback for scholarly research, and as such, this resource should be used with caution.

CULTURAL AND HISTORICAL RESOURCES

Aspects of the Victorian Book, at www.bl.uk/collections/early/victorian/intro
.html (accessed 16 April 2010).
The British Cartoon Archive, at www.cartoons.ac.uk (accessed 16 April 2010).
British History Online, University of London & History of Parliament Trust,
at www.british-history.ac.uk (accessed 16 April 2010).
*Dying Speeches and Bloody Murders: Crime Broadsides Collected by the
Harvard Law School Library*, December 2007, at broadsides.law.harvard
.edu (accessed 16 April 2010).
Jackson, Lee. *The Victorian Dictionary*, at www.victorianlondon.org (accessed 16 April 2010).
Literature, Arts, and Medicine Database, 2 November 2009, at litmed.med
.nyu.edu (accessed 16 April 2010).
Old Bailey Proceedings Online, December 2008, at www.oldbaileyonline.org
(accessed 16 April 2010).
Studies in Scarlet: Marriage and Sexuality in the U.S. and U.K., 1815–1914, at
vc.lib.harvard.edu/vc/deliver/home?_collection=scarlet (accessed 16 April
2010).
Thomas, Julia, et al. *Database of Mid-Victorian Illustration*, at www.dmvi
.cardiff.ac.uk (accessed 16 April 2010).
Women in the Literary Marketplace 1800–1900, at rmc.library.cornell.edu/
womenLit/default.htm (accessed 16 April 2010).

The Victorian Dictionary is an excellent resource for information about Victorian London. Created by author and librarian Lee Jackson, *The Victorian Dictionary* provides primary-source materials on forty broad topics such as "Advertising," "Childhood," "Disease," "Lighting," "Police," "Religion/ Spirituality," "Thames," and "Women." Each topic is broken down into narrower subtopics. "Women" is divided by "Children, Family, Husband and Friends," "Courtship, Marriage and Romance," "Education, Employment and Emancipation," "Health and Beauty," "In Public," and "Sexuality." The "Women" section also cross-references to "Childhood—Babies," "Crime—Prostitution," and "Health—Beauty Products." Relevant documents and topics are listed under each subcategory. Topics such as "dressing to match one's age," "gossips," "ladies on trains," "smoking," "a single woman," and "women acrobats" are listed under the "In Public" subcategory. Each topic then links to a primary-source document pertinent to that subject matter. In addition to browsing *The Victorian Dictionary*'s contents, you can search for words and phrases. This resource offers a bibliography of books, pamphlets, and journals used, as well as links to encyclopedias, genealogy, general Victorian sites, libraries and archives, museums, picture libraries, and public bodies with interests in Victoriana. To learn tidbits about Victorian life, you can click the links for "Random Page" or "Slang" to view a page from the dictionary or a Victorian slang term.

Scholars interested in book history and authorship should consult websites such as *Women in the Literary Marketplace 1800–1900* and *Aspects of the Victorian Book*. The Cornell University Library's Division of Rare and Manuscript Collections created ***Women in the Literary Marketplace 1800– 1900*** as an online exhibition on nineteenth-century women authors. The site has background information on the following topics: early role models, entering the literary market, learned poets, getting into print, Charlotte Brontë and George Eliot, sin and sensation, new women, education, journalism, activism, L. T. Meade, and the three-volume format. Each section comprises a brief essay, sample texts, and citations for selected primary sources. Although *Women in the Literary Marketplace* does not have deep content, it provides an excellent overview of the issues surrounding nineteenth-century female authors.

The British Library's ***Aspects of the Victorian Book*** offers information on book production and publishing during the Victorian age. Detailed introductions on "The Economic and Social Background to Victorian Print Culture" and "British Publishing 1800–1900" begin the production and publishing sections, respectively. Additional topics covered under "Production" include printing technology, illustration, lithography, 1880s wood engraving, photographically illustrated books, binding, and John Leighton bindings, while the novel, yellowbacks, penny dreadfuls, children's books, and magazines comprise the publishing section.

Related to book and publishing history are resources on the illustrative arts. Websites such as the *Database of Mid-Victorian Illustration* and *The British Cartoon Archive* will be useful for scholars interested in illustration and British cultural history. Created by Cardiff University's Center for Editorial and Intertextual Research, the **Database of Mid-Victorian Illustration (DMVI)** comprises "868 literary illustrations that were published in and around 1862." Illustrations by artists such as George du Maurier, Frederic Leighton, John Everett Millais, and James Abbott McNeill Whistler are included. Scholars may access the *DMVI* contents by keyword search, advanced search, or browse iconography. The first looks for keywords broadly in the database's contents and gives the option to order results by illustrator, author, engraver, source text, illustration title, date, and genre. The advanced search enables scholars to look for information by specific authors, titles, illustrators, engravers, places, publishers, work publication date, iconographic keywords, and genre, with the same sorting results as the basic search provides. The browse feature is organized by periods, geography, settings, people, activities, objects, and themes, each of which is further broken down into subcategories. Themes, for example, comprises "Society and Culture," "Travel and Tourism," "Religion," and "Narrative Themes." When you click on a subcategory such as religion, all images related to that theme display on the screen and a list of narrower topics is given. "Religion [General]," "Religious Services," "Religious Concepts," "Christianity," "Islam," "Judaism," and "Festivals and Feast Days" are listed under "Religion." Individual image records contain information on the work, image, iconography, and technical data. The images themselves are high-resolution so that scholars may zoom in to examine details. The *DMVI* also has a guide to the database and links to websites for project repositories, other visual and Victorian archive projects, and related academic sites.

The British Cartoon Archive is at the University of Kent's Templeman Library in Canterbury. The online catalog comprises almost 140,000 images sourced from the British Cartoon Archive, the National Library of Wales, the Library of the London School of Economics, and the John Rylands University Library of Manchester. Although the cartoons date from 1790 to 2003, the majority is from the twentieth and twenty-first centuries. Fewer than twenty-five hundred cartoons date from 1830 to 1910. Even so, it remains a useful resource for Victorian and Edwardian scholars. In addition to images, this site has cartoonist biographies, records for two thousand books on cartoons and cartoonists, and articles. Scholars may search *The British Cartoon Archive* by any text, artist, publication, date, title or caption, format, embedded text, notes, implied text, series, people depicted or referred to, subjects, reference number, collection, copyright, and location of artwork. The results display as thumbnail images along with options to narrow results by artist, publisher, depicted, referred to, and subject. Each image is accompanied by a record that includes a reference number, caption, embedded text, notes, and archival reference number, and additional details related to the image's size, technique, also published in, copyright holder, copyright contact details, and location of artwork. All cartoons are exact replications of their originals, so the database contains a mix of color, black-and-white, and grayscale images. Scholars may zoom in to view the details of each image and may request use in both educational and commercial contexts.

Scholars in need of historical primary and secondary sources should consult **British History Online**. Created by the History of Parliament Trust and the University of London's Institute of Historical Research, *British History Online* covers British history from the medieval period through the nineteenth century. The site's contents are organized by top sources for local history, historical geography, urban and metropolitan, parliamentary, and ecclesiastical and religious, and by region: east, London, midlands, north, Scotland, southeast, southwest, and Wales. Additionally, scholars may browse by classification, selecting from regions, subjects, and periods to retrieve documents that match the chosen facets. For instance, selecting London as region, economic history as subject, and nineteenth century as period limits to a list of four pertinent results: "City of London Livery Companies Commission. Report; Volume 1," "City of London Livery Companies Commission. Report; Volume 4," "Dictionary of Traded Goods and Commodities, 1550–1820," and "Memorials of the Guild Merchant Taylors—Of the Fraternity of St. John the Baptist in the City of London." You may also browse the documents by places, subjects, periods, sources, and maps. Text and advanced search options help scholars find resources that match particular terms. Subscribers to the site also have access to premium content including calendars of domestic state papers, Scottish and Irish state papers, and close rolls. Scholars must register with the site in order to save resources to a personal bookshelf. Although not comprehensive, *British History Online* is a phenomenal source for primary and secondary historical materials.

Resources such as *Dying Speeches and Bloody Murders: Crime Broadsides Collected by the Harvard Law School Library*, *Old Bailey Proceedings Online*, and *Studies in Scarlet: Marriage and Sexuality in the U.S. and U.K.* will be useful to scholars who need to understand the legal background of particular issues that emerge in nineteenth- and early twentieth-century literature. Each of these sources provides primary-source materials about crime and law throughout British history. ***Dying Speeches and Bloody Murders: Crime Broadsides Collected by the Harvard Law School Library*** comprises more than five hundred broadsides printed between 1701 and 1891 in Great Britain. The original broadsides are housed in the Harvard Law School Library. Scholars may browse the collection or use either the keyword or category searches. The keyword search looks for terms anywhere or specifically in title, name, date, site of publication, or subject, and supports both Boolean operators and wildcards. The category search allows scholars to combine up to three items in the following categories: crimes (as described in broadsides), year of publication, site of publication, printers, condemned, and victims. The browse options are alphabetically by title, name, subject, and form/genre.

Old Bailey Proceedings Online (***OBPO***) comprises full text to 197,745 criminal trials held at the Old Bailey, London's central criminal court, some of which were publicized in the broadsides digitized in *Dying Speeches and Bloody Murders*. This resource comprises Old Bailey proceedings from 1674 to 1913, the *Ordinary of Newgate's Accounts* from 1679 to 1772, and biographical details for around twenty-five hundred men and women executed at Tyburn. Transcripts, as well as page images of the original documents, are provided. The "About the Proceedings" section contains information on publishing history, value as a historical source, advertisements, associated records, and *Ordinary of Newgate's Accounts*, while the "Historical Background" section covers the following topics: crime, justice, and punishment; London and its hinterlands; community histories; gender in the proceedings; and the Old Bailey Courthouse. A glossary and *OBPO* bibliography are also included. The default search has fields for keyword(s), surname, given name, alias, offence, verdict, punishment, and time period with the option to search in specific text sections. Additional searches are for "Personal Details," "Ordinary's Accounts, 1679–1772," "Custom Search," "Associated Records, 1674–1834," and "Place and Map Search, 1674–1834." Both proceedings and Ordinary's Accounts may be browsed by date. In addition to more traditional search and browse options, *OBPO* allows scholars to generate statistics with the following fields: offence, verdict, punishment, defendant gender, defendant age range, victim gender, victim age range, keyword(s), and time period. This should be particularly useful for individuals who need to compare changes in crime rates over time.

The third legal studies website—***Studies in Scarlet: Marriage and Sexuality in the U.S. and U.K., 1815–1914***—focuses exclusively on relationships between men and women, whereas the previous two covered all manner of crimes and infractions. Drawn from the Harvard Law School Library's collections, *Studies in Scarlet* contains 420 published narrative accounts of trials that occurred between 1815 and 1914 in the United States, Great Britain, and

Ireland. Because these are narratives rather than court transcripts, they will be more useful for humanities scholars than lawyers. Cases such as Oscar Wilde's sodomy trial are included in this source. The search interface is quite simple. Two search boxes are provided with the option to specify whether terms appear in title, name/creator, subject, form/genre, or anywhere. Boolean operators and wildcards are supported. Scholars may also browse the alphabetical indexes for title, name/creator, subject, and form/genre. *Studies in Scarlet* maintains a search history for the duration of your session. *Dying Speeches and Bloody Murder*'s broadsides, *OBPO*'s court case transcripts, and *Studies in Scarlet*'s trial narratives complement each other nicely.

Created at New York University, the **Literature, Arts, and Medicine Database** is a multi-disciplinary resource that annotates works of art, literature, and the performing arts that pertain to illness experience, medical education, and medical practice. In September 2010, the database contained 143 art annotations, 237 film annotations, 2,498 literature annotations, two theater annotation, 89 artists, 1,565 authors, and 138 keywords. Art, literature, and performing arts are discrete sections of this resource, each of which includes information such as relevant annotations and biographical details of artists and authors. Scholars may also search across annotations, people, keyword (topic), annotator, or free text. Although the *Literature, Arts, and Medicine Database* is broader than the Victorian and Edwardian ages, forty works by nineteen Victorian authors and seven works by six Edwardian authors are annotated. The texts range from Charlotte Brontë's *Jane Eyre* to Rudyard Kipling's *Kim*, and from James Joyce's *Araby* to E. M. Forster's *Where Angels Fear to Tread*. Author entries provide information on sex, national origin, era, born, died, awards, and annotated works. Works entries comprise genre, keywords, summary, commentary, publisher, edition, place published, miscellaneous, annotated by, date of entry, and last revised. When the full text is freely available in the Web, a link is given. Scholars interested in representations of health and medical issues in literary texts should find the *Literature, Arts, and Medicine Database* an excellent resource.

CONCLUSION

As mentioned previously, this chapter does not discuss all relevant websites for the Victorian and Edwardian ages, but it does introduce you to many of the major open-access, online resources. At the time of publication, all of these resources were still available; however, given the ever-changing landscape of the Internet, it is highly probable that some of these will be short-lived and other websites will emerge on the scene. Websites such as the four scholarly portals—*Voice of the Shuttle, Literary Resources on the Net, The Victorian Web*, and *Victoria Research Web*—should continue to add links to new, relevant online resources. *NINES* will also play an increasingly major role in capturing emerging scholarship and digital resources, so scholars should regularly search and use the digital objects aggregated through that website as a means of staying current with online developments. The resources covered here are best used in conjunction with the print, microform, and subscription databases addressed in previous chapters.

NOTES

1. "Attributions of Authorship in the *Gentleman's Magazine*, 1731–77: A Supplement to Kuist," *Studies in Bibliography* 44 (1991): 271–302; "Attributions of Authorship in the *Gentleman's Magazine*, 1778–92: A Supplement to Kuist," *Studies in Bibliography* 45 (1992): 158–87; "Attributions of Authorship in the *Gentleman's Magazine*, 1793–1808: A Supplement to Kuist," *Studies in Bibliography* 46 (1993): 320–49; "Attributions of Authorship in the *Gentleman's Magazine*, 1809–26: A Supplement to Kuist," *Studies in Bibliography* 47 (1994): 164–95; "Attributions of Authorship in the *Gentleman's Magazine*, 1827–48: A Supplement to Kuist," *Studies in Bibliography* 49 (1996): 176–207; and "Attributions of Authorship in the *Gentleman's Magazine*, 1849–68, and Addenda, 1733–1838: A Supplement to Kuist," *Studies in Bibliography* 50 (1997): 322–58.

2. The *Unitarian Chronicle* was a supplement to the *Monthly Repository*, and the two combined are counted as one journal title.

3. OCR stands for Optical Character Recognition, which is a method of scanning printed texts using software programmed to recognize discrete characters.

Chapter Eleven

Researching a Thorny Problem

A wealth of information exists for well-known Victorian and Edwardian authors, so scholars researching the Eliots, Thackerays, and Wildes of the literary world should have few problems finding primary or secondary sources to support their research. Scholars of lesser-known authors will face a more challenging research trail. Empire writing is just one subset of the British literary tradition that was enormously influential in its day, but most of its writers and popular texts have received little critical attention. Throughout the nineteenth century and into the early twentieth century, as Britain transformed from a nation with colonies to an empire, the boundaries of what was considered "British" shifted. During this period, British citizens living abroad in the colonies wrote about their cultural experiences through both fictional and non-fiction works. Now-obscure texts such as Flora Annie Steel's novel *On the Face of the Waters* can pose unique problems for researchers. Although widely read in their time, these authors and their texts have largely been neglected for the past century.

This chapter discusses the difficulties of and suggests strategies for researching lesser-known texts written by British citizens abroad in the colonies. While the discussion focuses on empire writing, these tactics could be applied to any author or text. The resources addressed here follow the book's organizational structure. For example, reference sources come before major indexes. In your own research, feel free to consult sources in whatever order seems most appropriate. You may want to begin your research with the *Modern Language Association International Bibliography* and the *Annual Bibliography of English Language and Literature*, or you may find biographies a better place to start. Whatever order you choose, be thorough and use any and all relevant resources at your disposal.

Hailed as "the great novelist of India," Flora Annie Steel was a contemporary of Rudyard Kipling and was as widely read in the late nineteenth and early twentieth centuries; however, while Kipling remains a recognizable name to educated readers, Steel and her works have been largely unread and are under-studied today.[1] Indeed, Steel's writings "of India and Anglo-Indian life established her reputation as Rudyard Kipling's only serious rival."[2] Born Flora Annie Webster in 1847, she first moved to India in January 1868, just one day after marrying Henry Steel. Other than brief leaves to Britain, she remained in India until 1889, when her husband retired. Her experiences in India heavily influenced her writing, to which she would devote her life upon returning to Britain. Her best-known novel—*On the Face of the Waters*—was first published in 1896 and gives an account of the Indian Mutiny of 1857, or India's First War of Independence. This novel stands out from others about the mutiny, as she was "one of the first people to be given unlimited access to the huge archive of the mutiny, or rebellion, at Delhi."[3] Steel infused many of her other writings with her experiences in India, although her later works often addressed women's rights and human sexuality. As her obituary stated in the London *Times*:

> Lord Balfour (then Mr. Balfour) is reported to have said at the time that Mrs. Steel was the only Englishwoman who knew anything about real India. It is one thing to know India; it is another to be able to describe India, and yet a third to tell a thrilling and absorbing story within the limits of the facts of Indian history and Indian character.[4]

Given Steel's reputation, any scholar of Britain in India would be remiss in overlooking her literary contributions; however, until recently very little scholarly attention has been paid her.

A first step in researching Steel and her writings is to find out what background information exists by consulting the general literary reference sources discussed in chapter 2. While many of the bibliographies, biographies, and encyclopedias covered there may offer valuable research leads, this chapter does not discuss each and every one, but rather demonstrates how select sources can provide relevant background information and direct you to additional resources. In your own research, be sure to consult all pertinent resources so that you thoroughly assess the scholarship available on your author, text, or topic. While the sources discussed here may support your research, you may also need to consult other resources from chapter 2. This section specifically addresses major biographies such as the *Dictionary of Literary Biography* and the *Oxford Dictionary of National Biography*, select British or Victorian encyclopedias—*The Continuum Encyclopedia of British Literature*, the *Encyclopedia of the Victorian Era*, *The Oxford Encyclopedia of British Literature*, and *Victorian Britain*—and all editions of the *Cambridge Bibliography of English Literature* (1941, 1969, and 1999) and the *Bibliographies of Studies in Victorian Literature*. These resources are all discussed in more detail in chapter 2.

A search of the online *Oxford Dictionary of National Biography* reveals that there is a biography of Steel in the current edition and one in the 1937 *DNB*. Likewise, the *Dictionary of Literary Biography* has published two biographies of her: one from a volume on *British Short-Fiction Writers, 1880–1914: The Romantic Tradition* and another from the volume *Late-Victorian and Edwardian British Novelists, First Series*. While these biographies have complementary information, each takes a slightly different approach to describing Steel, her life, and her works. For more details about Steel's life, the book-length biographies identified in *WorldCat* below should be valuable resources. Written only eight years after her death, the 1937 *DNB* biography offers more personal insights into her life, but is based on only two obituaries, Steel's autobiography, and private information. The later biographies cite more secondary texts and primary sources from archives. These biographies and their lists of works cited give a clearer understanding of who Steel was and how she fits into literary history, and provide citations to additional resources, leading you further down the research trail.

Moving on to encyclopedias, look for information not only on Steel but also on the traditions and contexts in which she wrote. Steel's biographies indicate that her writings are infused with her experiences of living abroad, giving insights into Britain's colonization of India. This knowledge could help you identify possible avenues for research. Because she is a non-canonical author, many major British and Victorian encyclopedias do not have entries devoted to her. Even if a full entry has not been written on the author you are researching, always check any available indexes to see if he or she is mentioned within other entries. One encyclopedia—*The Continuum Encyclopedia of British Literature*—includes an entry for her, which at roughly two hundred words, merely gives a snapshot biography and does not add any real depth to our existing knowledge of Steel. However, that same encyclopedia has an excellent entry for "Colonial Literature," which defines and contextualizes the works of British citizens written in and about the colonies. While the entry does not explicitly mention her, Steel certainly fits into this literary tradition. Additionally, the entry concludes with a useful bibliography of works on British imperial literature, colonialism, orientalism, and empire.

In looking at other resources, we find that both *The Oxford Encyclopedia of British Literature* and the *Encyclopedia of the Victorian Era* have lengthy entries on "Orientalism," the latter of which mentions Steel's *On the Face of the Waters*. Each of these concludes with a bibliography of readings to add to our growing list of resources. Through entries such as these, you should begin to understand where Steel fits in English literary traditions and how best to approach her works. Our final encyclopedia, *Victorian Britain*, does not have entries on Steel or topics covered by the previous resources, but it does contain entries on "Anglo-Indian Literature," "India," and the "Indian Mutiny (1857)." The "Anglo-Indian Literature" entry briefly mentions Steel's major novels within the Anglo-Indian genre, and all three entries have short bibliographies. There are likely other relevant entries in these and other encyclopedias and companions, but this should give you a sense what types of entries to consult.

The next step is to look for citations to relevant books and articles in major bibliographies: *The Cambridge Bibliography of English Literature* (1941), *The New Cambridge Bibliography of English Literature* (1969), and *The Cambridge Bibliography of English Literature* (1999). Let's begin with *CBEL* (1941). Because the first edition stopped coverage at 1900, you only need to consult the volume for 1800 to 1900. The volume's organizational structure requires that you consult a significant number of sections, including "Bibliographies, Literary Histories and Special Studies, Prose-Selections, and Literary Memoirs and Reminiscences," "Prose Fiction: Bibliographies, Histories and Critical Studies," "British Imperial History" of the mid- and late nineteenth century, "Books of Travel," "Sanskrit and Indian Scholars," and "Literatures of the Dominion: Anglo-Indian Literature." Browsing through sections such as "Bibliographies, Histories, and Critical Studies" on prose fiction is an excellent way to identify relevant overviews of the British novel during a particular time period. Works on imperial history and travel can provide some historical and cultural context for the events Steel wrote about. While the "Sanskrit and Indian Scholars" section appears relevant, most of the works focus on the Sanskrit language and are not germane to researching Steel. The section for Anglo-Indian literature, however, includes citations to general works of reference, poetry, drama, fiction, translations, philology, history, biography and politics, geography, topography, travel, religion and philosophy, social, and miscellaneous. This section as a whole could be useful for finding historical information as well as identifying similar authors and texts to compare to Steel and her writings. A citation to Steel's *Wide-Awake Stories* is included in the fiction subsection.

In the *NCBEL* (1969), consult both volume 3 (1800–1900) and volume 4 (1900–1950). In this edition, the categories are significantly condensed. Scholars should consult "General Works" as well as general "Bibliographies" and "Histories and Studies" on the novel in both volumes. Additionally, the subsection of "Travel" on "Asia" is worth examining in volume 3, as is the section "Writers on travel, the countryside and sport" in volume 4. Because the *NCBEL* was published after the British Empire's decline, there is no section for Anglo-Indian literature as there was in the first edition. Neither volume contains any direct references to any works by or about Steel. The third edition of this standard bibliography, as discussed in chapter 2, currently comprises only one volume, which covers 1800 to 1900. As in the previous editions, scholars should consult general works on the novel, including bibliographies and histories and studies, and travel books on Asia. Additionally, the "Household Books" category is of interest only because it contains a citation to Steel's *The Complete Indian Housekeeper and Cook*. While there are no references in any *CBEL* edition to *On the Face of the Waters*, these bibliographies are still crucial research tools for identifying works that provide the cultural, historical, and literary contexts for Steel's works.

Even older bibliographies such as *Bibliographies of Studies in Victorian Literature 1965–1974* and *Bibliographies of Studies in Victorian Literature 1975–1984* are useful for locating books and articles about Steel's works. The former bibliography has one reference for Steel—Daya Patwardhan's *A Star of India: Flora Annie Steel, Her Works and Times* (Poona: A. V. Griha Prakashan, 1963)—and a review of Patwardhan's book by Benita Parry in *Modern Language Review* (62:324–25). Here Steel is described as a "writer of 'common-sense-romances' and Anglo-Indian fiction."[5] The latter Victorian bibliography has two entries for Steel—one that refers to Violet Powell's *Flora Annie Steel: Novelist of India* (London: Heinemann, 1981) and four reviews of that book, and a second that cites a fifth review of Powell's work. The benefit of a source such as *Bibliographies of Studies in Victorian Literature* is that its indexing will guide you to a very precise results set and those results are collocated with reviews, saving you time in seeking this information from disparate sources.

After consulting standard biographies, encyclopedias, and bibliographies, turn to catalogs such as *WorldCat* (see chapter 3) and major indexing databases such as *MLAIB* and *ABELL* (see chapter 4) to see if they cite works about Steel that were not in the reference sources you already examined. A subject phrase search for *Steel, Flora Annie* in *WorldCat* retrieves only five records, two of which are books written about Steel and her novels: Violet Powell's *Flora Annie Steel: Novelist of India* and Daya Patwardhan's *A Star of India, Flora Annie Steel: Her Works and Times*. The remaining results comprise a dissertation comparing Steel to Kipling and Forster, archival material for an annotated bibliography of British women's autobiographies from 1790 to 1950, and a microform set from Adam Matthew's *Colonial Discourses* series one, which covers women, travel, and empire. None of these materials are widely held. (See below information on using *WorldCat* to locate archival materials on Steel.)

Just as you searched broadly for reference information, you could use *WorldCat* to find more books on topics such as Anglo-Indian literature, orientalism, colonial literature, and the Indian mutiny. Knowing that there is at least one dissertation on Steel, it is worth finding out whether any other dissertations have been written about her. In *ProQuest Dissertations & Theses* (see appendix), a search retrieves a list of nine dissertations about Steel. While only one covers her exclusively, the remaining works, which compare her to other authors or situate her in a particular tradition, are also useful. Since dissertations are usually unpublished, you may or may not want to cite them; however, they can help to shape your thinking about a research topic and often contain highly valuable bibliographies.

As in *WorldCat*, *MLAIB* and *ABELL* should be searched to find additional secondary resources on Steel and her writings. Although some of the works cited in these indexes may have also been included in the print reference resources examined earlier, you should always check sources such as these to find current scholarship. Starting in *MLAIB*, search for *Steel, Flora Annie* as a "Person-About" search. This retrieves twenty-two results, including journal articles, dissertation abstracts, books, and book articles. Of these results, seven are for works about *On the Face of the Waters*. Examine the subject terms listed for each entry, not only to determine what the work is about but also to identify other potential search terms. Subjects such as "British imperialism," "in India," "treatment of English women," "fiction," "by colonial women writers," "relationship to British colonialism," "treatment of Indian women," "relationship to Anglo-Indian society," and "Indian mutiny" could be searched independently or in combination with each other to find additional articles and books.

Duplicating the searches for Steel and *On the Face of the Waters* in *ABELL* retrieves fifteen results for Steel, eight of which are on the novel in question. As with the *MLAIB* results, these contain a mix of books, book chapters, dissertation abstracts, and journal articles. Additionally, the *ABELL* results include book reviews, which are not in *MLAIB*. Rather than assume that *ABELL* repeats the citations listed in *MLAIB*, compare the two lists to determine how many unique results actually exist. A comparison reveals most of the results are unique, with only six citations appearing in both indexing sources; so in total, there are thirty-one articles, books, book chapters, dissertation abstracts, and reviews on Flora Annie Steel indexed in *MLAIB* and *ABELL*. This, along with the citations gleaned from print reference sources and *WorldCat*, should provide you with a decent base of scholarship to begin your work on Steel.

In addition to secondary sources, consider identifying any available primary sources that could give your research greater depth. Chapters 6 through 9 of this book all deal with various types of primary sources and how to locate them. As with previously discussed resources, this section does not cover each work that indexes or contains primary sources, but highlights several representative sources and how to use them for this particular research project. Start with the major meta-indexes—*C19: The Nineteenth Century Index* and *19th Century Masterfile*—to search across and within specific indexes such as the *Wellesley Index* and *Poole's*. In addition to these indexes, full-text collections such as *19th Century U.K. Periodicals* and the *Times Digital Archive* provide ready access to otherwise difficult-to-find primary sources. Then, to demonstrate how to search for manuscripts and archives, this chapter covers using the *Location Register of English Literary Manuscripts and Letters: Eighteenth and Nineteenth Centuries*, *Location Register of Twentieth-Century English Literary Manuscripts and Letters*, the British National Archives, and *ArchiveGrid*, and briefly addresses finding archival materials using *WorldCat*.

Both *C19* and *19th Century Masterfile* comprise numerous indexes and provide the interface to search across them simultaneously (see chapter 4). Since the two resources have minimal overlap, search both if they are available to you. In *C19* you can cross-search indexes such as the *Nineteenth Century Short Title Catalogue*, *British Periodicals*, *Poole's Index to Periodical Literature*, *Wellesley Index to Victorian Periodicals*, and *Palmer's Index to the Times*. A basic keyword search for *(Flora Annie or F. A.) and Steel* across all sources retrieves the following results: zero archives, sixty-four books, six newspapers, three official publications, 293 periodicals, and zero reference. While some of the results are not germane, most are for works either by or about Steel. A survey of the results reveals that most of the book, newspaper, and periodical entries are relevant and that all of the official publications are irrelevant. Because each index uses different terminology, search those with the best results individually to make sure that you did not inadvertently exclude something. Since many of these results are by Steel, it would also be useful to search for *Steel* and the title *On the Face of the Waters* to determine if any reviews or commentary on it were published in the late nineteenth and early twentieth centuries. Not surprisingly, this search retrieves entries for three editions of the book as well as twenty-five periodicals results, most of which are contemporary reviews. The reviews come from publications such as *Atlantic Monthly, Current Literature, Dial*, and *Imperial and Asiatic Quarterly Review and Oriental and Colonial Record*. These are valuable resources for understanding how *On the Face of the Waters* was received.

As previously discussed, *C19* and *19th Century Masterfile* have some overlap, but each incorporates different indexes, so if you have access to them, be sure to search both. Since you cannot search the indexes individually in *19th Century Masterfile* (*NCM*) and because the various indexes use different terminology, be particularly careful in selecting your search terms. Depending on your research topic, you may also need to search multiple terms for the same concepts in order to locate all relevant resources. If you simply want to find works Steel wrote, then browse the author index to find variants of her name: *Steel, F. A.*; *Steel, Flora A.*; and *Steel, Flora Annie*. The author index indicates that most entries are indexed under *Steel, F. A.* By selecting these from the index, you can easily identify works she wrote.

If you need information about Steel and her works in *NCM*, however, run separate searches for each variant to find all records both by and about Steel. A search for *Flora Annie Steel* retrieves sixty-two hits in multi-title periodical indexes, nineteen in book indexes and serial records, two in newspaper indexes, and two in periodical indexes with full-text links. Because Steel's name is fairly unique, these results should all be relevant; however, they are incomplete. Searching for *Flora A. Steel* retrieves a few more results—seventy-two in multi-title periodical indexes, nineteen in book indexes and serial records, ten in newspaper indexes, and two in periodical indexes with full-text links— but as the author index noted, most entries are under *F. A. Steel* rather than the fuller versions of her name. The search results increase dramatically when the terms are *F. A. Steel*: 249 in multi-title periodical indexes, ninety-five in book indexes and serial records, seventy-four in newspaper indexes, seven in periodical indexes with full-text links, and forty-seven in patent and government document indexes. While greater in number, these results are not all relevant. Results for steel and steel products are mixed in with writings by and about Flora Annie Steel. This is still a useful search, however, because many results on Steel are retrieved through this search but excluded from the others.

To find reviews of *On the Face of the Waters,* search for the title as an exact phrase in keyword (all fields). The results set is significantly smaller— thirty-two in total—all specific to the novel. With the exception of two records for the book itself, these records are all for book reviews. There is slight duplication for a few reviews, but most are unique records. Although *NCM* is an index, it uses link-resolving technologies, which connect the index to your library's holdings and enable you to search them easily. Additionally, *NCM* links to Google Books so you can identify an open-access digital copy. Select other records are labeled with the term "e-source," indicating that corresponding documents are available in subscription databases such as *JSTOR*. When the full text is not available in open-access or proprietary online sources or in print sources in your library, you will need either to request it through interlibrary loan or to travel to an institution that owns the resource. Unlike *NCM*, *C19* links to full text in other ProQuest products only, including sources such as the *American Periodicals Series* and *British Periodicals*.

You need not limit your searches in *NCM* only to Steel and *On the Face of the Waters*. Using this meta-index to research the novel's context could also provide relevant primary sources. Since the novel is about India's First War of Independence, you could begin by searching for *India independence*. Retrieving twenty-six total results, this search produces a useful but incomplete results set. Since that particular phrase may not have been widely used in the mid- to late nineteenth century, search under other possible names for the mutiny, including the Great Rebellion, the Indian Mutiny, the Revolt of 1857, the Uprising of 1857, and the Sepoy Mutiny. The term *Great Rebellion* retrieves more than four hundred results; however, because that label was applied to other historical events, such as the American Civil War, not all of these will be relevant. Adding the term *India* to the search greatly reduces the results set but increases their relevance. *Indian Mutiny* brings up nearly 150 results, but *India Mutiny* produces more than 230. Likewise, *Sepoy Rebellion* elicits different results than *Sepoy Mutiny*, with 189 and 107, respectively. You could continue looking for information on this topic using additional terms, and with each search you would retrieve different results. The lesson here is that because the language used to describe India's First War of Independence was not fixed, you must search creatively and always consider other possible words.

While indexes such as *C19* and *19th Century Masterfile* search a greater number of sources, they sometimes leave you with the challenge of then finding the full text. Digital archives and microform collections offer a smaller subset of information but have the benefit of immediately supplying the documents you seek. While a large and ever-growing number of online and microform archives are available, this chapter discusses search strategies and results for two: *19th Century U.K. Periodicals* and the *Times Digital Archive*. *19th Century U.K. Periodicals*, as discussed in chapter 7, is a full-text collection of periodicals published in the United Kingdom during the nineteenth century. Because some of the titles covered in this database were gleaned from *The Wellesley Index*, which is indexed in *C19*, you may be able to use this resource to find the full text for citations you have already uncovered.

As in the previous resources, begin your search for information about Steel. Keeping in mind that the database is full text without subject headings, search for both *Flora Annie Steel* and *F. A. Steel*. This search retrieves eight sources, which include both essays about Steel and accounts of her views on topics such as the condition of the troops in India in 1857, the position of Indian married women, and Indian social conditions. By adding the novel's title, *On the Face of the Waters*, you can easily identify which of the results pertain to that text. This reduces the results set to six; however, none are in-depth reviews of the novel. Even though the search did not produce many highly relevant results, *19th Century U.K. Periodicals* can still be useful for finding articles on the novel's historical and cultural context. A search for the *Indian Mutiny or Sepoy Rebellion* retrieves 2,171 results in the full text and 179 in document title, dating from 1857 to 1900. While the mutiny itself took place between 1857 and 1859, British authors continued to write about it at least through the end of the century. Articles published in the 1850s tend to provide contemporaneous accounts of the rebellion and its impacts, first-person accounts of the war, and political commentary, while most later works romanticize the events in fictional works. In addition to Steel's account, works such as F. R.'s "An Incident of the Indian Mutiny," Captain Charles Young's "The Mystery of the Mountain: A Strange Story of the Indian Mutiny," Lucy Taylor's "Sahib and Sepoy; or, Saving an Empire," and Captain Leonard Brayley's "The Beleaguered Garrison" are among the many fictional accounts of the Indian Mutiny.[6] These and other accounts could be compared to Steel's novel. If you wanted to pursue this line of research further, consider searching under other possible names for the mutiny as discussed above in relation to *NCM*.

Another search tactic could be to research women in India in the later part of the nineteenth century, which would offer some context for Steel's experiences living there. If you limit to publications dating 1850 and later and search for *wom?n and India*, you will retrieve 178 results. To refine this further, consider adding the words *British* or *English* so that the results are about Anglo-Indian women rather than Indian women. This type of search retrieves results such as the essay *English Women in India*, which was published in *The Calcutta Review*. Results such as these can provide insights into the world Steel lived in and wrote about.

A source such as *19th Century U.K. Periodicals*, which searches across multiple titles, certainly has its benefits, but also consider searching single-title resources such as *The Times Digital Archive 1785–1985* (see chapter 7). Archives for a particular publication have search options and limits specific to the newspaper or periodical in question. Because the sections are more or less uniform throughout the *Times* issues, it is easier to search for particular content types such as reviews, letters to the editor, and obituaries. A search for letters to the editor by *Flora Annie Steel or F. A. Steel* retrieves twenty-one results, twenty of which were written by Steel. These letters cover diverse topics such as women's suffrage, the health of the army in India, and gold thread workers and embroiderers in Delhi. Letters such as these can help you understand Steel's stances on various issues, many of which she incorporated into her fiction. The section limiters can also be used to find Steel's obituary. Since the *Times*, or any other individual newspaper or journal, is not necessarily representative of all viewpoints, consult multiple publications whenever possible.

The final resource category deals with locating archives and manuscripts. Both the *ODNB* and the *DLB* entries include brief discussions of Steel's papers and archives; however, consult other sources to make sure you have identified all possible materials.[7] These biographies reveal that, while uncollected, some of her papers are held at the National Record of Archives, the Harry Ransom Humanities Research Center at the University of Texas at Austin, the Macmillan Archive at the British Library, and the R. I. B. Library of Reed Book Services. Knowing that papers already exist in these locations, check their online catalogs and finding aids to learn more details about their holdings. For instance, a search of the *National Register of Archives* for Flora Annie Steel as a personal name reveals that some of her correspondence and literary papers are listed in the *Location Register of Twentieth Century English Literary Manuscripts*, two diaries and papers are held privately, and the British Library holds her correspondence with Macmillan from 1892 to 1927. Unlike published materials, which are generally available in multiple locations, these materials are unique and require you to travel to the disparate locations if you wish to read all of Steel's papers.

Knowing that some of Steel's manuscripts are listed in the *Location Register of Twentieth Century English Literary Manuscripts*, consult that resource to determine the exact nature of the correspondence and literary papers (see chapter 9). The *Location Register* includes fourteen entries under Steel's name. The papers are held in various libraries around Great Britain, including the Library of Manchester at John Rylands University, the Birmingham Reference Library, the Brotherton Library in Leeds, the Fawcett Library at City of London Polytechnic, the National Army Museum Library, the Richmond Central Library, the British Library, the Bodleian Library, the University of St. Andrews Library, the University of Edinburgh Library, and Manchester Central Library. Each location holds a selection of Steel's letters, including two letters from Steel to Bram Stoker at the Brotherton Library, three letters from Steel to W. F. Tillotson & Son at the Library of Manchester, and her correspondence in the Macmillan Archive at the British Library. These and the other letters listed in the *Location Register* reveal different information about Steel and her writings. Unfortunately there is no single major archive of Steel's collected materials. The online version of the location register lists these fourteen entries plus a fifteenth that was in the 2003 supplement. Because Steel's writing life spanned both the nineteenth and twentieth centuries, you should also check the *Location Register of English Literary Manuscripts and Letters: Eighteenth and Nineteenth Centuries*, as some authors are included in both. In Steel's case, however, she is not listed in the location register for the eighteenth and nineteenth centuries, but only in the twentieth-century set.

Since Steel's papers are not collocated in one archive, you may also want to search a resource like *ArchiveGrid* if it is available at your library (see chapter 9). A search for *"Flora Annie Steel" ~4*, which creates a proximity search for Steel's name, retrieves nine results. The results represent holdings from Columbia, the Morgan Library and Museum, Harvard, Stanford, UCLA, Yale, and the University of Texas at Austin. The results reveal how widely Steel's papers have dispersed, and these are only papers held within the United States. Although discussed previously in terms of locating books about Steel, *WorldCat* (see chapter 3) is also useful for identifying archival sources. To do so, limit type to "Archival Materials" and search for *Steel Flora Annie* as a subject. Doing so retrieves four records for three works: *An Annotated Bibliography of British Women's Autobiographies, 1790–1950: Research and Reference Materials, 1968–1998*; English literary agent William Morris Colles's *Papers, 1888–1928*; and autograph collector E. H. Smith's *Collection, 1888–1934*. While none are entirely about Steel, these collections still contain unique documents regarding Steel. By searching online catalogs and in both the location registers, which cover British archives, and a United States-centric source like *ArchiveGrid*, you have a better chance of identifying all extant manuscripts and archival materials related to Steel.

As mentioned previously, when researching a lesser-known author, it is important to consider other angles for inquiry. For Steel and her writings, topics such as Britain in India, late nineteenth-century British women, the British Empire, the Sepoy Rebellion, and fictionalizations of the Indian Mutiny could all prove to be useful search topics. Because scholars have already written some secondary literature about Steel, take care to consider existing arguments, but because the body of scholarship on her is relatively small, you may find that no one has taken the approach that most interests you. One of the great benefits of writing on lesser-known authors is that finding a gap in the scholarship is much easier than with a well-studied author such as Kipling. Other authors of empire writing may have even less written on them, which means not only that there is plenty of room for new scholarship but also that secondary and even primary sources may be difficult to find, or non-existent. In situations where there are little to no outside resources for your author or text, researching their context becomes increasingly important.

This chapter walked you through one possible research path, and there are doubtless other approaches you could employ. Remember that regardless of your approach, research is a recursive process. You may find yourself searching one topic in multiple resources from a variety of angles, or consulting one or two sources repeatedly. Whatever your topic, keep in mind that your first search may not be your best and will very likely not be your last. The sources and strategies discussed in this book are intended to build on one another and equip you with the skills and tools necessary to research Victorian and Edwardian literature.

NOTES

1. *The Times*, "Mrs. F. A. Steel. The Novelist of India," April 15, 1929.

2. *Dictionary of Literary Biography*, s.v. "Flora Annie Steel (2 April 1847–12 April 1929)" (by Julie English Early).

3. *Dictionary of Literary Biography*, s.v. "Flora Annie Steel (2 April 1847–12 April 1929)" (by Rebecca J. Sutcliffe).

4. *The Times*, "Mrs. F. A. Steel. The Novelist of India," April 15, 1929.

5. Robert E. Freeman, ed. *Bibliographies of Studies in Victorian Literature 1965–1974* (New York: AMS Press, 1981), 171.

6. F. R., "An Incident of the Indian Mutiny," *Chatterbox,* no. 16:121; Charles Young, "The Mystery of the Mountain: A Strange Story of the Indian Mutiny," *The Boy's Own Paper* (May–September 1897); "The Beleaguered Garrison," *Stories of Pluck: A High Class Weekly Library of Adventure at Home & Abroad, on Land & Sea,* no. 30 (1895 and 1900): 1.

7. *Dictionary of Literary Biography*, s.v. "Flora Annie Steel (2 April 1847–12 April 1929)" (by Julie English Early). *Dictionary of National Biography*, s.v. "Steel [née Webster], Flora Annie" (by Rosemary Cargill Raza).

Appendix

Resources in
Related Disciplines

This book introduced you to major tools for locating primary and secondary sources for Victorian and Edwardian literature and described strategies for searching online catalogs and databases. With a few exceptions, the resources have been specific to literature and focused on authors, texts, genres, and literary movements. Literature, however, has never been written in a vacuum, nor should it be studied in one. Victorian and Edwardian authors were influenced by the cultural, economic, political, religious, and social practices that surrounded them, and often incorporated these ideas into their writings. Because of this, your research may lead you into the sources of art, history, psychology, and other disciplines as you develop a fuller understanding of the author, text, or topic you are studying. This appendix is not designed to provide a detailed assessment of the research sources and strategies specific to each discipline. It is intended to introduce you to major atlases, chronologies, dictionaries, encyclopedias, handbooks, guides, bibliographies, and indexes as appropriate for each discipline or area of study, including general resources, art, historical atlases and geographical resources, history, language and linguistics, literary terms and theory, music, philosophy, religion, science and medicine, social sciences, and theater. These lists are not comprehensive, nor are they intended to be. Each resource fulfills one of the following four roles:

1. Give background information or define key terms (dictionaries, encyclopedias, and handbooks);
2. Provide specialized information for a particular field (atlases and chronologies);
3. Introduce a discipline's reference literature (guides); and

4. Serve as a finding aid to secondary scholarship and primary-source materials (bibliographies and indexes).

Altogether the resources discussed here should help you understand the issues at stake in a particular discipline, its core terminology, and its major research tools. Many include highly valuable bibliographies that will direct you to seminal works and further readings. Search your local library catalog or a union catalog such as *WorldCat* to identify relevant books available either at your library or through interlibrary loan. The research strategies covered in chapters 1 and 3 should assist you in searching both library catalogs and the databases discussed below.

GENERAL RESOURCES

Guides

Kieft, Robert, ed. *Guide to Reference.* Chicago: American Library Association, 2008. www.guidetoreference.org (accessed 19 April 2010).
Formerly titled *Guide to Reference Books* and edited by Robert Balay, this resource is a bibliography of standard reference sources across the disciplines. The works are categorized into six overarching categories: "General Reference Works," "Humanities," "Social and Behavioral Sciences," "History and Area Studies," "Science, Technology, and Medicine," and "Interdisciplinary Fields." Each category is then subdivided into specific disciplines; for instance, "General Humanities," "Art and Architecture," "Design and Applied Arts," "Languages, Linguistics, Philology," "Literature," "Music," "Philosophy," "Religion," "Sports and Recreation," and "Theater and Performing Arts" comprise the "Humanities." These disciplines further break down into subdisciplines, and each reference source entry contains a citation and an annotation. Contents may be searched or browsed.

Balzek, Ron, and Elizabeth Aversa. *The Humanities: A Selective Guide to Information Resources.* 5th ed. Engelwood, CO: Libraries Unlimited, 2000.
Balzek and Aversa's guide comprises a useful introduction to the humanities and overview of general humanities reference sources. Additionally, it covers assessing information in principal sources for philosophy, religion, mythology, folklore, visual art, performing arts, and language and literature. This is an excellent starting point for any humanities-related research.

Lester, Ray, ed. *The New Walford: Guide to Reference Resources.* 3 vols. London: Facet Publishing, 2005.

The British equivalent to the *Guide to Reference* (see above), *The New Walford* succeeds *Walford's Guide to Reference Material*, which was published in eight editions between 1959 and 2000. The new edition has volumes for the sciences, technology, and medicine; the social sciences; and the arts, humanities, and general reference. An annotated bibliography of reference resources is given for each discipline and its subdisciplines. Volume 3, which covers the arts, humanities, and general reference, is forthcoming.

Indexes and Bibliographies

Academic Search Complete. Ipswich, MA: EBSCO Publishing. Available online at www.ebscohost.com.
This general, multidisciplinary database comprises full text for more than 7,100 periodicals and indexing for nearly twelve thousand publications. Although not specific to literature, it indexes selected content from more than five hundred literature and literary criticism journals.

Academic OneFile. Farmington Hills, MI: Gale Cengage. Available online at www.gale.cengage.com.
This general database provides articles from more than thirteen thousand journals—more than half of which are peer-reviewed—from the sciences, social sciences, humanities, and arts. Although not exclusively a literature database, it contains more than 350 literary studies and more than sixty general humanities journals. *Academic OneFile* also offers full text for eight reference works, including *English Literature from 1785* and *Merriam Webster's Encyclopedia of Literature.*

Arts & Humanities Citation Index. Philadelphia, PA: Thomson Reuters. Available online via various vendors.
Indexes articles, bibliographies, editorials, letters, and reviews from 5,500 major arts and humanities journals and select science and social science journal articles from 1980 to the present. This resource supports cited reference searching, which enables scholars to determine which works have been cited and where. Available from Thomson Reuters as a stand-alone product or as part of the *Web of Science*, and through EBSCO as *Arts and Humanities Search (AHSearch).*

Essay and General Literature Index. New York: H. W. Wilson, 1984. Annual. Also available online at www.hwwilson.com.
Essay and General Literature Index Retrospective: 1900–1984. New York: H. W. Wilson, 1900–1984. Annual. Available online at www.hwwilson.com.

Available in both print and online, *EGLI* indexes literature published in single-author and multi-author collections from Britain, Canada, and the United States from the humanities and social sciences. In its online format, the *EGLI* offers both current and historic content, depending on which components your library has subscribed to: *EGLI* covers 1985 to the present, and *EGLI Retrospective* covers 1900 to 1984. Currently more than three hundred sources are indexed in *EGLI*, including selected serial and annual publications. *EGLI* is particularly useful for locating essays, reviews, criticism, and creative works published in book collections that are not generally found in journal article indexes and bibliographies.

Humanities Index. New York: H. W. Wilson, 1984. Annual. Available online
    at www.hwwilson.com.
With six hundred major scholarly journals and select specialized magazines, *Humanities Index* includes humanities publications from 1984 to the present. Its volumes were published annually in print until 2004. Retrospective coverage from 1907 to 1984 is available in the *Humanities and Social Sciences Index Retrospective.*

WilsonWeb OmniFile. New York: H. W. Wilson. Available online at www
    .hwwilson.com.
A general database, *WilsonWeb OmniFile* indexes more than 3,500 journals in the arts, humanities, sciences, and social sciences and has full text for more than 1,750 titles. Indexing extends from 1982 to the present. Includes materials from the following databases: *Education Full Text, General Science Full Text, Humanities Full Text, Readers' Guide Full Text, Social Sciences Full Text, Wilson Business Full Text, Applied Science & Technology Full Text, Art Full Text, Biological & Agricultural Index Plus, Index to Legal Periodicals Full Text,* and *Library Literature & Information Science Full Text.*

ProQuest Dissertations & Theses. Ann Arbor, MI: ProQuest. Available online
    at www.proquest.com.
Indexes doctoral dissertations and master's theses from 1637 to the present. Includes citations to 2.4 million dissertations from all disciplines, with full text for 1.2 million. Full text is primarily available for post-1997 dissertations with some retrospective coverage of older works.

British Humanities Index. Bethesda, MD: CSA, 1962. Quarterly. Also available online at www.csa.com.
Indexes and abstracts for more than 370 humanities journals, magazines, and newspapers published primarily in the United Kingdom. *BHI* includes subject

areas such as art, cinema, gender studies, history, language, literature, philosophy, poetry, and theatre from 1962 to the present. Available as a quarterly print publication and as an online database.

ART

Dictionaries, Encyclopedias, and Handbooks

Oxford Art Online. New York: Oxford University Press, 2007–2010. Available online at www.oxfordartonline.com.

This online database provides the interface to search across four major art reference sources: *Grove Art Online* (the online version of Grove's *Dictionary of Art*, see below); *The Oxford Companion to Western Art*; *The Concise Oxford Dictionary of Art Terms*; and *The Encyclopedia of Aesthetics*. In total, *Oxford Art Online* contains the full text to roughly fifty thousand entries on all aspects of art and artists. Scholars may search across all or select sources, or may search them individually. If your library does not subscribe to this resource, it may own print versions of the aforementioned reference works.

Chilvers, Ian, ed. *The Oxford Dictionary of Art and Artists.* 4th ed. New York: Oxford University Press, 2009.

Now in its fourth edition, this work comprises entries on Western art and artists from ancient Greece to the present. Entries cover galleries, materials, movements, museums, styles, and techniques as well as artists, collectors, critics, dealers, and patrons, and tend to be brief, ranging from one paragraph to one page in length. The previous edition was titled *The Concise Oxford Dictionary of Art and Artists.*

Chilvers, Ian, ed. *The Oxford Dictionary of Art.* 3rd ed. New York: Oxford University Press, 2004.

Comprises three thousand entries on Western and Western-inspired art and artists, and covers the art of ancient Greece and Rome, Europe from the thirteenth century to the present, and the Americas, Australasia, and other non-European countries from the eighteenth century to the present. Also includes biographies for writers, administrators, patrons, collectors, and dealers, and non-biographical entries on museums and galleries; academies, schools, and other institutions; exhibitions and prizes; styles, groups, and movements; materials, tools, and techniques; and miscellaneous terms. Entries are brief, ranging from one paragraph to one page.

Turner, Jane, ed. *The Dictionary of Art.* 34 vols. New York: Grove, 1996.

A long-time standard of art reference, *The Dictionary of Art* is available in thirty-four print volumes and online as part of *Oxford Art Online* (see above). In total, it comprises forty-five thousand entries, covering biographies, people groups, civilizations, geographic locations, styles, schools, groups, movements, building types, materials and techniques of art, art patronage, and theoretical and general issues. Entries cross-reference to one another and have bibliographies. Appendixes—"List of Locations," "List of Periodical Titles," "Lists of Standard Reference Books and Series," and "List of Contributors"—are included in volume 33, and volume 34 serves as the set's index and contains an appendix to "Non-Western Dynasties and Peoples."

Guides

Arntzen, Etta, and Robert Rainwater. *Guide to the Literature of Art History*. Chicago: American Library Association, 1980.
This detailed, annotated bibliography covers general reference resources such as bibliographies, directories, sales records, visual resources, dictionaries and encyclopedias, and iconography; general primary and secondary sources for historiography and methodology, sources, and documents, and histories and handbooks; the particular arts including architecture, sculpture, drawings, painting, prints, photography, and decorative and applied arts; and serials such as periodicals and series. The work concludes with an author-title index and a subject index. Although somewhat dated, it is a useful introduction to art history reference literature.

Ehresmann, Donald L. *Fine Arts: A Bibliographic Guide to Basic Reference Works, Histories, and Handbooks*. 3rd ed. Englewood, CO: Libraries Unlimited, 1990.
Provides an excellent overview of reference works such as bibliographies, library catalogs, indexes, directories, dictionaries and encyclopedias, iconography, and historiography of art history, and addresses histories and handbooks for prehistoric and primitive art, Western art history periods, national histories and handbooks of European art, Oriental art, new world art, and art of Africa and Oceania (with Australia). The works discussed here relate to architecture, sculpture, and painting.

Marmor, Max, and Alex Ross. *Guide to the Literature of Art History 2*. Chicago: American Library Association, 2005.
Supplementing Arntzen and Rainwater's *Guide to the Literature of Art History* (see above), Marmor and Ross's resource updates the art history reference

literature. Entries are organized into the following categories: "Bibliography"; "Directories"; "Sales Records"; "Visual Resources"; "Dictionaries and Encyclopedias"; "Iconography"; "Historiography, Methodology, and Theory"; "Sources and Documents"; "Histories and Handbooks"; "Architecture"; "Sculpture"; "Drawings"; "Painting"; "Prints"; "Photography"; "Decorative and Applied Arts"; "Periodicals"; "Series"; "Patronage and Collecting"; and "Cultural Heritage." Concludes with an index of people, titles, and subjects.

Indexes and Bibliographies

Art and Design Databases. Bethesda, MD: CSA. Available online at www
    .csa.com.
This resource enables simultaneous searching across *ARTbibliographies Modern*, *Avery Index to Architectural Periodicals*, and *Design and Applied Arts Index*. For more detail on each index or bibliography, see entries below.

Art Abstracts. New York: H. W. Wilson. Available online via various vendors.
Art Index Retrospective: 1929–1984. New York: H. W. Wilson. Available
    online at www.hwwilson.com.
Provides indexing and abstracting for more than 450 art periodicals, yearbooks, and museum bulletins. International in scope and coverage, *Art Abstracts* cites publications from 1984 to the present. Includes the following subjects: advertising, archaeology, architecture, art history, crafts, film, folk art, graphic arts, interior design, and video. Indexing from 1929 to 1984 is available in *Art Index Retrospective*.

ARTbibliographies Modern. Bethesda, MD: CSA. Available online at www
    .csa.com.
Comprises abstracts for books, dissertations, essays, exhibition catalogs, exhibition reviews, and journal articles on both modern and contemporary art since the invention of photography in the late nineteenth century. *ARTbibliographies Modern* includes publications from 1974 to the present with select citations from the late 1960s. Contains entries relevant to areas such as art history, conservation and restoration, folk arts, illustration, philosophy and art, photography, symbolism, and woodwork.

Avery Index to Architectural Periodicals. Bethesda, MD: CSA. Available
    online at www.csa.com.
Emphasizing architecture and design, this resource indexes more than seven hundred periodicals from 1934 to the present with select citations from as far back as 1741. Covers archaeology, architectural design, furniture and

decoration, green design, historic preservation, history of architecture, interior design, landscape architecture, sustainable development, and urban planning.

Bibliography of the History of Art/International Bibliography of Art, at library.getty.edu/bha (accessed 19 April 2010).
Formerly as a subscription resource, the *Bibliography of the History of Art/ International Bibliography of Art* is now an open-access resource through the Getty Research Institute. Including citations to articles from more than twelve hundred journals, this is considered "the world's most comprehensive bibliography of scholarly writing about the history of western art." It comprises the *BHA* from 1990 to 2007 and the *IBA* from 2008 and 2009.

Design and Applied Arts Index. Bethesda, MD: CSA. Available online at www.csa.com.
This index provides citations for articles, news, and reviews published from 1973 to the present. Covers design and applied arts broadly from the mid-nineteenth century onward for subjects such as interior design, ceramics, textiles, furniture, typography and type design, advertising, landscape architecture, and design history.

HISTORICAL ATLASES AND GEOGRAPHICAL RESOURCES

Atlases

Barraclough, Geoffrey, ed. *The Times History of the World*. New ed. London: Times Books, 1999.
O'Brien, Patrick K., ed. *Oxford Atlas of World History*. New York: Oxford University Press, 1999, 2002.
These two standard historical atlases comprise maps of and contextual information on world history from the earliest times to the present day. Both are excellent, reliable sources for maps representing agricultural, economic, environmental, military, political, social, territorial, and trade developments throughout history.

Falkus, Malcolm, and John Gillingham, eds. *Historical Atlas of Britain*. New York: Continuum, 1981.
Specific to the British Isles, this atlas covers the political, social, and economic history of Britain from 4000 BC through AD 1981. Maps are accompanied by scholarly text discussing topics and issues represented in the maps. Contents are organized both chronologically and thematically.

Gilbert, Martin. *The Routledge Atlas of British History.* 4th ed. New York: Routledge, 2007.
Provides maps of the British Isles, including England, Ireland, Scotland, Wales, and British colonies, from 50 BC to AD 2006. The 173 chronologically organized maps depict economic, social, political, territorial, and military issues, such as wars and treaties, alliances, industry and trade growth, and famine and plague.

Porter, A. N., ed. *Atlas of British Overseas Expansion.* London: Routledge, 1991.
Comprises maps and narrative discussions of Great Britain's formal empire and its informal presence around the globe. Almost 140 maps depict Britain's territories and involvement in the world from the late fifteenth century through the 1980s. Concludes with topic-specific bibliographies and an index.

Royal Geographical Society. *Atlas of Exploration.* New York: Oxford University Press, 1997.
Covers global exploration from the earliest time until the present. Contents are organized in the following categories: "Early Exploration"; "Asia"; "Africa"; "Central and South America"; "North America"; "The Pacific, Australia, and New Zealand"; "The Arctic"; "The Antarctic"; "Oceanography"; "Exploration Today"; and "Biographical Details." The atlas also contains a time chart of exploration and an index.

Dictionaries, Encyclopedias, and Handbooks

Cohen, Saul B., ed. *The Columbia Gazetteer of the World.* 2nd ed. 3 vols. New York: Columbia University Press, 2008.
Provides brief descriptions for approximately 170,000 places in the political world, the physical world, and special locations such as national parks, ports, mines, canals, shopping malls, fortified lines, and mythic places. Entries may contain the following information: agriculture; changed or variant names and spellings; cultural, historical, and archeological points of interest; demography; distance to relevant places; industry, trade, and service activities; longitude, latitude, and elevations; official local government place-names; physical geography; political boundaries; pronunciations; and transportation lines.

Howgego, Raymond John. *Encyclopedia of Exploration.* 4 vols. Potts Point, NSW, Australia: Hordern House, 2003–2008.
This four-volume set is a guide to the history and literature of colonization, exploration, and travel through 1940. The four volumes address, respectively: to 1800; from 1800 to 1850; oceans, islands, and the polar regions from 1850

to 1940; and continental exploration from 1850 to 1940. Entries conclude with a brief bibliography, and each volume has its own indexes.

Mills, A. D. *A Dictionary of British Place-Names*. New York: Oxford University Press, 2004.
Comprising more than 14,400 entries, this dictionary gives the meaning and origins of British place-names from the earliest times to the present day.

Parker, Sybil P., ed. *World Geographical Encyclopedia*. 5 vols. New York: McGraw-Hill, 1995.
Each of the five volumes covers a different geographical region, with volume 4 focusing on Europe. Entries are specific to countries and comprise a geopolitical summary and discussion of the natural environment, population, economics, and historical and cultural profile. A lexicon, great routes and voyages of discovery, an index, and world statistics are also in volume 5.

Room, Adrian. *Nicknames of Places*. Jefferson, NC: McFarland, 2006.
Includes 4,600 nicknames, alternative names, and secondary names for places used around the globe. Contains an index and seven appendixes for regional nicknames, road and street nicknames, Romany names of places, renamed countries, Roman names of European towns and cities, English county names, and astronomical names.

Room, Adrian. *Placenames of the World*. 2nd ed. Jefferson, NC: McFarland, 2006.
Surveys the origins and meanings of 6,600 country, city, territory, natural feature, and historic site names. The preface has a useful discussion of place-name study basic principles, classification, naming patterns, and frequency. Also includes a bibliography and three appendixes for common place-name words and elements, major place-names in European languages, and Chinese names of countries and capitals.

Speake, Jennifer, ed. *Literature of Travel and Exploration: An Encyclopedia*. 3 vols. New York: Fitzroy Dearborn, 2003.
Covers individuals, geographical entities, and thematic topics related to travel and exploration in more than six hundred entries. Topical entries are grouped into categories such as "Genres and Publication," "Journey Types and Routes," "Maritime and Circumnavigation," "Miscellaneous and Literary," "Organizations and Societies," "Publishers and Publishing," "Science and Travel," and "Themes and Issues." Entries have references and further reading and cross-reference to related entries. The final volume has an index to the set.

Waldman, Carl, and Alan Wexler. *Encyclopedia of Exploration.* Vol. 1. New
    York: Facts on File, 2004.
Waldman, Carl, and Jon Cunningham. *Encyclopedia of Exploration.* Vol. 2.
    New York: Facts on File, 2004.
This two-volume encyclopedia covers explorers in its first volume, and
places, technologies, and cultural trends in the second. Volume 1 also in-
cludes an index of that volume and four appendixes for "Explorers by Most
Relevant Occupation," "Explorers by Region of Activity," "Explorers by
Sponsoring Country or by Nationality/Native Land," and "Explorers in
Chronological Order by Birth Date." Volume 2 has a cumulative index for the
set, a chronology of exploration, further readings, and an appendix of maps
to routes and world regions.

HISTORY

Chronologies

Mellersh, H. E. L, and Neville Williams, eds. *Chronology of World History.*
    4 vols. Santa Barbara, CA: ABC-CLIO, 1999.
This chronology comprises more than seventy thousand entries tracing world
history from 3000 BC to AD 1998. Entries are categorized into four broad
categories—"Politics, Government, and Economics"; "Science, Technology,
and Medicine"; "Arts and Ideas"; and "Society"—and are divided into four
volumes. Volume 3 (1776 to 1900) and volume 4 (1901 to 1998) are germane
to Victorian and Edwardian scholars. Each volume has its own index to
names, titles, places, events, and subjects, and a title index for works of art,
literature, music, dance, theatre, and scholarship.

Dictionaries, Encyclopedias, and Handbooks

Arnold-Baker, Charles. *The Companion to British History.* 2nd ed. New
    York: Routledge, 2001.
Provides an overview of all aspects and time periods in British history in
12,500 entries. Entries are generally brief and may cross-reference to one
another. Concludes with appendixes to "English Regnal Years," "Selected
Warlike Events," and "Genealogies and Diagrams."

Cannon, John, ed. *The Oxford Companion to British History.* Rev. ed. New
    York: Oxford University Press, 2002.
Covering two thousand years of British history, this companion contains more
than four thousand entries on cultural, economic, feminist, military, political,

scientific, and social history. Although most entries are brief, some provide essay-length overviews. Also contains maps, genealogies, and a subject index.

Connolly, S. J., ed. *The Oxford Companion to Irish History.* Rev. ed. New York: Oxford University Press, 2007.
Addresses all aspects of Irish history from prehistory to the present. While entries are primarily brief, some offer in-depth treatment of subjects. Concludes with maps of both modern and historical Ireland and a subject index.

Lynch, Michael, ed. *The Oxford Companion to Scottish History.* New York: Oxford University Press, 2001.
Another of the Oxford companions, this work treats two thousand years of Scottish history in a combination of brief and in-depth entries. In addition to the entries, it contains a classified contents list, an abbreviations list, a glossary, a chronology, maps, genealogies, a guide to further reading, and an index.

Olson, James S., and Robert Shadle, eds. *Historical Dictionary of the British Empire.* 2 vols. Westport, CT: Greenwood Press, 1996.
Outlines the rise and fall of the British Empire from the late fifteenth century to the late twentieth century in two volumes. Entries are arranged alphabetically and have brief lists of references for further study. Includes an index and three appendixes on medals and orders of knighthood, a glossary, and a selected bibliography of recent scholarly works, 1980–1995.

Panton, Kenneth J. *Historical Dictionary of London.* Lanham, MD: Scarecrow Press, 2001.
Covers the economic trends, institutions, people, political forces, and social values that have characterized London from the times of the Roman Empire to the year 2000. Includes maps, chronologies, appendixes to London local government authorities and World Wide Web addresses, and a bibliography on topics such as: "Arts and Entertainment"; "Autobiography and Biography"; "Commerce and Industry"; "Government and Politics"; "The Law"; "Local Studies: Areas North of the River Thames"; "Local Studies: Areas South of the River Thames"; "Museums, Exhibitions, and Galleries"; "The Natural Environment"; "Religion, Burial Grounds, and Places of Worship"; and "Reference Works."

Guides

Fritze, Ronald H., Brian E. Coutts, and Louis A. Vyhnanek. *Reference Sources in History: An Introductory Guide.* 2nd ed. Santa Barbara, CA: ABC-CLIO, 2004.

Introduces scholars and students to history reference literature. In total, 930 reference sources are discussed, covering history and its subdisciplines from all time periods. The entries are organized into the following chapters: "Guides, Handbooks, and Manuals for History," "Bibliographies," "Book Review Indexes," "Periodical Guides and Core Journals," "Periodical Indexes, Abstracts, and Guides," "Guides to Newspapers, Newspaper Collections, and Newspaper Indexes," "Dissertations and Theses," "Government Publications and Legal Sources," "Dictionaries and Encyclopedias," "Biographical Sources," "Geographical Sources and Atlases," "Historical Statistical Sources," "Archives, Manuscripts, Special Collections, and Digital Sites," and "Microforms and Selected Microform Collections." Concludes with an index.

Loades, David, ed. *Reader's Guide to British History*. 2 vols. New York: Fitzroy Dearborn, 2003.
This essential resource is a guide to British history from all time periods. Entries are arranged alphabetically and introduce the themes, changes, and controversies related to particular topics. Each entry begins with a select bibliography and concludes with cross-references as appropriate. Volume 1 contains alphabetical and thematic lists of entries, and volume 2 has a booklist index and a general index.

Indexes and Bibliographies

Brown, Lucy M., and Ian R. Christie, eds. *Bibliography of British History, 1789–1851*. Oxford: Clarendon Press, 1977.
Lists resources on British history from 1789 to 1851. Works are organized into the following broad categories: "General Reference Works," "Political History," "Constitutional History," "Legal History," "Ecclesiastical History," "Military History," "Naval History," "Economic History," "Social History," "Cultural History," "Local History," "Wales," "Scotland," "Ireland," and the "British Empire." Each section is then divided into subcategories. The volume concludes with an index of persons, subjects, and titles.

Hanham, H. J., comp. and ed. *Bibliography of British History, 1851–1914*. Oxford: Clarendon Press, 1976.
Comprises a detailed bibliography of resources on British history from 1851 to 1914. The works are organized into the following broad categories: "General," "Political and Constitutional History," "External Relations," "Armed Forces," "Legal System," "Churches," "Economic History," "Social History," "Intellectual and Cultural History," "Local History," "Wales," "Scotland,"

and "Ireland." Each of these is subdivided into narrower topics of inquiry. The volume concludes with an index of persons, subjects, and titles.

Historical Abstracts. Ipswich, MA: EBSCO, 1955. Available online at www .ebscohost.com.
Historical Abstracts is the major bibliography of world history from 1450 to the present, excluding the United States and Canada. Begun in 1955, it currently comprises more than six hundred thousand entries for journal articles, books, and dissertations. In addition to history, disciplines such as anthropology, literature, multicultural studies, and political science are included. *Historical Abstracts* was previously issued quarterly as a print bibliography in two parts—Part A covering "Modern History Abstracts, 1775–1914" and Part B covering "Twentieth Century Abstracts, 1914–2000"—as well as an online resource. Currently it is only available as an online database through EBSCO. *Historical Abstracts* is discussed in more detail in chapter 5.

Bibliography of British and Irish History. Turnhout, Belgium: Brepols, 2010. Available online at www.brepols.net.
Formerly a free online resource known as the *Royal Historical Society Bibliography*, as of January 1, 2010, the *Bibliography of British and Irish History* (*BBIH*) is only available online by subscription through a collaboration between the Institute of Historical Research, the Royal Historical Society, and Brepols Publishers. *BBIH* is an essential source for identifying historical writing about the British Isles, the British Empire, and the Commonwealth from 55 BC to the present. Comprising more than 476,000 records for books, journal articles, review articles, and unpublished theses on London history, this resource attempts to be as comprehensive as possible for publications since 1900. It should be highly useful to scholars because of features such as in-depth subject indexing and direct linking to *Oxford Dictionary of National Biography*, *Who Was Who*, and the National Register of Archives.

LANGUAGE AND LINGUISTICS

Dictionaries, Encyclopedias, and Handbooks

Brown, Keith, ed. *Encyclopedia of Language and Linguistics.* 2nd ed. 14 vols. Boston: Elsevier, 2006. Available online at www.sciencedirect.com.
A standard source for language and linguistic research, this encyclopedia is available as a fourteen-volume print set and an online encyclopedia. It covers thirty-six linguistic areas such as foundations of linguistics, semiotics, morphology, semantics, text analysis and stylistics, religion and language, trans-

lation, languages of the world, language maps, lexicography, and linguistic anthropology. Most entries have cross-references and a bibliography. The final volume comprises a glossary, a list of languages, and appendixes for language maps; lists of abbreviations and logical symbols used; examples, transcriptional conventions, and the IPIA alphabet; a subject classification of entries; contributors; and a subject index.

Crystal, David. *A Dictionary of Linguistics and Phonetics.* 5th ed. Oxford: Blackwell, 2003.
Defines more than five thousand terms arranged in more than three thousand entries specific to linguistics and phonetics. Entries include cross-references as appropriate.

Fawley, William J., ed. *International Encyclopedia of Linguistics.* 2nd ed. 4 vols. New York: Oxford University Press, 2003.
Provides detailed entries on comparative, descriptive, formalist, functionalist, historical, and typological linguistics. Entries end with a bibliography of further readings on the topic. Includes extensive cross-referencing, a thorough index, and composite entries to help scholars understand disciplinary connections among entries.

Kay, Christian, Jane Roberts, Michael Samuels, and Irené Wotherspoon. *Historical Thesaurus of the Oxford English Dictionary.* 2 vols. New York: Oxford University Press, 2009.
The *Historical Thesaurus of the Oxford English Dictionary* (*HTOED*) analyzes the words comprised in both the *Oxford English Dictionary* (see below) and *A Thesaurus of Old English* (Jane Roberts, Christian Kay, and Lynne Grundy. 2nd ed. 2 vols. Atlanta, GA: Rodopi, 2000). Contents are organized into three major sections: "The External World," "The Mental World," and "The Social World." Volume 1 contains the classified entries, while volume 2 has an alphabetical word list that cross-references to entries in the first volume. In total, more 797,120 meanings are included in this monumental work.

McArthur, Tom, ed. *The Oxford Companion to the English Language.* New York: Oxford University Press, 1992.
Defines the terminology of literary, common, and colloquial English. Entries may be essay-like, dictionary-style, or biographical. In addition to the entries proper, it has an index of persons and a map of English throughout the world.

Momma, Haruko, and Michael Matto, eds. *A Companion to the History of the English Language.* Malden, MA: Blackwell Publishing, 2008.

This single-volume companion to English comprises fifty-nine essays in nine broad categories: "Introduction," "Linguistic Survey," "English Semantics and Lexicography," "Pre-history of English," "English in History: England and America," "English in History: English Outside England and the United States," "Literary Languages," "Issues with Present-Day English," and "Further Approaches to Language Study." Concludes with a glossary of linguistic terms and an index.

Partridge, Eric. *A Dictionary of Slang and Unconventional English.* Ed. Paul Beale. 8th ed. New York: Macmillan, 1984.
A standard source, this dictionary comprises slang and cant, colloquialisms, solecisms and catachreses, catchphrases, nicknames, and vulgarisms primarily from British English. Entries contain the keyword, part of speech, definition or explanation, register, and dating. Cross-references to the main text and the appendix are included throughout. This edition covers English words used from the 1600s through the 1970s. Partridge's dictionary has since been complemented by *The New Partridge Dictionary of Slang and Unconventional English* (Tom Dalzell and Terry Victor, eds. 2 vols. New York: Routledge, 2006), which addresses slang from 1945 to the early twenty-first century.

Romaine, Suzanne, ed. *The Cambridge History of the English Language.* Vol. 4. New York: Cambridge University Press, 1998.
Volume 4 of the six-volume *Cambridge History of the English Language* covers the history and development of English from 1776 to 1997. Chapters comprise an introduction to the English language, "Vocabulary," "Syntax," "Onomastics," "Phonology," "English Grammar and Usage," and "Literary Language." Concludes with a glossary of linguistic terms, bibliography, and index.

Simpson, J. A., and E. S. C. Weiner. *The Oxford English Dictionary.* 2nd ed. 20 vols. New York: Oxford University Press, 1989. Also available online at www.oed.com.
Currently available in its second edition, the twenty-volume *Oxford English Dictionary* (*OED*) is essential for understanding how word meanings and usages have shifted over time. The print version comprises 291,500 entries, while the online edition has more than 600,000 entries. Entries include pronunciation, spellings, etymology, and quotations illustrating the word's usage throughout history. *OED* editors are working on the third edition, but Oxford does not anticipate it being published prior to 2018.

Wright, Joseph, ed. *The English Dialect Dictionary: Being the Complete Vocabulary of All Dialect Words Still in Use, or Known to Have Been in Use during the Last Two Hundred Years*. 6 vols. London: Henry Frowde, 1898–1905. Reprint, New York: Hacker Art Books, 1962.

Explicates English dialectical words used or known during the eighteenth and nineteenth centuries in England, Ireland, Scotland, and Wales. Entries provide the geographical location for the word's usage, phonetic pronunciation, and etymology. The sixth volume also has a supplement to the previous volumes, a bibliography, and the English dialect grammar.

Guides

DeMiller, Anna A. *Linguistics: A Guide to the Reference Literature*. 2nd ed. Reference Sources in the Humanities Series. Englewood: Libraries Unlimited, 2000.

Comprises an annotated bibliography of sources for linguistics, allied research areas, and languages. Because linguistics is not exclusive to the English language, the resources discussed here address all languages and linguistic groups.

Indexes and Bibliographies

Linguistics and Language Behavior Abstracts. Bethesda, MD: CSA, 1973. Also available online at www.csa.com.

This crucial resource for locating scholarly literature on linguistics and languages is published from 1972 to the present in its online form and 1968 to present in print. International in scope, *LLBA* indexes and abstracts more than 438,000 books, book chapters, book reviews, conference papers, dissertations, and journal articles in thirty-two languages. It covers a wide variety of subfields within linguistics, including discourse analysis/text linguistics, history of linguistics, language classification, lexicography/lexicology, morphology, philosophy of language, poetics/literary theory, and semiotics.

LITERARY TERMS AND THEORY

Dictionaries, Encyclopedias, and Handbooks

Cashmore, Ellis, and Chris Rojek, eds. *Dictionary of Cultural Theorists*. New York: Arnold Publishers, 1999.

Covers biographies of contemporary social and cultural theorists. Entries comprise key works, concepts and terms, pivotal influences, theorists with shared intellectual concerns, a biographical sketch, summary of major contributions, and a brief bibliography.

Makaryk, Irena R., ed. *Encyclopedia of Contemporary Literary Theory: Approaches, Scholars, Terms.* Toronto: University of Toronto Press, 1993.
The entries are organized into approaches, scholars, and terms of contemporary literary theory, and are accompanied by bibliographies of primary and secondary sources. Within each section entries are listed alphabetically.

Harmon, William. *A Handbook to Literature.* 11th ed. Upper Saddle River, NJ: Prentice Hall, 2009.
This specialized dictionary defines literary terms, movements, and genres. Includes an outline of both British and American literary history and appendixes for monetary terms and values; Nobel Prizes for Literature; Pulitzer Prizes for fiction, poetry, and drama; and a proper names index.

Groden, Michael, Martin Kreiswirth, and Imre Szeman, eds. *The Johns Hopkins Guide to Literary Theory and Criticism.* 2nd ed. Baltimore: Johns Hopkins University Press, 2005. Available online at litguide.press.jhu.edu.
Covers literary theory and criticism from classical antiquity through the present day. The 241 entries address "individual critics and theorists, critical and theoretical schools and movements, and critical and theoretical innovations of specific countries and historical periods." Entries provide thorough discussions of their topics, cross-references, and bibliographies of further readings. Indexes to names and topics conclude the volume.

MUSIC

Dictionaries, Encyclopedias, and Handbooks

Kennedy, Michael. *The Oxford Dictionary of Music.* 2nd ed. New York: Oxford University Press, 2006.
This work has brief entries for musical terms, musicians, movements, styles, and works. Entries for people contain a biography and a bibliography of major compositions. Cross-references are included as appropriate. The dictionary uses American nomenclature rather than British.

Latham, Alison, ed. *The Oxford Companion to Music.* New York: Oxford University Press, 2002.
Provides both definitional and essay-length entries on music and musicians. While non-Western and popular music are also included, the primary focus is Western music. Entries cover musical terms, movements, forms, musicians, periods, and other related topics. Concludes with a select index of persons mentioned but not given their own entry.

Nettl, Bruno, and Ruth M. Stone, eds. *The Garland Encyclopedia of World Music*. 10 vols. New York: Garland, 1998–2002.
Serves as an introduction to the music and culture of particular regions, outlines major issues and processes, and offers a detailed account of individual music cultures. The set is organized by geographic regions, with each of the following receiving its own volume: Africa; South America, Mexico, Central America, and the Caribbean; the United States and Canada; Southeast Asia; South Asia: the Indian Subcontinent; the Middle East; East Asia: China, Japan, and Korea; Europe; and Australia and the Pacific Islands. The final volume addresses ethnomusicologists at work, lists resources and research tools, and provides a general glossary and an index.

Oxford Music Online. New York: Oxford University Press, 2007–2009. Available online at www.oxfordmusiconline.com.
This resource is an online portal to current and forthcoming music reference titles. While the platform was designed to support additional resources, currently the following titles are available: *Grove Music Online* (the online version of *The New Grove Dictionary of Music and Musicians*, see below), the *Encyclopedia of Popular Music*, *The Oxford Companion to Music* (see above), and *The Oxford Dictionary of Music* (see above). In addition to biographies and subject entries, *OMO* has an abbreviations guide, essential twentieth-century reading list, an opera roles index, music timelines, topical guides, research resources, and a guide to musical examples in *Grove Music Online*.

Randel, Don Michael, ed. *The Harvard Dictionary of Music*. 4th ed. Cambridge, MA: Belknap Press of Harvard University Press, 2003.
Includes entries for musical terms, musicians, and musical instruments from Western and non-Western cultures. It also covers popular music. Entries vary widely in length with longer ones containing brief bibliographies.

Sadie, Stanley, ed. *The New Grove Dictionary of Music and Musicians*. 2nd ed. 29 vols. New York: Grove, 2001.
A standard reference source for music research, this dictionary covers music and musicians from the earliest times through the twentieth century. Entries are on composers, performers, scholars, major individuals in other arts, patrons, people working in the business of music, musical terminology, genres and forms, instruments, institutions, geographic areas, and topics such as postmodernism and recital. Longer entries have section divisions, and many entries have cross-references and bibliographies of print and audio/visual resources. Volume 28 comprises appendixes to private collections, congress reports, music dictionaries and encyclopedias, historical editions, libraries, periodicals, sound archives,

illustration acknowledgements, music example acknowledgements, and contributors. Volume 29 is an index to composers, performers, and writers.

Taruskin, Richard, ed. *The Oxford History of Western Music.* 6 vols. New York: Oxford University Press, 2005.
Provides a narrative overview of Western music history from the earliest times through the late twentieth century. Each of the first five volumes covers a particular era. Victorian scholars should consult volume 3 (the nineteenth century) while Edwardian scholars will find that volume 4 (the early twentieth century) better suits their needs. Volume 6 comprises a chronology, bibliography, and master index to the set.

Guides

Brockman, William S. *Music: A Guide to the Reference Literature.* Littleton, CO: Libraries Unlimited, 1987.
This annotated bibliography, while somewhat dated, overviews music resources. The contents are categorized as "General Reference Sources," "General Bibliographical Sources," "Bibliographies of Music Literature," "Bibliographies of Music," "Discographies," and "Supplemental Sources" such as current periodicals and composer societies.

Crabtree, Phillip, and Donald H. Forster. *Sourcebook for Research in Music.* 2nd ed. Bloomington: Indiana University Press, 2005.
Now in its second edition, this resource introduces the reference sources available to musicians and music scholars and is an excellent starting point for any music research. The work's contents are organized into the following chapters: "Introductory Materials," "Basic Bibliographical Tools for Research in Music," "Area Bibliographies and Other Reference Sources," "Dictionaries and Encyclopedias of Music," "Sources Treating the History of Music," "Current Research Journals in Music," "Editions of Music," and "Miscellaneous Sources." Concludes with an index to authors, editors, compilers, and translators, and a title index.

Foreman, Lewis, ed. *Information Sources in Music.* Munich: K. G. Saur, 2003.
Identifies the best, most efficient sources and strategies for music research. The book addresses topics such as institutions, societies, and broadcasting stations; dealers and auctions; women in music; early music revival; standard reference sources and collected editions; music periodicals; music in newspapers and non-music periodicals; and theses. Describes traditional resource types and discusses them in context of their use and current issues in music research.

Steib, Murray. *Reader's Guide to Music: History, Theory, Criticism*. Chicago: Fitzroy Dearborn, 1999.
Comprises roughly five hundred essays on English-language critical literature on music-related topics. Each essay focuses either on a composer or a topic and has a bibliography. The work concludes with a booklist index and a general index to individuals, topics, and works mentioned in the entries. This is an excellent starting place for any scholar beginning music research.

Indexes and Bibliographies

RILM Abstracts of Music Literature. New York: RILM International Center, 1967. Available online via various vendors.
With more than 550,000 citations, *RILM Abstracts of Music Literature* (*RILM*) provides comprehensive access to books, conference proceedings, dissertations, Internet resources, journal articles, and research-based sound recordings and films related to classical, popular, and traditional music. Covers music and subdisciplines such as historical musicology, sound sources, and music in liturgy and tradition. From 1967 to 2008, a print version was published; however, now *RILM* is available online only.

International Index to Music Periodicals. Ann Arbor, MI: ProQuest. Available online at iimp.chadwyck.com.
The *International Index to Music Periodicals* (*IIMP*) comprises citations to nearly 800,000 articles from 445 international music periodicals. While most entries date from 1996 onward, roughly 25 percent of the articles date from 1874 to 1995. Covers popular and scholarly music and a variety of areas such as performance, musical theatre, theory, and composition. It also includes a glossary, opera synopses, music fundamental terms, and pronunciation guides.

PHILOSOPHY

Dictionaries, Encyclopedias, and Handbooks

Borchert, Donald M., ed. *Encyclopedia of Philosophy*. 2nd ed. 10 vols. Detroit: Macmillan Reference USA, 2006.
Now in its second edition, this highly respected encyclopedia addresses philosophers and philosophical schools of thought in more than two thousand entries. Comprises ancient, medieval, and modern philosophy and philosophers, and philosophical subfields such as "epistemology," "philosophy of mind, cognitive science," "metaphysics," "philosophy of language," "continental philosophy," "feminist philosophy," "ethics," "social and political philosophy,"

"philosophy of religion," "Indian philosophy," and "philosophical perspectives and movements." Entries include valuable cross-references and bibliographies. The final volume is composed of an appendix of additional articles, a thematic outline, bibliographies, and an index.

Bunnin, Nicholas, and Jiyuan Yu. *The Blackwell Dictionary of Western Philosophy*. Malden, MA: Blackwell, 2004.
Provides concise definitions for terms and individuals from ancient Greece to the present in Western philosophy. Entries cross-reference to one another and frequently end with a brief illustrative quotation. Additionally, it has references to further readings.

Craig, Edward, ed. *Routledge Encyclopedia of Philosophy*. 10 vols. New York: Routledge, 1998.
Covers all branches of philosophy from the Anglo-American perspective in more than two thousand entries. Entries may be "signpost" entries that provide subject overviews, thematic entries, or biographical information. Arranged alphabetically, entries offer a topic overview, a table of contents, cross-references within and to other entries, and a bibliography of references and further reading. Volume 10 comprises an index to the entire set.

Stanford Encyclopedia of Philosophy, at plato.stanford.edu (accessed on 19 April 2010).
The *Stanford Encyclopedia of Philosophy* (*SEP*) is an open-access, peer-reviewed encyclopedia created and maintained by experts in the field. The site's browseable table of contents lists existing, assigned, and projected entries. Additionally, scholars may search across all contents. Entries cover topics and people related to philosophical inquiry, have detailed bibliographies, link to other Internet resources, and cross-reference to related entries.

Critchley, Simon, and William R. Schroeder, eds. *A Companion to Continental Philosophy*. Malden, MA: Blackwell Publishers, 1998.
Comprises more than fifty essays on Continental philosophy from Kant through the twentieth century. Has a solid introduction to Continental philosophy, and the essays themselves are organized into the following categories: "The Kantian Legacy," "Overturning the Tradition," "The Phenomenological Breakthrough," "Phenomenology, Hegelianism and Anti-Hegelianism in France," "Religion without the Limits of Reason," "Three Generations of Critical Theory," "Hermeneutics," "Continental Political Philosophy," and "Structuralism and After." Concludes with an analytical index.

Dematteis, Philip B., Peter S. Fosl, and Leemon B. McHenry, eds. *British Philosophers, 1800–2000*, vol. 262, *Dictionary of Literary Biography*. Detroit: Gale Group, 2002.

This *Dictionary of Literary Biography* volume (see chapter 2) comprises biographies of thirty-two British philosophers who lived between 1800 and 2000. Includes philosophers such as John Austin, John Stuart Mill, Henry Sidgwick, and Herbert Spencer.

Honderich, Ted, ed. *The Oxford Companion to Philosophy*. 2nd ed. New York: Oxford University Press, 2005.

Comprises more than two thousand brief and in-depth entries on philosophers, arguments, doctrines, ideas, movements, schools, theories, traditions, and worldviews. Entries cross-reference to one another and have brief bibliographies. Concludes with maps of philosophy, a chronological table, and an index and list of entries.

Horowitz, Maryanne Cline, ed. *New Dictionary of the History of Ideas*. 6 vols. New York: Charles Scribner's Sons, 2005.

From abolitionism to Zionism, this encyclopedia covers the history of ideas from around the globe, spanning antiquity through the twenty-first century. Encompasses diverse disciplines such as anthropology; area and ethnic studies; communication and cultural studies; history; literature; performance, music, and the visual arts; philosophy and religion; politics, law, and economics; science, engineering, and medicine; and women's studies. Includes a detailed essay on "Historiography," a reader's guide, and an index.

Popkin, Richard H., ed. *The Columbia History of Western Philosophy*. New York: Columbia University Press, 1999.

Comprises essays on the history and development of Western philosophical traditions. The essays are organized into the following broad categories: "Origins of Western Philosophic Thinking," "Medieval Islamic and Jewish Philosophy," "Medieval Christian Philosophy," "The Renaissance," "Seventeenth-Century Philosophy," "Eighteenth-Century Philosophy," "Nineteenth-Century Philosophy," "Twentieth-Century Analytic Philosophy," and "Twentieth-Century Continental Philosophy." Contains several epilogues on the history of philosophy, a names index, and a subject index.

Guides

Bynagle, Hans E. *Philosophy: A Guide to the Reference Literature*. 3rd ed. Westport, CT: Library Unlimited, 2006.

This annotated bibliography overviews philosophy and introduces reference resources for general philosophy research, history of philosophy, branches of philosophy, and miscellanea. Primarily covers Western philosophy from all time periods with selective resources for non-Western philosophies.

Indexes and Bibliographies

The Philosopher's Index: An International Index to Philosophical Periodicals and Books. Bowling Green, OH: Philosopher's Information Center. Available online via various vendors.
Indexing journal articles, books, book chapters, and book reviews from 1940 onward, *The Philosopher's Index* contains more than 436,000 abstracts for philosophy and its subfields. Areas of study include "Aesthetics," "Axiology," "Metaphilosophy," "Metaphysics," "Philosophical Anthropology," "Philosophy of Education," "Philosophy of Epistemology," "Philosophy of Ethics," "Philosophy of History," "Philosophy of Language," "Philosophy of Logic," "Philosophy of Religion," "Philosophy of Science," "Political Philosophy," and "Social Philosophy." *The Philosopher's Index* is available both in print and online.

RELIGION

Dictionaries, Encyclopedias, and Handbooks

Bowker, John, ed. *The Oxford Dictionary of World Religions*. Oxford: Oxford University Press, 1997.
Provides brief entries for people, places, practices, and terminology associated with the world's religions. Many entries have short bibliographies for further reading. A topic index and an index of Chinese headwords conclude the volume.

Jeffrey, David Lyle, ed. *A Dictionary of Biblical Tradition in English Literature*. Grand Rapids: Eerdmans, 1992.
Comprises more than nine hundred entries regarding the Bible's influence on English literature. Entries fall into six categories: "Biblical Proper Noun," "Common Noun," "Concept," "Common Quotation or Allusion," "Parable," and "Familiar Terms in Hebrew, Greek, and Latin, in the Latter Case Drawn from the Vulgate Text of the Bible." The entries vary in length from one paragraph to several pages and frequently have cross-references and bibliographic citations. Includes bibliographies on biblical studies, the history of biblical interpretation, and the biblical traditions in English literature.

Jones, Lindsay, ed. *Encyclopedia of Religion*. 2nd ed. 15 vols. Detroit: Mac-
    millan Reference USA, 2005.
Now in its second edition, this standard religion encyclopedia comprises
more than three thousand entries on religion and religious practices from
around the world. Although some entries were carried over from the first edition, many were completely revised, added, or at least had their bibliographies revised in the second edition. Entries tend to be lengthy, with detailed
bibliographies of further readings. Volume 15 includes a guide to abbreviations and symbols, an appendix of twenty-one additional articles, a synoptic
outline of contents, and an index.

New Catholic Encyclopedia. 2nd ed. 15 vols. Detroit: Thomson Gale; Wash-
    ington, DC: Catholic University of America, 2003.
Comprising seventeen thousand entries in fourteen volumes plus a fifteenth
volume for the index, the *New Catholic Encyclopedia* surveys the doctrines,
history, and organization of Christianity from its Judaic roots to the early
twenty-first century. Additionally, its entries address scripture, theology, pa-
trology, liturgy, church history, canon and civil law, philosophy, biography
and hagiography, and the social sciences in terms of their impact on the
Catholic Church. Entries cross-reference to one another and have bibliographies of further readings.

Skolnik, Fred, ed. *Encyclopaedia Judaica*. 2nd ed. 22 vols. Detroit: Macmillan
    Reference USA, 2007. Also available online at www.gale.cengage.com.
As the standard encyclopedia for Judaism, this resource covers Jewish life
and culture in twenty-two volumes. Entries range in length from a single
paragraph to several pages, include cross-references as appropriate, and
frequently offer brief bibliographies. Volume 22 comprises an index to
twenty-two thousand subjects and a thematic index organized by "History," "Religion," "Jewish Languages and Literature," "Jews in World
Culture," and "Women." Each category is further divided into more narrowly defined subtopics. The *Encyclopaedia Judaica* is available both in
print and online.

Guides

Dillon, Martin, and Shannon Graff Hysell, eds. *ARBA In-Depth: Philosophy
    and Religion*. Westport, CT: Libraries Unlimited, 2004.
Although the title indicates coverage of both philosophy and religion, this
guide primarily focuses on reference sources in religion. The first section
focuses on philosophy and is organized by resource type. The second section

addresses religion and breaks down into general works, Baha'i Faith, Bible studies, Buddhism, Christianity, Hinduism, Islam, Judaism, Native American religions, occultism and witchcraft, Shinto, Sikhism, and Taoism. Concludes with an author/title index and a subject index.

Johnston, William M. *Recent Reference Books in Religion: A Guide for Students, Scholars, Researchers, Buyers, and Readers*. Rev. ed. Chicago: Fitzroy Dearborn, 1998.

Introduces scholars to reference books on the world's religions, Christianity, other prophetic religions, Asian religions, and alternative approaches. It also contains a glossary of types and functions of reference books, introductions to the postmodern revolution in reference books and reference books as self-teachers, and appendixes to the author's favorite reference books and references books that "cry out to be written." Concludes with five indexes to titles, authors, topics, persons, and places and an addendum to works published in 1996 and 1997.

Indexes and Bibliographies

ATLA Religion Database. Chicago: American Theological Library Association. Available online via various vendors.

Produced by the American Theological Library Association, the *ATLA Religion Database* is the major index for journal articles, book reviews, and essay collections in religion studies. It comprises more than 1.7 million records covering diverse topics such as "Bible, archaeology, and antiquities," "human culture and society," "church history, missions, and ecumenism," "pastoral ministry," "world religions and religious studies," and "theology, philosophy, and ethics." *ATLA* indexes resources for all major religions and major denominations. While more than half of the contents are in English, many other languages are represented as well.

Index Islamicus. Leidin, The Netherlands: Brill. Available online via various vendors.

Available in print and online, the *Index Islamicus* is the major bibliography for Islam and the Muslim world. With coverage beginning in 1906, this database comprises 377,000 records from more than three thousand periodicals. The print volumes provide detailed indexes for names and subjects, which carry over into the online product. Because *Index Islamicus* surveys Islamic Studies broadly, areas such as history, history of science, the arts and humanities, and the social sciences are included.

SCIENCE AND MEDICINE

Dictionaries, Encyclopedias, and Handbooks

Bynum, William F., and Roy Porter, eds. *Companion Encyclopedia of the History of Medicine*. 2 vols. New York: Routledge, 1993.
This two-volume set comprises seventy-two essays on the history of medicine. Excepting the introduction, the essays are organized into the following categories: "The Place of Medicine," "Body Systems," "Theories of Life, Health, and Disease," "Understanding Disease," "Clinical Medicine," "Medicine in Society," and "Medicine, Ideas, and Culture." Essays include both footnotes and further reading lists. An index to the set concludes the second volume.

Gossin, Pamela, ed. *Encyclopedia of Literature and Science*. Westport, CT: Greenwood Press, 2002.
This brief encyclopedia comprises more than 650 entries on interdisciplinary studies involving literature and science. The entries range from fifty to 3,500 words in length and address methodologies, scientists, themes, theories, and writers and their works. Entries have cross-references and short bibliographies. Concludes with a selected bibliography and an index.

Heilbron, J. L., ed. *The Oxford Companion to the History of Modern Science*. New York: Oxford University Press, 2003.
Tracing the history and development of science from around 1550 to through the early twenty-first century, this companion's entries fall into broad areas such as "historiography of science," "organization and diffusion of science," "the body of scientific knowledge," "apparatus and instruments," "uses," and "biographies." Entries contain bibliographies and frequently cross-reference to one another. Additionally, it contains a thematic listing of entries, a guide to further reading, Nobel Science Prize winners, and an index.

Hessenbruch, Arne, ed. *Reader's Guide to the History of Science*. Chicago: Fitzroy Dearborn, 2001.
This guide to secondary literature on the history of science covers "Alternative Sciences," "Analytical Concepts," "Astronomy and Astrophysics," "Chemical Sciences," "Earth Sciences," "Education," "Engineering and Technology," "General Themes," "Individuals," "Life Sciences," "Literature of Science," "Mathematical Sciences," "Medical and Health Sciences," "Medicine and Society," "National Histories," "Physical Sciences," "Sciences in 'pre-modern' Cultures," "Scientific Instruments," "Social Sciences," and "Societies and Institutions." The entries offer a list of books with occasional journal articles and

a discussion of each work's merits. Internal finding aids include a thematic list, a booklist index, a general index, and cross-references.

Lerner, K. Lee, and Brenda Wilmoth Lerner, eds. *Gale Encyclopedia of Science*. 3rd ed. 6 vols. Detroit: Gale, 2004.
Now in its third edition, the *Gale Encyclopedia of Science* provides reference information for all scientific fields of study. Entries may be one-to-two paragraph entries or lengthier, in-depth discussions that last for several pages. Most entries cross-reference to others and have brief bibliographies of further readings. A general index concludes the sixth volume.

McGraw-Hill Dictionary of Scientific and Technological Terms. 6th ed. New York: McGraw-Hill, 2003.
Comprises 110,000 science- and technology-related terms with 125,000 definitions. The entries may include the term, field of study, definitions, cross-references, synonyms or variants, chemical formulas, and pronunciation. Appendixes for "U.S. Customary System and the Metric System," "International System," "Conversion Factors for the Measurement Systems," "Units of Temperature in Measurement Systems," "Symbols for the Chemical Elements," "Chemical Nomenclature," "Symbols in Scientific Writing," "Periodic Table of Elements," "Mathematical Signs and Symbols," "Mathematical Notation," "Fundamental Constants," "Elementary Particles," "Schematic Electronic Symbols," "Geologic Time Scale and Related Aspects," "Classification of Living Organisms," and "Biographical Listings" conclude the volume.

McGraw-Hill Encyclopedia of Science and Technology. 9th ed. 20 vols. New York: McGraw-Hill, 2002. Also available online at www.accessscience.com.
Available as an eighteen-volume print set and online though *Access Science*, this encyclopedia is a standard reference source for the sciences and technology. The current edition comprises 7,100 alphabetically arranged articles. Entries tend to be in-depth and provide an excellent overview for any given topic. Volume 20 concludes the set and contains information on scientific notation, a topical index, an analytical index, and study guides for the following areas: agriculture, forestry, and soils; anthropology and archeology; astronomy; biological and biomedical science; chemistry; computing and information science; earth science; electronics; engineering and technology; environmental science; mathematics; medicine; paleontology; physics; and psychiatry and psychology.

Marcovitch, Harvey, ed. *Black's Medical Dictionary*. 42nd ed. London: A&C Black, 2009.

Now in its 42nd edition, *Black's Medical Dictionary* defines more than five thousand medical terms and concepts. Contains appendixes for "common tests and procedures," "travel and health," "measurements in medicine," "health economics," "complementary and alternative medicine," and addresses of professional organizations.

Selen, Helaine, ed. *Encyclopaedia of the History of Science, Technology, and Medicine in Non-Western Cultures.* 2nd ed. 2 vols. New York: Springer-Verlag, 2008.
Provides detailed articles on the history and development of science, technology, and medicine in non-Western cultures and, as such, is a nice complement to the other similar resources. Entries cross-reference to one another and conclude with references of further readings. The second volume contains an index.

Guides

Hurt, Charlie Deuel. *Information Sources in Science and Technology.* Englewood, CO: Libraries Unlimited, 1998.
Although somewhat dated, this guide should still be useful for researching the history and development of science and technology and identifying relevant reference resources for various disciplines. The bibliography covers multidisciplinary sources, biological sciences, physical sciences and mathematics, engineering, and health and veterinary sciences. The volume concludes with an author/title index and a subject index.

Indexes and Bibliographies

The History of Science, Technology, and Medicine. Dublin, OH: OCLC, 1975. Available online at www.oclc.com.
Comprising four major research tools—*Isis Current Bibliography of the History of Science, Current Bibliography in the History of Technology, Bibliografia Italiana di Storia della Scienza*, and Wellcome Library citations—this is the premier bibliography for science, technology, and medicine history. Includes more than 295,000 citations for journal articles, books, conference proceedings, dissertations, maps, serials, and other materials from 1975 onward.

Scopus. New York: Elsevier. Available online at www.scopus.com.
Covering life sciences, physical sciences, health sciences, and social sciences and humanities, *Scopus* comprises 38 million records with half from 1996

onward and the other half pre-1996. Although *Scopus* has humanities content, it is largely a sciences and social sciences database. Because it includes historic materials from institutes such as the American Physical Society and the Royal Society of Chemistry, and from journals such as *Nature* and *Science*, it should be useful for historic as well as contemporary journal literature.

See also volume 1 of *The New Walford: Guide to Reference Resources* (see above).

SOCIAL SCIENCES

Dictionaries, Encyclopedias, and Handbooks

Darity, William A., ed. *International Encyclopedia of the Social Sciences.* 2nd ed. 9 vols. Detroit, MI: MacMillan Reference USA, 2008. Also available online at www.gale.cengage.com.
Now in its second edition, the nine-volume *International Encyclopedia of the Social Sciences* comprises nearly three thousand entries. It covers diverse disciplines such as anthropology, economics, education, history, political science, psychology, and sociology. Entries cross-reference to one another and conclude with brief bibliographies. Finding aids include an alphabetical article list and an index.

Smelser, Neil J., and Paul B. Baltes, eds. *International Encyclopedia of the Social and Behavioral Sciences.* 26 vols. New York: Elsevier, 2001. Also available online at www.sciencedirect.com.
Comprising more than 3,800 entries, this encyclopedia covers overarching topics, disciplines, intersecting fields, and applications within the social and behavioral sciences. The entries range between two thousand and five thousand words and include extensive cross-referencing and thorough bibliographies of further readings. Volume 25 is a name index to the set, while volume 26 comprises a classified list of entries and the encyclopedia's subject index.

Kuper, Adam, and Jessica Kuper, eds. *The Social Science Encyclopedia.* 3rd ed. 2 vols. New York: Routledge, 2004.
Much shorter than the *International Encyclopedia of the Social and Behavioral Sciences*, this encyclopedia contains roughly five hundred entries about the social sciences broadly, including anthropology; cognitive psychology and cognitive science; cultural studies; demography; economics; education; evolution; gender; geography; health and medicine; history; industrial relations and management; language, linguistics, and semiotics; mental health;

methods of social research; philosophy; political theory; politics and government; psychology; social problems and social welfare; and sociology. Entries cross-reference to one another and have lists of further readings. The second volume ends with an index to the set.

Guides

Aby, Stephen H., James Nalen, and Lori Fielding. *Sociology: A Guide to Reference Information Sources*. 3rd ed. Westport, CT: Libraries Unlimited, 2005.
Now in its third edition, *Sociology* addresses reference and information sources for sociology, its subdisciplines, and related fields of study. Organized according to general social science reference sources, sociology, and sociological fields such as marriage and the family, rural sociology, and women's studies.

Herron, Nancy L., ed. *The Social Sciences: A Cross-Disciplinary Guide to Selected Sources*. 3rd ed. Greenwood Village, CO: Libraries Unlimited, 2002.
A standard reference source for the social sciences, *The Social Sciences* surveys reference literature for the following social science and related disciplines: political science, economics, business, history, law and justice, anthropology, sociology, education, psychology, geography, and communication. May cover resources for essays, guides and handbooks, bibliographies, indexes and abstracts, dictionaries and encyclopedias, almanacs, biographical sources, directories, area studies, statistics, and guides to electronic sources for each discipline. There is some variation in resources categories among the represented disciplines.

Jacoby, Joann, and Josephine Z. Kibbee. *Cultural Anthropology: A Guide to Reference and Information Sources*. 2nd ed. Westport, CT: Libraries Unlimited, 2007.
Surveys reference resources in anthropology, its subfields, and related disciplines. The contents are organized according to "general and social science sources," "general anthropology reference sources," "methods and practice," "subfields of anthropology," "research areas," "humanities related fields," "area and ethnic studies," and "supplemental resources."

Li, Tze-chung. *Social Science Reference Sources: A Practical Guide*. 3rd ed. Westport, CT: Greenwood Press, 2000.
Now in its third edition, this guide introduces social science reference materials. The resources are organized into the following broad categories: "Social Sciences in General" and "Subdisciplines of the Social Sciences." General resources are further divided according to "Reference Sources in an

Electronic Age," "Research Resources in the Social Sciences," "Access to Sources," "Sources of Information," "Statistical Sources," "Periodicals," and "Government Publications," while subdisciplines include cultural anthropology, business, economics, education, geography, history, law, political science, psychology, and sociology. Concludes with an appendix to cited URLs, a name and title index, and a subject index.

O'Brien, Nancy P. *Education: A Guide to Reference and Information Sources.* 2nd ed. Englewood, CO: Libraries Unlimited, 2000.
Provides an excellent introduction to education reference literature. Resources are organized in the following categories: "General Education Sources"; "Educational Technologies and Media"; "Early Childhood, Elementary, and Secondary Education"; "Higher Education"; "Multilingual and Multicultural Education"; "Special Education"; "Adult, Alternative, Continuing, and Distance Education"; "Career and Vocational Education"; "Comparative and International Education"; "Curriculum, Instruction, and Content areas"; "Education Administration and Management"; "Education History and Philosophy"; "Education Research, Measurements, and Testing"; and "Educational Psychology." The section on education history and philosophy should be particularly useful. Concludes with indexes to author, titles, and subjects.

See also volume two of *The New Walford: Guide to Reference Resources* (see above).

Indexes and Bibliographies

Social Sciences Citation Index. Philadelphia, PA: Thomson Reuters. Available online at www.thomsonreuters.com.
Available independently or as part of the *Web of Science*, the *Social Sciences Citation Index* provides bibliographic and citation searching. It currently indexes nearly twenty-five hundred journals from fifty disciplines. Citations date from 1987 to the present.

Social Sciences Index. New York: H. W. Wilson, 1983. Annual. Available online at www.hwwilson.com.
Formerly a print index, the *Social Sciences Index* is available online through H. W. Wilson and supports the social sciences broadly. Specific disciplines such as anthropology, economics, ethics, gender studies, geography, law, political science, and urban studies are included. This resource is available as *Social Sciences Index*, *Social Sciences Abstracts*, and *Social Sciences Full Text*, all of which rely on the indexing of the former and cover from 1983

onward. Older volumes may also be searched in *Humanities & Social Sciences Index Retrospective, 1907–1984* (see above) or *Social Sciences Index Retrospective: 1907–1983.*

See also the entry for *Scopus* above.

THEATER

Dictionaries, Encyclopedias, and Handbooks

Banham, Martin, ed. *The Cambridge Guide to Theatre.* New ed. New York: Cambridge University Press, 1995.
Provides an alphabetical listing of theater terms. Topics may be addressed in brief, one-paragraph entries or those several pages in length. Select entries have cross-references and bibliographies.

Hartnoll, Phyllis, ed. *The Oxford Companion to the Theatre.* 4th ed. New York: Oxford University Press, 1983.
In need of an update, this companion comprises brief entries on theater history through 1980. Entries cross-reference to one another, and the work has a guide to further readings on theater: "Reference Works," "General Histories," "Classical Drama and Theatre," "Great Britain," "Ireland," "Europe," "United States of America," "Asia," "Dramatic Forms," "Playhouses and Forms of Staging," "Techniques of Stagecraft," "Acting," and "Theatre Criticism."

Hochman, Stanley, ed. *McGraw-Hill Encyclopedia of World Drama: An International Reference Work in 5 Volumes.* 2nd ed. 5 vols. New York: McGraw-Hill, 1984.
Although somewhat dated, this encyclopedia remains an excellent resource for studying theater around the globe. Entries cross-reference to one another, contain bibliographies, and cover biographies, anonymous plays, theatre companies, genres, and in-depth studies of select topics. The final volume offers a glossary, a play title list and index, and a general index to the set.

Pavis, Patrice. *Dictionary of the Theatre: Terms, Concepts, and Analysis.* Trans. Christine Shantz. Toronto: University of Toronto Press, 1998.
Originally written in French, *Dictionary of the Theatre* defines terms related to dramaturgy, text and discourse, actor and character, genres and forms, staging, structural principles and aesthetic questions, reception, and semiology. Entries have cross-references and further reading lists. Concludes with a thematic index and bibliography.

Trapido, Joel, ed. *An International Dictionary of Theatre Language*. Westport, CT: Greenwood Press, 1985.
Provides brief definitions for approximately fifteen thousand theater terms.
Many entries include source citations that match with works listed in the
bibliography at the end of the volume.

Guides

Simons, Linda Keir. *The Performing Arts: A Guide to the Reference Literature*. Englewood, CO: Libraries Unlimited, 1994.
Focusing on theater and dance, this work provides an overview of bibliographic guides, bibliographies, catalogs, indexes, dictionaries, encyclopedias,
companions, biographical sources, handbooks and yearbooks, directories,
review sources, chronologies and histories, electronic discussion groups, core
periodicals, libraries and archives, and professional organizations and
societies in those disciplines.

Indexes and Bibliographies

International Index of Performing Arts. Ann Arbor, MI: ProQuest. Available
online at iipa.chadwyck.com.
The *International Index of Performing Arts* (*IIPA*) indexes and abstracts more
than 250 periodicals and contains more than 500,000 records. *IIPA* covers
journal literature from and about the arts and entertainment industry, circus
arts, dance, festivals and conferences, film, magic and illusionism, mime,
musical theater, and opera. Results date from 1864 to the present.

International Bibliography of Theatre and Dance. Ipswich, MA: EBSCO
Publishing, 1984. Available online at www.ebscohost.com.
Since 1984, the *International Bibliography of Theatre and Dance* has provided indexing and abstracting for books, book chapters, dissertation abstracts, and journal articles in theater and dance. This annual bibliography
began as the *International Bibliography of Theatre* under the auspices of the
American Theatre Research Society and then continued by Brooklyn College's Theatre Research Data Center until 1999. Currently it is only available
online through EBSCO.

Bibliography

Adams, James Eli, Tom Pendergast, and Sara Pendergast, eds. *The Encyclopedia of the Victorian Era.* 4 vols. Danbury, CT: Grolier Academic Reference, 2003.

Balzek, Ron, and Elizabeth Aversa. *The Humanities: A Selective Guide to Information Resources.* 5th ed. Engelwood, CO: Libraries Unlimited, 2000.

Brake, Laurel, and Marysa Demoor, eds. *Dictionary of Nineteenth-Century Journalism.* London: British Library, 2009. Also available online at c19index.chadwyck.com.

Brantlinger, Patrick, and William B. Thesing, eds. *A Companion to the Victorian Novel.* Malden, MA: Blackwell, 2002. Also available online at www.blackwellreference.com.

Cronin, Richard, Alison Chapman, and Antony H. Harrison, eds. *A Companion to Victorian Poetry.* Malden, MA: Blackwell, 2002. Also available online at www.blackwellreference.com.

Davis, Philip. *The Oxford English Literary History.* Vol. 8. New York: Oxford University Press, 2002.

Dictionary of Literary Biography. Detroit, MI: Gale Cengage, 1978. Also available online at www.gale.cengage.com.

Graham, Walter. *English Literary Periodicals.* New York: Thomas Nelson and Sons, 1930.

Griffiths, Dennis, ed. *The Encyclopedia of the British Press 1422–1992.* New York: St. Martin's Press, 1992.

Harmon, William. *A Handbook to Literature.* 11th ed. Upper Saddle River, NJ: Prentice Hall, 2009.

Harner, James L. *Literary Research Guide: An Annotated Listing of Reference Sources in English Literary Studies.* 5th ed. New York: Modern Language Association of America, 2008.

Houghton, Walter E. "Introduction." In *The Wellesley Index to Victorian Periodicals, 1824–1900.* Vol. 1. Toronto: University of Toronto Press, 1966.

Kastan, David Scott, ed. *The Oxford Encyclopedia of British Literature.* 5 vols. New York: Oxford University Press, 2006.

Kemp, Sandra, Charlotte Mitchell, and David Trotter, eds. *The Oxford Companion to Edwardian Fiction*. New York: Oxford University Press, 2002.

Kieft, Robert, ed. *Guide to Reference*. Chicago: American Library Association. Online at www.guidetoreference.org.

Marcuse, Michael J. *A Reference Guide for English Studies*. Berkeley: University of California Press, 1990.

Matthew, H. C. G., and Brian Howard Harrison, eds. *Oxford Dictionary of National Biography*. Rev. ed. 61 vols. New York: Oxford University Press, 2004. Also available online at www.oxforddnb.com.

Simpson, J. A., and E. S. C. Weiner. *The Oxford English Dictionary*. 2nd ed. 20 vols. New York: Oxford University Press, 1989. Also available online at www.oed.com.

Index

About the Author

Melissa S. Van Vuuren is an assistant professor and English librarian at James Madison University. Her research interests lie in Victorian and Edwardian literature and in learning and memory within print and digital cultures.